Teaching to Exceed the English Language Arts

Timely, thoughtful, and comprehensive, this text directly supports pre-service and in-service teachers in developing curriculum and instruction that both addresses and exceeds the requirements of English language arts standards. It demonstrates how the Common Core State Standards' as well as other local and national standards' highest and best intentions for student success can be implemented from a critical, culturally relevant perspective firmly grounded in current literacy learning theory and research.

The third edition frames ELA instruction around adopting a justice, inquiry, and action approach that supports students in their schools and community contexts. Offering new ways to respond to current issues and events, the text provides specific examples of teachers employing the justice, inquiry, and action curriculum framework to promote critical engagement and learning. Chapters cover common problems and challenges, alternative models, and theories of language arts teaching. The framework, knowledge, and guidance in this book shows how ELA standards can not only be addressed but also surpassed through engaging instruction to foster truly diverse and inclusive classrooms.

The third edition provides new material on:

- adopting a justice, inquiry, and action approach to enhance student engagement and critical thinking
- planning instruction to effectively implement standards in the classroom
- teaching literary and informational texts, with a focus on authors of color
- integrating drama activities into literature
- teaching informational, explanatory, argumentative, and narrative writing
- supporting bilingual/ELL students
- using digital tools and apps to respond to and create digital texts
- addressing how larger contextual and political factors shape instruction
- fostering preservice teacher development.

Richard Beach is Professor Emeritus of English Education at the University of Minnesota, USA.

Ashley S. Boyd is Associate Professor of English at Washington State University, USA.

Allen Webb is Professor of English Education and Postcolonial Studies at Western Michigan University, USA.

Amanda Haertling Thein is Associate Provost for Graduate and Professional Education, Dean of the Graduate College, and Professor of English Education at the University of Iowa, USA.

Teaching to Exceed in the English Language Arts

A Justice, Inquiry, and Action Approach for 6–12 Classrooms

Third edition

Richard Beach, Ashley S. Boyd, Allen Webb, and Amanda Haertling Thein

NEW YORK AND LONDON

Cover image: © Mindi Rhoades

Third edition published 2023
by Routledge
605 Third Avenue, New York, NY 10158

and by Routledge
4 Park Square, Milton Park, Abingdon, Oxon, OX14 4RN

Routledge is an imprint of the Taylor & Francis Group, an informa business

© 2023 Richard Beach, Ashley S. Boyd, Allen Webb, and Amanda Haertling Thein

The right of Richard Beach, Ashley S. Boyd, Allen Webb, and Amanda Haertling Thein to be identified as authors of this work has been asserted in accordance with sections 77 and 78 of the Copyright, Designs and Patents Act 1988.

All rights reserved. No part of this book may be reprinted or reproduced or utilised in any form or by any electronic, mechanical, or other means, now known or hereafter invented, including photocopying and recording, or in any information storage or retrieval system, without permission in writing from the publishers.

Trademark notice: Product or corporate names may be trademarks or registered trademarks, and are used only for identification and explanation without intent to infringe.

First edition published by Routledge 2012
Second edition published by Routledge 2016

Library of Congress Cataloging-in-Publication Data
Names: Beach, Richard, author. | Boyd, Ashley S., author. | Webb, Allen, 1957– author. | Thein, Amanda Haertling, author.
Title: Teaching to exceed in the English language arts : a justice, inquiry, and action approach for 6-12 classrooms / Richard Beach, Ashley S. Boyd, Allen Webb, and Amanda Haertling Thein.
Other titles: Teaching to exceed the English language arts common core state standards
Description: Third edition. | New York, NY : Routledge, 2022. | Revised edition of: Teaching to exceed the English language arts common core state standards : a critical inquiry approach for 6-12 classrooms | Includes bibliographical references and index. |
Identifiers: LCCN 2022004370 (print) | LCCN 2022004371 (ebook) | ISBN 9781032011455 (hardback) | ISBN 9781032008424 (paperback) | ISBN 9781003177364 (ebook)
Subjects: LCSH: Language arts (Secondary)—Curricula—United States—States. | Language arts (Secondary)—Standards—United States—States.
Classification: LCC LB1631 .B356 2022 (print) | LCC LB1631 (ebook) | DDC 428.0071/273—dc23/eng/20220421
LC record available at https://lccn.loc.gov/2022004370
LC ebook record available at https://lccn.loc.gov/2022004371

ISBN: 978-1-032-01145-5 (hbk)
ISBN: 978-1-032-00842-4 (pbk)
ISBN: 978-1-003-17736-4 (ebk)

DOI: 10.4324/9781003177364

Typeset in Minion and Gill Sans
by Apex CoVantage, LLC

Please access the book's wiki site http://englishccss.pbworks.com for further resources.

Contents

Preface vii
Acknowledgments xi

Section I
Theoretical Frameworks/Foundations of English Language Arts Instruction 1

1 Justice, Inquiry, and Action 3

2 Planning English Language Arts Instruction 21

3 Contexts, Standards, and Teacher Freedom 41

Section II
Implementing and Exceeding the ELA State Standards 65

4 Teaching Literature 67

5 Teaching Nonfiction 87

6 Teaching Writing 107

7 Writing and Enacting Narratives, Drama, and Poetry 127

8 Implementing Digital/Media Literacy Standards 143

9 Implementing Speaking and Listening Standards 165

10 Implementing the Language Standards 181

Section III
Evaluation, Assessment, and Reflection   **203**

11   Assessing Students' Learning   205

12   Fostering Teacher Reflection and Professional Development   227

Index   *239*

Preface

This book is about meaningful teaching of secondary English language arts in today's world, teaching that addresses and moves forward from Black Lives Matter, from the COVID pandemic, from global climate change, and the so many other urgent issues that touch students' lives and create the need and opportunity for their voices to be heard. The book explores traditional approaches to teaching English and sets forward an approach founded on justice, inquiry, and action. The book addresses all strands of the English language arts including classic, contemporary, multicultural, international, and young adult literature. Drawing on critical literacy, cultural studies, youth participatory action research, school literacy projects and more, *Teaching to Exceed* addresses writing, drama, language, technology, speaking and discussion, and English teacher professional development.

Following up on the first two editions, *Teaching to Exceed* also addresses implementing the 6–12 Common Core State Standards (CCSS) ELA standards in ways that are critical, meaningful, and successful. The book is rich with alternative models and theories of language arts teaching articulated through the voices and experiences of innovative teachers working with the truly diverse students of today's classrooms.

Today, districts and schools differ in the degree of attention paid to the CCSS. Preservice teachers may be in states, districts, and/or schools that demand close, daily attention to standards or in states, districts, and/or schools that pay little or no attention to the standards. However, this book will be useful to you as it draws on and sets forward exemplary English language arts instruction in ways that model some of the finest and most current teaching in our field, as well as addressing and exceeding official standards.

In this book, we frame ELA instruction around adopting a justice, inquiry, and action approach based on students addressing topics that matter in their lives, schools, communities, nations, and worldwide. We show students asking questions that matter, engaging in research, drawing on diverse texts and resources, exploring multiple perspectives. We report on teachers and students finding ways to have their voices heard, effectively communicating their beliefs and ideas, educating others, taking action in their lives, schools, and via the Internet, in their communities and beyond.

We also believe in the need to develop ELA instruction based on the current context in which students live and through your use of digital/media tools that shape your instruction and daily interactions. We also believe in the need to build language instruction based on understanding diversity, and relations between language, society, and power.

We also stress using open-ended, formative assessment to build supportive relations with students to foster growth. We prepare prospective teachers to understand how schools and classrooms work, to both use and think critically about standards and traditional approaches, and to develop diverse ideas about what language arts classes can accomplish. Readers of this book will benefit greatly from the examples of veteran ELA teachers describing in their own words their use of innovative instruction for engaging students.

OVERVIEW

The structure of the book is based on a critical inquiry framework.

Section I Theoretical Frameworks/Foundations of English Language Arts Instruction is a theoretical introduction to a justice, inquiry, and action approach and its applications to planning instruction to address state English language arts standards. The opening chapter on "Justice, Inquiry, Action" critically examines traditional approaches including cultural literacy, forms, skills, and processes for fostering a justice, inquiry, and action framework built on critical pedagogy, critical literacy, cultural studies, youth action, youth participatory action research, and school action literacy projects. The second chapter on planning activities is based on considering students' emotions to identify relevant topics and issues; employing questioning to focus on fairness and justice; fostering students' adoption of alternative perspectives; and promoting ways for students to address topics or issues by taking actions. It considers lesson planning and shows how to set high expectations. The third chapter examines the larger social and cultural contexts, the role of state and Common Core ELA standards in an unequal society, and ways to move beyond censorship to create teacher freedom.

Section II Implementing and Exceeding the ELA State Standards includes descriptions of specific frameworks and methods related to teaching literature, nonfiction, and writing; writing and enacting narratives, drama, and poetry; implementing digital/media literacy standards, speaking/listening standards, and language standards. Each chapter in this section includes examples of teachers employing innovative instruction activities designed to engage students in critical inquiry instruction.

Section III Evaluation, Assessment, and Reflection describes formative and summative assessment methods of evaluating student work designed to foster their growth in literacy practices over time. The book then concludes with activities designed to enhance preservice teachers' reflection on their instruction as well as resources for their long-term professional development.

The book also includes a companion website, *exceedingelastandards.pbworks.com*, with resources, units and activities, and further reading for each of the book's chapters.

NEW IN THE THIRD EDITION

The third edition provides new material on:

- adopting a justice, inquiry, and action approach that foregrounds teaching that matters, student engagement, critical thinking, and having their ideas heard
- planning instruction that holds high expectations for all students, supports student choice, and meeting and exceeding expectations and standards

PREFACE

- addressing how larger contextual and political factors shape instruction, for example, the impact of censorship on literature instruction
- fostering critical response to literature, with a focus on literature/young adult literature by authors of color
- enhancing reading instruction based on fostering student engagement with comprehension practices
- teaching information, explanatory, and argumentative writing based on use of topics or issues of interest to students
- engaging students through having them create narratives or portray or enact in drama activities
- using current digital tools and apps to foster supportive discussions and create digital texts
- improving discussions through facilitation practices as well as use of dramatic inquiry activities
- focusing on languaging instruction to support bilingual/ELL students through use of translanguaging activities
- employing formative assessment practices to provide supportive feedback and preparing students for summative assessments
- fostering preservice teacher development through supportive feedback and access to professional development resources, including the book's wiki site http://exceedingela standards.pbworks.com.

Acknowledgments

We'd like to thank teachers Tracy Becker, Elizabeth Erdmann, Steffany Maher, Josie Morris, Rebecca Oberg, Jeff Paterson, Marguerite Sheffer, and Molly Vanish, and for their contributions to this book. We'd also like to thank our editor at Routledge, Karen Adler, for her steadfast support for this revised edition, and Emily Dombrovskaya, for her editorial assistance.

Section I

Theoretical Frameworks/Foundations of English Language Arts Instruction

1

Justice, Inquiry, and Action

We are living in a remarkable time, a brave new world. We have survived a global pandemic that has killed millions, disrupted all our lives, impacted the way we work, learn, and are with each other. The pandemic has shown us that all humans across the planet are connected, that our lives can change, and change quickly and dramatically. In this sense, the pandemic is a practice run for what is already happening as global warming raises temperatures and sea levels, melts polar ice, accelerates storms and droughts, fosters wildfires and refugees, and threatens, unless we act quickly and effectively, human civilization and life on earth.

Pandemic and climate crises both magnify existing inequalities of power, income, race, nationality, gender, and age. We have seen pandemic and climate crises foster the worst political demagoguery—and the finest compassion and best collaboration.

As teachers, we are committed to working with our students and colleagues to understand the present and past and build the future. The work of the teacher emerges from hope. Hope that by helping our students inquire into the world, they can better understand it, and once we understand it, work to improve it. We believe teachers enhance lives and deepen and improve our relations with each other and our environment. Through learning, we can build a better world and achieve justice.

Justice, inquiry, and action are guiding principles as ancient as Socrates and as relevant to the present as Black Lives Matter, #MeToo, and Fridays for the Future.

We, the authors of this book, Richard, Ashley, Allen, and Amanda, all of us were secondary English teachers. All of us have devoted our lives to the teaching of English, and, as we have become professors of English education, to preparing and supporting English teachers. We believe that the teaching of English is enormously important, valuable to individuals and to the local, national, and planetary community.

In English classes, we recognize the power of the imagination. English classes are places to listen to, attempt to understand and put ourselves in the place of others, like and unlike ourselves. Literature plays an important role. We consider ethical questions about how people and communities should be treated. We engage in anti-racist, anti-sexist, and pro-justice teaching. We go beyond individualist thinking to explore the social web of challenges and possibilities our students confront and navigate. More than in any other discipline, in English language arts we can imagine better and worse ways to be with each other in the world, dystopias and utopias, reimagined systems, better worlds, and what we need to do, and not do, to get there.

DOI: 10.4324/9781003177364-2

Through English language arts teaching we empower. We help our students value and utilize their language, experience, and voice. We help them think about the world in complex and critical ways and analyze depictions, representations, mass and social media, news, and visual and political rhetoric. We help them find ways to be heard, to make a difference. We teach them how words matter, among them democracy, freedom, equality, compassion, understanding, peace, and mutual respect. These, and other words, are important in English teaching. Reading, writing, speaking, listening, acting are our tools.

The first two editions of *Teaching to Exceed* centered on helping teachers think critically about and exceed the Common Core State Standards (CCSS) for the English language arts in middle school and high school, standards now adopted by more than 40 states.

The book became an English teacher "bestseller" because teachers appreciated our critical approach, an approach based on professional English teacher knowledge, educational research, and a great deal of real-world experience. The CCSS continues to play a role in this third edition. We know the Standards well and will help you use and think critically about them, but they have transitioned to the background as they have in the schools.

Instead of focusing first on the Standards, this book has a greater ambition: to help you become the most caring, capable, and impactful secondary English teacher that you can be. We write this book with the history of our profession in mind, with a deep knowledge of standards, curriculum, and traditions, but with the context of our remarkable present moment at the center of our attention. And we build this third edition, and the vision of secondary English teaching that we invite you to join us in, around three words: justice, inquiry, and action.

A TEACHER EMPLOYING INQUIRY-BASED ELA INSTRUCTION

Josie Morris teaches English Language Arts in a suburban school in North Carolina. She was concerned that many of her students live in a bubble of privilege and at a time when racial unrest was constantly on the news and when Black Americans are continuing to die at the hands of police officers. Therefore, she wanted to expand her teaching to address this social injustice and have her students move beyond traditional texts and tropes to expand their understanding of race and racism. She wondered how she could help her students discern their privileges, understand systemic oppression, and channel their learning into social action. Similar to Borsheim-Black and Sarigianides (2019), she felt, "as White teachers, we must shoulder the responsibility for interrupting racism in our classrooms" (p. 3). How, though, could she achieve her goals? What resources could she use to serve as a mirror, a window, and a sliding glass door for her students (Sims Bishop, 1990)? What opportunities to act in their schools and communities could she give them?

We begin this book with Josie's questions because we believe she is onto something that is important for teaching English. As students read, write, and learn about the world, we think that questions, more than answers, are at the heart of good English teaching. Josie's questions in particular are those of an inquiry teacher: How do good teachers bring the experience, emotions, and backgrounds of their students to the classroom? How do good teachers help students understand historical and social contexts in relevant ways? How do good teachers help students use their knowledge for action?

Let's consider Josie's questions in the context of different beliefs and approaches to teaching English that you may be familiar with. And let's also keep in mind: What other questions, issues, identities, perspectives, theories, and resources are starting points for meaningful English teaching?

APPROACHES TO TEACHING ENGLISH LANGUAGE ARTS

As an English teacher, you draw on various theories, approaches, and practices every day. For example, in teaching a literary text, you make more or less conscious decisions about your focus. Should you focus on teaching the form of the short story, play, novel, or poem; emphasizing literary terms; teaching author biography, literary history, and movements; focusing on reading comprehension skills; modeling interpretative strategies; focusing on students' prior knowledge and differing interpretations; addressing characters and their relationships; exploring historical context; or exploring social, cultural, political, or ethical issues or questions?

These different approaches have been around for many years, and all could be considered "traditional," even though some are likely more familiar and others perhaps new to you. Some approaches have been institutionalized in textbooks, curriculum guides, habits and local school traditions, and state and local standards. Many approaches have been developed by teachers researching in their own classrooms, sharing ideas at professional conferences, and publishing articles in teacher journals. There have been—and still are—controversies and arguments over different approaches. The way we have ourselves been taught in school or at the university often becomes how we imagine English *should* be taught.

This chapter aspires to help you understand different approaches to teaching English. Rather than simply repeating the way you have been taught, or blithely accepting the approach in the textbook or in the standards or in your local school, we believe you need to recognize, name, and think critically about different approaches, including the justice, inquiry, and action approach we advocate. Having a clearly defined set of beliefs about teaching English will help you justify your use of innovative curriculum and instruction both in your student teaching and in your own classroom. You may then be less likely to simply conform to the traditional teaching practices operating in the schools than those teachers who do not have a well-defined set of beliefs and attitudes (Smagorinsky et al., 2004).

The goal is for you to develop a self-aware approach that you believe in, that inspires the best from you and your students. Rather than relying on standards makers, textbook publishers, or others, we want YOU as the English language arts professional to be the one to make informed choices about content and best teaching practices. What is, and what should be,

Focus on ELA Curriculum Frameworks	Instructional Goals
Privileged cultural knowledge	• Acquiring knowledge about and valuing certain literary texts
Knowledge of literary and rhetorical forms	• Analyzing the organization and techniques employed in texts
Skills, processes, and procedures	• Employing skills, processes, and procedure for comprehending and creating texts
Critical Inquiry	• Fostering critical analysis of texts and events from different perspectives

FIGURE 1.1 Curriculum Frameworks for Teaching English Language Arts

your focus in English language arts? How will students learn best in your classroom? How do you best provide your students with the knowledge and tools they need to understand the world they live in, and shape that world to be more just and sustainable?

As summarized in Figure 1.1, we examine three different traditional approaches to teaching English. Each approach employs particular instructional methods consistent with its goals. (The teachers we describe are based on individuals that we have known, though perhaps a bit exaggerated to serve as prototypes.)

ENGLISH LANGUAGE ARTS AS PRIVILEGED CULTURAL KNOWLEDGE

Michael has an enthusiasm for great literature that goes back to his college days. He teaches 12th grade British Literature and hits all the classics "from Beowulf to Virginia Woolf," as he puts it. His Freshman Language Arts classes linger on *The Odyssey*, *Romeo and Juliet*, and *Great Expectations*, all taught in full text, not in excerpts from a textbook. He wants students to be "culturally literate," and acquainting them with "their heritage," with the classics and canonical authors, is the very purpose of high school English teaching, as Michael sees it.

Michael's familiar approach stresses English language arts as cultural knowledge acquired largely through literature deemed essential by textbooks or tradition. This approach has been debated for years, including during the "culture wars" of the late 20th century when traditionalists armed with Ed Hirsch's *Cultural Literacy* (1987) and Allan Bloom's *Closing of the American Mind* (1987) argued that knowledge of a specific set of texts is needed to participate in society.

There is much to be gained from the study of the "Great Books." Yet this model takes for granted that particular texts cherished by certain groups—often those of White, Western, male, upper-middle-class people—should be considered as more essential for "cultural literacy" than those of other groups. Moreover, literary canons have always been in flux. Given the long history of education, the use of English or American literature as the content for the school curriculum is relatively recent. In the mid-19th century, the British government developed a British literature curriculum designed to subtly impose British/Christian values to maintain its authority over India. Rather than resort to the use of only military control that included examples of virtuous Englishmen to the religiously diverse people of India exploited by English colonizers, this curriculum was, in fact, the first time English literature was used as a school curriculum anywhere in the world (Viswanathan, 1989).

The curriculum commonly taught in today's middle and high schools is mostly "new," if we use "new" to refer to before the last hundred years. Even Shakespeare! His plays were rarely taught in the 19th century because they were considered "scandalous" and "indecent." Plays introduced as school texts in the 20th century frequently went in and out of favor, or were substantially censored (portions of *Romeo and Juliet* considered "vulgar" are still missing from most high school textbooks!).

Literary works that now seem like permanent fixtures such as *To Kill a Mockingbird*, or *Of Mice and Men*, or *The Great Gatsby*, or *Fahrenheit 451*, or *The Diary of Anne Frank* were all newcomers not so long ago, added to make the curriculum more relevant and appealing to young people. This awareness that secondary English teachers do not inherit an ancient, fixed, or perfect canon is knowledge that can free us to keep making choices as well as rethink traditional works in new ways.

The English language arts cultural tradition approach can fail to recognize diversity and a range of communities that value different literary works. For example, Hirsch (1987) posits that all students should be familiar with certain "classic" works of American literature. However, his proposed list excludes much of women's literature, multicultural literature, young adult literature, working-class literature, films, graphic novels/comics, popular songs, and digital literature—all works that can have value in English instruction.

Hirsch's cultural literacy model also privileges the acquisition of specific and isolated bits of information about literature instead of acquiring rich and contextualized knowledge or skills of critique and critical inquiry. Especially given the dramatically more culturally diverse school populations of America in the 21st century, a cultural knowledge/literacy model that ignores the prior knowledge, experience, and linguistic richness that diverse American students bring to the classroom is problematic (Saifer et al., 2011).

The National Council of Teachers of English creates standards that are used in the accreditation of colleges and universities certifying teachers. These "Standards for the Initial Preparation of Teachers of English Language Arts 7–12," revised in 2021, offer a similar critique of the "Privileged Cultural Knowledge" approach. Rather than identifying any specific texts or specific national literary traditions, teacher candidates are expected to:

> apply and demonstrate knowledge and theoretical perspectives about a variety of literary and informational texts—e.g., young adult, classic, contemporary, and media—that represent a range of world literatures, historical traditions, genres, cultures, and lived experiences.
> (National Council of Teachers of English, 2021, p. 1)

These standards also stress justice in English language arts, specifically a "coherent, relevant, inclusive, and antiracist/antibias instruction that critically engages all learners."

As an activity in critical inquiry and justice-seeking, you could have your students examine how their own textbooks present the "literary canon." Comparing their textbooks with textbooks from different time periods or with alternative textbooks with specific focuses—such as Holt, Rinehart, and Winston's *African American Literature* textbook (1998), created for the Detroit public schools—may be illuminating. In addition, many resources can be found online, including older textbooks, tables of contents, literary histories, and whole texts in digital archives.

Given the diversity of both traditional and new texts available online, you and/or your students can now construct your own textbooks, and students can write about what they learn from the process. In addition, you and your students can consider incorporating works that appeal to them, including new young adult literature, texts, or films that address gender identity, the #MeToo movement, Black Lives Matter, the climate crisis, the global pandemic, etc.

Following the model of Critical Canon Pedagogy (Dyches, 2018), you could also have students explicitly study the construction of the canon as "the most frequently taught literature selections in secondary classrooms as well as the 'canon wars'" (p. 549). Through this investigation, students can recognize the lack of diversity and relevance of the canon. Dyches (2018) closes her unit by having students "restory" a work from the canon, which involves their work to "reimagine" and "to provide more inclusive stories and effect more participatory realities" (p. 543).

MOVING BEYOND A BANKING MODEL OF INSTRUCTION

A narrow "Great Books" or "cultural literacy" approach risks a static model of instruction, where repetition without attention to justice and inquiry impedes learning. Paulo Freire (1972) describes what he calls "the banking model" of education in which "the scope of action allowed to the students extends only as far as receiving, filing, and storing the deposits" (53)—deposits of information made by the teacher into the student. Instead, Freire sets forward a "problem posing" model of inquiry, where learners are free to ask, explore, experiment. "Knowledge emerges only through invention and re-invention," he writes, "through the restless, impatient, continuing, hopeful inquiry human beings pursue in the world, with the world, and with each other" (53). To "tell" is to rob the learner of her capacity for inquiry.

It is important to know that standardized tests in America do NOT require knowledge of specific literary works. Language arts standards do NOT require any specific literary texts be taught. The Common Core State Standards stress that "texts need to be selected around topics or themes that generate knowledge and allow students to study those topics or themes in depth" (Common Core State Standards, 2010, p. 58). (We discuss selecting literature based on meaningful topics and thematic analysis in Chapter 5.) The CCSS do include a list of "Exemplars of Reading Text Complexity, Quality, and Range" (Appendix B); though these texts are meant to serve as examples of text complexity and quality given how they "expressly do not represent a partial or complete reading list" (Appendix B, p. 2). Appendix B may be misinterpreted by districts as required, or even thought to be necessary for use with standardized tests, but this is not the case (Goering & Connors, 2014). The skills cultivated in analyzing texts on the Exemplars list can be developed with many other texts, including those that are more relevant to students and reflect their identities.

Because students in the past were often given less demanding texts based on assumptions about their "reading level," we believe that students certainly need to know how to read and understand more challenging "complex texts," a key focus of the reading/literature CCSS. At the same time, it is equally important that the texts and themes you choose are engaging and relevant. Some canonical texts may require cultural or historical knowledge your students do not yet have. And, there are many kinds of "text complexity" that students need to experience, not only the complexity of language structures, but also the complexity of plot, character, and theme and complexity in the portrayal of historical and cultural contexts.

In this book we are not calling for eliminating canonical works. Instead, in developing curriculum, we believe teachers need to move beyond limited ideas of the canon, and beyond the CCSS list of exemplar works. Teachers need also to select texts and materials that will be engaging based on your students' particular cultural backgrounds and interests, and on the justice and inquiry questions that guide your instruction. Every class you teach also has significant variation in reading background and ability. As a teacher, you will want to attend to your students' backgrounds and prior knowledge, with the goal of supporting them as they extend to new ideas and information.

Josie Morris, the previously mentioned teacher in North Carolina, determined to expand her students' thinking about race and racism, might share Michael's enthusiasm for literature, but she chose works that she felt were relevant to the contemporary moment and could offer her students lessons on justice. Considering her questions from earlier, Josie decided to engage her students in reading *All American Boys* (Reynolds & Kiely, 2015), a young adult novel that confronts police brutality, White privilege, and systemic oppression.

Prior to any reading, she asked her students to note the privileges they possessed simply by being members of their community, their school, and their families. They unpacked the notion of privilege, especially White privilege, and collaboratively built definitions of related terms. As they read, students investigated concepts such as stereotypes and institutional racism and located popular media examples. They ended the unit with their social action projects in which they developed an action to address an issue in the book. Some students created an "anti-stereotype" campaign and hung materials around the school; another group wrote a rap against police brutality and shared it with their school officer and other local stakeholders (Boyd & Miller, 2020).

In this example, Josie used *All American Boys* in her district-required "argumentation" unit. She chose, however, a work from outside the traditional canon and crafted assignments that cultivated students' argumentative skills throughout. For example, students argued why their chosen topic needed to be addressed in their social action projects. As they examined stereotypes in media, they defended how these were harmful and who they damaged. Hers is one model of how teachers can work outside the canon to offer their students opportunities to read relevant texts and design responses for justice and action.

ENGLISH LANGUAGE ARTS AS KNOWLEDGE OF LITERARY OR RHETORICAL FORMS

Jasmine, a different prototypical English teacher representation, is fascinated by the structures of texts. Her students learn about the forms of literature and writing. Her literature curriculum moves sequentially from the elements of the short story, to different forms of poetry, to features of drama, and to the structure of the novel. Jasmine's students also memorize different literary terms from allusion to symbol. When she teaches writing, her class is broken into units by different formal categories, or "rhetorical modes": the argumentative essay, the expository essay, the description paper, comparison and contrast, the personal narrative—the only paper where "I" is allowed, Jasmine makes clear—the literary analysis paper, the research paper, etc.

Jasmine's approach based on forms and literary elements is called, appropriately, "formalism" and it was the dominant approach to teaching English beginning in the late 1940s. Still today, English language arts textbooks for literature and composition are often organized around learning specific literary and compositional forms, for example, teaching the five-paragraph essay. Yet, we believe that an over-emphasis on forms, structures, and terms can bore students, deprive them of personal and subjective experiences associated with responding to and creating texts, and limit opportunities to inquire into questions of justice and explorations of ways to take action.

Questions of content, context, and audience, what the literature is about, what it means to the reader—to your students!—can fall to the wayside in a formalist approach to English teaching. Drawing on narrow traditions of literary scholarship and a limited understanding of the approach of the "New Critics," this kind of curriculum has appealed to textbook companies because potentially complicated or controversial questions don't get in the way of their books being adopted by states and school districts. This formalist curriculum also appeals to the testing industry because, say, the form of a sonnet, the difference between a metaphor and a simile, or the formal components of a research paper is knowledge that can be "isolated" and "reliably" tested by multiple-choice questions.

As we will explore in this book, to a significant degree, a number of the Common Core State Standards reflect an emphasis on learning elements and forms based on a formalist approach to English language arts. The CCSS writing standards are organized around specific argumentative, explanatory, informational, and narrative forms or modes. Likewise, the literature standards address the specific features of different forms of literature and the use of specific types of figurative language. Computers reading student essays may be able to recognize when a student names a specific literary term or follows the format of a specific type of paragraph organization, but computers can't evaluate the student's ideas, the strength of argument, or quality of language—the elements of writing that really matter.

In the context of justice, inquiry, and action where questions and ideas matter, learning about forms does not become an end but rather a means to enhance reading and writing in meaningful ways. Good teaching emphasizes meaning, questions that matter, diverse and individual perspectives, not memorization and repetition of forms. When meaning comes first, form still matters; the question becomes how does the form of the text impact or influence its meaning.

Let's return to Josie for a moment and how she experimented with different forms to have her students respond thoughtfully to *All American Boys* (Reynolds & Kiely, 2015). Throughout the unit, students composed journal entries to explore complex questions about racism and society. They also wrote letters to the character with which they identified most in the text, asking questions and weighing the character's action. In the novel, Quinn, a White adolescent male, witnesses an instance of police brutality against Rashad, but doesn't speak up or report his knowledge of the incident. Students considered how difficult it is sometimes to do the right thing and empathized with their own situations. They studied graffiti as an art form, which was central to one of the novel's characters' protests. They also considered the best form to communicate their social action, whether through posters, song lyrics, or written reports. They discussed the most effective ways to reach their target audience as they designed their strategies in their groups.

Josie's work included a study of form, but not as an isolated entity. While she studied the form of the novel with her students (as used by different authors), she translated this to students' decisions about their own forms. So, while she again shared an enthusiasm for form with Jasmine, her emphasis was on form for a purpose—emerging from her students' engagement in inquiry, justice, and taking action. Students wrote with purpose, and used forms and modes of writing appropriate to context and audience, rather than just learning forms for forms' sake.

ENGLISH LANGUAGE ARTS AS LITERACY SKILLS, STRATEGIES, OR PROCESSES

In the middle school across the street from Michael and Jasmine, Alexis and Santiago, two other fictional representations, carry on their own debate about how to teach English. Santiago's mantra is "skills, skills, skills." In Santiago's class, instruction is organized around the teacher modeling a reading or writing skill, and the students practice the skill first under Santiago's guidance and then complete homework handouts and worksheets independently. Santiago views reading and writing as a set of skills or strategies that can be transported from one text or context to almost any other. Santiago has separate reading lessons on breaking words down into syllables, identifying word roots, using context clues, previewing, predicting, skimming, scanning, paraphrasing, identifying main ideas, etc.

When it is time for writing, Santiago's students learn rules for spelling, capitalization, punctuation, the differences between different noun cases (subjective, objective, possessive), forming perfect tenses, using correlative conjunctions, reflexive and intensive pronouns, phrases and clauses, misplaced and dangling modifiers, the function of verbals (gerunds, participles, infinitives), aligning case and number, using verbs in the indicative, imperative, interrogative, conditional, and subjunctive moods—and more.

In the lunchroom, Alexis tells Santiago that his approach could also be called "skill, drill . . . and kill." "Where is the life in your teaching? Where is a sense of personal involvement?" Responding to Alexis, Santiago (correctly) points out, "Hey, all of these skills are specifically listed in the Common Core Standards for middle school English! These are just the things that they are going to test! And now that our evaluations as teachers are tied to student test scores you are taking a risk if you ignore students' skills!

If Santiago's mantra is "skills, skills, skills," Alexis talks about "process, process, process." Alexis believes that writing and reading are interactive as students create and work with their own texts and develop their own interpretations of their reading. In Alexis's classroom, students learn and practice "the writing process" steps—prewriting, organizing, revising, editing, and publishing. Drawing on Nancie Atwell (1987), Alexis calls her classroom a "workshop" where students write about topics that matter to them. Alexis also sees reading, like writing, as a continuous and recursive process of developing meaning. Students bring their prior knowledge to reading so that the meaning of the text emerges from a transaction between what the students already know and the words on the page. Alexis believes meaning evolves as students discuss the text with each other and the teacher to then return to the text for rereading to find new understandings.

"My students are doing lots more reading and writing than your students and all their reading and writing are going to better prepare them to pass whatever tests the state throws at them," Alexis tells Santiago. "And besides, I want them to become readers and writers for a lifetime!"

Skills versus process are two models of English teaching often in conflict. Years ago, extensive research on teaching traditional school grammar showed acquiring the skill of naming parts of speech had no impact on improving writing (Hillocks, 1984). The process model emerged to emphasize students actually writing—rather than memorizing parts of speech—and teachers supporting that writing at different phases of the composing process. In the process model, skills were to be taught "in context"—rather than having the whole class learn about, say, noun–verb agreement, the "skill" is only taught to those students whose actual writing shows that they need to learn it. In that sense, the process model is a significant advance over a purely skill-based approach.

We will have more to say about the process approach. For now, we want to point out that, with all the richness a process approach provides, it also runs risks. As with a formalist approach, conforming to a set or specific process can oversimplify the complexity of reading and writing.

A particular procedure or strategy can become an end in itself rather than opening to the actual diversity of students and to different ways to understand materials and reach audiences. Sometimes skills, processes, or strategies are taught for their own sake, in isolation from issues and questions that matter. Maren Aukerman (2013) describes this as "pedagogy as procedures" where the teacher is primarily concerned with the students employing certain processes or strategies in particular ways consistent with the teacher's instruction. Instead, Aukerman (2013) describes "pedagogy as sense-making" through dialogic exploration of alternative meanings of experiences and texts.

Focusing primarily on "inferring the main point" of a text as itself the primary goal of a strategy lesson, while not unimportant, can limit the extent to which students explore alternative meanings of a text, inquire into relationships and ethics, make judgments, consider implications. Rather than having to conform to specific processes or strategies set by their teacher in certain predetermined ways, a "pedagogy as sense-making" invites students to engage in dialogic talk and writing in unpredictable, unfolding "events-in-the-making" ways (Roth, 2014). A seemingly "off-task" classroom discussion of a novel may result in students sharing unique insights about the novel that their teacher never anticipated would occur.

Of course, the teacher needs to be aware of the skills and processes that students are employing or lacking and address them in the context of demonstrated need. However, skills and processes should not be the end goals of instruction. Focus on skills or processes separate from content and meaning can decontextualize instruction and fail to address social and cultural contexts where questions of justice, inquiry, and action arise.

In Josie's study of *All American Boys* and students' social action projects, the students developed the skills they needed appropriate to their project selection, such as in drafts of letter writing that ensured their arguments were suited to their audience, be that their peers or school leaders. The process of project selection and implementation, however, was a messy and recursive one. For example, some students researched avenues they thought would be helpful but then could not determine a tangible action, so they switched directions. Or, others sent emails to inquire about local resources and didn't hear back, so they changed plans and explored other paths.

Honoring the authentic processes required in writing, planning, and organizing, Josie had to determine ways to give students' "credit" for their work, which often came in the form of portfolios that showed drafts and revisions. In so doing, she illustrates for us how skills and processes can come together in an authentic approach drawing on justice, inquiry, and action to make a difference.

Activity: Recalling Previous Experiences with Different English Language Arts Curriculum Models

Think back over your English language arts experiences as a student. What was your experience with these traditional approaches—cultural knowledge, forms of literature and writing, skills, and processes? How did they enhance or limit your engagement? How do your experiences with these approaches impact your thinking about the purposes of English instruction? Which of these models do you believe you may adopt in your own teaching and why?

ENGLISH LANGUAGE ARTS AS JUSTICE, CRITICAL INQUIRY, AND ACTION

In contrast to the previously described curriculum models, in this book, as you can see, we are putting forward an approach to the English language arts much like Josie's, one that centers on justice, critical inquiry, and taking action. We believe our approach allows students to use and develop academic skills and thinking to examine human, interpersonal, and lived-world questions, to better understand others through literature and cultural study. Reading, writing, speaking/listening, media/digital literacy, and language help us address well-being, justice, democracy, and sustainability.

Our focus on justice, critical inquiry, and action is not just something we cooked up. It draws on important and established practices and traditions in our profession. Critical pedagogy is an educational philosophy and movement guided by passion and principle and committed to helping students develop awareness and consciousness of freedom, inequality, and justice. Paulo Freire, mentioned above, is often identified as the founder of critical pedagogy. In his best-known book, *Pedagogy of the Oppressed* (1972), he argues:

> Education either functions as an instrument that is used to facilitate integration of the younger generation into the logic of the present system and bring about conformity or it becomes the practice of freedom, the means by which men and women deal critically and creatively with reality and discover how to participate in the transformation of their world.
>
> (p. 34)

His "problem posing" approach emphasizes "acts of cognition, not transferals of information" (p. 67). Friere believed that, "the teacher is no longer merely the-one-who-teaches, but one who is himself [or herself] taught in dialogue with the students, who in turn while being taught also teach" (p. 67). And that,

> in problem-posing education, men [and women] develop their power to perceive critically the way they exist in the world with which and in which they find themselves; they come to see the world not as a static reality, but as one in process, in transformation.
>
> (p. 71)

Alternative perspectives emerge through co-inquiry and working as a co-collaborator with students. In his teaching, Maha Bali (2014) notes that he tries to:

> treat students as peers in a learning community. In my first day of class, I quote Jesse Stommel's online learning manifesto, "Content-expertise does not equal good teaching . . . Once a course begins, the growing expertise of the students, and not the teacher, should be the primary focus." . . . Critical pedagogy, for me, is not about knowing how to do everything right, or getting it right the first time, or every time. It is about putting faith in our learners to take control of their learning, and teach us, each other, and themselves in the process.

This "problem posing" method mentioned above challenges dominant myths and received thinking and critically considers ideology, steps for creating a better world (Freire, 1972; Giroux, 2011; hooks, 1994; Apple, 1995).

In addition to *critical pedagogy*, our approach also draws on *critical inquiry*. *Critical inquiry* calls for a question-based approach to teaching that fosters engaged learning, rich understandings of self and others, and an empowered sense of citizenship. Rather than posing questions that simply encourage your students to find particular kinds of information, critical inquiry requires that students pose their own questions that shape the content and process of their learning. As Thomas and Brown (2011) note,

> Our educational system is built upon a structure that poses questions to find answers ... Yet finding answers and memorizing facts do little to inspire students' passion to learn ... We propose reversing the order of things. What if, for example, question were more important than answers? ... What if students were asking questions about things that really mattered to them? ... Every answer serves as a starting point, not an end point. It invites us to ask more and better questions.
>
> (pp. 81–82)

Posing such questions presupposes that students have a genuine need to engage in inquiry about a problem or issue—that they do not already have answers.

Our approach also draws on *critical literacy* which encourages students to pose questions about multiple meanings and differing perspectives, underlying messages and theories, and ways in which reading and writing serve different audiences and interests (Lewison et al., 2014). Critical literacy attempts to connect current and past events in the world and students' lives, where the world can be as small as the classroom or as large as the international stage (Janks, 2013). It also supports students' enhancing their sense of agency as they help make changes in the world.

Reading carefully is often called "close reading." As we describe in more detail in Chapters 4 and 5 on reading, there has been considerable debate about the different meanings of the concept of "close reading." Some accounts assume that students should just focus on the text itself—as if the meaning of a text resides solely "within" a text (Coleman & Pimental, 2012). Other accounts recognize the need for students to apply their prior knowledge, experiences, attitudes, and purposes for reading (Fisher & Frey, 2014; Lehman & Roberts, 2013). In this book, we use the words "text" and "reading" to mean literary works *and* the full range of social and cultural production. For us, close reading entails both close analysis of the use of language, images, video, or audio in a text and application of prior knowledge, contexts, experiences, attitudes, and purposes. As Aukerman (2012) notes:

> As I see it, a reader who reads critically must read with a sense of textual authority and must recognize that (a) her or his own reading of a text is one of many possible understandings (the multiplicity of perspectives); (b) the readings we produce depend on our histories and social locations (the contingency of interpretation); and (c) writing/reading text is never a neutral act (the ideological nature of texts/readings). Thus, to teach critical literacy is to invite students to inhabit positions of textual authority in which their work with texts is anchored in these recognitions.
>
> (p. 42)

Students move from inferring a text's meaning to applying different perspectives to then challenging the text in responding to texts. Troy Hicks (2013) cites Ernest Morrell's description of four stances involved in critically responding to texts:

- Reading upon text: Attempting to understand the context of the piece, who the author is, and with what authority he/she has to speak about the topic.

- Reading within text: Following the logic of the argument and the evidence that the author uses to make claims. In other words, does the logic hold up given the evidence that has been presented and the claims being made?
- Reading beyond text: Extending the text by asking questions and comparing to what others have said—do the claims made hold up in the broader ways that the topic is discussed? Does it make sense in the field of study?
- Reading against text: Pushing against the text by asking questions and contrasting it to what others have said—do you agree or disagree with the claims that the author is making? Why? Are there critiques you can (and should) make? This will likely require multiple readings!

Cultural studies is another field of knowledge that informs our approach. Cultural studies adopts perspectives to examine traditional "canonical" culture and literary and informational texts, popular culture, film, the Internet, advertising, public discourse, and everyday practices (Carey-Webb, 2001; Hammer & Kellner, 2009; Jenkins et al., 2006). Cultural studies also include a focus on multiculturalism, anti-racism, gender and identity studies. Literature, videos, speakers, informational texts from diverse perspectives, including multicultural, women's, world, young adult, postcolonial, working class, and different religious backgrounds provide students with alternative perspectives that serve to develop their thinking and questioning. Cultural studies calls for making connections between texts and/or events. Examining these connections leads students to infer *patterns* and engage in analysis. For example, in studying a series of television ads by oil and coal companies touting their contributions to economic growth and employment, students may pose questions as to "what's missing?" in these ads related to the environmental effects of fossil fuel emissions.

Another area we draw upon is the foundation of *youth action* in society and schools. And there are so many ways young people can educate others and take action. The history of social movements, especially in the United States, illustrates that young people have always been involved in creating social change. During the Civil Rights Movement, four Black men, then college students, began a sit-in movement that spread throughout the South, non-violently protesting lunch counters that served only White people. In 1963, the movement succeeded in Birmingham because school children joined the protests and went to jail in great numbers.

Objection to the Vietnam War for its cost and casualties was centered on college campuses, and after the shooting of four students at Kent State University college and high school students across the country walked out of their classes. More recently, youth such as Cameron Kasky and his peers started the #NeverAgain movement as 11th-graders and survivors of the Marjory Stoneman Douglas High School shooting. And, Greta Thunberg, a Swedish teenager inspired by the students of Marjory Stoneman Douglass, started climate protests that in September 2019, at over 4,500 locations in over 150 countries, led to 8 million young people demanding governments address the climate crisis—one of the largest protests in human history.

This tradition of youth action illustrates that young people are not only capable of creating change, but should be entrusted to do so. John Dewey's (1938) groundbreaking notions of experiential learning proffered that students learn by doing. Freire's (1972) previously mentioned problem-posing education involved students in naming and addressing a justice-related issue of interest. Many teachers and scholars have drawn on this work to examine how youth action can be engendered in school contexts.

There are several branches of this type of work, including *youth participatory action research* (YPAR) (Cammarota, 2016). In YPAR projects, students become trained researchers who generate a question, enact rigorous methods to ascertain information, and present their findings and solutions to their target audience. Much of the work involving YPAR and similar approaches emphasize the role of writing in action and students developing a public voice. Marciano and Warren (2018), for example, describe their work with high school students writing to "facilitate change in their schools and community" (p. 485). In their study, students tackled support systems across local high schools, examined the type and content of courses offered in different schools, and analyzed extracurricular activities and sports funding.

Borsheim and Petrone (2006) described how they re-conceptualized the conventional research paper assignment in a tenth grade English classroom to develop an assignment that tasked students with critically analyzing their school and community and composing writing to effect change. One group addressed "juvenile crime" and another "the legacy of the Ku Klux Klan and racism in the community" (p. 80). Students in this study undertook participant interviews, archival inquiry, surveys, and internet data collection. Despite the authors' initial hesitation that critical research often means: "students are likely to ask questions that some people prefer they not ask about topics that some people prefer they not address," they asserted, "we were motivated by the belief that this approach is more authentic, worthwhile, and relevant to students' lives" (p. 82). They created space for action within orthodox curricular requirements and successfully engaged their students in their local society while re-envisioning an established curriculum component.

Others who include youth action in their classrooms incorporate writing but expand the products of students' work to include a full range of texts for which we advocate from our cultural studies framework. Students create videos, social media posts, blogs, and other web-based platforms as well as songs, performances, and flyers. Epstein (2010), who engaged students with *social action literacy projects*, documented middle school students' efforts in which they were required to "articulate social concerns through written, visual, and oral texts and as a result, 'make a change' in their community" (p. 363).

This body of work suggests numerous benefits in allowing youth to identify issues and areas that concern them as starting points to effect change. Our approach rests heavily on the pillar of the *youth action* because we encourage the use of critical teaching methods (*critical pedagogies*) to have students question their worlds (*critical literacy*) and to design responsive texts (*cultural studies*) to attempt to make change.

CONTRASTING PERSPECTIVES AS ESSENTIAL TO JUSTICE, INQUIRY, AND ACTION

Our approach focuses on learning in context, rather than in the abstract or in isolation. Recently, learning theory has focused on the social aspects of learning—how *through and because of* participation in literacy activities with others as social phenomena, students are best acquiring language, genres, discourses, and tools (Pennycook, 2010). Thus, the notion that one teaches students to "read" or to "write" as generalized sets of skills ignores the variations in how "reading" and "writing" are employed in different ways in different kinds of social contexts (Street, 1995).

Recognizing learning as social includes awareness of how to enrich and extend student contexts and understanding. In classroom discussions, it often happens that students seek consensus on problems or issues they are addressing. However, analysis of high school students' argumentative writing found that when students did achieve consensus, they often did not explore the problem or issue in sufficient depth because they shared the same or similar perspectives on the problem or issue (Ryu & Bloome, 2014). Without exposure to dissenting, alternative perspectives, students may all too readily agree on how to think about a specific problem or issue.

On the other hand, when students did not achieve consensus, either because they were applying different, alternative perspectives, or because they were challenging each other's thinking, they were more likely to engage in a richer and more complex discussion. Respectful disagreements with each other can lead students to recognize and critically examine their assumptions. Rather than seeking consensus, teachers can help foster a supportive, open-minded community where students acknowledge, work through, and benefit from other's views and ideas.

It is often easier to look for one definitive explanation than it is to understand complexities. For example, it is easier to understand a person or character's lack of success due to "laziness" than it is to understand it as a host of complex, competing factors. As Sheridan Blau (2003) notes, "readers who read texts looking for secure and certain answers to their questions may also read the world with a similar passion for certainty and with a similar intolerance for the moral complexity and ambiguity that resists simplistic formulations" (p. 213). Molly Vanish, an English teacher at Washburn High School in Minneapolis, emphasizes the value of ongoing conversations in her classroom.

> I think that it's important that they have conversations about where they are coming from and what they connect with and what they don't because often we just have a whole bunch of white noise in our heads and we don't know what we believe or what it is that we actually know. So before I jump in and try to bring in either another speaker who's an expert on the topic or try to say something about it myself, I try to get the students to get their heads spinning to think about what they know about things like feminism, dictatorship, women's rights, and reproductive justice. They then have a better understanding once we have that conversation and then bring in another perspective and have them talk about it. It's interesting because I don't think students think about the diversity of opinions in the classroom, so it's important to get those opinions out.
>
> I think the English class is a great place to do it because when you have a text it is easier to do that than when it's something personal. One of the conversations we had earlier this year was about Hemingway's "Up in Michigan," which is a short story—it was in a series of about ten stories. At the end of it, there's a kind of ambiguous possibility that there could be some kind of an acquaintance rape, but that's ambiguous. And that's a really hot issue now in terms of how to deal with rape on campus, and so it was interesting to have that conversation because it was a safe space to do it, because it was in the context of these two characters that the students' don't know instead of being about a situation with someone the students do know so it made it a little bit of a safer space for multiple opinions.
>
> And then after hearing those opinions, I process that and determine what resources do I need to bring in to broaden the conversation, and those resources are everywhere, for example, I just found an article in *The New York Times* yesterday in the Magazine about what college campuses are doing in terms of education, so bring in those things to have students have conversations about it.

> For some issues it's hard because I don't want that one voice who thinks differently to be shut down. By starting to talk about a book or a text it encourages a safe space and then students know how to talk about something that's hard to talk about and not interrupt each other when they want to push back on something. (Beach et al., 2016, p. 13).

Molly here reinforces one of the beautiful aspects of teaching literature, given how it allows students a way to discuss and wrestle with difficult topics, scaffolding them through characters' lives and affording a way 'in' for talking about—and acting on—real world social issues. We return to a description of leading class discussions as an important topic in Chapter 9.

Developing your students' skill at taking different perspectives means that instruction cannot be standardized, teaching in the same way in all contexts. Instead, you need to ground perspective-taking in the unique aspects of your students' own experiences, identities, and community contexts (Beach et al., 2015). Understanding the complexity of multiple, alternative, and contrasting perspectives is one of the most interesting, meaningful, and enjoyable aspects of teaching English.

THE BREADTH AND DEPTH OF SOCIAL ACTION

We realize that encouraging your students to understand multiple perspectives on an issue, research it, and take action may sound both appealing and challenging. We want to assure you that there are myriad ways youth can engage in their communities and that action comes in many forms. Often when we mention social action, people think of large-scale protests in streets. While that is certainly a valid form, so is educating others, interpersonal communication and behavior, conducting local action, and even cultivating online action. The Canadian Teachers' Federation's (2010) spectrum of action may prove valuable here to you and your students, as it posits a range from *indirect action*, in which activists attempt to influence those with the power to make change, such as writing letters to local lawmakers, to *direct action*, which is actually completing the action oneself, such as creating an LGBTQIA+ club at a school to support students and create allies.

Any effort to address an injustice, which may seem big or small, to make change for the better, is a step in the direction we advocate. As you teach and reflect on your lessons, you will want to make modifications and perhaps implement different iterations with each new group of students. You might then find that your comfort level increases as you learn what strategies, opportunities, and processes work best for you, your students, and your community. We encourage you to be brave in adopting a justice-and action-based critical inquiry approach and to continuously reflect upon your own goals, values, texts, and methods.

Activity: Identifying an Issue or Topic for Adopting These Approaches

Come up with an issue or topic that could be a starting point for a justice, inquiry, and action approach that students may be interested in addressing, particularly in terms of ones they are facing in their own lives. What are some questions students might explore? What are some texts they might study? What activities or assignments might you use? How might students engage in action taking?

SUMMARY

This chapter examines traditional frameworks for the teaching of English language arts, cultural knowledge, forms, skills, and processes. We put forward our approach drawing on the best frameworks and also focus on justice, inquiry, and action. As the rest of the book will show, there are as many ways to engage in justice, inquiry, and action teaching as there are teachers and classrooms. To provide you with additional resources associated with each chapter in this book, we've created a website that contains links to resources, instructional activities, and further reading for each chapter: *exceedingelastandards.pbworks.com*

REFERENCES

Apple, M. W. (1995). *Education and power*. Routledge.

Atwell, N. (1987). *In the middle: Writing, reading, and learning with adolescents*. Boynton/Cook.

Aukerman, M. (2012). "Why do you say yes to Pedro, but no to me?" To Santiago a critical literacy of dialogic engagement. *Theory Into Practice, 51*(1), 42–48.

Bali, M. (2014, September 9). Critical pedagogy: Intentions and realities [Web log post]. Retrieved from http://tinyurl.com/pmxp3l6

Beach, R., Johnston, A., & Haertling-Thein, A. (2015). *Identity-focused ELA teaching: A curriculum framework for diverse learners and contexts*. Routledge.

Beach, R., Thein, A. H., & Webb, A. (2016). *The English language arts Common Core state standards: A critical inquiry approach for 6–12 classrooms*. Routledge.

Blau, S. (2003). *The literature workshop: Teaching texts and their readers*. Heinemann.

Bloom, A. (1987). *Closing of the American mind*. Simon & Schuster.

Borsheim-Black, C., & Sarigianides, S. (2019). *Letting go of literary whiteness*. Teachers College Press.

Borsheim C., & Petrone, R. (2006). Teaching the research paper for local action. *English Journal, 95*(4), 78–83.

Boyd, A., & Miller, J. (2020). Let's give them something to talk (and act!) about: Privilege, racism, and oppression in the middle school classroom. *Voices from the Middle, 27*(3), 15–19.

Cammarota, J. (2016). Social justice education project (SJEP): A case example of PAR in a high school classroom. In A. Valenzuela (Ed.), *Growing critically conscious teachers: A social justice curriculum for educators of Latino/a youth* (pp. 90–103). Teachers College Press.

Canadian Teachers' Federation & The Critical Thinking Consortium. (2010). *Social action projects: Making a difference K–1*. Canadian Teachers Federation and The Critical Thinking Consortium.

Carey-Webb, A. (2001). *Literature & lives: A response-based, cultural studies approach to teaching English*. National Council of Teachers of English.

Coleman, D., & Pimental, S. (2012). *Revised publishers' criteria for the Common Core State Standards in English language arts and literacy, grades 3–12*. Common Core Standards Initiative. Retrieved from www.corestandards.org/assets/Publishers_Criteria_for_3-12.pdf

Common Core State Standards. (2010). Common Core State Standards for English language arts & literacy in history/social studies, science, and technical subjects. Council of Chief State School Officers and the National Governors Association.

Dewey, J. (1938). *Experience and education*. Macmillan.

Dyches, J. (2018). Critical canon pedagogy: Applying disciplinary inquiry to cultivate canonical critical consciousness. *Harvard Educational Review, 88*(4), 538–564.

Epstein, S. (2010). Activists and writers: Student expression in a social action literacy project. *Language Arts, 87*(5), 363–372.

Fisher, D., & Frey, N. (2014). *Close reading and writing from sources*. International Reading Association.

Freire, P. (1972). *Pedagogy of the oppressed*. Herder & Herder.

Giroux, H. (2011). *On critical pedagogy*. Continuum.

Goering, C. Z., & Connors, S. P. (2014). Exemplars and epitaphs: Defending young adult literature. *Talking Points, 25*(2), 15–21.

Hammer, R., & Kellner, D. (Eds.). (2009). *Media/cultural studies: Critical approaches*. Peter Lang.

Hicks, T. (2013, September 18). My digital reading practices, Part 3. [Web log post]. Retrieved from http://tinyurl.com/m58uwv6

Hillocks, G. (1984). What works in teaching composition: A meta-analysis of experimental treatment studies. *American Journal of Education, 93*(1), 133–170.

Hirsch, E. D. (1987). *Cultural literacy: What every American needs to know*. Vintage Books.

Holt, Rinehart, and Winston. (1998). *African American Literature*. Author.

hooks, B. (1994). *Teaching to transgress: Education as the practice of freedom*. Routledge.

Janks, H. (2013). *Doing critical literacy: Texts and activities for students and teachers*. Routledge.

Jenkins, J., Clinton, K., Purushotma, R., Robison, A., & Weigel, M. (2006). *Confronting the challenges of participatory culture: Media education for the 21st century*. MIT Press.

Lehman, C., & Roberts, K. (2013). *Falling in love with close reading: Lessons for analyzing texts—and life*. Heinemann.

Lewison, M., Leland, C., & Harste, J. C. (2014). *Creating critical classrooms: Reading and writing with an edge*. Routledge.

Marciano J. E., & Warren, C. A. (2018). Writing toward change across youth participatory action research project. *Journal of Adolescent & Adult Literacy*, 62(5), 485–494.

National Council of Teachers of English. (2021). *NCTE standards for the initial preparation of teachers of English language arts 7–12 (initial licensure)*. Author.

Pennycook, A. (2010). *Language as local practice*. Routledge.

Reynolds, J., & Kiely, B. (2015). *All American boys*. Simon & Schuster.

Roth, W-M. (2014). *Curriculum in the making: A post constructivist perspective*. Peter Lang.

Ryu, S., & Bloome, D. (2014, December 6). On the dialectical relationship of theory, methodology and classroom practice in the formative-design experimental study of argumentative writing. Paper presented at the meeting of the Literacy Research Association, Marco Island, Florida.

Saifer, S., Edwards, K., Ellis, D., Ko, L., & Stuczynski, A. (2011). *Culturally responsive standards-based teaching: Classroom to community and back*. Los Angeles: Corwin Press.

Sims Bishop, R. (1990). Mirrors, windows, and sliding glass doors. *Perspectives: Choosing and using books for the classroom*, 6(3), ix–xi.

Smagorinsky, P., Gibson, N., Moore, C., Bickmore, S., & Cook, L. S. (2004). Praxis shock: Making the transition from a student-centered university program to the corporate climate of schools. *English Education*, 36, 214–245.

Street, B.V. (1995). *Social literacies: Critical approaches to literacy in development, ethnography, and education*. Longman.

Thomas, D., & Brown, J. S. (2011). *A new culture of learning: Cultivating the imagination for a world of constant change*. CreateSpace.

Viswanathan, G. (1989). *Masks of conquest: Literary study and British rule in India*. Columbia University Press.

2

Planning English Language Arts Instruction

As the teacher, your knowledge, interests, and passionate commitment to what you are teaching are vital to your students' success and your decisions about instruction. At the same time, the best teachers know their students' reading and media interests, outside school activities, the issues they care about, the challenges they face, and their academic abilities and prior knowledge. Teachers should seek to uncover and build on their students' strengths and the intriguing, challenging, and inspiring aspects of their lives, rather than finding limitations, deficits, or faults.

It is essential that students know why and what they are studying matters in their lives. In our justice, inquiry, and action model, we encourage you to explore with your students questions and issues of fairness, decency, rights, equal treatment or opportunity—questions that people care about and debate, thus the questions that are controversial and important. Understanding the past matters, especially when it helps us understand today and tomorrow, when the past becomes a "history of the present" (Foucault, 1977).

In the same way, imaginatively exploring the future means the most when it gives insight into the world we live in now. Develop curricular units that are relevant, that begin with resonant issues, ideas, and questions, that move into young adult and classic novels, poetry, films, images, writing assignments, and that include school or community actions. In this way, you provide students with thoughtful, new, and empowering perspectives.

PLANNING BASED ON LIVED-WORLD EVENTS

It is important to plan activities based on what is going on in the larger world. In teaching in a rural alternative school in Michigan during the Iraq War, Jeff Paterson noted that military recruiters frequently visited his students. Many of his students knew soldiers serving in Iraq, and, indeed, two of his seniors were already married to American soldiers stationed in the Middle East (Webb, 2011). Stacy, a 17-year-old student, told the rest of the class that the night before her husband had told her during his call that he had just witnessed a fellow soldier shot by a sniper. Jeff reports,

> I was prepared to teach a lesson on war, but I had been thinking of war in some measure in an abstract sense—war as literature. I was prepared to push my own agenda and call for tolerance

and understanding, but this incident left me at a loss. What was I going to teach ... my students about what was happening on the other side of the world that was, at the same time, so connected to them and their isolated, but not so sheltered, lives in middle America?

Further, this event forced me to acknowledge my limited knowledge of the situation in Iraq. I was prepared to walk the students through *Sunrise Over Fallujah*, a young adult novel written by Walter Dean Myers (2009) about a young soldier's experiences in Iraq. The novel showed us that some of America's soldiers in Iraq are scared and confused, and that war is bad, often unnecessary—the novel is a fine example of the kind of war literature we should be teaching today. But even still, the time we had together in this class was precious and the need to address the topic urgent. Once the subject was opened, students wanted to find answers: why were we there? Is the war worth the staggering debt and deaths? The reality check that Stacy was giving us meant I needed again to rethink my approach to dealing with the conflict in my classroom. We just couldn't simply read a couple of books and move on to the next topic.

I realized that I was not capable of being the one with all of the answers in this class. I decided that we would need to engage in research together. As a class, we set out to develop a better understanding of the situation in Iraq. The idea was to attack the topic from many different angles. Students would become experts in their chosen area. For example, the two military wives expressed an interest in researching the effect of war on the soldiers. Another student wanted to examine stereotypes of Iraqis. Another wanted to research war profiteers. I discovered that some students—students who had lost interest in traditional schooling—were in fact eager to investigate this issue that was in the news and touched some of their lives (Webb, 2011, p. 103).

Jeff began by having his students examine their own and common stereotypes and negative attitudes toward Arabs. They watched and wrote about a video from *This American Life* about an Iraqi, Haider Hamza, who sets up a booth "Talk to an Iraqi" about life in Iraq before and after the American invasion. They read *Sunrise over Fallujah* (Myers, 2009) and a collection of blogs by a young Iraqi woman, "Riverbend." Students engaged in research and recorded what they were learning by video camera, created a class online social media discussion to make their work more broadly available, and wrote multi-genre papers.

Looking back on his class's critical inquiry into the war, Jeff notes:

We took a break from being distracted by classic novels, plays, and poetry and took a good hard look at something horrible that is actually happening in our world. We found a counterbalance to the distractions from a pop culture and mainstream media that encourages us to believe that everything is fine ... I want to believe that the students in English 12 left with a file of information from that semester stored in their brains, and when the time comes to make an informed choice or opinion about their world, that they can access those files and use the information stored there.

(Webb, 2011, p. 111)

As Jeff's example illustrates, an inquiry, justice, and action-oriented approach often involves non-linear teaching and a more diverse engagement with texts, research, online resources, and digital tools than more familiar content. We have found that this example, even though it is from a few years ago, still has contemporary resonance as many families have had experience in the Mideast wars and recruiters are still active in schools. Teachers can develop similar approaches to teaching with current topics, such as Black Lives Matter and climate change. When students hear about these issues on social media, in conversations at home, and on the news, they have questions. Such topics also deeply touch their own lives, like the military wives above. Many of our students have experienced racial profiling, and others are well acquainted with how their agriculturally based families have been affected by disruptions to weather patterns. They are eager to share their stories and to dig into research and address these contemporary problems. The opportunity to do so, however, is not often offered in schools. We encourage you to engage youth with meaningful texts and topics.

As a new teacher, you are likely to start with a textbook, a curriculum guide, and/or classroom sets of individual works. Literature textbooks are typically organized by literary genres (i.e., short story, poetry, drama, novel) or traditions (i.e., American, British, or world literature) or themes (i.e., "finding common ground," "the struggle for freedom," "heroes and quests"). Composition textbooks are typically organized around different writing modes (i.e., description, narration, comparison & contrast, persuasion) or subskills (grammar, topic sentences, punctuation). Any of these resources can offer starting points that can directly lead into or be incorporated within an inquiry, justice, and action approach.

As you develop familiarity with your students and the resources you have at hand, you will be better able to plan curriculum and instruction. As we discussed in Chapter 1, our approach is to focus on ideas and issues that connect different works. Skills, knowledge of traditions, forms, and processes can emerge from a curriculum with purpose and meaning. As you begin teaching, you may find yourself picking through and prioritizing existing texts and curriculum resources based on the topics you want to explore, then finding additional materials, developing sustained units, and fostering student communication and actions beyond the classroom.

The Internet offers enormous possibilities for extending reading, writing, and making a difference. Becoming an inquiry, justice, and action teacher takes more than simply reading this book—though knowing the theory and having many examples is vital. Your growth as a teacher takes place over time, step-by-step, as you extend, experiment, and gain confidence as well as knowledge and experience.

HOW DO I PLAN ACTIVITIES?

In Chapter 1 we described teaching students to engage in inquiry, justice, and action teaching. This framework, which we further elaborate below, calls for certain approaches to developing, planning, and implementing curriculum—the focus of this chapter.

Our approach is based on the use of four basic practices:

1. Valuing emotion to identify relevant topics and issues;
2. Using questioning to focus on fairness and justice;
3. Examining and adopting different perspectives; and
4. Finding ways to inform others/take action.

Though we have numbered and put these curriculum development and planning practices in a certain order, the order they might take place in is not fixed or rigid. Instead, the whole process is developmental, recursive, and creative. And, as we will discuss in the next chapter, our approach is also shaped by the students we are teaching and the standards we are meeting.

1. VALUE EMOTION AS A PATHWAY TO RELEVANT TOPICS AND ISSUES

Discovering key topics and issues to explore when teaching often emerges from emotional responses to reading, viewing, issues students learn about, or specific local, national, or international events.

Students experience doubt, pain, frustration, puzzlement, concern, indignation, or anger. These emotions can be starting points for asking "how come" or "why is it that . . . ?" as a means of "disrupting the commonplace" (Lewison et al., 2014, p. 7). Emotions may lead us to ask why we feel a certain way, such as a sense of frustration with how we or others—or a character we read about—are treated. Emotions are often a clue that something isn't right or fair. Thus emotions can be a pathway to developing questions of justice and action taking.

Students can draw on their own experiences and knowledge to identify emotions and raise issues. Sometimes issues that seem relatively insignificant or personal to you or other adults can actually be of great importance to students and valid starting points. Often, issues that touch their worlds also tie closely to unfair treatment based on gender, economic status, racism, mental health, employment issues, or local environmental problems. Engaging students in critical inquiry involves posing questions based on their concerns, interests, and passions about issues in texts and in their lived worlds (Rothstein & Santana, 2011).

Identifying these problems or issues leads students to adopt a critical stance. A critical stance is an attitude or orientation willing to ask questions about and challenge the status quo, to, as Lewison et al. (2014) define it, "disrupt the commonplace" (p. 5). They identify four dimensions associated with adopting a critical stance: consciously engaging, entertaining alternative ways of being, taking responsibility to inquire, and being reflexive.

Planning her teaching of *1984* (Orwell, 1984) to 12th-grade students at Jefferson High School in Bloomington, Minnesota, Elizabeth Erdmann described students' interest and concern about the amount of online data that was being compiled about them. Her students recognized how technology might be used as a form of social control similar to that portrayed in the novel. Adopting a critical inquiry approach in this classroom involved students exploring technology, rights, and freedom issues.

Teaching *1984*, she built on connections between the students' lived world observations and issues and problems portrayed in the text.

> With Winston, he is just writing in a little diary, and that's a big deal, but with these students, who knows what they are doing? They are taking pictures of themselves; they are writing things on Facebook and making movies. It's all going to a gigantic square in Arizona—it's all being stored somewhere. It's all for consumers—all of these people are being marketed to, so it's controlling how they think. They are the thought police—the thought police are the capitalists. Like the people they are making fun of in the story, making them insecure.
>
> I show them a Frontline documentary about the secret state of North Korea which shows how the government controls the people. So then I asked them how do you know that you don't know whether this is happening to you—think of the pop-ups on your computers and the TV ads when you fill up gas is a tele-screen in your face. How do you know that you're not in North Korea? They say because we have free speech here.
>
> It made the literature meaningful when students were able to notice parallels between *1984* and current examples of institutions acquiring personal information, including their school.

Their emotional reactions led to increased analysis of the topic of privacy, government, marketing, technology, and surveillance. (Beach et al., 2016, p. 61).

As you create a safe classroom where emotions can be shared, you will likely discover that emotions and ideas change and evolve. Sometimes emotions emerge that may be difficult for students to deal with. Students trust their English teachers and, at times, share, reveal, or make evident things in their lives that are difficult, even traumatizing. Supportive listening without judgment, encouraging reading and writing on related topics, connecting students with others, including mental health professionals, and finding ways to take action in their own lives and communities are all basic and important dimensions of English teaching. (As you likely know, as a teacher, you are a "mandatory reporter," required to alert appropriate authorities in your school about issues of criminal abuse or neglect impacting your students.)

The challenging topics addressed in an inquiry, justice, and action curriculum can also bring up difficult emotions. If you focus on topics such as racism and oppression as we encourage you to do in this book, White students may feel "guilty" or may think you are trying to make them feel "guilty." The same exploration may lead students of color and White students to feel "angry."

These emotions are important topics for validation and inquiry. For example, students learning about genocides or the nightmare future created by business-as-usual climate change may feel "overwhelmed" or "hopeless."

Rather than shutting down learning about difficult topics, as the current attack on critical race theory (CRT) advocates, it is important to learn from emotional reactions. Why do we feel "guilty," "angry," "overwhelmed," or "hopeless"? How do these emotions help us think about and better understand issues of fairness and justice? How do they lead us to think or act differently?

The *crucial* response to all of these difficult emotions is to understand them and find ways to draw on them to move forward—the key is that third word of our approach: action. Finding ways to put the energy of these important and difficult emotions to work involves taking action to address inequality, unfairness, or threats to our environment. Doing so creates change and generates more positive emotions. This includes listening to students and addressing the issues in their lives in your curriculum. Great English teachers don't shy away from difficult topics or feelings. Instead, they create a safe classroom where such topics can be addressed respectfully and productively, supporting individuals, embracing diversity, and fostering democracy.

2. ASK QUESTIONS TO BRING FOCUS TO JUSTICE AND ACTION

In a justice, inquiry, and action approach, posing questions is not only a crucial part of close and careful reading, but it also invites students into the curriculum-making process. Students can collaboratively construct questions about a topic or issue by listing questions in groups or as a class. They can then sort the questions into categories or prioritize those questions they perceive to be the most significant or relevant to addressing their concerns, interests, and passions.

Based on their questions, students come to better understand the problem or issue they are exploring in increasingly specific terms. For example, students reading *To Kill A Mockingbird*

(Lee, 1960) might begin with a question such as "why was lynching prevalent in the first half of the 20th century in the American South?" As teachers encourage them to become more specific, students might ask questions such as, "what specific groups of Whites in the American South were engaged in lynching and what reasons did these groups give for participating?" Specific questions might connect with current issues, for instance, "how does the criminal justice system treat minoritized racial groups in our country today?"

You can also use student questions to generate readings or develop issues to focus on when reading—often called a "point-driven stance." For example, if students are interested in gender inequity, perhaps you teach *Romeo and Juliet* with a focus on gender roles and relate that to treatment of women today. Are the expectations for Juliet to marry different from today? In what ways? How is each treated differently by their parents? Canonical works can therefore become creatively connected to your students' questions. It may require some additional inventiveness on your part to select texts that help students think critically about their topics and questions, but you can find them!

A justice, inquiry, and action approach can focus on significant problems or issues facing society such as economic inequality, racism, climate change, health care, and immigration. At the same time, English teachers should recognize that for students, certain problems or issues that seem relatively insignificant or personal to an adult can actually be major issues in their lives; for example, the fact that they are experiencing high levels of stress, given the college admissions process, or finding it difficult to find healthy foods in their neighborhoods. Therefore, it is useful to have students draw on their own experiences and knowledge to identify problems or issues rather than on prepackaged, "safe" issues typically found in curriculum or writing textbooks.

Students are more likely to generate effective questions when they formulate them in small face-to-face or online groups that allow for sharing ideas, revising, and clarifying. Reporting out to the whole class can lead to prioritizing what the class as a whole wants to address (Virgin, 2015) (for resources on having students pose questions: *rightquestions.org/education*).

For planning activities to foster students' adoption of a critical stance in responding to literature, film, or other reading, you can pose questions such as the following:

- What emotions do the events we are reading about bring up for you? How do those emotions help you better understand the text and how you should respond to it?
- How do problems portrayed in texts you are reading or viewing connect with your own life and experiences or issues in our community or world? How might those problems or issues be addressed?
- What additional research or reading could we do to help us better understand these issues and what to do about them?
- How are different types of characters portrayed, and are these portrayals fair or representative of different groups of people?
- Whose point of view is most valued in the text? What other points of view might there be in the text, and how do they compare or contrast?
- What points of view are not in the text but might help us better understand it? How could we learn more about these "excluded" points of view?
- How are human institutions (family, school, organizations, activities, or economic or social systems) portrayed? How should they be changed or improved?

- How is nature or the natural environment portrayed? How does that portrayal relate to what is happening to nature or the environment today? What can we do about that?
- What issues in the text might connect to our families, school, community, country, or world? What organizations in our school, community, country, or world are addressing these issues? How could we get involved?
- How can we share what we are learning with others, family members, other students, or other communities in person or online?
- What is the history of issues or problems we see in this text? How can we learn more?
- What issues of inequity, justice, or decency come up in the text? What kinds of social or political responses or remedies might be important to address the inequalities?
- What questions does the text raise about the way we live or ought to live, about fairness or human rights? What rights do people have? Where are these rights listed, and how are they protected? What rights should people have?
- What would an ideal community look like? How do we get closer to it?

Complex and controversial issues and texts can foster student inquiry. For example, in teaching the Disney film, *Pocahontas* (Gabriel & Goldberg, 1995) in a high school English class, a teacher wanted her students to critique the stereotyped representations of Native Americans (Lewis & Dockter, 2008). Two African American students in the class voiced strong responses to the hyper-sexualization of Pocahontas, a critique that reflected their prior knowledge of stereotypes of African Americans. Or, students may respond to the memoir *The Things They Carried* (O'Brien, 2009), portraying the difficult experience of American soldiers in the Vietnam War. They may then have questions about why small-town community members supported the war and the perception that going to fight was the main character's "patriotic duty." These "indeterminate situations" create doubts, include contradictions, and foster questions (McCann, 2014).

It is also crucial to note that students will likely need scaffolding in designing questions to address issues in ways that lead to action. For example, if questions are left at the topic level, such as genocide, students may not be able to think of an action that can feel sufficiently successful. Most of the public would agree that genocide is a problem, so what could be done to address a part of this topic in a way that helps with a more specific piece or related problem (Boyd & Darragh, 2019)?

Developing a question such as "How can we help local refugees who left their country to escape genocide?" would move the topic to a related, local problem and thus more manageable. Students can research and design actions based on that inquiry. Justice, inquiry, and action should not lead to hopelessness (Boyd, 2017; Downey, 2005). As students narrow broad topics to an issue, to a specific problem that can be addressed, they increase their ability to be effective, to make a difference.

3. EXAMINE AND ADOPT DIFFERENT PERSPECTIVES

Students' perspectives are shaped by what they are familiar with, whom they know, and the range of ideas and perspectives they are exposed to. People are more likely to trust the media outlet that is consistent with their political affiliation, and then they access those outlets more frequently (Gottfried, 2021). Democrats may access CNN or MSNBC, while Republicans may access Fox News. As a result, they are gaining very different perspectives on current news events. If students only encounter beliefs and attitudes that reinforce their existing ideas, they are less likely to engage in inquiry.

Students may not be familiar with historical, institutional, or cultural perspectives necessary to understand a text, event, or issue. Together with the students, you can consider how more diverse perspectives could be heard and considered. Additional reading, viewing, or research can increase knowledge of context and perspectives. School or community members or representatives of different groups or organizations can be interviewed outside of class or can visit the class. If particular experiences or points of view are not available in your curriculum, that creates a powerful argument for funding the purchase of new materials. Discovering, researching, and carefully considering diverse alternative perspectives is an important part of student learning.

To acquire relevant sources of information, you can provide students with literary and media texts that bring perspectives they are not used to considering. You can create text sets (Elish-Piper et al., 2014), and use libraries and online resources. Starting with students' inquiry questions from above, you can select relevant materials that help them deeply explore the problem from a variety of perspectives. If students are interested in gender inequity, you could have them study court cases that established women's rights (e.g., *Orr v. Orr*, 440 U.S. 268). They could also examine YouTube videos of activists demanding equal pay (e.g., interviews with Megan Rapinoe) or view documentaries that explain the history of ideas or groups (e.g., Netflix's "Feminists: What were they thinking?"). You might also add to your text set works that complicate these perspectives, such as which women have gained from such movements and which are still struggling (including works such as Rebecca Walker's "I am the Third Wave.")

Moreover, students need to learn how to identify media sources, their funding, and the quality of documentation, evidence, and argument.

Adopting alternative perspective for responding to texts

You can also facilitate students' consideration of alternative experiences and viewpoints by assigning different perspectives to read a text (Appleman, 2015). For example, suppose students are reading a story written by an author in a dominant group. In that case, you could have them examine what else was happening during a particular era that is not included in the text, or consider whose story is not being told.

You might also assign them a particular perspective, such as from a minority or marginalized person, from which to read. How might a person who identifies as gender nonconforming read *Romeo and Juliet*, for instance? How does thinking from another person's viewpoint alter a reading, and how might this inform students' thinking about a related social topic? For example, you could ask them to read culturally diverse texts and then ask how a feminist might interpret a particular court case portrayed in a text. Encouraging students to conduct these alternate readings can help them develop empathy and more critical stances, beyond when a text or topic simply doesn't conform to their own positions or backgrounds.

Steffany Maher coupled her student's reading of *To Kill a Mockingbird* (Lee, 1960) with a historical investigation of lynching with Walter Dean Myers's (1999) young adult novel *Monster*, which explores the incarceration of a young African American man on trial for the murder of a store owner. Steffany points out that when students investigate contemporary American incarceration rates based on race they learn about disturbing racial discrimination still going on today. Reading a literary work about the past invites students to engage in inquiry and actions related to injustices in the present. The study of history then becomes a way to understand the world today as "a history of the present."

This approach better prepared Steffany's students to analyze arguments, make claims, and propose and act on solutions. They were able to analyze and take stands on a variety of topics, including the importance of the attempted lynching and trial scene in the novel, impact of lynching on African Americans, the fairness of the jury system in the Jim Crow era, on-going inequities in the criminal justice system, the school to prison pipeline, and the Black Lives Matter movement. Her students' critical stance and engagement with information and ideas prepared them for both formal argumentation and creative attempts at persuasion. (One student presented an argument through the format of a poem set to music and images.) Steffany says,

> Students were better able to relate the literature and these important issues to their own lives. They were thinking more deeply about the world around them and their places in it. They were also interested enough in the literature and involved enough in the class to contribute their responses to what they had read and learned. As a result, my classroom was a much more exciting place for me to be as well.

While Steffany's teaching of *To Kill a Mockingbird* is compelling and helps point out the problematic perpetuation of a racist narrative in the novel (Macaluso, 2017), many works commonly taught in English can become starting points for justice, inquiry, and action teaching. English teachers frequently examine the portrayal of witch-hunts in the play, *The Crucible* (Miller, 2003) to help students inquire into how Puritan religious beliefs led townspeople to believe that their peers were agents of the devil. They then infer parallels to the 1950s and 1960s, shaped by McCarthyism and anti-Communism, or the present-day treatment of government and corporate whistleblowers. Students reading *Things Fall Apart* (Achebe, 1958) might inquire into colonialism and its ongoing impacts in Nigeria or West Africa and in other places in the world, including in their own communities in North America.

Applying larger institutional, historical, and institutional perspectives

Students can examine how different institutional systems shape issues: families, schooling, government/political, legal, health care, business, science, community/neighborhood, environmental/ecological, communications/media, military, etc. Each of these systems is driven by certain goals and uses specific tools or strategies to achieve those goals (Engestrom, 2009). Students are often not aware of how various institutions and systems serve as invisible forces that structure and inform their beliefs and even their roles and identities. Institutions and systems rely upon specific forms of language, systems of reasoning, sets of values, and ways of viewing the world—different "discourses" (Gee, 2008).

As they adopt certain discourses as ways of knowing and thinking, people construct their identities—what Gee (2008) refers to as "identity tool kits." As a teacher, you adopt certain ways of knowing and thinking based on pedagogical theory and practice that shape your identity as a teacher. Readers of this book may come to think of themselves as justice, inquiry, and action teachers, or they may not. Students may also interrogate narratives constituting their identities based on race, class, and/or gender.

Students can also engage in critical inquiry into ways discourses are enacted through narratives and shape cultural beliefs and perceptions. Of course, advertising also promotes consumerism based on the assumption that acquisition of products and experiences contributes to personal happiness without considering broader impacts. For example, SUV or truck commercials portray how an

> energy-inefficient vehicle rumbles off the paved road, rambling through fields, streams, mountainsides, or across a desert landscape. In such a scene, the environment becomes a playground for humans, with little attention paid to what such activity might mean for the environment.
>
> (Damico et al., 2020, p. 684)

Moreover, students might examine how "stories-we-live-by" shape their beliefs about the need to take action to address the climate crisis (Damico et al., 2020; Stibbe, 2021) *storieswel iveby.org.uk*. Students can examine how the media promotes individualism or understanding human beings as separate from the environment.

In contrast, narratives from Indigenous cultures and groups promote harmony between humans and nature, as evident in videos from Canadian System Change Not Climate Change project: *canadians.org/systemchange*. Similarly, young people adopt environmental justice and activism narratives evident in Zero Hour *thisiszerohour.org*, the Sunrise movement *sunrisemovement.org*, Extinction Rebellion *rebellion.global*, and School Strike for Climate Australia *schoolstrike4climate.com*.

In adopting a justice, inquiry, and action approach, you, as a teacher, assume an important role in raising alternative perspectives or using relevant and diverse resources, particularly when you perceive students adopting limited or one-sided perspectives. In a study that hits close to home, pre-service teachers' perspectives on students in an urban school during and after their teacher education program were shaped by the degree to which they adopted a "social justice" approach (Whipp, 2013). Teachers who adopted a cultural/institutional perspective were more likely to employ culturally responsive, social justice pedagogies, while teachers who adopted an individualistic, "color-blind" perspective showed less use of social justice pedagogy.

4. COLLABORATE, INFORM OTHERS, AND TAKE ACTION

Whether by positive or negative example during the Covid pandemic, we all learned about the value of interactive learning, whether face-to-face or online. Teaching today, you want to involve students working together, learning from each other. That interaction may be through whole-class discussion, literature circles or group projects, or through redefined, non-linear activities such as writing workshops. For example, Stevens and Dugan (2010) describe a high school English class organized as a media lab in which groups of students collaboratively produced four genres of videos: a commercial, a public service announcement, an interview, and a documentary. The media lab learning space fostered collaborative, hands-on learning driven by the goal of producing a winning video shown on the school's TV news. In this class, when students asked the teacher, "'What are we doing today?'" the teacher asked the students "'What are you doing today?'" (Stevens & Dugan, 2010, p. 64). The students knew that producing successful videos depended on their ability to collaborate through co-planning with each other and the teacher.

This model of "autonomy support" results in increased engagement, motivation, and achievement (Patall et al., 2008). As Alfie Kohn (2010) notes, "What matters is not what we teach; it's what they learn, and the probability of real learning is far higher when the students have a lot to say about both the content and the process" (p. 22). Rather than imposing pre-packaged "content" onto students, it's better to build activities based on your students and their worlds as starting points to engage, develop skills, and inspire success. At the same time, invite students to go beyond their personal experience and local worlds to experience alternative perspectives through classic, popular, multicultural, and contemporary literature, film, informational text, or library/online research.

In English language arts, we highly and appropriately value the imagination, its capacity to help us understand the experience of others, its power to envision different futures, its motivation to foster action. In so many ways, writing is a powerful tool. Writing can be a form of inquiry, a way to learn more. Writing can also help formulate and articulate solutions. Students can address specific audiences and demonstrate that they are credible, knowledgeable, and propose solutions through their writing.

Students also need to understand how changes occur through appeals, organized efforts, established channels, and social actions and movements. As students learn about making change, they might pose questions such as:

> Who was involved in making change? What did they do? Were their actions successful? What would I change or do differently? What resources did they need? Did they engage allies and if so, how? How was their message forwarded?
>
> (Agarwal-Rangnath, 2013, p. 119)

When they launch their efforts to address a problem or issue, students can then pose questions such as:

> If so many people know about this problem, why does it still exist? Who might be benefiting from the situation as it currently exists? What values might be motivating them? What do they want or need? Has anyone tried to block solutions? How? What happened? What's already being done? What still needs to be done? What should be our goals for the project? Who will be involved in the project? Who will the project help/support? What more information do we need? What challenges do we face? How do we connect with others with the same goal? How do we connect with others who may not think the same way?
>
> (Agarwal-Rangnath, 2013, pp. 119–120; adapted from Schmidt, 2007)

When students identify their purpose and audience in a rhetorical context, they can address audiences who have the power or authority to make change; and in so doing, formulate arguments using reasons or evidence to support their proposed solutions, drawing on multiple perspectives, and responding to counter-arguments. They may decide to use different multimodal tools, for example, use of charts, graphs, videos, websites, etc.

Students may also use a range of different modes to voice resistance and the need for change. For example, a teacher in San Francisco had her students employ what she defined as "positive graffiti" to express their concerns (Agarwal-Rangnath, 2013). Students engaged in a field trip to the Angel Island site where Chinese immigrants wrote poems about their experience of oppression and imprisonment. Students wrote their own poems about injustice, homesickness, guilt, consolations, and obligations based on what they learned. They also studied the work of graffiti artist, Banksy, who uses his graffiti art to express resistance to status quo problems or issues. Based on study of his graffiti, students also created graffiti-like images to accompany their poems; the images were then displayed to the class. (For more on devising activities based on issues in local communities, see *Learning in local communities* on the website.)

Students can consult the work of the famous American political scientist Gene Sharp and his list of *198 Ways to Engage in Nonviolent Action www.aeinstein.org/nonviolentaction/198-methods-of-nonviolent-action/*). Many of these actions involve writing, formal statements, media communications, group presentations and performances, symbolic public acts, drama, music, guerilla theater, and many other forms of direct action potentially appropriate to English language arts students.

Another approach to taking action is counter-storytelling—when students address stereotypical or negative portrayals and representations by creating alternative narratives (Johnson & Rosario-Ramos, 2012). For example, newspaper and online crime reports are often associated with urban neighborhoods. Students could create counter-narratives to these stereotypical media representations by, for example, portraying instances of neighbors or organizations in urban or low-income neighborhoods providing positive support for others in their neighborhood.

Allen, one of the co-authors of this book, frequently has his students engage in public writing, share what they are learning with others online, lead community education activities, and participate in "service learning" projects.

After studying various aspects of and perspectives on the climate crisis, including reading climate fiction or "cli-fi," Allen has his students write a "Climate Justice Manifesto." The manifesto is a genre that we rarely ask students to write in, but it shouldn't be. A manifesto is "a clear and conspicuous public declaration of the views of the issuer on a matter of great public importance." There is a rich and diverse tradition of manifestos from the Declaration of Independence to the Port Huron Statement. (See Wikipedia "Manifesto" for a long list.)

Allen encourages students to include several elements in their manifesto but also welcomes them being written in different genres. He asks that their manifestos include some analysis of the history and urgency of the climate crisis, its justice dimensions, and a call to action including specific steps, and a vision of how a just and sustainable future society should be organized.

He tells his students:

> You are writing about the greatest issue human beings and, perhaps, all life on Earth has ever faced. Show that you have a serious knowledge of the facts, issues, and justice issues. Write in a powerful and stirring public voice and use language that appeals to and draws others to your position. Be thoughtful, courageous, passionate, and visionary.

Some manifestos have been written as poetry, songs, letters to corporate executives, or other young people. Writing their manifesto helps Allen's students not only better understand, connect, and clarify the issues, but it also establishes their stance and empowers them to speak out. His students publish them online, and have also read from their manifestos at public rallies, spoken from them on public panels, shared copies from tables set up around the school, sent them to corporations they have worked for, and addressed professional organizations (assignment and manifestos at *bit.ly/31FrZhX*).

There are so many other ways to create public writing and presentations. Allen's students have also written climate change-related poetry, short stories, persuasive essays, and a children's book that they shared face-to-face and online. Their public writing also includes blogs, wikis, and climate crisis "culture jams" distributed via social media.

Working in groups, his students created an online climate change cookbook for young people featuring recipes and information about food justice and carbon footprints. They also organized public events including showing climate change documentaries at a local school and serving on a panel afterward to lead discussions. They also held a public tree planting event, led community reading discussion, and created a climate change "teach-in" where students, teachers, and community members spoke.

One way to think about action taking is "service learning." The concept goes back to John Dewey and early 20th century Progressivism and Pragmatist ideas about education. Service-learning is incorporated into many secondary and university programs and classes by tying what students are learning in school with volunteering in the community, often for specific non-profit, service, or activist organizations. A key component is tying back what students learn from their volunteer work to critical thinking in the classroom. The potential ties with language arts are, perhaps, obvious.

Students studying *Of Mice and Men* (Steinbeck, 1993) could work in their community with organizations supporting migrant workers, the homeless, people with mental disabilities, farmworkers, etc. Students reading works addressing domestic violence from *Taming the Shrew* or "The Birthmark" (Hawthorne) to *Speak* (Anderson, 2011) could work with organizations from the YWCA to RAINN or other organizations addressing rape or domestic violence. Mental health, poverty, climate change, racism—virtually any important social issue comes up in literature read in secondary schools and could tie to organizations. Joining organizations, creating local chapters in the school or community is one of the most powerful ways to take action and absolutely a fit with service learning.

LESSON PLANNING

Justice, inquiry, and action teaching is an unfolding and recursive process driven by posing further questions, more deeply exploring texts and issues, and finding new ways for students to examine feelings, critically inquire, communicate, and act on what they are learning.

Universities preparing teachers and school districts monitoring them often focus on lesson plans as the center of instruction. We want to register some reservations.

In this chapter on "planning," you may have noticed that we don't begin by focusing on delivering individual lessons. Our approach to lesson planning is meant to be both critical and suggestive, rather than prescriptive. We profoundly believe that individual lessons are not stand-alone activities to be dropped willy-nilly into random classrooms. Rather, they depend on the issues and ideas being explored in units more largely conceived and on the dynamics of the students and their special teacher.

The first question is not *how* you should teach but *what* you teach. As we have been describing, *what* is not static or simply given by the textbook or curriculum guide, but needs to evolve from teacher and student interest and passion, and involve inquiry, questions of inclusion and justice, and taking action. Certainly, *how* and *what* are intimately tied together: good teaching is not simply carrying out a set of steps or activities regardless of the content. The *how* emerges from the *what*, from inquiring into meaningful questions about living and acting rightly.

As we discussed in Chapter 1, English language arts lesson planning that simply finds clever ways to teach decontextualized skills, be that naming parts of speech or different forms of composition, fails to develop a rich, evocative, or meaningful curriculum. Lessons without broader context are not only less likely to engage students, but they are also less likely to be effective in enhancing student skills—the skills that stick are ones that are learned through practice in a social and meaningful context.

Lesson plans come in many different formats, each with somewhat differing open and hidden assumptions about what students should be learning and doing. Consistent with the focus of this book, we believe that a good lesson plan begins with an *overview* of how a particular day or multi-day activity relates to the course or unit curriculum, themes, or issues. Then move on to meaningful learning *goals* addressing important intellectual and emotional content and ethical, justice questions and ideas the students will explore so specific skills or specific texts may be addressed but as means rather than as ends in themselves.

A lesson plan may include *standards* that are expected to be met—in Chapter 3 we extensively inquire into how to address standards in meaningful ways; just as with skills they need to tie to learning that matters. There are so many *activities* that have value, including but not limited to drawing on students' prior knowledge, incorporating writing, choice, reader response, thematic instruction, carefully focused discussion, group work, etc. Actions certainly include the full range of ways students can educate others and take action on what they are learning.

A lesson plan should also include *accommodations* specific to the different student learning levels, styles, and special needs present in the class. We also think it important that a lesson plan includes *extensions* as follow-up activities that develop and expand on the lesson and encourage continued learning, often learning independent of the teacher. We like to see *assessment* go beyond fill-in-the-blank rubrics to include support for critical, careful, and generous student self-assessment focused on continued learning and growth, rather than grading, sorting, and ranking. Finally, every lesson plan should include *reflection*—what went well, what could be improved. Involving students in the reflection enriches their understanding and increases a sense of ownership and motivation.

All of these appropriate lesson planning dimensions are richly developed and include real-world examples throughout this book. However, rather than any "silver bullet" instructional method, it is your judgment, passion, and freedom that will engage your students to transform their lives and the world we all share.

HIGH EXPECTATIONS AND HELPING STUDENTS DO THE WORK

Since the reading and work in your class is going to be meaningful and important, we agree with you that your students should be doing the reading and homework. Too often, secondary students skate around reading assignments, using Spark Notes or other online summaries, talking to other students, rephrasing what other students have said in the discussion, slipping under the radar, etc. Your classes will always have students with diverse reading levels, even in "ability grouped" classes in low or high levels or tracks. So a critical part of lesson planning is answering these two questions: (1) how do you support students reading texts that are difficult for them? And, (2) how do you ensure students do their homework? Here are some starting points:

- Preview the reading. What do students need to know about the context or telling of the story before they start to read it?
- Start the reading by the teacher reading the beginning of the story aloud in class. Pause at key moments to ask questions and check for understanding.
- The teacher reading aloud makes texts significantly easier for students to understand; students reading aloud often does not have this advantage.
- Provide students with reading questions to help them focus on and understand difficult passages. Expect them to write answers to the questions and/or expect to have the questions addressed during class discussion.
- Invite students to write their questions about the reading. These questions can then be discussed in pairs, small groups, or by the whole class.
- Begin class discussion of a text by asking students questions about basic information about the main characters and the plot action before moving to more complex or difficult questions or questions higher on "Bloom's Taxonomy."
- Reading sections together from the data projector can model careful and critical reading.
- Providing knowledge about the genre of texts—while avoiding being too technical—can help students better understand what they are reading.
- Incorporating readers' theater events, creating scripts, and using drama activities increases comprehension and motivation.
- Be sure that reading homework is clearly assigned. Homework calendars, a class blog or website with reading assignments listed, repeating assignment instructions at the beginning and end of class, assigning students a partner to communicate with when they miss class—all of these can increase the likelihood students do the reading.
- Be sure homework is well integrated into class activities; for example, if students are assigned reading that reading should be discussed or addressed in class the next day.
- Students need to know that homework is important. Talk frequently about their learning that comes from doing the homework and why it is useful to what you are doing in class. Avoid point systems, petty rewards, or grade threats and focus on their learning. Teach students how to do homework and the study skills they will need for academic success.
- Written homework can be fun, creative, and involve high-level thought. A key measure of this is how you feel responding to the homework: truly creative and intellectually meaningful homework is something the teacher looks forward to reading. Don't assign homework that will bore you!
- Homework needs to be closely monitored. Collect homework from individual students at their desks—create a moment where they come face-to-face with you every time homework is assigned. Return homework that you have responded to quickly, preferably the next day.

- All students need to be held accountable for doing homework. When students don't have their homework, be sure you let them know that you expect it. Meet with them after class, find them during your "prep" period, call them at home, and develop contracts. Your personal relationship with each student is vital to inspiring students to do the work in your class. When a few students get away with not doing homework, the atmosphere in the whole class will deteriorate.
- Inform parents or guardians about homework expectations, and tell them that their child is falling behind. Enlist their help, support, and involvement (but don't blame them for students not doing the work in your class—that is your responsibility and that of the students, not the parents or guardians).
- When several students are not turning in homework, it is important to have whole-class discussions about the homework. "I noticed several people did not have the homework done, what is going on?" might be one way to start such a discussion. Involve students with helping each other with the homework and supporting each other with turning it in. Learn from your students, don't blame them. When students are not doing their homework, that does not necessarily mean that they are lazy or don't care. Instead, it is important information for the teacher that something is not right either with the curriculum, the homework itself, or the way it was assigned. Language about expectations is important, and, often, teachers and students misunderstand each other.
- Don't be insulted if students tell you that the reading is "boring"—what they may mean is "I don't understand the reading," and, as a teacher, you have lots of ways to help make reading interesting and understandable.
- When students complain: "This is too much work." They might really mean: "I am not interested in the work." Students who enjoy and are interested in what they are doing are willing to work hard—don't assign less work, make the work more interesting.
- When students misbehave or act out, it is so easy to start to think that "they just don't care" but it might really mean "I believe I can't do the work" or "I don't understand the assignment." or "I don't know why this assignment is important."
- If the teacher tells the class: "I will notice when you do not do the work and I will talk to you about it personally." Students may say: "The teacher is a hard a—!" But they might really be thinking: "The teacher cares about me."
- If the teacher says, "Students of your age (or level) really should be able to take responsibility for turning in homework on your own." The students might think this means, "The teacher doesn't care if I succeed or fail."
- When students say: "I hate writing." They might really mean: "I am afraid I will be criticized."
- When teachers write a lot of comments on papers, it might mean to teachers: "I really care about my student's writing." However, to students, it could come across as: "The teacher wants to tear us apart."
- When students say: "I hate reading," they might really mean: "I don't yet know how to read very well."
- When teachers believe: Students from that family, economic, or cultural background can't do homework. They might be communicating to students, "You are not capable. We believe there is no hope for your success."
- "Students are not allowed to take books home" might send the message: "We are convinced our students will fail to learn, and we don't care if they learn or not."

- "What grade did I get?" might not really be about grades, but mean instead "Do you like me? Do you approve of my work?"
- The question "When will you pass our papers back?" can drive even conscientious teachers crazy, but it might really mean "The assignment I turned in meant something to me."
- When students say, "Did I miss anything when I was gone?" Teachers receive: "My class means nothing to them, they think we never do anything important." But students might really mean: "I like this class and am sorry I missed it."

These examples can help you think about listening, focusing on the students, attending to their deeper thoughts and concerns, and responding in ways that help them become involved and successful.

As we describe next in Chapter 3, the contexts in which we teach are marked by increasing inequality. Whereas some students have support at home for doing homework, other students may have daunting responsibilities. Sometimes schools exhibit lowered expectations for students in poverty and/or students of color. How often, for example, are students from upper social classes told that they can't take their books home for fear they will lose them?

Yet working-class kids or kids of color are often told that. We align with scholars who maintain that high expectations are crucial for *all* students' success, especially students of color (Ladson-Billings, 1995), and thus we support maintaining academic rigor in your classroom. Allowing students to "check out" or not to do work actually reproduces the inequity we strive to work against. Still, it is important to create meaningful homework, communicate achievable expectations, be flexible, create alternative assignments and due dates, know your students' situations, and, depending on those situations, at times to have work done in school rather than at home.

> **Activity: Addressing Issues or Problems with Students**
>
> Drawing on your own passions and interests, come up with an issue or problem you might like to explore with your students. Then, make a list of ideas for each of the four curriculum planning steps from above, and describe how you would develop that teaching in a language arts classroom at a grade level and student population of your own choosing. How might you support your students' success?

SUMMARY

In this chapter, we set forward a four-part model for planning English language arts curriculum and instruction based on an inquiry, justice, and action framework:

1. Valuing emotion to identify relevant topics and issues;
2. Using questioning to focus on fairness and justice;
3. Examining different perspectives; and
4. Finding ways to collaborate, inform others/take action.

We set forward ways to support your students as you set high expectations, and we examine lesson planning and provide many examples throughout this book.

REFERENCES

Achebe, C. (1958). *Things fall apart*. William Heinemann.
Agarwal-Rangnath, R. (2013). *Social studies, literacy, and social justice in the common core classroom: A guide for teachers*. Teachers College Press.
Anderson, L. H. (2011). *Speak*. Square Fish.
Appleman, D. (2015). *Critical encounters in secondary English: Teaching literary theory to adolescents*. Teachers College Press.
Boyd, A. (2017). *Social justice literacies in the English classroom: Teaching practice in action*. Teachers College Press.
Boyd, A., & Darragh, J. (2019). Critical literacies on the university campus: Engaging pre-service teachers with social action projects. *English Teaching: Practice & Critique*, 19(1), 49–63.
Damico, J. S., Baildon, M., & Panos, A. (2020). Climate justice literacy: Stories-we-live-by, ecolinguistics, and classroom practice. *Journal of Adolescent & Adult Literacy*, 63(6), 683–691.
Downey, A. L. (2005). The transformative power of drama: Bringing literature and social justice to life. *English Journal*, 95(1), 33–39.
Engestrom, Y. (2009). Learning and expanding with activity theory. In A. Sannino, H. Daniels, & K. D. Gutiérrez (Eds.), *Learning and expanding with activity theory* (pp. 303–328). Cambridge University Press.
Elish-Piper, L., Wold, L. S., & Schwingendorf, K. (2014). Scaffolding high school students' reading of complex texts using linked text sets. *Journal of Adolescent and Adult Literacy*, 57(7), 565–574.
Foucault, M. (1977). *Discipline and punish: The birth of the prison*. Pantheon.
Gabriel, M., & Goldberg, E. (1995). *Pocahontas*. [Motion picture]. United States, Disney.
Gee, J. (2008). *Sociolinguistics and literacies: Ideology in discourses*. Routledge.
Gottfried, J. (2021, July 1). Republicans are less likely to trust their main news source if they see it as "mainstream"; Democrats more likely. Pew Research Center. Retrieved from http://t.ly/mp1Q
Johnson, L. R., & Rosario-Ramos, E. M. (2012). The role of educational institutions in the development of critical literacy and transformative action. *Theory Into Practice*, 51(1), 49–56.
Kohn, A. (2010). "EJ" in focus: How to create nonreaders: Reflections on motivation, learning, and sharing power. *The English Journal*, 100(1), 16–22.
Ladson-Billings, G. (1995). Toward a theory of culturally relevant pedagogy. *American Educational Research Journal*, 32, 465–491.
Lee, H. (1960) *To kill a mockingbird*. Pan Books.
Lewis, C., & Dockter, J. (2008). Mediascapes and social worlds: The discursive construction of critical engagement in an urban classroom. Paper presented at the National Council of Teachers of English. San Antonio, TX.
Lewison, M., Leland, L., & Harste, J. C. (2014). *Creating critical classrooms: Reading and writing with an edge*. Routledge.
Macaluso, M. (2017). Teaching To Kill a Mockingbird today: Coming to terms with race, racism, and America's novel. *Journal of Adolescent & Adult Literacy*, 61(3), 279–287.
McCann, T. M. (2014). *Transforming talk into text: Argument writing, inquiry, and discussion grades 6–12*. Teachers College Press.
Miller, A. (2003). *The crucible*. Penguin.
Myers, W. D. (1999). *Monster*. HarperCollins.
Myers, W. D. (2009). *Sunrise over Fallujah*. Scholastic.
O'Brien, T. (2009). *The things they carried*. Houghton Mifflin.
Orwell, G. (1984). *1984*. Signet.
Patall, E. A., Cooper, H., & Robinson, J. C. (2008). The effects of choice on intrinsic motivation and related outcomes: A meta-analysis of research findings. *Psychological Bulletin*, 134, 270–300.
Rothstein, D., & Santana, L. (2011). *Make just one change: Teach students to ask their own questions*. Harvard Education Press.
Schmidt, L. (2007). *Social Studies that sticks: How to bring content and concepts to life*. Heinemann.
Steinbeck, J. (1993). *Of mice and men*. Penguin.
Stevens, L. P., & Dugan, M. (2010). The dynamic design of learning with text: The grammar of multiliteracies. In D. L. Pullen & D. R. Cole (Eds.), *Multiliteracies and technology enhanced education: Social practice and the global classrooms* (pp. 53–60). Information Science.
Stibbe, A. (2021). *Ecolinguistics: Language, ecology and the stories we live by*. Routledge.

Virgin, R. (2015). Teaching students to ask rich questions. *ASCD Express, 10*(9). Retrieved from www1.ascd.org/ascd-express/vol10/1009-virgin.aspx.

Webb, A. (2011). *Teaching the literature from today's Middle East*. Routledge.

Whipp, J. L. (2013). Developing socially just teachers: The interaction of experiences before, during, and after teacher preparation in beginning urban teachers. *Journal of Teacher Education, 64*(5), 454–467.

3

Contexts, Standards, and Teacher Freedom

In thinking about addressing ELA standards within schools, it's important to consider the larger societal forces shaping perceptions of schools. Unfortunately, there has been a misimpression created by the media and by politicians that American public schools do a poor job educating students. There are certainly important and troubling differences in achievement levels between different social classes and racial groups in our society, though outside-of-school economic forces and policies have a significant influence on students (Berliner & Glass, 2014). Much of this "opportunity gap" is not simply the fault of schools or teachers, but deeply related to dramatically increasing economic inequality in America overall. Static wages for most low-income people since the 1970s and increased concentration of wealth at the top 1% have widened the gap between upper-income families and middle-income families (Fry & Kochhar, 2014).

THE IMPACT OF RACIAL AND SOCIOECONOMIC STATUS ON SCHOOLING

When measured by accumulated wealth rather than income, differences between racial groups are dramatic: average White households' wealth is 13 times that of Black households and ten times that of Hispanic households (Kochhar & Fry, 2014). These disparities have various historical roots, including institutional racism in the form of residential redlining and school segregation—African American and Latino students continue to be in highly segregated schools with twice the poverty concentration of schools attended by Whites and Asians.

In an address at Columbia Teachers College in New York on May 18, 2011, Linda Darling-Hammond (2011, May 21), distinguished professor of education at Stanford and former president of the American Educational Research Association, made some important remarks still true today:

> We live in a nation that is on the verge of forgetting its children. The United States now has a far higher poverty rate for children than any other industrialized country (25 percent, nearly double what it was thirty years ago); a more tattered safety net—more who are homeless, without healthcare and without food security; a more segregated and inequitable system of public education (a 10:1 ratio in spending across the country); a larger and more costly system of incarceration than any country in the world, including China (5 percent of the world's population and 25 percent

of its inmates), one that is now directly cutting into the money we should be spending on education; a defense budget larger than that of the next twenty countries combined; and greater disparities in wealth than any other leading country (the wealthiest 1 percent of individuals control 25 percent of the resources in the country; in New York City, the wealthiest 1 percent control 46 percent of the wealth and are taxed at a lower level than in the last sixty years). Our leaders do not talk about these things. They simply say of poor children, "Let them eat tests."

Moreover, while there is lots of talk of international test score comparisons, there is too little talk about what high-performing countries actually do: fund schools equitably; invest in high-quality preparation, mentoring and professional development for teachers and leaders, completely at government expense; organize a curriculum around problem-solving and critical-thinking skills; and test students rarely—and never with multiple-choice tests.

Since 2014, the majority of students in American public schools have been from non-White racial backgrounds and are increasingly Latinx and immigrants. Yet, 80% of the teaching staff is Euro-American. As Kincheloe (2001) noted 20 years ago, when school culture and curriculum is alien, it is harder for students to succeed:

> For students who live outside these wider cultural relationships, it becomes extremely difficult to understand why the school requires particular tasks to be performed or why certain knowledge is important. A cultural outsider may feel bewildered by the demands of the school. Growing up in the mountains of rural Tennessee, I witnessed dirt-poor but savvy mountain children capable of brilliant out-of-school accomplishments fall victim to their cultural exclusion from the discourse community of schooling.
>
> (p. 649)

Of course, it is essential that English language arts teaching and learning become relevant to all students, particularly students from backgrounds and cultures outside the dominant culture (Janks, 2014). Our curriculum can emerge from the lives, cultures, and issues that matter to all of our students. Unfortunately, when White middle-class cultural norms are the "ideal," students of color or different social or ethnic backgrounds are positioned as "culturally deprived," "at risk," and "disadvantaged," (or even "threatening" and "dangerous") (Baldridge, 2014). When students are positioned by their schools or teachers as being "limited," having "deficits," or placed in low tracks, they are likely to resist, for instance, by "off-task" acts during class; refusing to do homework; or engaging in challenging behaviors, language, or dress (Johnson & Vasudevan, 2012).

English Language Learners (ELL) students face particular challenges. Some struggle with speaking English. Even when spoken language is well developed, reading and writing can lag behind. These students may also not have access to or experience with specific academic literacies valued in schools (Zwiers et al., 2014). They may perceive little purpose or value in school, given the lack of connection between traditional instructional methods and their own lives (Lent & Gilmore, 2013). Low-income ELL students often do not have access to books, are often excluded from advanced courses, and often don't attend college (Kanno & Cromley, 2013).

During the Trump era, there was the loss of union jobs in the American "Rust Belt," the fanning of racial antagonisms, the building of walls, the rise of nativism, and the opioid epidemic. These critical issues in the lives and worlds of White working- and middle-class

Americans can also be key starting points for English language arts inquiry curriculum, raising questions of justice and taking action.

ADDRESSING ISSUES OF INEQUALITY IN THE ELA CLASSROOM

All American students should learn about issues of increasing inequality and develop an understanding and appreciation for diverse cultures. With the increasing skill at using communications technology generated by the COVID pandemic, more can be done so that students can learn about the experience and points of view of students in different contexts. The use of Google classroom, Messenger, Zoom, and other interactive tools create opportunities to collaborate with teachers working in diverse settings. These tools can also bring students together across racial and economic divides, opening dialogue, learning from each other, and developing greater understanding.

Building around inquiry into common themes of justice and developing strategies for action taking, students could communicate, learn, and develop connections with students in schools very different from their own. Students could communicate across differences in rural schools, schools in different regions of the country, and schools in districts in different economic or ethnic communities. They could examine issues of increasing poverty in their suburban, urban, and rural demographics and lifeways. *Epals.com* is also a resource English teachers can draw on to establish digital "pen pal" relationships between classes of students around the world.

The National Council of Teachers of English has taken a strong stand against racism in education. The 2018 Statement on Anti-Racism to Support Teaching and Learning sets forward four recommendations for English language arts teachers:

> 1) actively identify and challenge individual or systemic acts of racism and other forms of discrimination and bigotry in educational institutions and within our profession, exposing such acts through external communications and publications; 2) express strong declarations of solidarity with people of diverse human and cultural backgrounds to eradicate forms of racism, bias, and prejudice in spaces of teaching and learning; 3) promote not only cultural diversity and expanding linguistic knowledge, but explicitly push for antiracism by participating in ongoing professional development for educators to succeed in countering racism and other forms of bigotry; 4) support the enforcement of laws and policies that provide sanctions against racial and ethnic discrimination in education.
>
> (Moore et al., 2018, pp. 4–5)

Multicultural literature in the curriculum falls short of the presence of multicultural children in the schools. The text exemplars recommended by the CCSS make that pretty clear. Out of the 171 texts recommended for elementary children in Appendix B, only 18 or 10% are by authors of color; only a few of these books feature low-income children of color (Gangi & Benfer, 2014). Of the 129 text exemplars for English language arts grades 6–12, only 31 (24%) of these are by authors of color—and this is a generous count as the "of color" authors we counted included writers from ancient China, from Africa and India, as well as American writers. And, those writers of color that are included are more likely to be suggested for shorter works (poems) rather than for longer works (novels or plays).

Another issue that matters to young people is the climate crisis. Increasing droughts, storms, wildfires, floods, increasing heat and polar vortices, and rising sea levels raise profound intergenerational justice questions. Young people recognizing the danger of climate change are emerging as perhaps the most powerful force pushing countries and world leaders to act. Increasingly aware of the risks presented to their future by climate change and the necessity of reducing its severity, young people are motivated by the possibility of creating a greener, cleaner, and safer future than we are currently hurtling toward. Young people's voices from all countries, social and ethnic groups, and all political backgrounds are breaking through political gridlock, overcoming lobbying and misinformation of self-interested corporations and fossil fuel barons, fostering public will, and creating the social movement necessary to preserve their future.

Richard and Allen, two of the co-authors of this book, are also co-authors of *Teaching Adolescents about Climate Change: Reading, Writing, and Making a Difference*, a book that provides teachers with a climate-related language arts curriculum based on justice, inquiry, and action (Beach et al., 2017) (the book's website includes resources on teaching about climate in ELA classrooms *climatechangeela.pbworks.com*.)

THE NEED FOR TEACHER PREPARATION IN CULTURALLY RESPONSIVE TEACHING

According to research on teacher preparation, a key factor in whether teachers adopt social justice approaches was whether they had cross-cultural experiences either before or during teacher preparation. These experiences are essential to employing "culturally-responsive-teaching" that draws on a range of students' cultural backgrounds in planning multicultural instruction (Grant & Sleeter, 2009). O'Byrne and Smith (2015) draw on Banks and McGee Banks (2013) to identify five dimensions of effective multicultural education for their preservice teachers that they believe should be addressed in their methods courses:

> *Content integration*: Content integration deals with the extent to which teachers use examples and content from a variety of cultures in their teaching.
>
> *Knowledge construction*: Teachers need to help students understand, investigate, and determine how the implicit cultural assumptions, frames of reference, perspectives, and biases within a discipline influence the ways in which knowledge is constructed.
>
> *Prejudice reduction*: This dimension focuses on the characteristics of students' racial attitudes and how they can be modified by teaching methods and materials.
>
> *Empowering school culture and social structure*: Grouping and labeling practices, sports participation, disproportionality in achievement, and the interaction of staff and students across ethnic and racial lines must be examined to create a school culture that empowers students from diverse racial, ethnic, and gender groups.
>
> *Equity pedagogy*: An equity pedagogy exists when teachers modify their teaching in ways that will facilitate the academic achievement of students from diverse racial, cultural, gender, and social class groups.
>
> (p. 176)

Addressing these dimensions means that teachers need to have "'an understanding and appreciation of every student's background and culture'" (p. 178) so that, as another teacher noted "everyone's individuality [is] is to be recognized and incorporated into his or her learning experience'" (p. 178). Acquiring knowledge of students' cultures, as another teacher noted, involves having a "'basic understanding of those cultures to determine how best to form a bonding relationship with each student'" (p. 179).

It is not that you as a new teacher must know everything before you have your own classroom, but that you are prepared with dispositions, background, theory, and strategies that facilitate continued learning. Through listening to your students, you learn about their worlds and their concerns. You then learn how their lives are rich with language, experiences, relationships, events, media, culture, as well as challenges created by inequality, racism, violence, oppression, and the climate crisis as the #MeToo, Black Lives Matter, and Fridays for the Future movements have called out. All of these can be starting points for discussion, reading, writing, sharing, curriculum development, inquiry into questions of fairness and justice, and student-driven activism.

A justice-and action-oriented inquiry approach positions the teacher as an ally in the search for answers to student-driven questions and fosters a different kind of student–teacher relationship, valuable to students of all backgrounds. Analysis of student success in urban schools focuses on the need for students to perceive their teachers as having a personal concern or interest in them. To counteract students' disaffection, boredom, and alienation from school, teachers need to build supportive, personal relationships with students through reciprocal respect of the value of students' experiences and perspectives as contributing to their learning (Wallace & Chhuon, 2014). Teaching that engages with student passions and interests, for exploring questions that matter to students, better positions students for taking action.

Activity: The Influence of Student Populations on Curriculum and Instruction

Describe the student ethnic and social class population of a school that you attended and/or are working in for your practicum. To what degree did or does the school's language arts curriculum and instruction build on these students' cultural background experiences and knowledge—for example, the types of texts students are reading in their classes or the topics for students' writing assignments? How as a teacher, could you find out more about your students' cultural background experiences and knowledge for the purposes of planning instruction?

UNDERSTANDING AND IMPLEMENTING COMMON CORE STATE STANDARDS

In our diverse and unequal country, the same or very similar Common Core State Standards (CCSS) have been adopted by most states. We provide some background and suggest lines of analysis of the CCSS that we believe will enable you to make sound decisions about their implementation.

At the time of this third edition (2022), the degree to which the standards are impacting instruction varies from state to state, and even school district to school district. In some schools the CCSS is understood to guide curriculum and daily instruction; in other schools the CCSS is more in the background. Yet, in both contexts, there is often confusion and misunderstanding about the standards. Regardless of the place of standards in the school you teach in, it is important for you to understand and think critically about the CCSS and how they are best implemented.

The CCSS emerged from different "standards-based" reform efforts that began in the 1980s to address a public perception that many high school students lacked the abilities and skills associated with their success in college. There was also concern that this problem was particularly acute in lower-income communities where people of color are overrepresented. The CCSS were initiated by the National Governors Association and the Council of Chief State School Officers working with Achieve, Inc. and in "partnership" or "consortia" with education publishers (e.g., Pearson Corporation, McGraw-Hill) and standardized testing companies (Education Testing Service, ACT, College Board).

The introduction of the CCSS in 2010 occurred in the midst of a larger school reform movement responding to the failures of George Bush's No Child Left Behind (NCLB). Rather than directly addressing the issues of inequality, racism, unequal resources, and funding that we have described, reformers blamed schools and teachers. The movement included the adoption of testing to evaluate teachers, the push for market-based privatization of schooling through charters, challenges to teacher unions and tenure, and reduction of school funding. There were also increases in child poverty rates, increases in college costs and debt that affect teachers' debt burden, in an economy that was and is slow to recover from the Great Recession (Karp, 2013–14), and most recently, the COVID epidemic. The factors have placed additional burdens on teachers. Diane Ravitch (2014) posited that the standards were rolled out quickly and superficially so that they were never fully implemented in terms of specific instructional activities. She also critiqued the CCSS as not based on any research into learning English language arts skills or on experience in real classrooms with real students. It is, as she says, the "translation" of the standards by teachers that will make all the difference.

Advocates for adopting a standards-based approach argue that standards enhance student achievement. However, you will be interested in learning that there is precious little research behind the standards and no solid evidence that adopting standards will necessarily improve student achievement. For instance, there is no strong correlation between National Assessment of Educational Progress (NAEP) scores and high state standards (Mathis, 2010). There is also no strong correlation between international test performance and countries with national standards (Tienken, 2008). Countries such as the Nordic countries or Canada have no national standards, but their students score well in international reading tests (Mullis et al., 2006). Likewise, research suggests that standards may have negative effects on non-White students' performance and dropout rates (Mathis, 2010).

If the adoption of standards increases student achievement, then one would expect that scores on the NAEP tests would increase over time. However, results of the NAEP test scores for 2019–20 test results for achievement found that 13-year-olds test scores for lowest-performing students, particularly Black and Latinx students, actually declined from 2012, the first decline in NAEP scores since testing began in the 1970s (Meckler, 2021). In contrast, scores for higher-performing students did not decline, a reflection of disparities between these groups of students.

While these issues around the standards certainly create some serious problems, as we shall see, there are valuable ideas in the standards and thoughtful, critical thinking teachers, who act wisely, can use them to create inquiry, justice, and action instruction.

First, it is important to be clear that the "abstract descriptions of academic abilities" in the CCSS do not specify *what* or *how* to teach English language arts. There are no specific texts, no "canon," or special "privileged cultural knowledge" required by the CCSS. Indeed, the CCSS do not create a common, core, required, or national curriculum of any kind. The Introduction to the CCSS makes clear,

> A great deal is left to the discretion of teachers and curriculum developers. The aim of the Standards is to articulate the fundamentals, not to set out an exhaustive list or a set of restrictions that limits what can be taught beyond what is specified herein.
>
> (p. 2)

As Rebecca Sipe (2009) notes, "standards provide a definition of what is possible, but *standards are not curriculum documents*" (p. 41, emphasis in original). Nor do they specify, describe, or set forward any general or specific teaching methods. It is teachers as "knowledgeable and engaged professionals [who] are the most important factor in the improvement of adolescent literacy" (p. 41).

The CCSS on writing standards emphasizes argumentative writing and requires attention to audience, purpose, and rhetorical context. A study of the teaching of argumentative writing in 31 English language arts classrooms found that what counted as argument and effective argumentative writing varied from classroom to classroom. As a result, the types of activities the teachers and students engaged in varied, leading to different trajectories of writing development made available to the students (Newell et al., 2015). A focus on argumentative writing is a logical and natural part of an inquiry, justice, and action approach.

The CCSS explicitly state that they support learning in English the skills necessary to participate in a democracy—thus, the CCSS can most certainly be used to justify and support an inquiry, justice, and action approach. Terms like "asking and answering questions," "information," "argument," "claims," and "persuasion" appear again and again throughout the Common Core State standards.

At the same time, English teachers may have to help others understand that participation in a democracy includes students developing their own ideas and voices and exploring issues of justice. Strangely, the language of the CCSS does not emphasize developing personal or critical stances. It concerns us that the word "voice" appears in the CCSS only in relation to verb tense. It makes us wonder how democratic debate can proceed when none of these terms appear even once in the document: "unequal," "unfair," "justice," "injustice," "equality," "inequality," "oppression," "fairness," "truth," "ethics," or "ethical."

Making curriculum politically "safe"—if that is the intent of the language of the CCSS—makes English teaching less meaningful and less interesting to students, undermines developing them as citizens, further isolates them from the "grownup" world, and, indeed, lowers the standards of what we expect.

Standards need to be implemented in the context of a rich, meaningful, and relevant curriculum of the kind that a justice, inquiry, and action curriculum fosters. Too often schools attempt to implement English language arts curriculum by teaching one standard at a time, or isolating standards as opposed to building increasingly sophisticated connections and understandings. Attempting to address individual standards in isolation shifts the goal of your teaching from fostering engaging learning that addresses the complexity of ideas and participation in any language arts activity, to an intellectually impoverished isolation of skills and knowledge in the name of "meeting a standard."

Activity: Studying the CCSS

Prepare a presentation to your class on one of the following topics/questions assigned to your group. Include the standard or the language that you are discussing.

- Select one or two anchor (non-grade-level) standards and describe how you would implement these standards based on the adoption of the justice, inquiry, and action framework described in Chapter 1.
- Compare and contrast an anchor standard with several related specific standards. Some schools only emphasize specific grade-level standards; some experts recommend only focusing on anchor standards. What is gained or lost by either approach? Talk about this both in general, and with specifics from the example you chose.
- Identify three anchor standards that you believe are important for students to achieve, provide reasons for their importance, and how you would implement them.
- Identify a standard that you believe would be difficult for a particular group of students to achieve, giving reasons why that standard would be difficult. Then, propose some activities designed to help students address these potential difficulties.
- Identify a learning progression between at least three different grade levels and talk about what you like and don't like about that learning progression. Drawing on your specific example, and your reading of other learning progressions, how would you judge the effectiveness of the learning progressions in the CCSS in general?
- Review the texts listed as text exemplars in the CCSS Appendix B. Assess what you believe would be the potential appeal/understanding or lack of appeal/understanding for these exemplars relative to certain groups of students, noting reasons for assessments. (Beach et al., 2016, pp. 37–38)

LEARNING PROGRESSIONS IN STANDARDS

As Diane Ravitch describes, the standards are built around a set of "abstract descriptions of academic abilities organized into sequences"—the fundamental organization of the standards is the creation of sets of *learning progressions* as "abstract" and un-researched. Grade-level-by-grade-level standards are based on a developmental hierarchy of theoretically increasingly more complex, sophisticated ways of addressing the same core skills.

For example, for the overarching anchor standard for interpretation of point of view or perspective, "assess how point of view or purpose shapes the content and style of a text," includes a series of increasingly more difficult standards for grades 6–12. So, the grade-level standards begin in the 6th grade with simply describing point of view in a text. This leads to a focus on describing competing points of view in grade 7, to interpreting how disparities between reader and character perspective results in dramatic irony in Grade 8. Then, for grades 9–10, students focus on how authors develop their perspective or stance in a text. Students in grades 11–12 are expected to use satire, sarcasm, irony, or understatement to convey multiple, alternative perspectives.

These high school grade level standards related to inferring authors' point of view or perspectives assume that high school students are cognitively better able to infer how an author's use of language represents a particular point of view or perspective than middle school students.

This may sound reasonable at a theoretical level, but the key question is: does it provide a meaningful way to understand the way students think and learn, and thus to organize curriculum and instruction? Clearly, one key assumption is that each new academic year simply builds systematically and reliably on students' learning in previous years. But, of course, in the highly complex and individualized learning that takes place in English language arts, it is nearly impossible to make such assumptions about your students' knowledge or abilities based on their previous instruction. To be simplistic, if, for example, students are having difficulty contrasting different characters' perspectives at the 8th-grade level, you may need to develop activities related to inferring characters' perspectives associated with achieving grade 7 standards.

However, there are several problems with the concept of a "learning progressions" continuum that identifies certain standards as appropriate for certain grade levels. This continuum is based on cognitive stage development models that presuppose that, at different age levels, students are cognitively capable, or incapable, of thinking in certain ways, in the case of English, of employing certain literacy practices. For example, based on notions of early adolescents' presumed egocentricity, that they have difficulty adopting perspectives other than their own, assumptions are made about their ability to adopt multiple, alternative perspectives. As teachers, of course, we know so many exceptions to this cognitive stage model of development that we may find it hard to accept, and, as researchers, we wonder how much sense such "stages of cognitive development" make in the real world. The appropriateness of the different learning progressions of language arts skills in the CCSS to students at specific grade levels are certainly *not* based on research!

Even if one accepts the idea of stage models of intellectual development, cognitive stage models fail to consider differences between students, texts, activities, and contexts. For example, students' ability to adopt characters' perspectives may vary according to individual differences within your class as well as differences due to the complexity of a text's language, the prior knowledge the text calls on, or students' understanding of or motivation to participate in your activity. Given this variation, it is difficult to make generalizations about your entire class's ability to address particular standards based on a lock-step, hierarchical continuum. Learning the literacy practices in English language arts requires a more holistic, recursive, and contextualized understanding.

The arbitrary nature of the grade-level learning progressions is evident in the following 6th, 7th, and 8th grade standards related to figurative language use:

- 6th grade. Interpret the *figurative and connotative meanings* of words and phrases as they are used in a text.
- 7th grade. Interpret the figurative and connotative meanings of words and phrases that are used in a text and describe in detail a specific *word choice* and its impact on meaning and tone.
- 8th grade. Explain an author's comparisons through *metaphors, allusions, or analogies* in a text and analyze how those comparisons contribute to meaning.

(Common Core Standards, 2010, p. 36)

If it is assumed that only by 8th grade students should study metaphors, does that mean that 6th graders may not learn to "interpret the figurative and connotative meanings" without studying metaphors?

Assuming that students, based on a presumed "learning progression" continuum, may not be able to engage in certain literacy practices, seriously underestimates students' abilities especially when they are engaged and motivated. Holding high expectations does not mean, for example, that 6th-grade teachers should only address "how an author establishes the point of view"—6th-grade teachers need to be aware of the whole range of complexity of meaning, up to and including the 12th grade standard of understanding "various layers of meaning."

In English one set of skills or one kind of knowledge does not always lead step-by-step to the next "level" of skills or knowledge. While these learning progressions may have "logical" appeal, they have no basis in empirical research and over-simplify students' literacy learning. Indeed, the specific progressions laid out in the standards are not necessarily related to how skills and learning are actually acquired. For instance, suggesting that "dramatic irony" is somehow age-appropriate for 8th graders and "taking a stance on a social issue" is age-appropriate for 9th or 10th graders has no logical basis.

Moreover, the idea that "taking a stance on a social issue" is an intellectually more advanced skill that somehow follows or is dependent on prior knowledge of "dramatic irony" is equally illogical. Students of all ages need to consider how authors take stances on issues and how the knowledge of the reader or audience may differ from the knowledge of characters in a story (dramatic irony). In this sense, we recommend at least using caution in applying learning progressions established by a presumed developmental continuum.

Rather than making instructional decisions based on simplistic grade-level-by-grade-level learning progressions, we recommend that you view the entire set of language arts standards holistically. Doing so means that you focus on designing those activities that are most likely to engage your particular group of students based on their unique needs, knowledge, abilities, and interests. Evoking student motivation by engaging in rich, complex, relevant, and meaningful learning is the best way to set high standards and to meet and exceed the Common Core State Standards.

STANDARDS AND TEXT SELECTION

As we repeatedly point out, the CCSS does not *mandate* any specific texts although it lists a series of exemplars. At the 2010 Annual Convention of the National Council of Teachers of English, NCTE members supported a resolution strongly supporting teacher decision making:

> The development and adoption of the Common Core State Standards and its inclusion of exemplar texts heightens the concern that the authority of teachers as professionals who make decisions regarding materials and practices in literacy education will be diminished.... Resolved that the National Council of Teachers of English reaffirm the rights of teachers and their students to draw from many diverse and dynamic sources—not only a list of exemplar texts—in the selection of classroom texts and materials; continue to endorse a school curriculum that honors cultural and socioeconomic backgrounds, language variety, and the interests and needs of the individual student; and continue to support and advocate for the inclusion of teachers at all levels of educational decision making.

A major focus of the CCSS involves encouraging students to read increasingly complex texts as they advance through grade levels. This focus on text complexity reflects a concern that during their secondary school experience, students are not reading difficult, complex texts so that they then struggle when they encounter such texts in college.

We certainly agree that students need to learn to read "complex" texts. We applaud the Common Core designers for recognizing the importance of contextual factors shaping "complexity." However, we also believe that given the highly subjective nature of individual students' transactional experiences with texts, it may be difficult to derive any valid and reliable measure of grade band "complexity." A text may have high or low appeal, and be easier or harder to read, for students based on their own prior knowledge, interests, needs, and cultural backgrounds. For example, some of Walter Dean Myers's young adult novels that are set in urban neighborhoods may have high appeal for students living in those neighborhoods and low appeal for students living in suburban neighborhoods, and thus be easier for one group of students to read than for another.

Applying different critical perspectives to a text also enhances the complexity of a text. While the Cinderella fairy tale is not a complex text, having students apply as a feminist analysis of Cinderella is a relatively complex task. In planning activities, you should therefore consider the complexity of both the text *and* the activity for responding to that text relative to your students' "zone of proximal development" (Vygotsky, 1986)—the space in which they are able to perform certain tasks easily and attempt to perform complex tasks with your assistance.

Providing texts that may be too difficult for students to read independently without support may be counterproductive, given that students may have difficulty even reading texts at their grade level. As P. David Pearson (2013) notes:

> I cannot imagine that the exhortation to teachers and students to try harder will succeed where serious efforts to bring students up to grade level expectations have failed . . . stretching the gap between ability and text challenge may be harder than we might imagine, at least in situations in which no teacher scaffolding is provided.
>
> (p. 258)

The meaning of a text lies not "in" a text but rather through the *transaction* of a reader and a text in a particular event or context. It is up to the reader to create text complexity as interpretative complexity (Wilhelm, 2015). Even with popular fiction such as fantasy or romance novels that might not be considered as "complex" can lend themselves to highly complex interpretations, texts that often have high appeal for students. As Smith et al. (2014) note:

> not considering interpretive complexity reinforces unwarranted distinctions between the reading students do in and out of school, marginalizing what students choose to read on their own despite the fact that such reading often works powerfully—in many instances more powerfully than in-school reading—to meet the goals that the Core articulates.
>
> (p. 155)

In selecting texts, it's essential to consider students' engagement and the issues the text raises. Wilhelm and Smith (2014) found that students can be highly engaged with certain texts depending on the nature of their experience—for example, a dystopian text helped them think about issues of political and governmental control.

In addition to whole classes reading the same work, English teachers can foster groups reading different books in literature circles. Students could also engage in independent reading, perhaps all from the same text set or around a common theme, thus creating choice, engagement, and opening up multiple perspectives and possibilities for dialogue.

Applying justice, inquiry, and action questions to a text enhances the complexity of students' shared, collaborative interpretations. Students then explore their concerns about certain problems or issues. For instance, students might find it interesting to inquire into how adolescents are shaped by advertising messages when reading *Feed* (Anderson, 2002), a science fiction work where young people receive advertisements directly fed into their brains.

To model people's collaborative interpretation of a problem or issue, you could have students study online shared responses or reviews of books, movies, songs, or video games to have them discuss reasons people are willing to engage in these shared responses (Beltramo & Stillman, 2015). A curriculum that explores common themes through a series of texts and materials leads to more complex thinking and interpretation than a curriculum that looks at individual texts in isolation.

Certain contemporary young-adult literature has become increasingly multimodal and intertextual, again enhancing text complexity through the use of online fan-based activities surrounding that literature (Gerber & Lesesne, 2011/2012). For example, in responding to the mystery novel, *Skeleton Creek* (Carman, 2009), readers are encouraged to go to a related site *www.sarah#ncher.com* to gain further perspectives from one of the key characters in the book, Sarah. Fans create Facebook pages *facebook.com/skeletoncreek* and fan sites such as Skeleton Creek is Real *skeletoncreekisreal.com* (Gerber & Lesesne, 2011/2012). And, in response to the *Hunger Games* (Collins, 2008) series, readers engage in interactions on fan sites such as Mockingjay.net *http://www.mockingjay.net* to share with fans new and remix/created alternative versions of the novels.

The "Exemplar Texts" list in the Common Core State Standards excludes texts, particularly young adult literature, portraying adolescent experiences that would be appealing to students, resulting in students becoming less engaged with their reading (Watkins & Ostenson, 2015). Rather than using the same text for all students in a class, one alternative is to use different texts varied according to students' needs and reading abilities through small-group/book club approaches and a selection of shorter texts associated with the use of inquiry-based instruction.

Ultimately, based on a host of factors, you will need to decide which, if any, of the "complex texts" on the "exemplar text" list are appropriate for your particular students. For instance, Faulkner's (1991) *As I Lay Dying* is not only a difficult text, but also fails to be engaging for most high school students. The novel addresses a narrow social group in the South and family issues specific to that context and historical period. It may lack relevance for students who have little prior knowledge of the context. As a teacher, you will need to balance the benefits of teaching a text against the potential frustrations students may face in trying to make sense of it.

In a similar vein, we want to point out that determining appropriate texts for your students cannot be adequately accomplished by relying on their "grade level" reading ability. For example, knowing that Sue, a ninth grader, is reading at a "fifth-grade level" as determined by scores on standardized reading tests does not provide you with enough information to assess Sue's reading abilities. These reading level categories do not consider variations in students' engagement with certain genres and modes of texts, their prior knowledge about a given text's content, or their purposes for reading.

All of this suggests that the use of a list of texts found in Appendix B of the CCSS has little meaning without considering the nature of the activities or context in which these texts would be used (Smith et al., 2014).

IMPLEMENTATION: STANDARDIZATION ≠ HIGH STANDARDS

If the standards are properly implemented, it should be up to you as the teacher, collaborating with your students, colleagues, and districts, to develop the curriculum and teaching approaches you will use. The needs, abilities, knowledge base, and interests of teachers and students vary from school to school, from classroom to classroom, and even within every classroom; they cannot and should not be standardized. As Christopher Tienken (2011) notes:

> Standardization is a Pollyanna [wildly optimistic] approach to policymaking. One cannot simply separate curriculum from culture, emotions, personal backgrounds, prior experiences, prior knowledge, and stages of cognitive and social development.... Mandating that everyone follow the same set of standards and perform at the same level of achievement guarantees that everyone will not get what they need and that certain groups of students, those that do not fit into the new system, will lose out. These latter students will be labeled "not proficient" or "in need" of academic remediation, when perhaps they just need more choices, more pathways, and more diversity of curricula within the system.
>
> (p. 61)

Enforcing the same learning on all students, as some have mistakenly advocated on the basis of "standards," slows down the most capable students and leaves behind those already struggling, creates inappropriate limitations on what students can accomplish, and in effect, dumbs down teaching and learning. The CCSS recognize that *standardization is not the same thing as holding high standards*.

Standardization of instruction in decontextualized, prescriptive ways is often promoted by certain organizations or publishers as a means to sell standardized curriculum materials or textbooks across districts and states (Surprise!). As Moore et al. (2014) note, these organizations are attempting to define how the CCSS should be implemented in a manner that is:

> anathema to the spirit and methods of critical literacy. To put it another way, the CCSS say "This is what literacy is. Use it this way." Critical literacy asks, "What is literacy for me, for us, for this community, this time, in this place, and how can it be used by all of us to reach our goals?"
>
> (p. 143)

Standardization may also lower rather than raise achievement if teachers teach the same content using the same methods regardless of differences in their classroom contexts or students (Kohn, 2010). Such homogenization often occurs when schools or districts adopt "teacher-proof," scripted curriculum programs or mandated textbook series that allow for little teacher development of their own curriculum.

Moving beyond a scripted or teacher-centered critical inquiry approach involves engaging students in dialogic, inclusive, and a wider range of competing perspectives and voices (Aukerman, 2012). Rather than attempting to arrive at a consensus perspective, as an advocate of justice, inquiry, and action teaching, you invite students to express alternative, dialogic perspectives (Heidebrink-Bruno, 2014). In doing so, students recognize that texts are not neutral in that they reflect their author's particular perspectives, discourses, or narratives and often serve to position the audience in limited ways (Janks, 2014, p. 2). When students' own perspectives are honored as valuable, just as those of the teacher or their peers are valuable, students become more confident about publicly voicing their critiques.

Use of narrow textbooks, pre-packaged or scripted curricula, mass-marketed worksheets, and one-size-fits-all-teaching or curriculum implementation do not fulfill the high expectations that all of us want and that the Common Core Standards envision. Out-of-date conceptions of English language arts fail to recognize advances in our field, evolving literary canons, emerging literary and social science scholarship, and changing literacy demands in the digital age will lead to improvement intended by these standards. Informed administrators and curriculum specialists understand this and work to support teachers' professional knowledge, research, decision making, risk-taking, and freedom to experiment, grow, and improve, year after year. (For more on strengths and limitations of the CCSS, see *Strengths and limitations of the CCSS* on the website).

Activity: Implementing the CCSS

Teachers may implement the CCSS based on misinterpretations of the CCSS listed below. Based on discussions of one or more of these approaches, explain why such a misinterpretation may have occurred and why this approach might be limited, ineffective, or ill-advised. Then, formulate some alternative approaches that would be richer or better than these approaches.

Finally, describe what you could do if, in a school setting, you were told that you needed to follow one or more of these approaches.

ELA teachers:

- must teach only text-dependent "close reading."
- must teach all students at the same grade level the same material at the same time.
- have to follow a scripted "teacher proof" instructional plan.
- are required to teach one standard per day, every day, always a different standard.
- are required keep a gradebook that separately grades every student on every standard.
- are required to teach long units, or even full semesters, focused on test taking skills.
- are required to teach only standards for a given grade level.
- are told they can only teach from the approved textbook.
- are told that they can only teach texts from the Common Core Standards list of text exemplars.
- are support personnel in a computer lab where students systematically work through an entirely online curriculum to meet the Common Core Standards. (Beach et al., 2016, p. 42)

IRA/NCTE Standards for the English Language Arts

1. Students read a wide range of print and nonprint texts to build an understanding of texts, of themselves, and of the cultures of the United States and the world; to acquire new information; to respond to the needs and demands of society and the workplace; and for personal fulfillment. Among these texts are fiction and nonfiction, classic and contemporary works.
2. Students read a wide range of literature from many periods in many genres to build an understanding of the many dimensions (e.g., philosophical, ethical, aesthetic) of human experience.
3. Students apply a wide range of strategies to comprehend, interpret, evaluate, and appreciate texts. They draw on their prior experience, their interactions with other readers and writers, their knowledge of word meaning and of other texts, their word identification strategies, and their understanding of textual features (e.g., sound–letter correspondence, sentence structure, context, graphics).
4. Students adjust their use of spoken, written, and visual language (e.g., conventions, style, vocabulary) to communicate effectively with a variety of audiences and for different purposes.
5. Students employ a wide range of strategies as they write and use different writing process elements appropriately to communicate with different audiences for a variety of purposes.
6. Students apply knowledge of language structure, language conventions (e.g., spelling and punctuation), media techniques, figurative language, and genre to create, critique, and discuss print and nonprint texts.
7. Students conduct research on issues and interests by generating ideas and questions, and by posing problems. They gather, evaluate, and synthesize data from a variety of sources (e.g., print and nonprint texts, artifacts, people) to communicate their discoveries in ways that suit their purpose and audience.
8. Students use a variety of technological and informational resources (e.g., libraries, databases, computer networks, video) to gather and synthesize information and to create and communicate knowledge.
9. Students develop an understanding of and respect for diversity in language use, patterns, and dialects across cultures, ethnic groups, geographic regions, and social roles.
10. Students whose first language is not English make use of their first language to develop competency in the English language arts and to develop understanding of content across the curriculum.
11. Students participate as knowledgeable, reflective, creative, and critical members of a variety of literacy communities.
12. Students use spoken, written, and visual language to accomplish their own purposes (e.g., for learning, enjoyment, persuasion, and the exchange of information).

FIGURE 3.1 IRA/NCTE Standards for English Language Arts

IRA/NCTE STANDARDS FOR THE ENGLISH LANGUAGE ARTS

The Common Core State Standards are not the only set of standards that English language arts teachers can draw on to develop curriculum and justify instruction. In 1996 the National Council of the Teachers of English (NCTE) worked together with the International Reading Association (IRA) (now the International Literacy Association (ILA) to create a powerful, flexible, and approachable set of language arts standards for curriculum and instruction in grades K–12 (International Reading Association & National Council of Teachers of English, 1996). These leading organizations of language arts teachers reaffirmed the standards in 2012. (As we have seen, NCTE also has standards for the preparation of language arts teachers.) The IRA/NCTE standards are appealing for many reasons (see Figure 3.1).

These standards emerge from deep knowledge of the discipline. Teachers played a major role in writing them. The standards are concise, reflected in the fact that their 12 standards can be printed on a single page.

The standards strongly support teacher decision making and freedom. The standards are national—teachers in any state, whether or not that state has adopted or revised the CCSS, can draw on and appeal to the IRA/NCTE standards. The standards do not break learning into a grade-level-by-grade-level, micromanaged, and artificial set of skills and learning progressions. Thus they are more true to content and content acquisition in English language arts, which is envisioned holistically from elementary school through high school. The IRA/NCTE Standards support diversity in language use and the value of students' home languages. The IRA/NCTE Standards are perfectly compatible with the justice, inquiry, and action approach we set forward in this book.

The IRA and NCTE published a 112-page booklet, *Standards for the English Language Arts* (International Reading Association & National Council of Teachers of English, 1996) now available free as a pdf online *bit.ly/3wTxUeR*, that more fully explains the standards and how they can be used. In 1996 NCTE also published a series of books on using the standards, including *Standards in Practice 6–8* by Jeffrey Wilhelm (1996) and *Standards in Practice 9–12* by Peter Smagorinsky (1996). Both books are rich with classroom examples. Drawing on the IRA/NCTE Standards can give teachers freedom—the topic we explore next.

CREATING TEACHER FREEDOM AND AUTONOMY

Throughout this book, we emphasize your ability in working with your students to develop curriculum and instruction in ways that are meaningful and make a difference. As we have explained, we don't believe your teaching should be dictated by traditional approaches, standardized textbooks, or even Common Core Standards. We believe controversial ideas should be explored, not avoided. Indeed, in a democracy, it is critical that all students are prepared to think critically about issues on which people disagree. Addressing controversy is central to developing justice, inquiry, and action-based curriculum and teaching. New teachers may be surprised to learn that surveys of secondary English teachers indicate that most teachers feel they have a good deal of freedom.

A survey of 339 public school English teachers regarding their text selection process indicated that most teachers demonstrated complete autonomy in selecting texts. Half noted that these selection decisions were often made at their district or department level (Watkins & Ostenson, 2015). Some teachers noted that they had more autonomy in their selection of shorter texts than with novels. While most also indicated that they employ a literature anthology, only 7% use it frequently, while the vast majority of teachers in the survey were using texts not included in the anthology.

The survey reported that teachers selected texts primarily based on their purpose for using a text, the text's relevancy to their curriculum, and writing quality, as well as a text's potential level of engagement. At the same time, they noted that certain texts were slated for teaching at certain grade levels. They also noted that there were constraints shaping text selection, such as the costs of purchasing class sets. Creative teachers can often find ways to obtain texts online, through libraries, sharing, or finding funds.

We tend to think of freedom to teach as something given to us in certain settings by either the traditions or practices of a given school, school leaders, department chairs, or colleagues. Regardless of the degree of freedom or lack of freedom that you believe you have, there are many ways that you can take action to develop the freedom you need to address controversial topics in real-world schools, public, private, or religious. Your freedom as a teacher is not simply given to you, it can be something you help create.

Even in the same school, there can be confusion. Allen visited a high school and spoke to three different English teachers about the amount of curricular freedom they had. One teacher told him that all the teachers had to teach the same books. Another teacher, in the same hallway, told him that they had a lot of freedom: "There is a long list of books and English teachers can choose any book on the list." A third English teacher, whose classroom was just around the corner from the first two, told him, "One thing I love about this school is that we can teach any book we want!"

Careful reading and examination of curriculum guides, state or national standards, or actual school or district policies often reveals more flexibility than teachers typically take advantage of. Scholars who study school policies talk about "phantom policies"—policies that teachers believe are the case but, in fact, don't even exist. When you are told about policies that limit what you teach, or texts that are "required," there are careful and diplomatic ways to explore policies and find wiggle room.

COMMUNICATION WITH PARENTS/GUARDIANS

Communication with parents/guardians can make a difference. We suggest, if possible, calling every parent/guardian in the first few weeks of school to

1. introduce yourself, and share something about your engagement in teaching,
2. ask them how you can best support their student,
3. let them know you will be discussing complex and controversial ideas in your class, and, if there are any concerns, alternative assignments are available,
4. explain that you try to have students' voices heard, and you help them find ways to become involved in the "real world," and that you
5. welcome discussion from your class continuing at home and parents or community members visiting or even speaking in your class.

Along with the phone calls—and especially if you can't make the phone calls work—write a letter home to parents with the same information. When Allen taught high school, his students were required to return the letter with the parent/guardian signature. On the rare occasion when, later in the semester, a parent/guardian had a question or concern about the class, it turned out to be useful to have the letter with that parent/guardian's signature. If the student had signed it in place of the parent/guardian, it turned out to change the nature of the concern.

When Ashley taught high school, she sent a similar note home and asked that the adult in the home respond with anything they would like her to know about their student. This opened the door to many relationships and the learning of important information about students and families. Providing parents/guardians at the beginning with the knowledge that your class will address controversial issues and that alternative assignments can be created is the best way to avoid censorship problems. Teachers may provide parents/guardians with written statements or permission slips during the semester when they are teaching specific texts or films that might for some reason be problematic, although be careful with this approach as it can raise red flags unnecessarily.

We can't overstate the value of this communication with parents/guardians early in the semester for all teachers, especially for interns and new teachers. Open communication with parents/guardians is an important way to support your students, develop relations and trust with the community, and expand your freedom.

SHARING YOUR TEACHING EXPERIENCES WITH OTHERS

Teachers typically don't want to brag about their accomplishments or those of individual students, but we think that we should all become more confident talking with others and in a public way about our and our students' accomplishments. Doing so can enhance trust and develop freedom. Inviting parents, visitors, and administrators to your classroom—even if those invitations are not taken up—can enhance community confidence in you as a teacher and support the teaching you believe in. (Don't worry; administrators know you are a new teacher and will not expect perfection.)

Presenting about your teaching at state or national NCTE or ILA conferences and/or publishing about your teaching in journals like *Voices from the Middle* and the *English Journal* adds to your reputation for professionalism. Obtaining positive attention for the school or in the local newspaper based on student learning and activities in your classroom can enhance your freedom.

Josie from our first chapter hosted a night for community members to view her students' graffiti art responding to their reading of *All American Boys*, and that communicated a message from the book relevant to its themes of racism and police brutality. Many people attended and engaged in dialogue with her students about the novel, and the night was covered by the local newspaper as well as highlighted on the school social media page. Josie later attended a national conference to share about her work and received financial support from her district. The recognition from these outlets bolstered her own confidence in her work and built trust in her from school leaders and parents.

COPING WITH CENSORSHIP

A fear of risk-taking, reluctance to stand up for what you believe in or even a lack of interest in new and challenging ideas is destructive to the teaching process and to the teacher as a person and professional, particularly in our current political context in which people are more likely to critique texts and curriculum they perceive as problematic.

When selecting texts, you may encounter censorship issues, particularly in assigning texts that deal with issues socially deemed as sensitive. Some parents/guardians may question certain works exposing students to ideas or scenes that they are not yet ready for, such as scenes reflecting sexual encounters, physical or emotional violence, or charged language.

Or there are concerns that specific texts can lead students to adopt negative behaviors or to assume problematic beliefs. For example, parents may assume that reading about characters using drugs will lead students to take drugs. Sometimes parents learn about these texts through conservative radio personalities or networks and have never read the texts themselves.

There are several issues to consider in relation to censorship. Proponents of censorship posit a causal relationship between reading texts perceived to be problematic and adverse effects. For example, a Texas legislator created a list of 850 books about race and sexuality such as *The Handmaid's Tale* by Margaret Atwood (1998) and *The Confessions of Nat Turner* by William Styron (1992) that he believed should not be available in schools. He claimed that these books "might make students feel discomfort, guilt, anguish, or any other form of psychological distress because of their race or sex" (Ross, 2021).

The call for censorship assumes that students reading about an assumed problematic behavior will then engage in that behavior. However, little research supports a causal relationship between reading about a behavior and engaging in it (Greathouse et al., 2020). Furthermore, many writers include material that parents or guardians might protest that, in fact, may actually serve to deter students from detrimental behaviors and expose behaviors' consequences and dangers. A study of youth's engagement with young adult literature found that "the books allowed teenagers to think through life's decisions about drugs, sex, and other moral complexities in advance, with some distance and assistance from others" (Ivey & Johnston, 2018, p. 147). Students also sought out peers and adults to talk with about issues in the material they were reading. They documented "books tend to reveal the consequences of bad choices through the eyes of characters with whom students identify" (p. 149), thereby allowing readers to grow and actually become more mature through their encounters.

In addition, developmental arguments treat all adolescents as the same by essentializing a vastly variant population (Lesko, 2012). When provided with choices, students will select texts that fit in their realm of understanding and will not engage with those they find troublesome (Gay & Johnston, 2018; Greenbaum, 1997). Most teenagers, however, are already familiar with (through media, if not through their own experiences) the topics that adults often wish to shield them from. Writers such as Laurie Halse Anderson and Jeff Zentner have shared how frequently they receive letters from young people who have read their books and relate to stories about sexual assault and poverty.

Perhaps most importantly, it is crucial to consider who is shielding whom from what. Parents or guardians with privilege often wish to uphold the dominant structure that seeks to limit exposure to diverse narratives that are framed as "sensitive" or "controversial." When teachers and schools submit to those demands, whose perspectives do they silence and whose do they value? When we avoid certain stories in classrooms, what messages are we communicating to students? When important social topics, especially those related to human rights, are framed as "controversial," we might ask: controversial to whom? (Crawley, 2020).

Diana Hess and Paula McAvoy (2012) encourage teachers to think about settled versus open issues—those that have been decided by courts of law already and have majority opinion and those that are being currently argued with a large backing (as opposed to a small faction). They argue that the "open controversies" rather than the "settled" ones make for the best teaching. They also describes issues that are "tipping," or changing as history changes. Conceptualizing issues in this way may help you make choices between controversial topics.

When stakeholders challenge a text, they may begin with a written message or phone call to the teacher or school administrator. Many teachers don't know that most school districts have established written policies and procedures for parents to challenge the use of texts. Typically, these procedures include administrators' involvement—so that you are not the primary target for complaints. If there are complaints, seek out these policies. School librarians or curriculum specialists in the central office may have more information. If, for some reason, you have a sense that a particular text or practice may draw attention, you can develop rationales in advance of complaints (Smagorinsky, 2007). For many texts, ready-made statements are already available online, and you can modify them to fit your situation.

Near the end of President Trump's term, a term marked, alas, by xenophobia and racist thinking especially in regard to the Black Lives Matter movement, Republican politicians and nativist groups began talking about the public schools and "woke" corporations being dominated by critical race theory. Apparently, the concern is that schools and corporations are recognizing racism as a feature of American social, cultural, and legal practices and trying to do something about it, rather than promoting a race-free narrative featuring White heroes.

Students, teachers, and schools should not be silenced by this kind of "culture war," often cynically promoted to confuse voters and win elections. There is no specific "Critical Race Theory Curriculum." High school English teacher Jennifer Martin (2014) recounts the following conversation with one of her students:

> Upon seeing my anthologies of African American literature, Mexican-American literature, Asian literature, among others on my bookshelf, a white student asked me, "Where are the books on white literature? I pointed to the Holt *Elements of Literature* textbooks for 10th and 11th grade, American and English literature respectively. "Most everything contained in those, and probably most everything you have been asked to read until now," I replied. The student thought about this and nodded.
>
> This portrait is not unrepresentative of the discourse of white students newly exposed to non-majoritarian texts. It speaks to the unmarked nature of whiteness and to my sense that many of the students, particularly white students, are uncritical of their school experiences in any collective sense and do not claim a standpoint of social justice. Most of my white students had not previously been asked to move beyond their personal experiences and question why they would expect only to read themselves in their classroom texts. This privileging of whiteness was reflected in the school culture.
>
> (p. 132)

Efforts to promote primarily the views of dominant groups are not new, and students can lead the way in addressing the issue. In two high schools in Jefferson County, Colorado, the local school board reviewed their new advanced placement US history curriculum because they perceived it as criticizing the way early American colonists treated the Native Americans (Gewertz, 2014). The board committee wanted a curriculum that would "'promote citizenship, patriotism, benefits of the free-market system, respect for authority' . . . [for] students to learn more about the 'positive aspects of the United States and its heritage'" (Gewertz, 2014, p. 1). Students responded by walking out of their schools. One student noted that "'I don't think my education should be censored... We should be able to know what happened in our past,'" while another student indicated the need for adopting a critical perspective on events in American history:

> As we grow up, you always hear that America's the greatest, the land of the free and the home of the brave... For all the good things we've done, we've done some terrible things. It's important to learn about those things, or we're doomed to repeat the past.
>
> (Gewertz, 2014, p. 1)

When choosing works, it is important to weigh reasonable concerns against your goals as a teacher. Providing students with sanitized stories does not align with what they already experience and it neglects a rich opportunity to engage them fully in navigating society and its challenges. Teaching addressing issues of race, critically inquiring into the canon of frequently taught and anthologized texts, and/or into the confusion and controversy over "critical race theory," creates opportunities for learning and informing others.

Note also that recent research (Crawley, 2020; Ivey & Johnston, 2013; Walter & Boyd, 2019) conducted with parents and guardians about potentially inflammatory texts actually found that many support their use in the classroom. While their voices are less often in the news, these adults noted the value of having conversations in classrooms about real-world topics. They expressed a desire to be informed of their students' curriculum to have the opportunity to communicate with their children about important issues. Furthermore, others described how, despite perhaps initial concerns, they came to realize that their students' reading engagement was enhanced through such texts and cultivated the development of skills beyond reading, such as oral fluency.

We believe that the greatest risk of censorship is not parents, community or school board members, or racist politicians, but self-censorship by teachers themselves. We are not suggesting that taking risks should jeopardize your job—teachers rarely lose positions because of the books they choose or the topics they address. Instead, we believe it means selecting issues and texts that matter, raising questions of justice, relevant to your students and to the issues before us.

There are many specific resources and organizations to support English teacher freedom. Statements justifying the teaching of specific works can be found ready-made online and be modified to fit your situation. Resources regarding censorship questions include the National Council of the Teachers of English (NCTE) Intellectual Freedom Center *www.ncte.org/action/anti-censorship*, the Electronic Freedom Foundation *www.eff.org*, the American Library Association (www.ala.org/bbooks), the American Civil Liberties Union *tinyw.in/5cqv*, the National Coalition Against Censorship (ncac.org), and the Freedom to Read Foundation *www.ftrf.org*. Teacher unions are also an important resource for support, including the National Education Association and the American Federation of Teachers.

REFERENCES

Anderson, M. T. (2002). *Feed*. Candlewick Press.
Atwood, M. (1998). *The handmaid's tale*. Doubleday.
Aukerman, M. (2012) "Why do you say yes to Pedro, but no to me?" Toward a critical literacy of dialogic engagement. *Theory Into Practice*, 51(1), 42–48.

Baldridge, B. J. (2014). Relocating the deficit: Reimagining Black youth in neoliberal times. *American Educational Research Journal, 51*(3), 440–472.

Banks, M. A., & McGee Banks, C. A. (2013). *Multicultural education: Issues and perspectives*. Wiley.

Beach, R., Thein, A. H., & Webb, A. (2016). *The English language arts Common Core state standards: A critical inquiry approach for 6–12 classrooms*, 2nd ed. Routledge.

Beach, R., Share, J., & Webb, A. (2017). *Teaching climate change to adolescents: Reading, writing, and making a difference*. National Council of Teachers of English/Routledge.

Beltramo, J. L, & Stillman, J. (2015). Why should students want to do a close reading. *Voices from the Middle, 22*(4), 9–14.

Berliner, D. C., & Glass, G. V. (2014). *50 myths and lies that threaten America's public schools: The real crisis in education*. Teachers College Press.

Carman, P. (2009). *Skeleton creek*. Scholastic Press.

Collins, S. (2008). *The hunger games*. Scholastic Press.

Common Core Standards. (2010). *Common Core State Standards for English language arts & literacy in history/social studies, science, and technical subjects*. Council of Chief State School Officers and the National Governors Association.

Crawley, S. A. (2020). "The sky didn't fall or anything": A mother's response to lesbian and gay-inclusive picture books in elementary schools in the United States. *Bookbird, 58*(1), 29–44.

Darling-Hammond, L. (2011, May 21). The service of democratic education. *The Nation*. Retrieved from www.thenation.com/article/160850/service-democratic-education

Faulkner, W. (1991) *As I lay dying*. Vintage.

Fry, R., & Kochhar, R. (2014). *America's wealth gap between middle-income and upper-income families is widest on record*. Washington, D.C.: Pew Research Center. Retrieved from http://tinyurl.com/m2g48p

Gangi, J. M. & Benfer, N. (2014, September 16). How Common Core's recommended books fail children of color. The Answer Sheet, *The Washington Post*. Retrieved from http://tinyurl.com/plwkbrz

Gay, I. & Johnston, P. (2018). Engaging disturbing books. *Journal of Adolescent & Adult Literacy, 62*(2), 143–150.

Gerber, H., & Lesesne, T. (2011/2012). In defense of young-adult texts: Engaged and electrate in the fan spaces of YAL. *Signal Journal, 35*(1), 11–15.

Gewertz, C. (2014, September 25). Colorado Students Protest School Board's History Proposal. [Web log post] Retrieved from http://tinyurl.com/n4akbnv

Grant, C. A., & Sleeter, C. E. (2009). *Turning on learning: Five approaches for multicultural teaching plans for race, class, gender, and disability*, 5th ed. Wiley.

Greathouse, P., Consalvo, A., Covino, K., David, A. D, Eisenbach, B., et al. (2020). When inclusion meets resistance: Resources for facing a challenge. *English Journal, 110*(1), 80–86.

Greenbaum, V. (1997). Censorship and the myth of appropriateness: Reflections on teaching reading in high school. *The English Journal, 86*(2), 16–20.

Heidebrink-Bruno, A. (2014, September 3). Critical pedagogy in classroom discussion: A #Digped discussion [Web log post]. Retrieved from tinyurl.com/lhrmhw2

Hess, D. E., & McAvoy, P. (2012). *The political classroom: Evidence and ethics in democratic education*. Routledge.

International Reading Association & National Council of Teachers of English. (1996). *Standards for the English language arts*. International Reading Association/National Council of Teachers of English.

Ivey, G., & Johnston, P. H. (2013). Engagement with young adult literature: Outcomes and processes. *Reading Research Quarterly, 48*(3), 255–275.

Janks, H. (2014). Critical literacy's ongoing importance for education. *Journal of Adolescent & Adult Literacy, 57*(5), 349–356.

Johnson, E., & Vasudevan, L. (2012). Seeing and hearing students' lived and embodied critical literacy practices. *Theory into Practice, 51*(1), 34–41.

Kanno, Y., & G. Cromley, J. G. (2013). English language learners' access to and attainment in postsecondary education. *TESOL Quarterly, 47*(1), 89–121.

Karp, S. (2013–14, Winter). What's wrong with the Common Core. *Rethinking Schools, 28*, 10–17.

Kincheloe, J. L. (2001). Introduction. In J. L. Kincheloe and D Weil (Eds.), *Standards and schooling in the United States*, Vol. 1 (pp. 1–89). ABC/CLIO.

Kochhar, R., & Fry, R. (2014). Wealth inequality has widened along racial, ethnic lines since the end of the Great Recession. *Pew Research Center* [Web log post]. Retrieved from www.pewresearch.org/fact-tank/2014/12/12/racial-wealth-gaps-great-recession

Kohn, A. (2010). How to create nonreaders: Reflections on motivation, learning, and sharing power. *English Journal, 100*(1), 16–22.

Lent, R. C., & Gilmore, B. (2013). *Common Core CPR: What about adolescents who struggle . . . or just don't care?* Corwin.

Lesko, N. (2012). *Act your age!: A cultural construction of adolescence*, 2nd ed. Routledge.

Martin, J. L. (2014). Critical race theory, hip hop, and Huck Finn: Narrative inquiry in a high school English classroom. *Urban Review, 46*(2), 244–267.

Mathis, W. (2010). *The "Common Core" standards initiative: An effective reform tool?* National Education Policy Center. Retrieved from greatlakescenter.org/docs/Policy_Briefs/Mathis_NationalStandards.pdf

Meckler, L. (2021, October 14). "Nation's Report Card" finds falling test scores, even pre-Covid [Web log post]. *The Washington Post.* Retrieved from https://www.washingtonpost.com/education/2021/10/14/nations-report-card-scores-falling/

Moore, J., Manning, L., & Villanueva, V. (2018). *Statement on antiracism to support teaching and learning.* National Council of Teachers of English. Retrieved from https://ncte.org/statement/antiracisminteaching

Moore, M., Zancanella, D., & Avila, J. (2014). Text complexity: The battle for critical literacy in Common Core State Standards. In J. Z. Pandya & J. Avila (Eds.), *Moving critical literacies forward: A new look at praxis across contexts* (pp. 129–145). Routledge.

Mullis, I. V. S., Kennedy, A. M., Martin, M. O., and Sainsbury, M. (2006). PIRLS 2006: Assessment Framework and Specifications, 2nd ed.. TIMSS and PIRLS International Study Center, Lynch School of Education, Boston College.

National Council of Teachers of English. (2021). NCTE standards for the initial preparation of teachers of English language arts 7–12 (initial license). Author.

Newell, G., Bloome, D., & Hirvela, A. (2015). *Teaching and learning argumentative writing in high school: Moving beyond structure.* Routledge.

O'Byrne, W. I., & Smith, S. A. (2015). Multicultural education and multiliteracies: Exploration and exposure of literacy practices with preservice teachers. *Reading and Writing Quarterly, 31*(2), 168–184.

Pearson, P. D. (2013). Research foundations of the Common Core State Standards in English language arts. In S. B. Neuman & L. B. Gambrell (Eds.), *Quality reading instruction in the age of Common Core Standards* (pp. 237–262). International Reading Association.

Ravitch, D. (2014). *Reign of error: The hoax of the privatization movement and the danger to America's public schools.* Vintage.

Ross, J. (2021, November 2). Minnesota authors land on list of 850 books targeted by Texas lawmaker as "distressing" for students. *Minneapolis Star Tribune.* Retrieved from http://t.ly/76sU

Sipe, R. (2009). *Adolescent literacy at risk?: The impact of standards.* National Council of Teachers of English.

Smagorinsky, P. (1996). *Standards in practice grades 6–8.* National Council of Teachers of English.

Smagorinsky, P. (2007). *Teaching English by design: How to create and carry out instructional units.* Heinemann.

Smith, M. W., Appleman, D., & Wilhelm, J. D. (2014). *Uncommon core: Where the authors of the standards go wrong about instruction-and how you can get it right.* Corwin.

Styron, W. (1992). *The confessions of Nat Turner.* Vintage.

Tienken, C. H. (2008). Rankings of international achievement test performance and economic strength: Correlation or conjecture?. *The International Journal of Education Policy and Leadership, 3*(4), 1–15.

Tienken, C. H. (2011). Common core standards: The emperor has no clothes, or evidence. *Kappa Delta Pi Record, 47*(2), 58–62.

Vygotsky, L. S. (1986). *Thought and language* (A. Kozulin, Trans.). MIT Press.

Wallace, T. L., & Chhuon, V. (2014). Proximal processes in urban classrooms: Engagement and disaffection in urban youth of color. *American Educational Research Journal, 51*(5), 937–973.

Walter, B., & Boyd, A. (2019). A "threat"—or "just a book"? Analyzing responses to *13 Reasons Why* in a discourse community. *Journal of Adolescent & Adult Literacy, 62*(6), 615–623.

Watkins, N., & Ostenson, J. (2015). Navigating the text selection gauntlet: Exploring factors that influence English teachers' choices. *English Education, 47*(3), 245–275.

Wilhelm, J. D. (1996). *Standards in practice grades 6–8.* NCTE.

Wilhelm, J. D. (2015). Teaching texts to SOMEBODY!: A case for interpretive complexity. *Voices from the Middle, 22*(4), 44–46.

Wilhelm, J. D., & Smith, M. W. (2014). *Reading unbound: Why kids need to read what they want and why we should let them.* Scholastic.

Zwiers, J., O'Hara, S., & Pritchard, R. (2014). *Common Core standards in diverse classrooms: Essential practices for developing academic language and disciplinary literacy.* Stenhouse.

Section II

Implementing and Exceeding
the ELA State Standards

4

Teaching Literature

When we wrote the first edition of this book, the Common Core State Standards were just rolling out, and teachers were nervous about the state of literary fiction in the English language arts curriculum. The standards include a substantial focus on teaching informational texts, and early interpretations of the standards had English teachers worried that non-fiction would replace fiction in the curriculum. And, although it's since become clear that the standards ask for an increase in informational texts across all core subjects rather than concentrating the increase in English classrooms, the call for an increase in informational texts led some to wonder—does reading literature in the English classroom still matter?

In this chapter, we will argue that, yes, reading literature not only matters but is central to teaching English—perhaps now more than ever. Literary texts have a vital role in critical inquiry. Literature stimulates our students' imaginations, raising whole hosts of questions about human and social relations, history, politics, and culture. Literature engages students in complex and critical thinking about the most pressing problems we face in our world today. And, literature asks students to consider—through the study of character—the deeply human ways people respond to such issues, given their histories, experiences, and identities in specific social, cultural, and historical contexts. Literature can be combined with non-fiction and other kinds of texts to inquire into justice-related themes. Finally, literature can be the basis of social action, serving as a springboard to motivate students to better their communities and society.

PHILOSOPHIES ON TEACHING LITERATURE

There have been quite a few philosophies on how and why we should teach literature over the years. Those philosophies align pretty closely with the curriculum frameworks for teaching English that we outlined in Chapter 1. As we ask you to think about the value of teaching literature, we think it's helpful to share a quick discussion of a few of these philosophies to consider the various ways that standards and standardization might encourage you to take up particular philosophies and how you might respond.

DOI: 10.4324/9781003177364-6

New Criticism

When English first came to be understood as an academic discipline, it was guided by the philosophy and practice of New Criticism—an approach that focused on the study of literature as a scientific, technical, and objective endeavor (Wimsatt & Beardsley, 1949). The goal of New Critical approaches to reading and teaching literature was (and is) for students to make focused, close reading of literary texts, especially poetry, often emphasizing literary devices (e.g., figurative language, symbolism) and poetic forms to determine the meaning the author "intended" the reader to take from the text.

Key to this approach is the idea that the text is static; the text and its meaning don't change over time and can be pinpointed through close textual analysis. New Critical approaches to teaching literature are certainly still with us today. We see them in standards documents that emphasize close reading and require students to provide textual evidence in their responses to literature. And, in literature anthologies, you'll find questions based on close reading associated with inferring certain predetermined "correct" answers. Standardized tests may involve close reading of passages and questions that are "text dependent," that supposedly don't draw on larger contexts or student background knowledge.

Reader response theory

In response and contrast to New Criticism, reader response theory (e.g., Rosenblatt, 1995) provided an entirely new philosophy for thinking about how readers make sense of literature. At the risk of simplifying a substantial and complex body of theory, we'll highlight a few key concepts from reader response theory. First, the author is thought of as the starting place for a text, but not the endpoint. Literature is written in a particular time and place by a particular person, but literature means new things as times change and language changes. Second, when a new reader reads a piece of literature, its meaning changes. That's because every reader has their own social and cultural history that interacts with their reading of the text. In short, meaning is made through a transaction of text, a reader, and a social and cultural context.

Teachers, educational scholars, textbook companies, and writers of standards have taken up reader response theory in a number of ways—some more useful than others, and some downright problematic. For instance, at one point, reader response theory was associated with "personal growth" approaches to teaching English that focused on students' identity development through the teaching of literature (Dixon, 1975). This approach can be seen in textbook units focused on, for instance, "Coming of Age." While this might sound like a useful approach, it tends to promote developmental and biological approaches to identity development that suggest that all young adults experience similar physical, psychological, and social crises on the way to becoming adults (Lesko, 2012). This approach assumes a sameness that discounts the diversity of lived experiences that youth bring to our classrooms.

Another way that reader response theory has been taken up is in instruction that asks students to connect their personal experiences to those of characters in literature. This approach is often seen in textbook questions meant to generate student engagement with unfamiliar texts—for instance, "Have you ever had to make a big decision? How did you make the decision, and what were its consequences?" Again, this sounds, on the surface, like a useful approach. However, it can become problematic when students are encouraged to connect with characters with whom they share little in common and, as a result, over-identify with characters experiencing oppression and racism. Similarly, it can also become limiting if not enough attention is devoted to historical context for the sake of universalism if students are not challenged to learn the politics and ideologies that shape a text.

To be sure, the justice, inquiry, and action approach we support is grounded in the fundamental tenets of reader response theory. But critical inquiry aims to help students understand that their responses to literature are rooted in social and cultural beliefs, practices, and dispositions. Adopting a critical inquiry stance invites them to reflect on how the meaning they construct with a text is shaped by their experiences with families and communities, as well as race, class, gender, nationality, religion, and so many other social categories. Students may also infer how their experiences reading a given text are shaped by norms operating in a specific classroom, school, and historical moment.

With all of this in mind, a justice, inquiry, and action approach to teaching literature suggests that reading literature matters because it engages students in careful and critical thinking about their own perspectives, those of their peers, and those represented in characters and situations in texts.

Such engagement helps students understand that a range of perspectives exists on complex problems and issues—perspectives that are grounded in peoples' social, cultural, and historical experiences. Moreover, such engagement helps students consider a wider range of perspectives, sometimes even questioning or reconsidering their perspectives. Acquiring these critical inquiry skills gained through reading literature is crucially important, now more than ever, as our students become adults faced with problems like racism; socioeconomic inequality; tensions over immigration policy, climate change, and the influence of social media; and public health crises.

Critical Inquiry

When employing a critical inquiry approach, students can apply critical perspectives that focus on the historical, institutional, and cultural perspectives to literary texts (Appleman, 2015). For example, responding to *To Kill a Mockingbird* (Lee, 1988—first published in 1960 and set in the early 1930s) requires defining the norms of Whiteness that operated in the segregated South and that created racial and class hierarchies. Examining the author's background and history can also lead to uncovering how the novel perpetuates a White savior narrative (Macaluso, 2017).

Because students generally lack the background knowledge needed to define these texts' historical and cultural contexts, they may benefit from readings or studying artifacts related to the worlds being portrayed in the works. For example, from engaging with *Pride and Prejudice* (Austen, 2009) and reading about the class hierarchy in early 19th century England, students gain an understanding that Elizabeth Bennett's family is simply middle class as opposed to the upper-class families represented by Darcy's family. As a result, the females in the Bennett family need to find husbands to ensure their financial future, something that does not concern the females in wealthier families who will simply inherit wealth.

Understanding these cultural contexts informs youth's ability to sympathize with characters and more deeply discern their motivations. It also allows them to evaluate the text, protagonists, and even authors from a more informed stance, both in the historical era in which they occurred and within their own.

In addition to applying historical and cultural perspectives, you may have students employ additional perspectives on literature that aid their understanding and analysis (Beach et al., 2021; Appleman, 2015). Engaging these perspectives can encourage students to embrace the critical inquiry approach and unpack narratives for how they create and/or reproduce power, reflect dominant historical narratives, or even expose their own positionalities. These perspectives prompt a deeper analysis and foster intentional connections to the world.

Numerous perspectives can be employed for any literary interpretation, including those typically associated with literary criticism (Appleman, 2014; 2015). We extend each, however, to note how you can employ them for critical purposes:

A *biographical* perspective focuses on how the author's life experiences may have influenced their writing, assuming that those experiences actually shaped their writing. While biographical perspectives have been around for a long time, as women's literature and literature by people of color have become more important, biographical approaches have taken on new relevance.

A *psychological* or psychoanalytic perspective focuses on how characters' psychological motives, needs, desires, or past experiences shape their actions—for example, the need for parental love or sexual fulfillment. Expanding this perspective to consider protagonists' mental health and potential struggles can be relevant to many texts in fostering understanding and empathy.

A *gender* perspective examines the portrayal of gender roles in texts and how readings uphold the gender binary. Closely related, applying a *feminist* lens critiques how sexist or patriarchal gender discourses position both women and men in limited ways.

A *class* or *Marxist perspective* focuses on how socioeconomic class differences shape characters' beliefs and actions. This stance also examines how social class appears in a text as a system that oppresses some and privileges others.

A *deconstructivist/poststructuralist* perspective examines how binary language categories, for example, "good" versus "evil," or "male" versus "female," are themselves problematic for conceptualizing experience. It allows readers to examine the social construction of groups, objects, or experiences.

A *postcolonial* perspective critiques the imposition of colonial, often Western, discourses that position colonized people as the passive "Other" who need to be controlled and taught Christianity, "civilization," "capitalism," or "democracy."

BROADER CRITICAL PERSPECTIVES AND ADAPTATIONS FOR LITERARY ANALYSIS

More recently, scholars have offered methods for critiquing literature that broadly engage students' critical dispositions around power and privilege and facilitate insights across a number of categories. Those posited specifically for analyzing canonical literature include *Critical Literature Pedagogy* (Borsheim-Black et al., 2014) which is an approach that involves "reading *with* and *against* a text," (p. 124, emphasis in original). Reading *with* a text denotes traditional analysis of theme, plot, and characters while reading *against* involves "reading between the lines to expose and interrupt embedded, dominant narratives, power dynamics, and perceived normalcy espoused by and hidden within the text, including its inclusion in school curricula" (p. 125).

This paradigm goes beyond reader response by asking students to "examine the ideologies of texts" (p. 130) and to transfer their understandings from textual analysis to their communities. Similarly, *Critical Canon Pedagogy* (Dyches, 2018) specifically asks students to explore the socially constructed nature of the canon (including who is left out) and its representations. From this approach, students might "restory" (Thomas & Stornaiuolo, 2016) a canonical text to include diverse perspectives, such as changing the race of Macbeth to a Black man to note how he would have been treated differently in the killing of Duncan (Dyches, 2018).

In addition to these broader critical approaches, English teachers have adapted specific perspectives developed in other fields, such as legal studies or social theory, to literary study. These critical approaches support our intent by drawing readers' attention explicitly to systems of oppression. The following are brief summaries of these different approaches.

A *youth lens* perspective takes into account "representations of youth in texts as they reflect assumptions tied to age as well as how those representations might intersect with conceptions of class, sexuality, race, gender, ability, and other social categories" (Petrone et al., 2015, p. 508). This approach examines how a work perpetuates or disrupts messages about teens by working against essentialized, linear, and often deficit views of young people. Using the youth lens to examine *The Hunger Games* (Collins, 2008), for example, would evaluate Katniss as representative of adolescence, her supposed evolution to adulthood, and would point out the contextual, rather than individually inherent, factors that influence her actions (Petrone et al., 2015).

A *critical race* perspective examines the ways racism and Whiteness are prevalent in a text. Using the tenets of critical race theory (Delgado & Stefancic, 2017), this stance explores how a text normalizes or deconstructs racism. It also critiques how liberalism operates within a text including how it presents colorblindness or meritocracy or where/how it invites the creation of counter-narratives. A text might even itself be a counter-narrative to traditional stories or histories, illustrating a perspective not known in mainstream discourse. Similarly aligned, a *critical Whiteness* lens explores how Whiteness as a system of domination is pervasive in texts, such as those from the canon, and how a text works to center Whiteness. Embodying anti-racism is the goal of this approach. For example, applying the lens of critical race theory to *To Kill a Mockingbird* (Lee, 1960) would help students detect how infrequently Black characters speak. Even though Tom Robinson and Calpurnia are central to the plot, they are not presented as multi-dimensional (Boyd, 2021). Readers also encounter them primarily through the perspective of White characters (Borsheim-Black & Sarigianides, 2019). One useful resource for historical and literary texts related to the portrayal of the history of slavery in American is the edited collection, *The 1619 Project: A New Origin Story* (Hannah-Jones et al., 2021) (for curriculum resources on The 1619 Project from The Pulitzer Center *t.ly/uC7y*). It is crucial to note that many states have recently passed legislation banning the teaching of critical race theory as well as instruction related to The 1619 Project.

We therefore encourage teachers to formulate strong rationales for this approach and for confronting historic and systemic racism. Articulating these rationales to administrators and school board members will help solidify the value of such an approach and help to preclude misunderstandings and misapplications of the theoretical perspective.

A *decolonial* perspective works to uncover the marginalization of certain voices and to re-center those. This perspective critiques the idea of universal knowledge and welcomes stories considered outside of those traditionally documented. An example of teaching from this lens is pairing *Of Plymouth Plantation* by William Bradford (2016), which details his first encounters with Native Americans with primary sources by the Wampanoag tribe. Bradford's work is often excerpted in American literature textbooks, but little is known from Squanto's point of view in this historic encounter.

A *queer* perspective can include either reading through the lens of LGBTQ identities or one outside of norms and binaries. The idea of queering a text, for instance, means reading against its conventionally accepted meaning (Britzman, 1995). Cart and Jenkins (2006) noted three stages of GLBTQ literature which were: homosexual visibility, gay assimilation, and queer consciousness/community. Literature can be read and critiqued for its representation of these categories as well as how it depicts individuals who identify as LGBT, noting any tropes or stereotypes used. Blackburn, Clark, and Nemeth (2015) posit a similar paradigm for reading with queer theory in which, in addition to sexuality and gender, readers notice "normative notions of families, homes and time" (p. 15). They apply this lens to *The Color Purple* to examine how Celie disrupts sexual norms and desires.

Finally, a *critical disabilities* stance involves examining texts in terms of how they reflect the social constructions of ableism and disability. Critical disabilities studies urge us to explore how disabilities are presented as undesirable and often isolating, thereby acquiring social consequences. This perspective also notes how ability is privileged in social interactions and physical situations. Dunn (2015) applies disabilities studies to critique traditional works such as "The Scarlet Ibis," (Hurst, 1960) and relates it to how the story focuses on the able-bodied individual and his learning for the sake of his brother, who was born with a disability. She analyses the story's messages for students, including one that conveys, "it is impossible to live a fulfilled life with a disability" (p. 73). As a result of the disability in the story, the character dies, further establishing the negative message for readers.

To develop critical questions for inquiry, groups of students could apply these different critical perspectives to the same text, perhaps a particularly older, canonical text. However, this approach can work with any text. Certain texts are more inviting of specific critical approaches, yet trying out a perhaps unexpected approach can have interesting results and can help students expose where important silences are in a text. For example, in studying a text without a character with a disability, you can have students read through a *critical disabilities* lens and help students document how ableism is constructed and privileged. Students will likely need an introduction to the theoretical components of each in order to apply these perspectives. Once they become familiar with these perspectives, you can extend their application from literature to the world, noting how, for example, a *critical race* lens offers an understanding of current events and movements.

Helping students to read through different lenses, from different perspectives, greatly enhances their understanding of texts and the world. It is a perfect fit with a justice, inquiry, and action approach.

Activity: Applying Different Critical Perspectives to a Literary Text

Based on a literary text you are reading for your course or on your own, apply some of the different critical perspectives to that text. Reflect on how applying these perspectives illuminated the text more clearly. For example, consider how in applying a gender

> perspective, you noticed how some of the female characters were portrayed based on a traditional male-gaze perspective highlighting their appearance.
>
> Then, consider how you would teach students to apply the perspectives you applied to the text through activities that drew on their lived-world experiences associated with adopting those perspectives, such as how they frame peers' perceptions through a gender perspective.

METHODS FOR TEACHING LITERATURE

While we have focused on theoretical approaches thus far in this chapter, many teachers want to know the "how" of teaching literature. What specific strategies or configurations can they use with students? For example, should novels be read whole-class, or should students choose their texts? What approaches help students dissect characters and plot? How can novel reading lead to the sort of action and inquiry we encourage throughout this text? While there is no one right approach, and you will have to determine how your students should read and engage based on your context (which includes their needs and preferences), we can offer some methods for reading literature with students.

Creating free-reading/book club experiences

A primary goal in teaching literature is to foster students' reading interests so that they become lifelong readers. One incentive to develop students' reading interests is to allow them to select their own books. Doing so allows them to inquire into areas of interest and determine how and why they enjoy certain titles over others. Providing students with choices addresses reading standards related to comprehending complex literary texts independently, and allowing students to select specific topics can lead them to take on an action developed from their reading. A classroom where students choose what they want to read is sometimes called a "reading workshop"—an approach richly described by Nancie Atwell in *The Reading Zone: How to Help Kids Become Skilled, Passionate, Habitual, Critical Readers* (2007).

A survey of students ages 12 to 17 found that students who are more frequent readers—who read books for fun on 5–7 days a week, reading 39.6 books annually—are more likely to rate themselves as enjoying reading (Scholastic, 2014). They also believe that reading for fun is important, have parents who are themselves frequent readers, are more likely to read a book of choice independently in school, engage in rereading, and have larger home libraries than is the case with less frequent readers who are reading only 4.7 books annually. Students ages 6–17 prefer to read books they select; 33% of students indicated that their classes include independent reading time, but only 17% have daily independent reading time; 52% posit that independent reading is one of their favorite parts of the school day.

To provide students with opportunities to choose texts, you can set up a free-reading program by setting aside certain days for students to select and read books by accessing print or online books through your classroom or school libraries. You can also have students share face-to-face or video book-talk recommendations, given the importance of peer recommendations. They can use the iOS Subtext *tinyurl.com/krr3j99* app that provides students with access to books and book recommendations by Subtext users and reviewers. Students could also make selections as a small book club and read around a central topic or theme of interest. Alternatively, students could first select the text of interest and be grouped with others who chose the same text. Groups could meet daily and rotate roles in a traditional literature circle format, or you could create certain tasks for groups to accomplish for their book.

You can have students make their own book choices as completely open, or within a variety of frameworks. Students might be provided with a text set related to a specific issue or set of issues from which they select what they want to read, either individually or in literature circles. Some companies have created for-profit programs to make money from student independent reading, best known is Accelerated Reader or AR. AR can be of value, though it can also be restrictive (holding students to certain "grade level approved" texts), be based on taking tests (students take simplistic multiple choice tests to "prove" their reading), and fail to foster community discussion or exploration of specific issues or ideas.

Fostering close-reading approaches

Regardless of whether students are reading a novel whole-class or in small groups, one literacy practice teachers want to develop is their ability to read a text closely (for a critique and more information on close reading, see Chapter 5). To examine the CCSS approach to close reading, Marguerite Sheffer, a high school English teacher in Oakland, California, undertook a teacher inquiry project. As her 11th-grade students were reading *Macbeth*, she formulated questions that specifically required them to study particular passages closely. Her questions emphasized attention to only the text itself and did not invite either the students' reactions to the text or consideration of the historical, cultural, social, or political contexts in which the text might be understood. Instead, she focused her students' writing on finding supporting evidence (Sheffer 2013a).

She found that the students "would combine their response (topic sentence) with their evidence and analysis to form a neat, structured paragraph." However, their writing was "unoriginal, and did not show that students were grappling with the complexities and the ambiguities of our complex text, Shakespeare's *Macbeth*." One reason for the lack of originality was that the students were looking for the most obvious, readily identifiable evidence that matched her "text-dependent questions" as opposed to more complex, nuanced evidence. She recognized that her use of "text-dependent questions" was actually undermining her attempts to foster students' formulating original interpretations.

This led her to have her students pose their questions based on "Costa's Leveled Questions: Level 1 questions (surface level), Level 2 questions (inferences) and Level 3 questions (connections)" for responding to *The Woman Warrior: Memoirs of a Girlhood Among Ghost* (Kingston, 1975/2010). She also had students reflect on the nature of their questions (Sheffer, 2013b). While the students did generate complex questions, initially, their discussions were quite limited, with students providing only initial, single answers. She then focused on the need to provide deeper answers through the use of stems: "'What other possibilities are there? What about . . .? Is this the only way to look at . . .?'" Analyzing her students' "close-reading paragraphs," in response to their questions, she noted an increased focus on different, more complex aspects of the text, reflecting more original writing than was the case earlier in the year.

Sheffer believed that the most important lesson she learned was that for students to do a meaningful deep reading of texts, they need to care about what they were doing, and they need to have a personal engagement with the questions they are exploring (Sheffer, 2013c). She recalls her lack of engagement in writing about *King Lear*, which she perceived to be "'about nothing.'" When her teacher picked up on her comment and suggested to her that she could actually write about why she perceived the play to be "about nothing," she found herself grappling with complex and interesting ideas. When one of her students described Malcolm Gladwell's (2010) *What the Dog Saw, And Other Adventures* as "boring" because it addressed seemingly "trivial" topics, she encouraged the student to write about why people were curious about such topics.

From these experiences, Sheffer recognized the need to value students' opinions and initial discomforts and not fully formed reactions which, when taken seriously, can ultimately lead to grappling in meaningful ways with complexities in texts. Sheffer believes that complex responses from students can actually be undermined by teacher scaffolding close reading tasks instead of having students generate their own questions.

Aligned with our inquiry approach in this book, students need to perceive that interesting questions are open-ended and debatable rather than closed or rhetorical with predetermined answers (Smith et al., 2014). To model posing your own questions, you might use the Critical Response Protocol (CRP) and have students asking each other: "What are you noticing?" (Beach et al., 2010, p. 27). Students are then asked to respond to the question, "What did you see that makes you say that?" The third question is, "What does it remind you of?"

Students can also infer intertextual connections between what they notice about images, texts, and phenomena, and their own lived experiences, current events, or other texts. The fourth question identifies emotions: answering the query, "How do you feel?" involves risk-taking, trust, and community-building, as students identify how a text has the power to activate certain emotions. These later questions take students beyond limited "text-dependent" understanding of "close reading" in the CCSS and toward richer, more complex, and more meaningful ways to read and respond.

> **Activity: Fostering Close Reading for Responding to Texts**
>
> Based on a text you are studying in your course or plan to use in your student teaching, generate some response activities that foster students' close reading responses to that text. These activities may include having them jot down responses or annotations as they are reading based on responding to some open-ended questions, having students share those responses or annotations in pairs prior to a discussion, and then engaging in small or large group discussions. As students respond, you may ask them to share how they were formulating their responses, for example, in responding to a character's addressing a problem or challenge or how they drew on their problem-solving thinking in their lived-world contexts.

EMPLOYING MULTIMODAL RESPONSES TO LITERATURE

Students can employ artwork or digital tools to create multimodal responses to texts, for example, using comics production apps such as Comic Life *tinyurl.com/kx3pnfg* to produce a comic book version of a text or artwork to visually portray settings, events, or characters.

For example, to visually respond to a novel's protagonist, Rebecca Oberg's students created a "body biography" (Smagorinsky & O'Donnell-Allen, 1998). They used butcher paper and coloring utensils to portray the traits associated with the character's heart (relationships with others), spine (his goals), and head (his thoughts). They also used color (associations with his character), symbolic objects, changes in actions through thought balloons, mirror images (how he perceived himself versus how others perceive him), quotes (an important quote about his identity), left and right arms (important decisions), left side (virtues), right side (vices), and stomach (motivational forces).

Students can also create digital book reports as book commercials or trailers *tinyurl.com/8enfexf* to encourage viewers to read their book and simultaneously illustrate how they consider purpose and audience (Hicks, 2015). Troy Hicks's daughter, Lexi, created a digital book report for *I Funny: A Middle School Story* (Patterson, 2013). She used a Glogster poster featuring the different characters in the book designed to provide her audience with a hook as to why they would want to read the book.

Other teachers have had students create memes to illustrate a response to a text. Faulkner (2014), for example, engaged her students with the three types of irony: situational, dramatic, and verbal, and tasked them with designing memes from *The Crucible* (Miller, 2003) illustrating the play. Many teachers have also incorporated social media as a way to solicit students' creativity, having students create: tweets at various points in reading, Snapchat messages between characters, hypothetical Instagram accounts to demonstrate a depth of understanding of a character's personality, or even TikTok videos in which students dress up as a character or author.

Book trailers, mentioned previously, can be created easily on TikTok as well. Students can also use Loom and Flipgrid to create video responses to texts and podcasts as a popular means of responding to literature. Such platforms can also be productive means for students to engage in awareness campaigns based on organizing and implementing projects that are often advertised and even carried out online.

INFERRING CHARACTERS' PERSPECTIVES FROM THEIR POINT OF VIEW

Interpreting conflicts or tensions between characters in the story involves inferring their perspectives or inner thoughts. The fact that a story is told from a first-person point of view means that readers are privy to that character's thoughts and feelings. Thus, readers engage in "mindreading" of characters' perspectives. In some sense, most literary works are like a detective novel in the sense that the reader follows the detective character's thinking processes as she or he sifts through various clues or interviews potential suspects.

Mind reading of characters' perspectives involves students intuiting or ascribing certain thoughts or feelings based on characters' or narrators' observable, explicit actions, e.g. a character is crying, so he must be upset. For example, because it is written in first person, Angeline Boulley's (2021) novel *The Firekeeper's Daughter* invites readers into the mind of the narrator Daunis after she witnesses a tragic murder and attempts to put the pieces together of what is negatively affecting her Ojibwe community. Readers uncover new individuals involved and their sordid attempts to cover up illicit behavior with each twist and turn.

Similarly, using a third person point of view provides readers with certain perspectives or information shared by the omniscient narrator such that characters may not know certain things known by the reader. For example, in the dystopian novel *Scythe* (Shusterman, 2016), the author shows how two young people apprentice for the position of a *scythe*, the person whose job is to decide who must die in an overpopulated world. Readers are privy to the experiences of each narrator, but those two do not necessarily know about one another's. Students could draw on point of view to analyze and respond to characters' actions and interpret the conflict (and feelings) between the two. They could also analyze the history provided by the external narrator in terms of what sort of justice this system promotes and its shortcomings.

CREATING DRAMATIC RESPONSES

You may also engage students in dramatic inquiry situations or dilemmas, where students adopt roles and attempt to address problems or issues based on their reading of a literary text. This approach can be part of a critical inquiry unit (Edmiston, 2014) as described in more detail in Chapter 7. For example, suppose students are studying the topic of income inequality. In that case, they could be told that they are members of a company whose mission is to address homelessness, requiring them to develop strategies to work with and support individuals without shelter. Or, students could be told that the gorillas in Uganda are being threatened with extinction due to poaching, requiring them to develop strategies to stop poachers. As these dramas unfold, you as the teacher can continually *frame and reframe events* by posing questions and adding new complications (for a description of dramatic inquiry activities *t.ly/r2QZ*).

This work requires that students continue to develop critical inquiry and problem-solving practices. They also need to conduct research, for example, studying various models for dealing with homelessness or researching the topic of gorillas in Uganda. In proposing the centrality of improvisation for agency and identity formation, Dorothy Holland and her colleagues (1998) have argued that improvisation is intended actions which are not a set response to a situation and that improvisation changes spaces to make them less restricted by, and more playful in relation to, both existing cultural norms and relationships with others.

Other ideas for incorporating improvisation in class for responding to literature include students reading a scene in a text and pausing their reading to enact what happens next, or they could enact what they think should have happened in a scene. For instance, students might learn about microaggressions and learn to recognize them in literary works. When they see one occur, they could then imagine what could have happened differently to address the scene. For instance, in René Watson's (2017) *Piecing Me Together*, the narrator, Jade, a young Black woman, is harassed in a store while shopping with her friend, Sam, who is White. Several onlookers do nothing. Readers could enact what the bystanders, or even Sam, could do in this instance.

Doing so involves adopting a "what if" inquiry stance through dialogue with others (Edmiston, 2014). Students may not know how events will unfold or how peers will respond to their talk in an improvisation. They may intend that their audience will respond in a certain manner, but may find that others respond in ways contrary to their intended responses, requiring them to adopt a different strategy.

Using improvisation and creative drama in the classroom requires students to adopt different perspectives to interpret alternative perspectives in ways that can challenge monologic thinking and their perspectives. When "in role," students commit themselves to act in a certain way and encounter the consequences of adopting certain actions or of not selecting other actions. They learn that the choices they make effectively construct identities and confirm ethical stances.

INTERPRETING USE OF LITERARY LANGUAGE

Students also draw on their literary knowledge to infer symbolic meanings of uses of literary language. Elizabeth Acevedo uses the metaphor of a lantern in her verse novel, *The Poet X* (2020), to represent how writing poetry provides light in the protagonist's world. In another example, in a study of literary interpretation, graduate students specializing in literature and first year college students with no specialization read a story about a "glittering" wedding ring that had fallen into a "mess of leaves" at the bottom of a dirty swimming pool (Levine, 2014).

During a think-aloud interview, one of the graduate students referred to that image, saying, "'Now that sounds like a symbol . . . a symbol of purity rising up out of the muck'" (p. 284). The first year college reader in the swimming pool study did not construct figurative interpretations, but did move beyond pure summary in one significant way: he made an affective evaluation of the image of the pool based on the imagery of the "'mess of leaves'" and similar details. He said, "'This is one terrible pool.'" (p. 284).

Many secondary students may be unfamiliar with the symbolic uses of literary language. To help them infer symbolic uses of language, you can have them draw on their emotions associated with everyday social interactions and relationships. The first year college student inferred the meaning of the leaves in the pool by applying what Levine (2014) describes as "affect-based evaluations" (p. 284). To do so, students first identify certain words or phrases that evoke certain emotions associated with the image of leaves in a swimming pool. They then assign certain positive or negative meanings to those words or phrases, for example, a negative response to the messy leaves. This leads to explaining their responses in terms of the larger meaning of the use of these words or phrases, for example, how the leaves function to portray negative connotations such as corruption.

Notice how the "symbolic meaning" in these examples is not something fixed or singular, or something that the teacher knows in advance. Instead, students drew on their prior knowledge and free associations to infer connotative interpretations. Too often in secondary classrooms literature teaching can become a hunt for "symbols" that the teacher "knows" and students try to guess at. That approach is trivializing, confusing, and off-putting. In your classroom, keep the exploration of "symbols" and connotative meaning fresh and organically meaningful. Symbols and literary devices should not distract from the personal and authentic ways your students respond to texts or from the important issues, topics, and questions literature raises.

TEACHING YOUNG ADULT LITERATURE

The strategies mentioned above can apply across literary genres and encourage students to respond to texts in a variety of ways. However, there are also methods that you can employ based on the genre or type of text you are teaching. For instance, as a teacher in a contemporary classroom, you will likely encounter canonical texts and contemporary general market texts and young adult literature. Young adult literature (YAL) has been defined in an array of different ways in the past 30 or so years.

In this book, we define YAL as literature written and marketed for teenagers. A relatively new phenomenon, YAL has come into its own in recent years and is currently one of the most lucrative divisions of most publishing houses. In the English language arts curriculum, YAL was once thought of primarily as useful in middle schools and as "gateway" literature (Coats, 2011), intended to engage students in reading and move them toward tackling "real" literature. However, in contemporary ELA classrooms, YAL has become what Coats (2011) calls a "destination" literature—something worth reading and studying in its own right (Hayn & Kaplan, 2012).

A critical inquiry approach to teaching YAL should foster careful consideration of audience and purpose and encourage students to consider the degree to which they affiliate or disaffiliate with the youth audience the author seems to be imagining in their work.

If we really want to treat young adult literature as destination literature, "teachers and scholars need to develop viable means for critiquing YAL that underscore unique and prominent qualities" of these texts (Thein & Sulzer, 2015, p. 53). Drawing on the interdisciplinary field of Critical Youth Studies (e.g. Lesko, 1996), Thein and Sulzer argue that because adults write YAL for youth, youth need to unpack the assumptions about and essentialized representations of adolescents in YAL in terms of adolescents' identities, needs, and desires. As mentioned earlier in our discussion of the Critical Youth Lens, adult norms are portrayed as the ideal that adolescents should emulate in some cases.

Students should consider how adolescents are represented in YAL, the author's purpose and imagined audience, and the extent to which they want to affiliate or disaffiliate with that audience. Questions to help guide this analysis are:

- What claims/observations about a given issue or topic (bullying, adolescent masculinity, etc.) are being made in the conversation between the narratee, the narrator, and the implied reader?
- Have you heard these claims before? Where?
- What is interesting, useful, or problematic about how these claims or observations are being expressed?
- What do these claims/observations seem to say about young people in general?
- How are these claims/observations similar to or different from your experience?
- To what extent are these claims/observations true?

(Thein & Sulzer, 2015, p. 52)

This approach actively recruits students to critically consider YAL as both a literary and economic phenomenon and leads adolescents "to generate the types of questions that young people are in the best position to answer" (p. 52). Approaching YAL this way differs from didactically teaching YAL with the goal of teaching students lessons about bullying, drug use, teen pregnancy, suicide, or any number of prototypical teen crises, because it allows students to question the universality of those crises and their depiction in literature. Reading this way allows youth to resist positionings that don't serve their needs and think critically about and perhaps change how they imagine their own identities.

YAL also captures the social issues of our world and can serve as a window, mirror, and sliding glass door (Sims Bishop, 1990)—reflecting readers' stances and cultivating empathy and understanding for individuals who may be different from them. Responding to YAL can then lead them to transform their worlds by using their responses as a springboard toward community and social action (Boyd & Darragh, 2019; Simmons, 2012). Josie, for instance, whose classroom we read about in Chapter 1, designed a social issues project in which she offered students a choice between several young adult novels, all centered on different issues such as racism or immigration policy. The choices included: *The Benefits of Being and Octopus* (Braden, 2018), *Blended* (Draper, 2020), and *Other Words for Home* (Warga, 2019).

Each day in the unit, students completed journal entries that were broad enough to apply and adapt to any book, such as: How is the protagonist in your novel alike and different from you? Or: Describe the most important scene you have read so far and justify your choice.

Throughout their reading and group meetings, students worked with their team of peers on designing a community action project related to the social issue presented in their novels.

For a book that examined immigration critically, they researched local agencies that helped individuals relocate and determined ways they could contribute. Another group that read about people with limited resources investigated a local organization that provided food, clothing, and shelter for families and contributed to a drive to solicit additional resources and support. Josie, however, hoping to point students toward systems that created such circumstances for people, continuously challenged them to think of how they could help materially and foster broader change. As a result, students wrote to legislators about policies that restricted undocumented individuals as well as argued for higher wages for local jobs. These examples illustrate how reading in book clubs, mentioned previously in this chapter, can be combined with YAL to engender justice, inquiry, and action.

TEACHING DRAMA

Another important literary genre is drama (see also Chapter 7 on engaging students in drama activities). Because play scripts are primarily dialogue, understanding plays by simply reading them rather than seeing them performed requires the reader to infer relationships between written dialogue and presumed actions. For example, in responding to *Hamlet*, students infer whether and how Hamlet plans to avenge his father's murder from his speeches.

Clearly, students benefit from attending live performances or even viewing film versions. Students who attended theater productions of *Hamlet* or *A Christmas Carol* had a higher level of knowledge about the story plot, vocabulary employed in the play, and measures of empathy and level of tolerance for others, compared to students who simply read or viewed movies of the plays (Greene et al., 2018. The results of this study point to the value of engaging students in attending theater productions and the use of drama activities in the classroom to develop student understanding of a play and enhance their ability to empathize with others' perspectives.

Rather than simply sitting through an entire film adaptation of a play, it will likely be more effective to have students closely and repeatedly view a single scene, perhaps from recordings of different productions. Students can then analyze the ways in which a director or film interprets the text through how actors perform roles or how a film version uses certain cinematic techniques, settings, music, lighting, or actors to convey meaning.

In one example, combining the viewing of clips with reading aloud the play *Fences* (Wilson, 1986), students were able to more deeply engage with the message the writer crafted. Students read on a physical set that included artifacts from the play so that they experienced a sense of context associated with their experience of the play (Beach & Beauchemin,

2019). The play portrays an African American family in the 1950s and a conflict between Troy, an ex-con and garbage pickup truck worker, and his son, Cory.

The son wants to attend college by obtaining a football scholarship, something that Troy refuses to support, leading to Cory leaving the family. In writing about their responses to this conflict, one student noted that Troy "wanted to do it in his way, and Cory wanted to it in his way . . . they never showed their feelings, and that was the biggest mistake both could have ever done in their entire life" (p. 119). Another student noted how Troy's time in prison was based on minor crimes that resulted in an excessive sentence:

> America has established a system that oppresses people of color in a way that forces some into crime, and subsequently, incarceration. August Wilson is uncovering the truth of the American experience that the American experience is not equal for everyone.
>
> (p. 119)

Through viewing, reading aloud, and reflecting, students more aptly engaged with the issue of justice in the play.

Students can engage in drama as a response to the issues or conflict in a play or theater production, such as a trial, debate forum, or city council/school board meeting. For responding to *Romeo and Juliet*, a teacher created a town meeting of the people of Verona to address the question as to who was to blame for the tragic deaths of Romeo and Juliet (Flynn & Forman, 2016).

By acting out specific scenes from plays, students are necessarily using performances to interpret the meaning of speech. Students can also create videos of certain scenes from a play. As mentioned previously, Flipgrid or other online sources can provide students with an engaging platform for recording and sharing videos. Because students may initially be reluctant to perform roles in front of their peers, you can have them engage in initial warm-up activities. For example, pairs of students can simply greet each other at various levels of formality, or practice blocking by adopting different nonverbal poses to convey alternative meanings.

For responding to Shakespeare plays, students can write annotations next to specific lines in the plays in which they rewrite these lines into their colloquial style. For example, 10th-grade students rewrote lines from *Romeo and Juliet*, related to Juliet's frustration with the Nurse regarding her previous visit with Romeo:

Juliet: I sent the Nurse out at nine and she said she'd return in half an hour. If only the Nurse were young and fast, not old and slow.

Enter Nurse.

Juliet: Hey, Nurse, why do you look so sad?
Nurse: I need a nap. I'm old and my bones hurt.
Juliet: SPEAK!
Nurse: Hold your horses; let me catch my breath.
Juliet: If you are so out of breath then how do you have breath to tell me that you are out of breath? Just tell me if it's good or bad news.
Nurse: Romeo's not a man, but he sure is handsome.
Juliet: I already knew that!

(Beach & Beauchemin, 2019, p. 161)

In rewriting lines, students are "double-voicing" (Bakhtin, 1981) the original language actions to create their alternative actions based on their interpretations of characters' roles and intentions in a play.

TEACHING POETRY

Poetry is another text form that warrants specific strategies for soliciting student's responses (see also Chapter 7 on writing poetry). You can build on students' interest in music lyrics and have students select online poetry from sites such as The Academy of American Poets *www.poets.org* or The Poetry Archive *www.poetryarchive.org*. In teaching poetry, the starting point should be fostering student experiences of reading and responding rather than extensive instruction about the features or structures of poetic forms.

Reading poetry from online sites immerses students in a world of poetry beyond a traditional textbook. So many of these sites are *alive*, connected to living poets and to poetry lovers. The Academy of American Poets, for instance, features a "National Poetry Calendar" where students can search for poetry events near them. This site also advertises poetry book clubs; accepts manuscripts from contemporary poets; gives poetry awards; produces a free podcast; offers a free newsletter; and provides reading recommendations, lesson plans, and resources for teachers. Other sites let students explore poetry in other ways, beyond what is possible in printed text. The American Verse Project *quod.lib.umich.edu/a/amverse* assembles volumes of American poetry published before 1920 and allows users to search for occurrences of words and phrases throughout the entire full-text archive—thousands of poems.

Rather than organizing poetry instruction around traditionally established poetic forms and literary language, in keeping with our critical inquiry approach, we suggest finding ways to help students inquire into the themes and issues that poetry powerfully raises or responds to. Spoken word poetry, for example, is a medium through which many activists share counternarratives and political messages.

Andrea Gibson, for example, is a powerful artist whose messages challenge gender norms. There are a number of youth slam poets whose work is inspiring and powerful, including Amanda Gorman, who famously performed "The Hill We Climb" at Joe Biden's presidential inauguration. Her work garnered attention for how to include spoken word in the classroom.

Students might also create their own spoken word poems in response to a text or issue. They could share these with the class or even at a community event night, raising awareness of certain issues or voicing their opinions on contemporary issues.

Students in Allen's ELA methods course recently reflected on how different approaches to poetry instruction result in different kinds of learning. This class of future secondary English teachers read the canonical poem "The Passionate Shepherd to His Love" written by Christopher Marlowe in 1599. Next, they discussed how traditional approaches focused on literary forms or close reading skills would address either providing knowledge of famous authors and texts, examining poetic language and structures, or decoding words and vocabulary. The future teachers in Allen's class also talked about how a reader response teacher would ask students about their personal responses to the poem, what it made them think or feel, and how the poem connected to their own experiences.

When future teachers speculated about how a critical inquiry teacher would approach the poem, they came up with several possibilities: secondary students might inquire into the social context of the poem—an exchange between an elegant man and refined lady—and how the work implicitly constructs class and gender roles to investigate what those roles may have been like during the time period. They also suggested ways students could investigate the differences between the real life of shepherds and rural workers in the 16th century and the "beds of roses/and a thousand fragrant posies" portrayed in the poem as well as the pastoral and bucolic setting related to the poem's "valleys, groves, hills and fields," of industrialization, urban expansion, and modernization. Any of these inquiries could be connected to looking at the same topics in the present.

Critical inquiry into poetry certainly begins with careful and engaging reading of poetic works. You can engage students in multiple readings, reading aloud, vocabulary study and close reading, literature circles, readers' theater and performance, rewriting across genres from sonnet to rap lyric or epic to slam poem, etc. A critical inquiry approach is especially relevant to poetic genre study when it examines how genres are culturally coded and how they structure ethical and political understanding of gender, class, social relations, and important issues.

Activity: Responding to Poetry

In thinking about creating activities for your students to respond to poetry, formulate your overall purpose related to how you want them to experience their own unique responses to a poem you are having them read. One purpose might be to have them recognize the need to reread a poem multiple times to reflect on how they generate new, alternative meanings with each rereading. Another purpose might be to have them visualize the meanings of images/metaphors for constructing meanings, while another purpose may involve verbally performing the poem in different ways to enact alternative meanings through variations in sound and pauses.

FINAL THOUGHTS ON TEACHING LITERATURE

As Allen's description of an inquiry approach to pastoral poetry indicates, justice, inquiry, and action approaches can be brought to any literary work. Works from the canon, young adult literature, drama, or poetry are all open to the various perspectives we described earlier in this chapter and through the response strategies we provided. For example, *Of Mice and Men* (Steinbeck, 1937) can be read through a disabilities studies lens for the messages communicated about people with special needs. Students can enact scenes to imagine more just treatment in the novel. Students might then design action projects to address inaccessibility or other social barriers or stigmas associated with people with disabilities.

A justice, inquiry, and action approach to literature therefore involves going beyond the work itself, with students asking social, cultural, and historical questions and engaging in additional research. This approach doesn't isolate the text, but seeks to bring together different genres to explore important questions. To the extent possible, it's the questions that organize curriculum, not the other way around. While some texts lend themselves more readily to such critical approaches, others may require more creativity to determine the angle to use with students. Regardless, we firmly believe that all literature can connect to the world in ways that encourage and excite students toward justice and action.

REFERENCES

Acevedo, E. (2020). *The poet X*. Harper Teen.
Appleman, D. (2014). *Critical encounters in secondary English: Teaching literary theory to adolescents*. Teachers College Press.
Appleman, D. (2015). *Critical encounters in high school English: Teaching literary theory to adolescents*, 3rd. ed. Teachers College Press/National Council of Teachers of English.
Atwell, N. (2007). *The reading zone: How to help kids become skilled, passionate, habitual, critical readers*. Scholastic.
Austen, J. (2009). *Pride and prejudice*. Middleton Classics.
Bakhtin, M. M. (1981). *The dialogic imagination: Four essays*. (Ed. M. Holquist, trans., C. Emerson). University of Texas Press.
Beach, R., & Beauchemin, F. (2019). *Teaching language as action in the ELA classroom*. Routledge.
Beach, R., Appleman, D., Fecho, B., & Simon, R. (2021). *Teaching literature to adolescents*, 4th ed. Routledge.
Beach, R., Campano, G., Edmiston, B. & Borgmann, M. (2010). *Literacy tools in the classroom: Teaching through critical inquiry, grades 5-12*. Teachers College Press.
Blackburn, M. V., Clark, C. T. & Nemeth, E. A. (2015). Examining queer elements and ideologies in LGBT-themed literature: What queer literature can offer young adult readers. *Journal of Literacy Research, 47*(1), 11–48.
Borsheim-Black, C., Macaluso, M. & Petrone, R. (2014). Critical literature pedagogy: Teaching canonical literature for critical literacy. *Journal of Adolescent & Adult Literacy, 58*(2), 123–133.
Borsheim-Black, C., & Sarigianides, S. (2019). *Letting go of literary whiteness: Antiracist literature instruction for white students*. Teachers College Press.
Boulley, A. (2021). *The firekeeper's daughter*. Henry Holt.
Boyd, A. (2021). Engaging white privilege, racial injustice, and intersectionality in the canon and young adult literature. In T. Hawley and P. Chandler (Eds.), *Handbook on teaching social issues*, 2nd ed. (155–162). Information Age Publishing.
Boyd, A., & Darragh, J. (2019). Critical literacies on the university campus: Engaging pre-service teachers with social action projects. *English Teaching: Practice & Critique, 19*(1), 49–63.
Braden, A. (2018). *The benefits of being an octopus*. Sky Pony Press.
Bradford, W. (2016). *Of Plymouth plantation*. CreateSpace Independent Publishing Platform.
Britzman, D. (1995). Is there a queer pedagogy? Or stop reading straight. *Educational Theory, 45*(2), 151–165.
Cart, M., & Jenkins, C. (2006). *The heart has its reasons: Young adult literature with gay/lesbian/queer content, 1969-2004*. Scarecrow Press.
Coats, K. (2011). Young adult literature: Growing up, in theory. In C. Jenkins, K. Coats, P. A. Enciso, S. Wolf (Eds.), *Handbook of research on children's and young adult literature* (pp. 315–330). Taylor & Francis.
Collins, S. (2008). *The hunger games*. Scholastic.
Delgado, R., & Stefancic, J. (2017). *Critical race theory: An introduction*, 3rd ed. New York University Press.
Dixon, J. (1975). *Growth through English: Set in the perspective of the seventies*, 3rd ed. National Association for the Teaching of English.
Draper, S. (2020). *Blended*. Atheneum Books for Young Readers
Dunn, P. A. (2015). *Disabling characters: Representations of disability in young adult literature*. Peter Lang.
Dyches, J. (2018). Critical canon pedagogy: Applying disciplinary inquiry to cultivate canonical critical consciousness. *Harvard Educational Review, 88*(4), 538–564.
Edmiston, B. (2014). *Transforming teaching and learning with active and dramatic approaches: Engaging students across the curriculum*. Routledge.
Faulkner, J. (2014). Faulker's fast five: Memes in the ELA classroom [Web log post]. Retrieved from https://juliefaulknersblog.com/memes-in-ela-classroom
Flynn, R., & Forman, S. (2016). Framing the narrative: A teacher-in-role strategy with Romeo and Juliet. Retrieved from https://community.schooltheatre.org/HigherLogic/System/DownloadDocumentFile.ashx?DocumentFileKey=8546687a-3bfb-4294-9541-dfa2ed6fd287
Gladwell, M. (2010). *What the dog saw: And other adventures*. Back Bay Books.
Greene, J. P., Erickson, H. H., Watson, A. R., & Beck, M. I. (2018). The play's the thing: Experimentally examining the social and cognitive effects of school field trips to live theater performances. *Educational Researcher, 47*(4), 246–254.
Hannah-Jones, N. & *The New York Times Magazine* (Authors), Roper, C., Silverman, I., & Silverstein, J. (Eds.) (2021). *The 1619 project: A new origin story*. One World.
Hayn, J. A., & Kaplan, J. S. (Eds.). (2012). *Teaching young adult literature today*. Rowman & Littlefield.
Hicks, T. (2013, September 18). My digital reading practices, Part 3 [Web log post]. Retrieved from http://tinyurl.com/m58uwv6
Holland, D., Lachicotte Jr., W., Skinner, D., & Cain, C. (1998). *Identity and agency in cultural worlds*. Harvard University Press.
Hurst, J. (1960). The scarlet ibis. *The Atlantic Monthly*.
Kingston, M. H. (1975/2010). *The woman warrior: Memoirs of a girlhood among ghosts*. Vintage.

Lee, H. (1988). *To kill a mockingbird*. Warner Books.
Lesko, N. (1996). Past, present, and future conceptions of adolescence. *Educational Theory, 46*(4), 453–472.
Lesko, N. (2012). *Act your age! A cultural construction of adolescence*. Routledge.
Levine, S. (2014). Making interpretation visible with an affect-based strategy. *Reading Research Quarterly, 49*(3), 283–303.
Macaluso, M. (2017). Teaching *to kill a mockingbird* today: Coming to terms with race, racism, and America's novel. *Journal of Adolescent & Adult Literacy, 61*(3), 279–287.
Miller, A. (2003). *The crucible*. Penguin.
Patterson, J. (2013). *I funny: A middle school story*. Little Brown & Company.
Petrone, R., Sarigianides, S. T., & Lewis, M. A. (2015). The youth lens: Analyzing Adolescence/ts in literary texts. *Journal of Literacy Research, 46*(4), 506–533.
Rosenblatt, L. (1995). *Literature as exploration*, 5th ed. Modern Language Association of America.
Scholastic. (2014). *The Scholastic Kids & Family Reading ReportTM*, 5th ed. Author. Retrieved from www.scholastic.com/readingreport
Sheffer, M. (2013a, October 27). Reading closely: What does it really mean? [Web log post]. Retrieved from http://tinyurl.com/n7u3bxs
Sheffer, M. (2013b, October 26). Getting closer to close reading [Web log post]. Retrieved from http://tinyurl.com/n8uud5p
Sheffer, M. (2013c, October 26). The close reading conundrum [Web log post]. Retrieved from http://tinyurl.com/qhfjwst
Shusterman, N. (2016). *Scythe*. Simon & Schuster.
Simmons, A. M. (2012). Class on fire: Using *The Hunger Games* trilogy to encourage social action. *Journal of Adolescent & Adult Literacy, 56*(1), 22–34.
Sims Bishop, R. (1990). Mirrors, windows, and sliding glass doors. *Perspectives, 6*(3), ix–xi.
Smagorinsky, P., & O'Donnell-Allen, C. (1998). Reading as mediated and mediating action: Composing meaning for literature through multimedia interpretive texts. *Reading Research Quarterly, 33*(2), 198–226.
Smith, M. W., Appleman, D., & Wilhelm, J. D. (2014). *Uncommon core: Where the authors of the standards go wrong about instruction – and how you can get it right*. Corwin.
Steinbeck, J. (1993). *Of mice and men*. Penguin.
Thein, A. H., & Sulzer, M. A. (2015). Illuminating discourses of youth through the study of first- person narration in young adult literature. *English Journal, 104*(3), 47–53.
Thomas, E. E. & Stornaiuolo, A. (2016). Restorying the self: Bending toward textual justice. *Harvard Educational Review, 86*(3), 313–338.
Warga, J. (2019). *Other words for home*. Balzer + Bray.
Watson, R. (2017). *Piecing me together*. Bloomsbury.
Wilson, A. (1986). *Fences: A play*. Plume.
Wimsatt, W. K., & Beardsley, M. C. (1949). The affective fallacy. *The Sewanne Review, 57*(1), 31–55.

5

Teaching Nonfiction

For many English teachers, there is a strong emphasis on teaching reading of nonfiction texts, which represents a real shift in how and what we teach in the English language arts classroom. And while many English teachers worry that increased time spent with nonfiction might mean less time reading literature, it is important to recognize that research suggests that students *do* need more experience and critical skills when it comes to reading nonfiction. Despite states adopting reading standards, this did not necessarily result in increases in reading test scores, and in some states there has been a reduction in those scores (Hock et al., 2015).

An analysis of 9.8 million students' reading of 330 million books in the 2013–14 school year, "What Kids Are Reading and Why It Matters" (from the Renaissance Learning company that produces the Accelerated Reader reading program that includes online quizzes for books), found that students are still reading relatively few nonfiction books.

It is also the case that Black, Latinx, and Native American 8th graders in 2018 had significantly lower reading test scores on the National Assessment of Educational Progress reading tests than White and Asian/Pacific Islander 12th graders, a pattern that has persisted since 1992 (Institute of Education Sciences, 2019).

Gender differences may also influence reading where boy students may prefer nonfiction texts, for example, for reading about sports, suggesting the need to include nonfiction texts in the ELA classroom (Smith & Wilhelm, 2002).

It is also the case that reading of online digital texts is increasing, as evident in students' reading each other's texts on their phones as well as websites. Studies suggest that if we as English teachers want our students to be able to read broadly and critically, we need to bolster their proficiency with nonfiction texts, both by introducing them to new text types and genres, and by helping students critically engage with the digital texts they already read. In this chapter, we explore each of these topics in an effort to help you and your students exceed the state nonfiction reading standards.

A review of research at part of the Reading for Understanding Initiative (RfU) found that, beyond learning to read in the early grades, from middle school on, students still need to acquire additional reading comprehension practices—for example, responding to specific disciplinary language (Pearson et al., 2020). Teachers have a major role in teaching reading based on their having knowledge about their students' reading practices as well as knowing how to assist students to enhance their reading practices (Hattie, 2009). Teachers can enhance

DOI: 10.4324/9781003177364-7

students' reading ability by supporting their metacognitive thinking related to decoding and problem-solving as well as providing them with feedback about their comprehension practices (Allington, 2011; Hock et al., 2015).

SELECTING ENGAGING, RELEVANT INFORMATIONAL TEXTS

As a teacher, you will want to select nonfiction texts that are complex, relevant, and engaging—something that can be a real challenge. One of the difficulties of teaching nonfiction, informational texts in the ELA classroom is that the excerpts provided in textbooks often fail to be engaging for students. We recommend that you think outside of the box in selecting nonfiction texts, exploring a range of sources and genres within the broad category of "nonfiction." (For recommended popular nonfiction texts, see *Recommended nonfiction texts* on the website.)

Thinking outside the box means going beyond print texts and considering the many types of nonfiction students encounter outside of school—newspapers, videos, magazines, websites, social media, and blogs. Students are more likely to be engaged in reading nonfiction when they have some purpose related to addressing a problem or issue in their lives; for example, their interest in the efficacy of the Covid vaccines on adolescents.

It's also important for students to access different texts about the same problem or issue so that they gain a range of different perspectives on a problem or issue. In studying shootings at Virginia Tech University, students read a range of different texts that rhetorically framed and actually shaped events in different ways from sites such as the American Rhetoric website *www.americanrhetoric.com* and the National Archives *www.archives.gov* (Beckelhimer, 2010).

GOING BEYOND NARROW NOTIONS OF "CLOSE READING" FOR CONTEXTUALIZING TEXTS

One issue associated with the Common Core Standards is that, in making recommendations to textbook publishers, two framers of the standards, David Coleman and Susan Pimentel (2012), recommended that textbook activities employ only "text-dependent" questions to foster what they defined as "close reading" of texts. Their notion of "close reading" assumed that the meaning can only be found "in" the text, leading to recommending against the use of pre-reading activities where students apply their prior knowledge to texts.

This recommendation reflects the adoption of New Critical literary analysis methods popular in the 1940s to 1960s that assumed the need to bracket out reader's unique prior experiences, knowledge, and goals for reading, a stance that was found to be empirically problematic by reading researchers and led to the rise of reader-response approaches in the 1970s and 1980s (see Sulzer, 2014 for a critique of this approach to literature found in CCSS-aligned textbooks).

Contrary to the use of "text-dependent" questions that presuppose that a text's meaning is "in" a text, synthesizing texts involves not only the ability to attend to specific aspects of the use of language, images, audio, and video constituting a text, but also the ability to contextualize the text based on one's purpose, knowledge, experiences, attitudes, and needs—for example, relating an essay to the topic or theme students are studying.

Reading texts in different phases

A more productive and critical approach to close reading is one in which close reading is understood as unfolding in a series of different phases beginning with an initial reading to gain a general sense of the text's big ideas, followed by a second reading that involves more focused responses generated through posing and responding to questions; writing about and annotating the texts; and discussing texts to make claims and focus on evidence supporting those claims (Fisher & Frey, 2014).

Close reading, therefore, requires providing students with time to engage in reading, rereading, and responding to texts with specific questions, goals, and purposes in mind, as opposed to simply an initial reading followed by responding to a few questions tethered to the "four corners" of the text. This includes noting certain patterns in a text related to the use of similar words, repetitions, or contradictions that add up to a focus on key ideas or themes (Kain, 1998) *t.ly/FaXV*.

During these different phases of reading, you can encourage your students to continually reflect on and monitor whether they are successfully making inferences based on their purposes and questions for reading the text. If they sense that they are not acquiring the relevant meanings, they might then recognize that they need to reread the text with their purposes and questions in mind. As students reread, you can prompt them to focus on the writer's use of certain organizational features or rhetorical devices, as well as concepts and ideas that they do not understand. At the same time, from rereading the text, they may revise their purposes or questions to entertain alternative perspectives on the problem or issue they are addressing.

Close reading also entails the need to avoid simply scanning a text—a practice often associated with reading online texts—by engaging in "slow reading" that involves establishing a relationship with a text so that students pause to savor and reflect on the meaning of a text (Newkirk, 2011; Mickics, 2013). To do so, students learn to apply "rules of notice" (Rabinowitz, 1998) to infer the meaning of specific salient features of a text: the title, subtitles, first and final sentences, detailed descriptions of key events, etc. Close reading also involves *inferring certain consistent patterns* in or across different texts related to the repetition of certain key concepts or words, positions or stances, or use of evidence or reasoning (Lehman & Roberts, 2014).

APPLICATION OF METADISCURSIVE PRACTICES FOR CONTEXTUALIZING TEXTS

Effective comprehension of texts involves the use of metadiscursive practices, meaning how, when, where, and why a learner adopts reading and writing practices in a particular context, such as a discipline (biology vs. literature), a kind of text frame (descriptive vs. argument), or a task (summary vs. critique) (Catterson & Pearson, 2017, p. 465).

Students acquire these practices by reflecting on how they are contextualizing the text based on applying their use of language, ways of organizing texts, and their prior knowledge of the topic or issue (Hattan & Alexander, 2020). This suggests the importance of selecting and sequencing different texts that each provides relevant background knowledge for subsequent texts (Willingham, 2015). If students are reading about the contemporary denial of voting rights, it is useful that they have read about the civil rights movement and the passage of voting rights legislation as portrayed, for instance, in the movie *Selma* (DuVernay, 2014) (DVDs of this movie have been provided to all schools by Paramount Pictures *selma4students.com* along with curriculum materials *tinyurl.com/p8y987k*).

As students are reading a text, you may have them connect a text to certain related texts or experiences. For example, in reading reports about the adverse effects of climate change related to wildfires, flooding, extreme weather events, excessive heat, droughts, etc., you may have them reference local examples of those effects in their own communities or lives. At the same time, rather than have students evoke this knowledge or experience during or after reading a text, you may also have them share or write about this knowledge or experience prior to reading a text, prior knowledge or experience that serves as a framework or scaffold for responding to the text.

Students are also applying equally important social/cultural knowledge and experiences for contextualizing texts. It is often assumed that, given experiences with reading comprehension texts, the meaning of a text is constructed by inferring what a text is "saying"—the overall key idea or thesis of a text. However, it is also important for students to apply and infer writers' underlying social and cultural stances associated with a text. In responding to essays around gender discrimination, students need to infer how their attitudes about gender shape their inferences about a writer's stance on gender equality.

Students also learn to contextualize texts by writing texts based on reflecting on formulating purposes for their writing to achieve uptake from audiences. A review of research studies on combining reading and writing instruction found that writing instruction benefitted students' decoding, vocabulary, and writing strategies (Graham et al., 2018).

USING THINK-ALOUD RESPONSES FOR RESPONDING TO NONFICTION TEXTS

In using think-alouds, students pair up and share their responses to a text as they read, as opposed to summarizing or interpreting a text on their own at the culmination of the reading (Beck, 2018; Wilhelm, 2013). Students may also note what intrigues them, connections they find with other texts, or difficulties they are having in reading a text. Partners simply react with positive support and then the students switch roles.

Making their thoughts explicit helps students actively formulate reactions to words or ideas that they have difficulty understanding. Because students may have difficulty making their thoughts explicit, you may need to model the think-aloud process for students. Students can also engage in think-alouds before they begin a text, reporting their purposes or expectations for reading a text, what they may expect to learn from a text, and issues on which they may focus (Wilhelm, 2013). Some questions that students can use in think-alouds include, "what are you doing?" or "what is going on in your mind?" Recordings of think-alouds, particularly when dictated using speech-to-text software programs such as Dragon Speaking that create transcripts, can be assessed in terms of the range of different responses.

Activity: Learning to Model Think-Alouds for Your Students

To learn to effectively model think-alouds for your students, it is useful to engage in your own think-alouds with a partner in your methods courses. Select a partner and

> a relatively short text. Then, share your explicit thoughts with your partner as you are reading through the text—what Elbow (1973) described as "movies of your mind" (p. 85)—stopping at certain set places in the text. Rather than attempt to interpret the text, share how you are thinking about the text, including difficulties in comprehending the text. Your partner should simply provide you with supportive nonverbal or verbal feedback to encourage you to continue with your think-alouds. Then, switch roles. When you're both done, step back and reflect on how you will model the process of doing think-alouds for your students

TEACHING VOCABULARY

It is often the case that vocabulary is taught in a decontextualized manner as a set of isolated words on worksheets or in a discussion where students need to identify correct definitions. This approach is contrary to the notions that the meanings of words depend on the contexts in which they are employed, suggesting the need for a contextualized approach to vocabulary instruction (Beck et al., 2013).

Another practice related to reading comprehension involves acquiring knowledge of vocabulary associated with specific topics or disciplines (Pearson et al., 2020). For learning to read texts in their science, social studies, and math classes, students need to acquire specialized vocabulary in those disciplines. They also need to know how to acquire the meaning of unfamiliar words through learning the meanings of new words.

One study examined the effects of one year of reading instruction on 9th-grade students with low reading abilities, half of whom were from economically disadvantaged homes (Solis et al., 2018). Instruction focused on the level of comprehension: *surface* level related to decoding letters and words, *propositional* level focused on the context for word meaning, and *situation* level involving connecting to prior knowledge. Students engaged in writing "walk-in slips" summarizing responses to a paragraph related to a topic about which they were reading. Students also engaged in previewing texts to activate related prior knowledge to predict what they would learn from a text.

As they were reading, students shared inferences about main ideas as well as citing evidence from the text to support their inferences, and responding to questions regarding who, when, where, and why. They also worked in pairs to read lists of keywords to each other in less than 15 seconds. Over the period of one year, students demonstrated significant improvement in vocabulary but only small improvements in comprehension, suggesting that just one year of instruction may be insufficient for helping students with low reading ability levels.

For teaching vocabulary, teachers can provide students with a list of words that students indicate as being familiar or unfamiliar, leading to their studying unfamiliar words and to students writing a definition of the word related to how they are used in certain contexts (Hock et al., 2015). Students then share their definitions to generate a composite definition followed by writing new sentences employing those words.

Students can also engage in vocabulary instruction using the web-based DictionarySquared *doi.org/10.23641/asha.9765161* (for a video description: *dictionarysquaredresearch.sc.edu*) (Adlof et al., 2019), use of Snappy Words *www.snappywords.com* for creating visual maps with words and synonyms, or use of the Flocabulary *www.flocabulary.com* tool for embedding words into contexts; for example, adding visual images or songs to words (Csillag, 2016).

ACQUIRING EFFECTIVE ONLINE READING FOR RESPONDING TO NONFICTION TEXTS

Students are increasingly reading online nonfiction texts, reading that involves processes that differ from reading print texts; for example, locating relevant information on a website page differs from the linear, left to right processing of print texts (Leu et al., 2011). Reading a web page also requires the ability to locate relevant information by selecting and clicking on certain links or icons rather than others, based on the specific purpose for reading.

Similarly, in reading blog posts or online articles that contain hyperlinks, students need to know when and why they should click on various links to acquire further information about a topic. This requires that students have a clear sense of purpose for locating icons or links by reading for relevancy (Kress, 2009).

Further, students' ability to engage in effective online reading can differ according to their access to computers or digital devices in their schools and homes, and according to their access to peers or family members who can assist them in using digital tools—differences related to access to digital devices and support between students from higher and lower-income families (Leu et al., 2014).

All of this suggests the need for instruction focused on online reading processes that include:

- *formulating purposes* for reading online texts to focus on relevant information. For example, if students are searching for information on the adverse effects of consuming sugar, they need to identify what information they are seeking to select relevant texts.
- *selecting links* relevant to their purposes for reading. Online texts include numerous hyperlinks to other texts. Students, therefore, need to know which links to click on and which to ignore relative to acquiring needed information based on their purposes for reading. Students can use social bookmarking tools such as Diigo to collect and store relevant links.
- *evaluating* the relevancy and validity of information acquired. As previously noted, students need to continually assess the relevancy and validity of the information they are acquiring. If they determine that the information is irrelevant to their purposes, they need to keep searching. If they recognize that the information is suspect, they need to find alternative sources.
- *synthesizing and formulating* the information acquired (Coiro et al., 2014). As they acquire information, students need to continually synthesize that information. (Beach et al., 2016, p. 80).

(For more on reading online texts, see *Reading online texts* on the website.)

Online sources for accessing nonfiction texts

By accessing informational, nonfiction texts online, students learn to select and use online search engines and databases effectively, appropriately, and critically. Students often initially go to Google, Yahoo, Bing, Chrome, or YouTube for their searches, but often lack search strategies skills to limit or focus their search results or to use more specific search tools—for example, Google Advanced Search *www.google.com/advanced_search* or Custom Search *www.google.com/cse/docs*.

In using these tools, it is important that students become critical consumers, recognizing that certain companies employ "search optimization" tools so that their sites obtain high rankings on Google, Safari, Bing, or Chrome—sites that often contain ads. In one survey, 76% of teachers indicated that using these search engines gave students the false impression that they were accessing scholarly, vetted content, and 71% believed that their students failed to access a range of different informational sources (Purcell et al., 2012).

Students therefore also need to learn to use databases through their libraries' sites, such as InfoTrac Junior Edition, Academic Search Premier, Gale Group, CQ Researcher, General Reference Center Gold, or EBSCO Academic Search Premier. To identify certain relevant databases for specific disciplines, students can use the Library of Congress's Ask a Librarian *tinyurl.com/14ev* site to obtain information based on academic databases.

Another useful resource for information is Wikipedia. To determine the validity of Wikipedia entries, students can look at the revision histories on entries to note deletions and additions, as well as Talk Pages for discussions of misinformation (Jenkins, 2006). Middle school students may benefit from using the iOS Qwiki *tinyurl.com/kc3oape* app given its use of revised entries, images, and videos. Students can learn to be contributors to Wikipedia, creating and updating pages for institutions, programs, or people they know in their own community, including for their school.

For current events or news, students can access sites such as Newsela *newsela.com*, Tween Tribune *tweentribune.com* (which filters articles by 5–8 and 9–12 grade levels and provides Spanish translations), CNN Student News, Slate, PBS NewsHour Extra, or Time for Kids, as well as news curation apps—Flipboard, Zite, Learnist, Zinio, Pearltrees, Google Currents, LiveBinders, Scoop.it!, Pinterest, Educlipper, and Storify. Students might also view TED talks using the TED under 20 site, leading students to engage in creating their own TED talk presentations. You can also subscribe to the free CoreStand *www.corestand.com* service or Jim Burke's Digital Textbook *tinyurl.com/oedtctd* to acquire articles based on grade-level differences.

Assessing online search results

When students are searching for information, they need to know how to assess the validity, source, and relevancy of that information. This requires that they investigate the writer who or the organization that created a particular webpage as well as the extent to which the claims provided are supported by evidence or valid reasons. To address the writing standard "Gather relevant information from multiple print and digital sources, assess the credibility and accuracy of each source, and integrate the information while avoiding plagiarism" (Common Core Standards, 2010, p. 41), students need to identify the author or organization noted on the "about us" page on a website to assess their credentials and the objectivity or bias in the information provided.

To help students recognize the need to vet websites, you can send them to sites such as the Martin Luther King site *www.martinlutherking.org* which is operated by White supremacists and contains racist misinformation about Dr. Martin Luther King. For critically analyzing false claims on these hoax sites, students can employ Roland Paris's C.L.E.A.R. model *aix1.uottawa.ca/~rparis/critical.html* for analysis of claims the author is making, logical structure of the argument, evidence provided, assumptions the author makes, and alternative arguments; or sites such as Howard Reingold: Critical Thinking *criticalthinking.iste.wikispaces.net* or Critical Thinking on the Web *austhink.com/critical*.

Teaching online reading using reciprocal teaching

To teach students the use of these different ways of responding to online informational texts, you can employ Reciprocal Teaching methods that focus on your modeling of various practices for responding to a text, students modeling of practices for each other, and discussing and reflecting upon the use of certain practices (Brown & Palincsar, 1989). The central idea behind Reciprocal Teaching is that demonstration and scaffolding of practices result in a gradual release of responsibility to students for their own learning.

You can assist your students in this question-asking and assessment process by modeling your own responses as you read online texts. Using a data projector, you can display different kinds of web pages and digital texts for your students and, as a group, you and the class can discuss how you find yourselves reading online texts. You can then pose questions such as:

- How do we best read this kind of page or document?
- When do you slow down to study specific sentences or images?
- How do you read the images with the texts?
- What role do links play in giving this page authority or meaning?
- If you had this page on your own computer, what might you do with it?
- How might you keep track of the information on this page? (Beach et al., 2016, p. 80)

Given differences between print and online reading comprehension, Leu and his colleagues have modified comprehension methods for use with online texts (Leu et al., 2011; 2014). These modifications encompass many of the strategies we've discussed so far in this chapter: teachers model questioning, locating, critically evaluating, synthesizing, and communicating practices through formulating questions/problems and reflecting on how they search for and assess relevant material using search strategies.

Both teachers and students model responses to texts for each other, describing the practices they employ to locate, assess, and synthesize what they learn from online material (for videos of students modeling practices: *www.newliteracies.uconn.edu/iesproject/videos*). Teachers and students can share their syntheses on blogs, wikis, Twitter, IM'ing, or class websites. The fact that students assume teacher roles enhances their sense of agency since they can share their expertise with others.

Students begin to work on their own through the use of individual or collaborative inquiry units based on their own questions in which they are still modeling practices for each other. To assess students' growth in uses of practices, you can have students list the practices they learned, why these practices are important, and how they might use them for understanding online reading (for more description of these assessment techniques *www.newliteracies.uconn.edu/IRT*).

After students complete their shared readings, they can discuss whether and how a text fulfilled their purposes or expectations, how they will apply what they learned to work on a project or activity, and what kinds of questions they might formulate to respond to key moments in a text (Filkins, 2010). This activity is likely to work best if there is initial modeling by the teacher, or the use of a "fishbowl" to observe and learn from students using the process. Helping students slow down and carefully examine sentences and arguments is especially important for difficult pieces. Examples of videos of a teacher engaging her students in close reading activities can be found at *tinyurl.com/mcuymw3* (Jones, 2014).

To help students organize material from their reading, a digital inquiry tool, *tinyurl.com/k5zglk2*, was devised to scaffold students reading related to identifying perspectives shaping their reading, locating information based on questions for use of search terms, evaluating the validity and trustworthiness of sources, identifying claims made in texts related to their own arguments and counter-arguments, synthesizing the information related to pro/con perspectives, and organizing their own writing (Coiro et al., 2014) (for instructions on the use of the tool *tinyurl.com/k4z45tm*).

One useful online tool for planning discussions around readings that address essential questions is Commonlit *www.commonlit.org*. This site includes pre-selected texts relevant to one of 14 themes associated with questions. These texts are appropriate for different reading levels for middle-school students. On their site, you first select a theme, for example, "growing up." You are then provided with questions related to that theme, for example, "What does it mean to be grown-up?" By selecting that question, you can then access texts identified by the Lexile® Text Measurement System according to a student's reading level: beginning (grades 4–5), intermediate (grades 5–6), and advanced (grades 6–7), to access free PDFs. While these different options may be somewhat restrictive, they do provide you with ready access to relevant texts associated with certain themes; you may also draw on material from this site to create your own questions and related text. It may be the case that you can also have students make some of these decisions themselves regarding the themes or questions they want to address.

Digital note-taking responses

Students can take notes about their reading using digital note-taking tools or apps such as Evernote, iOS, Android OneNote, or Android PhatPad. In doing so, it is important that they learn how to reformulate or translate the text into their own words rather than simply regurgitating the language of the text. Students are more likely to formulate their interpretations if they have a clear sense of purpose for taking notes, for example, responding to questions they have generated for reading a text. One approach to fostering reformulation or translation of the text is to have the student restate or summarize key points in the left column of a page, while offering their own interpretations of those key points on the right side.

Students can also use NoodleTools *www.noodletools.com* notecard templates to copy/paste digital text, put the text into their own words, add annotations to specific parts of a text, and define how the text relates to their own prior knowledge (Lapp et al., 2015). They can then tag these note cards by topic and place them on a virtual map to create an essay outline that draws out relationships between the notecard topics.

Digital annotations/comments

Students can employ annotation tools as described in Chapter 8 for responding to texts *tinyurl.com/6oqgm2m*, for example, Diigo Sticky Notes, Evernote, VoiceThread, iAnnotate,

A.nnotate, or Viewbiz; A.nnotate, AnnotDoc Lite, or WebNotes iOS apps; or Adobe Reader, iAnnotate pdf, or PDF Annotation Android apps. So that students focus on certain organizational features of texts, teachers have to help them attend to the use of problem/solutions, cause/effect, or comparison/contrast structures (Csillag, 2016). For example, in reading essays about the topic on the use of wind turbines in California, students used Diigo stickynoes to share their sticky-note annotations, to react to others' annotations, and to formulate responses (Castek & Beach, 2013). They then used these annotations to write summary responses to the essays, writing that often reflected different dialogic perspectives on the pros and cons of use of wind turbines.

To model types of annotations, students could access the UDL Cast Studio *udlstudio.cast.org/library* which contains texts with questions and visuals. Students can use highlighting tools for responding to texts (Casillag, 2016). They can also employ Easybib's Scholar *www.easybibscholar.com* or DocentEDU Chrome extension for yourself or students creating annotations related to adding related information or questions.

Similar to annotations, the use of comments in Microsoft Word or Google Docs involves creating Word or Google Docs files to then add comments in different colors for focusing responses to specific parts of a text or sharing comments with peers.

Graphic organizers or maps

Graphic organizers or digital maps are effective for visually organizing information and making inferences about nonfiction texts (Lapp et al., 2015). For example, using the Text Box feature in Word, students can summarize different key points or ideas in a text or respond to different questions about a text such as:

- What I know about the document before reading
- What I need to learn as I read
- What I learned about the document and its author (Lapp et al., 2015, p. 69) (for an example: *www.corwin.com/miningcomplextext/6-12*).

Graphic organizers or digital maps can also be used to identify text structures—sequential, descriptive, cause/effect, comparison/contrast, or problem/solution (Lapp et al., 2015). For example, students might use overlapping Venn Diagram circles to engage in a comparison/contrast analysis to identify, for example, aspects of "weather" and "climate."

Activity: Assessing Students' Ability to Engage in Online Reading Practices

You can view examples of middle school students engaging in online reading practices by going to the Online Research and Comprehension Assessments (OCRA) *www.orca.uconn.edu* site; for a video on the use of OCRA for analysis of students' practices *tinyurl.com/p8ugnjt*. You can also have your own students use this tool by sending an email to AccessORCA@gmail.com with your name, title, school district, state, country, the approximate number of students who will be taking the assessment, and your contact information.

> You can practice scoring students' work on the Let Me Try *tinyurl.com/oxdt8tf* section in which students are accessing the information on the topics of energy drinks, video games, snacks, contacts. First read a description of each of the practices associated with locating, evaluating, synthesizing, and communicating information. Then, as you view the videos, use the score point rubric below each video to score the student's performance as "acceptable" or "unacceptable." You can then select "Check Answers" to determine if your assessment is correct or incorrect.

INFERRING CONNECTIONS BETWEEN NONFICTION TEXTS

The state reading standards also focus on the importance of inferring connections between nonfiction texts as related to the CCSS reading standard "Analyze how two or more texts address similar themes or topics in order to build knowledge or to compare the approaches the authors take" (CCSS, 2010, p. 35).

As we discuss further in Chapter 11 on assessment, on the open-ended Spring 11th- grade PARCC practice tests *tinyurl.com/o48byp5*, two of the three sample tasks involve students' ability to infer connections between texts—excerpts from the novel, *Quicksand* (Larsen, 1928/2006) and *The Autobiography of an Ex-Colored Man* (Johnson, 1912/2008) written by American author James Weldon Johnson in 1912; and the "Declaration of Independence," written by Thomas Jefferson and a speech by Patrick Henry to the Second Virginia Convention in Richmond, Virginia (Wirt, 1817/2013). On these tasks, students are asked to compare and contrast the perspectives and stances between texts focusing on similar topics or themes; for example, inferring differences and similarities in African Americans' experiences in *Quicksand* and *The Autobiography of an Ex-Colored Man*.

One key aspect of inferring intertextual connections between texts involves comparing writers' adoption of alternative perspectives in the different texts; for example, differences based on gender in comparing *Quicksand* and *The Autobiography of an Ex-Colored Man*. You can pose the following questions designed to have students compare alternative perspectives:

- What is the perspective or stance that a writer takes on a problem or issue in this text?
- How does the perspective or stance in this text differ from the perspectives or stances taken in the other texts you have read?
- What are some possible differences in beliefs, attitudes, experiences, or knowledge that may lead these writers to adopt different perspectives or stances on this problem or issue?
- Given these different perspectives or stances, which perspectives or stances do you agree with or disagree with and why?

Tracy Becker developed a 12th grade English Language Arts course around Thomas Friedman's (2005) book *The World is Flat: A Brief History of the 21st Century*. Friedman argues that globalization caused by historical events and new technologies has created a world economy that is more than ever a "level playing field." Tracy explained:

> To jump-start our year and first unit, students will be introduced to *The World is Flat*. In brief, it suggests we are all living co-dependently as countries, where connections are continually made

all over the world. Because we are in a time where we can consider our world to be "flat," voices from around the world are important to our social, political, and economic understanding and outlook as future leaders.

Tracy's students then engaged in a number of explorations to more deeply understand the author's ideas and how they might be relevant to understanding world literature. On the website Tracy created about the class (https://tracybecker.wordpress.com/english-12/), she emphasized that:

> Each unit specifically addresses a social justice issue within our world today, preparing students to be more compassionate, empathetic, culturally aware, and attuned to a world that is more connected now than ever before . . . Ultimately, it is the aim of the course to educate global citizens, to prepare them for a future they can both understand and help lead.

The first unit, which she called "Voices from the Middle" involved a study of diverse texts from the Middle East. The students all read *Baghdad Burning: Girl Blog from Iraq* (Riverbend, 2005) a collection of blog posts made by a 24-year-old young woman in Iraq starting four months after the American invasion from the point of view of an Iraqi family. Reading this book, Tracy's students began their own blogs connected to one another by a class "blog roll" that made it easy to respond to each other. (For more on making connections between texts, see *Synthesizing and connecting texts* on the website.)

APPLYING GENRE KNOWLEDGE FOR UNDERSTANDING NONFICTION TEXTS

In reading nonfiction texts, students also apply the perspective of genre knowledge to understand how writers of different types of informational texts organize their texts in different ways. As previously noted, students acquire knowledge of these genres inductively through experiences with reading these different types of texts (Smith et al., 2014). When genre knowledge is made explicit for students, they can respond to the organizational features and logical development of ideas, for example, writers' use of opinion/example, claim/evidence, cause/effect, or problem/solution organizational strategies.

Students can then use that knowledge to critique problems in both the effectiveness of the organization as well as the logical development of ideas. For example, in having students respond to editorials or letters to the editor in a newspaper, students can note the use of the problem/solution organization, leading them to note that, for example, the nature of the problem has not been clearly identified, that reasons for the problem are not formulated, that the solutions proposed would not necessarily address the problem, or that there is little or no evidence provided that the solutions would effectively solve the problem.

Three important genre texts are biography, memoir, and autobiographical texts that can be integrated with the use of other nonfiction texts to provide students with personal perspectives on certain issues and problems. For instance, students could read biographical, memoir, or autobiographical texts such as *The Things They Carried* (O'Brien, 1999), *I Know Why the Caged Bird Sings* (Angelou, 2009), *Anne Frank: The Diary of a Young Girl* (1993), *Breaking Through* (Jiménez, 2002), *A Summer Life* (Soto, 2011), or *Bad Boy* (Myers, 2009), as well as examples on the Narrative.ly *narrative.ly* site or literacy autobiographies on the Digital Archive of Literacy Narratives *daln.osu.edu* site (Beach et al., 2015).

For responding to memoirs, teachers and students can become critical consumers of memoirs, given a boom in the young adult literature market with regard to "young reader" versions of memoirs originally written and marketed for a general market adult audience. Although it is true that these adapted texts are typically written at a simpler reading level than the original texts, the original texts are rarely written at markedly less accessible lexile levels. Instead, what these adapted texts often really offer are sanitized versions of the original texts that are stripped of complexity and make unfounded assumptions about what might be appropriate (or not) for young people.

For example, a comparative study of two different versions of Wes Moore's memoir—one written for adults (*The Other Wes Moore: One Name, Two Fates* (Moore, 2010)) and one written for adolescents (*Discovering Wes Moore* (Moore, 2012)) found that the version written for adults adopted a more critical perspective through portraying the challenges of institutional forces shaping Moore's experiences growing up in a difficult urban neighborhood, yet finding success as an adult, while the version for young adults adopted more didactic stances by emphasizing the need for "at-risk" adolescents to make responsible choices (Thein et al., 2013).

A recent example of this phenomenon is, ironically, a text written by a young adult, *I am Malala: The Girl Who Stood Up for Education and Was Shot by the Taliban* (Yousafzai, 2013). The mere title of the "young readers edition" provides a glimpse into the different stance that is forwarded by the two texts, *I Am Malala: How One Girl Stood Up for Education and Changed the World* (Yousafzai, 2014). While appearing nearly identical on the shelf, these two versions of Malala Yousafzai's story are markedly different in their narrative structure, political stance, and level of detail. Although you as a teacher might sometimes find that a young readers edition of a given memoir is in fact the best choice for your students, it is worth your time to carefully consider what that version offers—and fails to offer—in contrast to the general market version of the text. You might also consider incorporating comparisons of memoirs like those mentioned in this section into your instruction with your students.

ACQUIRING DISCIPLINARY LITERACIES IN READING NONFICTION TEXTS

Given a central focus of the CCSS on increased reading of informational texts, there was considerable concern voiced by literature teachers as to the assumed reduction in reading literary texts. However, the recommendation for a focus on reading informational texts does not lie exclusively in the domain of ELA and therefore should not dominate ELA instruction to the exclusion of literature. Instead the CCSS recommendation for increased reading of informational texts is intended to be applied across all subjects, particularly in social studies and science, associated with the ELA CCSS social studies and science standards.

In responding to informational texts in different subjects, students are applying knowledge of history/social studies, science, math, and technology associated with addressing the history/social studies, science, and technical information CCSS. Rather than assuming that certain reading comprehension strategies apply uniformly across all subjects, it is useful to recognize how people in different disciplines employ different reading practices unique to reading texts in their disciplines (Moje, 2011).

In a study of disciplinary reading practices, expert history readers read a text by analyzing the narrative organization of the text, the author's individual perspective, and credibility associated with knowledge about an event, comparing their own perspective with that of the author. By contrast, expert readers of science texts focused less on the author's own unique perspective and more on the use and presentation of empirical data as serving to confirm or challenge results of other studies on a particular topic or phenomenon (Shanahan et al., 2011).

One major challenge in reading science texts is students' lack of understanding of the use of certain scientific vocabulary descriptors used in the context of scientific research. The Reading Apprenticeship framework designed by Greenleaf et al. (2011) focuses on students engaging in inquiry-based discussion and metacognitive reflection on ways of reading science texts that differ from transmission models of science instruction focusing on students extracting information from their reading or teacher lectures. In applying the framework related to reading a text on molecular genetics and the evolution of lizards *www.ucmp.berkeley.edu/fosrec/Filson.html*, a teacher asked students to identify words that were related to evolution, work in pairs to define these words, and then share their definitions with the class. The students then analyzed images of lizards and were directed to their reading as useful in understanding the images. Student pairs then had to generate two questions about the text recorded on a whiteboard that would be used for discussion the next day.

It is, therefore, useful to engage in cross-disciplinary planning with colleagues who teach social studies and science to determine how they are fostering the use of particular disciplinary literacies in their classrooms to then assist your students in applying those literacies, for example, learning to critique historians or social scientists' perspectives in social studies nonfiction (Nokes, 2013) or to examine the presentation and validity of data in science reports.

EMPLOYING CRITICAL INQUIRY RESPONSE TO NONFICTION TEXTS: IDENTIFYING PROBLEMS OR ISSUES

In engaging in critical inquiry related to informational texts, it is important to provide students with a clear purpose for reading these texts, using front loading or pre-reading activities in which students identify problems or issues. In this work, students can pose what Wiggins and McTighe (2005) call "essential questions" associated with a critical inquiry stance.

For devising activities based on essential research questions, you can employ the Perspectives for a Diverse America site *perspectives.tolerance.org* that includes a framework for having students pose essential questions, recognizing the importance of students generating their own questions based on their concerns about certain problems or issues. Once students have formulated a question, for example, "what food choices have the highest impact on increased adolescent obesity?", they can extract specific search terms, for example, "adolescents," "diet," "obesity," and/or "food choices." By using Google Advanced Search, they can limit or control their searches by requesting a focus on "all these words," "this exact wording or phrase," "one or more of these words," etc.

In responding to different history texts using a cause/effect strategy to formulate certain causes for a particular event, for example, the persistence of segregation and Jim Crow laws in the American South in the 20th century, students could examine the validity of these explanations across these different texts. Some texts may focus more on the ways in which politicians exploited racial fears with their White, working-class constituents to perpetuate policies of segregation and Jim Crow laws. Other texts may focus on resentment in the South regarding the treatment of African Americans in the Reconstruction era. Still, other texts may focus on the fact that segregation occurred both in the South and in the North due to widespread institutional racism related to employment and housing discrimination. Examining the validity of these competing explanations relative to historical facts leads students to recognize that there are multiple explanations for a certain phenomenon.

IDENTIFYING WARRANTS UNDERLYING CLAIM-REASONS RELATIONSHIPS

In responding critically to argumentative texts, students need to infer the relationships between certain claims and then reasons or evidence for those claims, for example, the scientific evidence that climate change will have adverse impacts on the planet.

To assess the validity of these claim/reason–evidence relationships, students need to infer the warrants or premises linking the claim to the reasons or evidence. These warrants are the inferences or assumptions derived from cultural or personal experiences that are taken for granted by the writer, and sometimes by the argument, and they connect—explicitly or implicitly—the argumentative claim and its support.

It may be useful to describe them as "gap-filling" (Ennis, 1996) in that they fill the gap between the claim and the reason/evidence. Students learn to infer these logical relationships through practice engaging in verbal arguments about everyday problems in which they pose questions of "Why?, So What?, and Who says?" that "require support for claims" and "invite the consideration of competing arguments and multiple points of view" (McMann, 2010, p. 34).

To help students understand the concept of warrants, you can begin with if–then syllogism statements about familiar phenomena. For example, a student may note that it is going to rain since it is cloudy out. Underlying this statement is the warrant, when it is cloudy outside, then it is going to rain. The warrant can be challenged with evidence of instances of students experiencing cloudy days, but having no rain, hence the claim that it is going to rain since it is cloudy out is not valid. Or, an environmental organization may argue that if we develop more clean energy alternatives, then we will be less dependent on foreign oil. Underlying this if–then claim is the warrant that using more clean energy alternatives lowers foreign oil use. This warrant can certainly be challenged—while we may use more clean-energy alternatives, that does not necessarily mean that we will reduce oil use.

The strengths of claims and warrants—whether they are convincing to an audience, therefore depend on the believability and validity of the evidence. Students can assess the evidence based on the criteria of whether that evidence is:

- *Credible*—being consistent with accepted, scientific knowledge about a topic or issue or from an authoritative source. If students cite sources that are not credible, their evidence will not be taken seriously.
- *Sufficient*—providing enough evidence so that audiences are convinced of the validity of their claims. If students provide only one, limited bit of evidence, audiences may not be convinced in terms of the quality of the evidence.
- *Accurate*—providing evidence that is accurate and verifiable as well as sources being cited and properly quoted.

(Rex et al., 2010, p. 59)

USING READING TO LEARN ABOUT AND ENGAGE IN TAKING ACTION

Related to the third phase of our critical inquiry framework, in reading informational texts, students acquire knowledge about individuals or groups engaged in social or political action to change the status quo, knowledge that is useful for thinking about engaging in their own actions to critique and change the status quo.

For example, in reading Tim O'Brien (1999), *The Things They Carried*, students can discuss how O'Brien decided to take action regarding his opposition to the Vietnam War when he was drafted into the army after being accepted to graduate school (Beach et al., 2015). He then needed to decide whether he should escape from Minnesota to Canada to avoid being drafted or accept his call-up to go to Vietnam. In the book, he quits his summer job to travel north where he stays in a lodge on the Canadian border. In mulling over whether or not to escape to Canada, he envisions his small home-town peers and family members opposing leaving for Canada as an unpatriotic act of "draft-dodging" as well as the war protesters urging people to resist the draft. In the end, he reluctantly decides to accept the draft and go to Vietnam.

A key factor in his decision-making process is his consideration of how his peers and family members would define his identity based on his actions. Students could then draw comparisons to their having to make difficult decisions related to taking actions to cope with demands or changes in their lives, particularly in terms of voicing criticism of status quo problems or issues. Learning about people's or organizations' use of tools and resources helps students determine their own use of tools and resources for creating these texts.

As part of an ELA/social studies interdisciplinary unit that combined nonfiction with fiction texts to study urban neighborhoods, 9th grade students enrolled in Rebecca Oberg's English class at Roosevelt High School (a Minneapolis high school in which 82% of students qualify for free and reduced-cost lunch) engaged in a place-based analysis of portrayals of urban neighborhoods in literature as well as a study of their own neighborhoods. In this project, students addressed the essential questions outlined by Ms. Oberg: "What is a neighborhood? How do neighborhoods change over time? and How does the individual impact his/her neighborhood?" Ms. Oberg's students wrote and commented on "neighborhood blogs" (via Blogger) and used Google Docs to organize and share their writing. On their blog posts, they responded to prompts such as:

- How do the environment and neighborhood shape our identity? What identities, if any, are permanent and which do we have the power to change? What roles do neighborhood and community play in shaping who we become?
- What is your identity? Make a top 10 list of words to describe
- What is your neighborhood? Make a top 10 list of words to describe. (Beach et al., 2016, p. 87)

Students also wrote responses to *Days of Rondo* (Fairbanks, 1990), an autobiographical recollection of growing up in the 1930s and 1940s in a predominantly African American neighborhood of St. Paul, Minnesota. The author describes the impact of the construction of an interstate highway during the 1960s that destroyed the neighborhood and displaced the neighborhood's residents. In response to the novel, students wrote blog posts in the form of a letter to a character/resident of the Rondo neighborhood posing questions regarding the demise, memories, and positive aspects of their experiences in the neighborhood.

INSTRUCTIONAL ACCOMMODATIONS FOR ELL AND SPECIAL LEARNING NEEDS STUDENTS

One of the major needs related to reading instruction involves providing accommodations for ELL and special learning needs students. Given that many ELL students are from different cultural backgrounds, they may lack relevant backgrounds for reading texts (Calderón & Slakk, 2018). ELL students also may struggle with language issues associated with vocabulary, something we discuss in more detail in the teaching language Chapter 10.

For ELL and special learning students, text-to-speech (TTS) tools can be helpful for listening to texts (Csillag, 2016). Students using Macs can go to "System Preferences" then "Dictation & Speech" and then "Text to Speech" to highlight text. For using iPads or iPhones, they go to "Settings" then "Accessibility," then "Speak Selection." In Windows, they go to "Start," then "Control Panel," then "Speech," and then "Text-to-Speech" tab. They can also install iSpeech *www.ispeech.org* as an extension for Chrome.

SUMMARY

In this chapter, we described methods for assisting students in responding to nonfiction texts through the use of close reading processes that involve rhetorical analysis of a writer's sense of purpose and audience. Given that much of the reading of nonfiction texts includes online texts, we posited the need for instruction in both accessing and responding to online texts in ways unique to processing these texts. We also describe approaches for critiquing how nonfiction texts frame problems and issues, the alternative perspectives adopted in these texts, and the role texts can play in making changes.

REFERENCES

Adlof, S. M., Baron, L. S., Scoggins, J., Kapelner, A., McKeown, M. G., Perfetti, C. A., Miler, E., Soterwood, J., & Petscher, Y. (2019). Accelerating adolescent vocabulary growth: Development of an individualized, web-based, vocabulary instruction program. *Language, Speech, and Hearing Services in Schools, 50,* 579–595.

Allington, R. L. (2011). *What really matters for struggling readers: Designing research-based programs,* 3rd ed. Pearson.

Angelou, M. (2009). *I know why the caged bird sings.* Ballentine.

Beach, R., Johnston, A., & Thein, A. H. (2015). *Identity-focused ELA teaching: A curriculum framework for diverse secondary classrooms.* Routledge.

Beach, R., Thein, A. H., & Webb, A. (2016). *The English language arts Common Core state standards: A critical inquiry approach for 6-12 classrooms,* 2nd ed. Routledge.

Beck, I. L., McKeown, M. G., & Kucan, L. (2013). *Bringing words to life: Robust vocabulary instruction.* Guilford Press.

Beck, S.W. (2018). *A think-aloud approach to writing assessment: Analyzing process & product with adolescent writers.* Teachers College Press.

Beckelhimer, L. (2010). From Hitler to hurricanes, Vietnam to Virginia Tech: Using historical nonfiction to teach rhetorical context. *English Journal, 99*(4), 55–60.

Brown, A. L., & Palincsar, A. S. (1989). Guided, cooperative learning and individual knowledge acquisition. In L. B. Resnick (Ed.), *Knowing, learning, and instruction: Essays in honor of Robert Glaser* (pp. 393–451). Lawrence Erlbaum Associates.

Calderón, M. E., & Slakk, S. (2018). *Teaching reading to English learners, Grades 6-12: A framework for improving achievement in the content areas.* Corwin.

Castek, J., & Beach, R. (2013). Using apps to support disciplinary learning and science learning. *Journal of Adolescent and Adult Literacy, 56*(7), 544–554.

Catterson, A. K., & Pearson, P. D. (2017). A close reading of close reading: What does research tell us about how to promote thoughtful interrogation of text? In K. Hinchman & D. Appleman (Eds.), *Adolescent literacies: A handbook of practice-based research* (pp. 457–475. Guilford Press.

Coiro, J., Kiili, C., Hämäläinen, J., Cedillo, L., Naylor, R., & O'Connell, R., & Quinn, D. (2014, December 4). Digital scaffolds for reading multiple online sources and writing an argumentative text. Paper presented at the meeting of the Literacy Research Association, Marco Island, Florida. Retrieved from https://uri.academia.edu/JulieCoiro/Papers

Coleman, D., & Pimentel, S. (2012). *Revised publishers' criteria for the Common Core State Standards in English language arts and literacy, grades 3–12*. Washington, DC: National Governors Association/Council of Chief State School Officers. Retrieved from www.corestandards.org/assets/Publishers_Criteria_for_3-12.pdf

Common Core Standards. (2010). *Common Core State Standards for English language arts & literacy in history/social studies, science, and technical subjects*. Washington, DC: Council of Chief State School Officers and the National Governors Association.

Csillag, J. (2016). *Differentiated Reading Instruction: Strategies and technology tools to help all students improve*. Routledge.

DuVernay, A. (Director). (2014). *Selma*. [motion picture]. United States: Paramount Pictures.

Ehrenreich, B. (2011). *Nickel and dimed: On (not) getting by in America*. Picador.

Ennis, R. H. (1996). Critical thinking dispositions: Their nature and assessability. *Informal Logic, 18*(2–3), 165–182.

Fairbanks, E. (1990). *Days of Rondo*. Minnesota Historical Society Press.

Filkins, S. (2010). *Supporting student comprehension in content area reading*. National Council of Teachers of English. Retrieved from http://tinyurl.com/2768c3a

Fisher, D., & Frey, N. (2014). *Text dependent questions: Pathways to close and critical reading*. Corwin.

Frank, A. (1993). *Anne Frank: Diary of a young girl* (A. J. Pomernas & B. M. Mooyaart, Trans.). Bantam.

Friedman, T. (2005). *The world is flat: A brief history of the 21st Century*. Farrar Strauss & Giroux.

Graham, S., Xinghua, X., Angelique, A., Ng, C., Brendan, B., Harris, K. R., & Newark, J. (2018). Effectiveness of literacy programs balancing reading and writing instruction: A meta-analysis. *Reading Research Quarterly, 53*(3), 279–304.

Greenleaf, C. L., Litman, C., Handon, T. L., Rosen, R., Boscardin, C. K., Herman, J., Schneider, S. A., Madden, S., & Jones, B. (2011). Integrating literacy and science in biology: Understanding teaching and learning impacts of Reading Apprenticeship professional development. *American Educational Research Journal, 48*, 647–717.

Hattan, C., & Alexander, P. A. (2020). Prior knowledge and its activation in elementary classroom discourse. *Reading and Writing, 33*, 1617–1647.

Hattie, J. (2009). *Visible learning: A synthesis of over 800 meta-analyses relating to achievement*. Routledge.

Hock, M. F., Brasseur-Hock, I. F., & Deshler, D. D. (2015). Reading comprehension instruction for middle and high school students in English language arts: Research and evidence-based practices. In K. L. Santi & D. K. Reed (Eds.). *Improving reading comprehension of middle and high school students* (pp. 99–118. Springer.

Institute of Education Sciences. (2019). *Reading performance*. Author. Retrieved from https://ies.ed.gov/

Jiménez, F. (2002). *Breaking through*. HMH Books for Young Readers.

Jenkins, H. (2006). *Convergence culture: Where old and new media collide*. NYU Press.

Johnson, J. W. (1912/2008). *The autobiography of an ex-colored man*. Bibliolife.

Jones, L. (2014, September 19). Case study of a teacher: Engaging students in text analysis (Part 1) [Web log post]. Retrieved from http://tinyurl.com/mcuymw3

Kain, P. (1998). How to do close reading. Writing Center at Harvard University. Retrieved from https://writingcenter.fas.harvard.edu/pages/how-do-close-reading

Kress, G. R. (2009). *Multimodality: A social semiotic approach to contemporary communication*. Routledge.

Lapp, D., Wolsey, T. D., Wood, K, & Johnson, K. (2015). *Mining complex text: Using and creating graphic organizers to grasp content and share new understandings*. Corwin.

Larsen, N. (1928/2006). *Quicksand*. Dover.

Lehman, C., & Roberts, K (2014). *Falling in love with close reading: Lessons for analyzing texts—and life*. Heinemann.

Leu, D. J., McVerry, J. G., O'Byrne, W. I., Kiili, C., Zawilinski, L. Everett-Cacopardo, H., Kennedy, C., & Forzani, E. (2011). The new literacies of online reading comprehension: Expanding the literacy and learning curriculum. *Journal of Adolescent & Adult Literacy, 55*(1), 5–14.

Leu, D. J., Forzani, E., Rhoads, C., Maykel, C., Kennedy, C., & Timbrell, N. (2014). The New Literacies of online research and comprehension: Rethinking the reading achievement gap. *Reading Research Quarterly, 50*(1), 37–59.

McMann, T. (2010). Gateways to writing logical arguments. *English Journal, 99*(6), 33–39.

Mikics, D. (2013). *Slow reading in a hurried age*. Belknap Press.

Moje, E. B. (2011). Developing disciplinary discourses, literacies and identities: What's knowledge got to do with it? In M.G. L. Bonilla & K. Englander (Eds.), *Discourses and identities in contexts of educational change: Contributions from the United States and Mexico* (pp. 49–74). Peter Lang.

Moore, W. (2010). *The other Wes Moore: One name, two fates*. Spiegel & Grau.

Moore, W. (2012). *Discovering Wes Moore*. Ember.

Myers, W. D. (2009). *Bad boy*. HarperCollins.

Newkirk, T. (2011). *The art of slow reading: Six time-honored practices for engagement*. Heinemann.

Nokes, J. D. (2013). *Building students' historical literacies: Learning to read and reason with historical texts and evidence*. Routledge.

O'Brien, T. (1999). *The things they carried*. Bantam.

Pearson, P. D., Palincsar, A. S., Biancarosa, G., & Berman, A. I. (Eds.). (2020). *Reaping the rewards of the Reading for Understanding Initiative*. National Academy of Education.

Purcell, K., Rainie, L., Heaps, A., Buchanan, J., Friedrich, L., Jacklin, A., Chen, C., & Zickuhr, K. (2012, November 1). *How teens do research in the digital world*. Pew Research Center's Internet & American Life Project. Retrieved from www.pewinternet.org/Reports/2012/Student-Research.aspx

Rabinowitz, P. J. (1998). *Before reading: Narrative conventions and the politics of reading*. The Ohio State University Press.

Rex, L. A., Thomas, E. E., & Engel, S. (2010). Applying Toulmin: Teaching logical reasoning and argumentative writing. *English Journal, 99*(6): 56–62.

Riverbend. (2005). *Baghdad burning: Girl blog from Iraq*. The Feminist Press at CUNY.

Shanahan, C., Shanahan, T., & Misischia, C. (2011). Analysis of expert readers in three disciplines: History, mathematics, and chemistry. *Journal of Literacy Research, 43*(4), 393–429.

Smith, M. W., Appleman, D., & Wilhelm, J. D. (2014). *Uncommon core: Where the authors of the standards go wrong about instruction—and how you can get it right*. Corwin.

Smith, M. W., & Wilhelm, J. (2002). *"Reading don't fix no Chevys": Literacy in the lives of young men*. Heinemann.

Solis, M., Vaughn, S., Stillman-Spisak, S. J., & Cho, E. (2018). Effects of reading comprehension and vocabulary intervention on comprehension-related outcomes for ninth graders with low reading comprehension. *Reading & Writing Quarterly, 34*(1), 537–553.

Soto, G. (2011). *A summer life*. University Press of New England.

Sulzer, M. A. (2014). The common core state standards and the "basalization" of youth. *English Teaching: Practice and Critique, 13*(1), 134–154.

Thein, A., Sulzer, M. A., & Schmidt, R. (2013). Evaluating the democratic merit of young adult literature: Lessons from two versions of Wes Moore's memoir. *English Journal, 103*(2), 52–59.

Wiggins, G. J., & McTighe, J. (2005). Understanding by design, 2nd ed. Pearson.

Wilhelm, J. (2013). *Improving comprehension with think aloud strategies, 2nd ed.: Modeling what good readers do*. Scholastic Press.

Willingham, D. T. (2015, April 27). Does the Common Core help boost reading comprehension? Retrieved from http://tinyurl.com/pvyvoge

Wirt, W. (1817/2013). *Sketches of the life and character of Patrick Henry*. CreateSpace Independent Publisher.

Yousafzai, M. (2013). *I am Malala: The girl who stood up for education and was shot by the Taliban*. Little, Brown & Co.

Yousafzai, M., with McCormick, P. (2014). *I Am Malala: How one girl stood up for education and changed the world*. Young Readers Edition. Little, Brown & Co.

6

Teaching Writing

In this chapter, we describe methods for teaching writing in ways that go beyond an approach that focuses on teaching the formal structures that are central to the writing standards in most state standards. We perceive writing as a way of thinking and acting consistently by recognizing writing as "way[s] of being and acting in the world in a particular time and place in relation to others" (Bawarshi, 2003, p. 123).

Students often struggle with writing because they are often more likely to be assigned summary or worksheet writing than extended writing that simply requires students to complete forms or worksheets (Applebee & Langer, 2011). All of this reflects the larger problem that students engage in little or no extended writing of any kind in schools (Graham, 2019; Applebee & Langer, 2011).

One survey found that students were writing an average of only 1.6 pages in their English classes and only 2.1 pages in their other subjects, with only 8% of class time devoted to writing more than a paragraph (Applebee & Langer, 2011). Across the four core subjects (English, science, math, and social science/history) on average, only 7.7% of classroom time was devoted to writing a paragraph or more. Another study of 41 L1 and 26 L2 students found that 88% of "low-performing" L1 students and 89% of L2 students wrote no more than a paragraph (Wilcox & Jeffery, 2014).

Writing functions as an important tool for fostering learning, given how writing requires focusing attention on formulating ideas or portraying experiences in ways that enhance literacy practices. Unfortunately, students' writing is often limited to correct answer worksheets or quizzes instead of more open-ended writing (Graham, 2019). Students benefit from writing to learn based on how writing enhances thinking about a topic or issue leading to generating new connections between those ideas and applying those ideas to novel contexts (Graham et al., 2020).

The increased use of digital writing has meant that students can now readily interact with audiences within and beyond the classroom, employing the use of writing as an interactive social practice in ways that enhance their enjoyment of writing, something we emphasize in this chapter. However, a survey research study found that "nearly half of the high school students reported that they enjoyed writing for their personal goals, but disliked assigned school writing" (Addison & McGee, 2016, p. 66). Only 28% of students looked forward to completing school writing assignments.

DOI: 10.4324/9781003177364-8

USE OF WRITING TO FOSTER CRITICAL INQUIRY

Central to the focus on critical inquiry in this book involves moving away from traditional writing instruction revolving primarily around the five-paragraph expository essay. Teachers often teach the five-paragraph essay, assuming they need to prepare students for standardized, mandated state writing tests that may include expository essay writing. This formalist instruction in writing expository essays often focused on simply creating a single draft and then editing that draft based on conforming to the five-paragraph-theme template as a matter of filling in the template boxes as opposed to emphasizing the development of ideas and structures that correspond with purposes (Applebee & Langer, 2011; Hillocks, 2002) (see Figure 6.1).

There are several limitations to a major focus on teaching formulaic thinking associated with writing the five-paragraph essay (see Figure 6.1).

The assumption that the essay should begin with an overall thesis statement and that paragraphs should begin with a topic sentence limits students' ability to generate and organize ideas according to their intentions (Kittle & Gallagher, 2021). Imposing a formulaic, single structure onto students also conflicts with their extensive experiences with using alternative styles and structure in online platforms employing multiple, alternative modes of composing.

Suppose the primary focus of their writing in high school revolved around the use of the five-paragraph theme. In that case, they may then experience a disconnect when their college instructors expect them to engage in more open-ended thinking and composing. For example, one college assignment asked students to identify issues or challenges in their lives to then share their thinking in response to readings about these issues or challenges in class discussion (Kittle & Gallagher, 2021). Thinking about how to address this prompt requires that

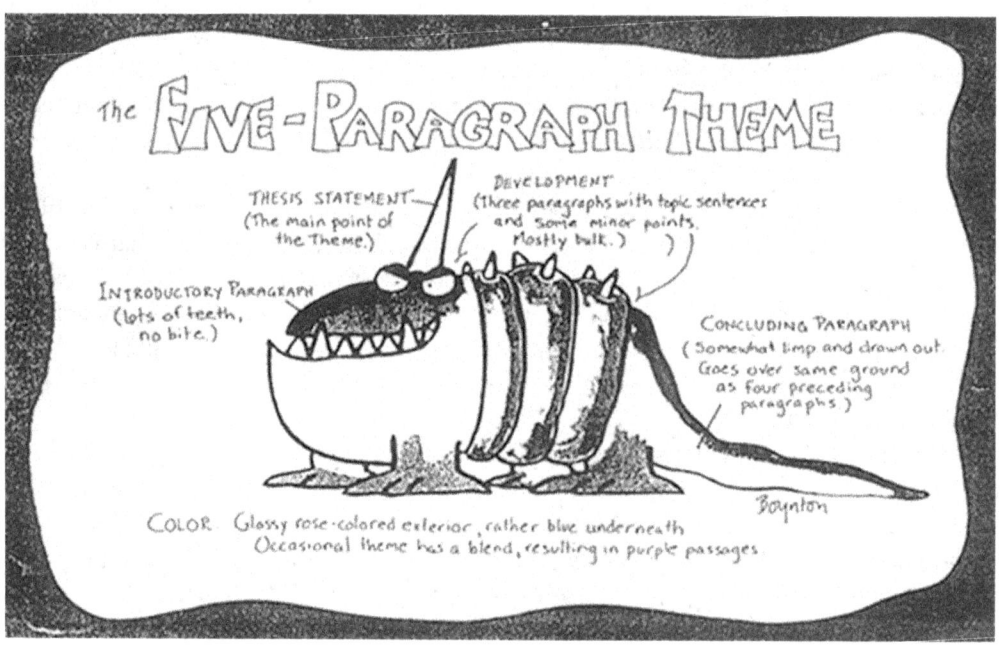

FIGURE 6.1 The Five-Paragraph Theme (used with permission of Sandra Boynton)

students define their focus, determine their audience and overall purpose, adopt a believable persona, identify ideas, employ research to gain relevant evidence for their claims, and sequence their ideas, etc. This thinking process requires students to go beyond adhering to a formulaic structure such as the five-paragraph essay.

Students are more likely to be motivated to engage in critical inquiry when writing about topics, issues, or events within specific social/cultural contexts about issues or experiences that interest them or impact their daily lives.

The extent to which standards reflect a focus on writing in different contexts varies across different states. A comparison of writing standards in Michigan, California, New York, Kentucky, and Texas found that the California standards that were revised from their previous standards included a focus on skills, creativity, process, genre, social practice, and sociopolitical discourses (Wilcox et al., 2021). In contrast, the Michigan standards focused only on skills, processes, and genre. One reason for this shift in the California standards to a focus on the use of language in different social and cultural contexts has to do with California's highly diverse student population related to the need to value the use of non-standard student language/dialects across different contexts for writing.

COMPONENTS OF EFFECTIVE WRITING ASSIGNMENTS

Rather than simply assigning a topic or issue for students to address in their writing, it is also important to provide students with the following specific aspects of the rhetorical context in which they are writing.

Sense of purpose

Students need a clear sense of purpose for their writing related to addressing a problem or issue in ways that would lead them to adopt a critical stance. Providing students with a sense of purpose for argumentative writing goes beyond asking students to write about a problem or issue. Instead, it asks them to consider how their writing may convince their audience, given the limitations of the status quo, to believe or do something related to changing the status quo. Students are also more likely to have a sense of purpose when they need to write about their lives through freewriting, autobiographies/diaries, or essays/blog posts about issues in their lives, as well as, for ELL students, writing in their home language (Flores, 2018).

Basing writing on students' experiences

Related to creating a sense of purpose, it is also important to contextualize writing based on connections to students' everyday experiences. Unfortunately, the CCSS's primary focus on argumentative, explanatory, and informational writing has resulted in a decline in standards related to narrative writing from 35% in grade 4 to 30% in grade 8 to 20% in grade 12 (Wilcox et al., 2021) (see our discussion of teaching narrative writing in Chapter 7).

College seniors perceived their most meaningful writing completed during their college experience when they were able to connect with their personal lives to their writing as a means of building connections with their instructors and engaging in writing as social action

(Eodice et al., 2017). Steffany wanted to find ways to help her 10th-grade students engage with and construct meaning from their study of *To Kill a Mockingbird* (Lee, 1961):

> I focused on several cultural studies issues inside one piece of literature. I wanted to help students connect their personal responses to the issues prevalent in the text and then relate these issues to their own lives. I noticed that Atticus was a single parent, and it occurred to me that the issue of single parenting may shape the daily experience of many of my students' lives.
>
> As teachers, we know that single parents and blended families are common in our nation today. I assigned the first several chapters of *To Kill a Mockingbird* for the students to read at home. When they came to our next class, before discussing anything, I had them write a free-response journal entry about their reading for that day. We then spent that class time focusing on single fathers. We looked at clips from the films *Finding Nemo*, *The Pursuit of Happiness*, and *To Kill a Mockingbird*. Each clip focused on a single father and his interaction with his child.

Including informal writing

It is also useful to include informal writing as freewriting, note-taking, or annotations, as noted elsewhere in this book, for articulating and reflecting on responses and ideas. In using freewriting, students can write for a few minutes non-stop and then loop or circle back to infer a key idea or concept and then continue to freewrite about that idea or concept (Elbow, 1973). In using informal writing to learn, students need to initially adopt a tentative stance by taking up "passing theories" (Kent, 1993) or hypothetical hunches about a topic that they can then test by seeking out supporting or conflicting evidence.

For responding to texts or presentations or in discussions, students can use free note-taking tools/apps: Apple Notes, Simplenote, Google Keep, Drafts 5, Zoho Notebook, Penultimate, Microsoft OneNote, Evernote, inClass, or Joplin. Students can also record their oral think-alouds in response to a text using text-recording apps to create a transcript. It's important that informal writing not be assessed to avoid students not being concerned about conforming to certain norms that might inhibit their thinking.

Students benefit most from informal writing to generate alternative, novel thoughts about a topic or issue. To encourage students to adopt alternative perspectives in their informal writing, you can ask them to consider how other people they know as well as the authors they are reading might think about a topic or issue.

Acquiring relevant, valid, credible information

The quality of writing argumentative, explanatory, and informational texts depends on students' ability to cite relevant, valid, and credible information as evidence to support their claims or explanations. To help students conduct effective search strategies for acquiring information, you can provide them with instruction on formulating keyword topics, using search engines and library databases, analyzing sources, and validating their information.

In conducting online searches, students experience a number of difficulties. They will often first turn to search engines like Google, Safari, Duck Duck Go, Yahoo Search, or Ask/Teoma, which produce many results, but may not be relevant or scholarly. Students may also initially go to Wikipedia, which also provides a lot of useful information, but should not be students' final, definitive source, given that not all information on the site is accurate. With help from media center staff, you can steer students to library sites such as InfoTrac Junior

Edition, Academic Search Premier, Gale Group, CQ Researcher, or General Reference Center Gold. Advanced students can use Google Scholar and Book searches and many of the electronic scholarly databases.

Once they acquire certain texts, they need to know how to cite references using the Modern Language Association (MLA) (2009) style guidelines typically used in literature or the arts and the American Psychological Association (APA) (2009) style typically used in social sciences. Students can develop their skills with these style guidelines by using free tools such as StudentABC's Citation Creation Machine, Citation Builder, CiteULike, Connotea, Citation Machine, or Zotero.

Organization of writing based on genre features

Students gain familiarity with features of genres they are using for their writing by reading examples of these genres, such as reading examples of college application essays.

How students organize their writing based on these genre features depends on their sense of the rhetorical context shaping their decisions about using certain features. For example, seventh-grade students collaboratively constructed a letter to be read at their local school board arguing against closing their school (Sheehy, 2003). While students orally shared different, competing arguments to develop ideas for their letter/statement, the use of the letter genre served to unify their writing around a single message for their audience—members of the school board (Sheehy, 2003). Therefore, knowledge of the letter genre helped them effectively focus their attention on conveying their position to their audience.

You may also provide students with some basic organizational structures related to logical relationships between ideas, for example, cause/effect, comparison/contrast, or problem/solution relationships. Understanding these different structures can help students organize their thinking at the draft phase. For example, having identified a problem, students can then identify reasons for the problem followed by proposed solutions and reasons that these solutions may address the problem.

Criteria for self-reflection

In your assignment prompts, you may include criteria constituting your expectations related to the effective use of organizational features. For example, students need to provide supporting reasons or evidence for their claims and consider their purpose, audience, and stance. For example, students are writing a biographical profile of a favorite relative. You can assess them using specific descriptions and their accuracy and depth of information about the relative.

> **Activity: Reflecting on Previous Writing Assignments to Generate Engaging Writing Assignments**
>
> Recall some previous writing assignments from your college or secondary school classes. What was it about those assignments that engaged you or did not engage you? Was it the topic or issue you addressed or the type of writing that was meaningful to you? What things did the teacher do to make the assignments engaging or not engaging?

> Based on these reflections, generate a writing assignment for students consistent with the need to provide a clear sense of purpose and that draws on students' experiences; includes informal writing; involves the use of relevant, valid information; identifies relevant genre conventions; and includes criteria for self-reflection.

TEACHING ARGUMENTATIVE WRITING

There is a major focus on teaching argumentative writing in the state ELA standards. In argumentative writing, students examine evidence or information for formulating and testing out claims to then formulate their evidence or information in ways that convince their audience of the validity of their claims. Central to effective argumentative writing assignments is the extent to which students have a clear sense of the rhetorical context in terms of their:

- purpose based on a strong concern about and interest in addressing a certain issue that concerns them.
- use of alternative perspectives related to knowing that they may actually influence their audience to agree with their position on their issue so that writing has some social purpose.
- stance or point of view on a topic or issue.
- claims based on formulating valid claims based on supporting reasons and evidence.
- warrants or assumptions related to the relationships between claims and reasons/evidence.
- counter-arguments to refute alternative perspectives on an issue.
- mode or genre related to achieving a positive audience uptake, for example, the need to include visual images of the effects of phenomena to document those effects.
- request to an audience for the need to take action to address a certain issue.

You can have students analyze argumentative essays or editorials to identify a writer's use of these components. For examples of students' argumentative writing, see Schulten (2020) t.ly/VFMt.

To engage students in critical inquiry through argumentative writing, students can identify problems and issues in their own lives or that characters are experiencing, leading them to adopt a critical stance to challenge status-quo norms.

To reflect on their stance or point of view related to claims, and request to adopt a belief or action within a particular rhetorical context, Rex et al. (2010) have students address the following questions:

> 1. Point of view: How do I see and understand what I'm looking at? What in my experience makes me care about this issue, idea, circumstance, or condition? How does this way of caring influence me toward thinking about it? How does my relationship with my readers and my current situation influence where I stand?
> 2. Claim: What is true and should be known about this subject? What is important to understand about this issue, idea, circumstance, or condition for this situation at this moment?
> 3. Request: What should readers understand about this subject? What would or should readers think is important? How would or should they feel? How would or should they act?
>
> (p. 58)

Students may then define their stance or point of view on their issue related to a concern for continued, future flooding in their community associated with climate change, leading to their claim associated with a request for the need to address climate change as something that impacts their own lives.

The limitations of a formalist approach to teaching argumentative writing

One limitation of the CCSS argumentative writing standards is that they can reify a formalist focus on the structure of claims, reasons, and evidence. For example, of the six model essays on writing about literature, four of them are five-paragraph essays (Rejan, 2017). One reason for the CCSS on organizational structures as opposed to using writing to generate knowledge to influence audiences is that writing instruction in secondary education often revolves around grades and assessments based on criteria, rubrics, or writing assessments that reify formalist writing (Rejan, 2017).

Given this formalist approach to teaching argumentative writing, interviews with both college and 6–12 writing teachers found that the college writing teachers were critical of their incoming college students' lack of experience with composing processes (Fanetti et al., 2010). They perceived students as lacking the ability to develop ideas based on the critical inquiry approach related to entertaining alternative perspectives. One teacher, who was a member of The Ohio State University Argumentative Writing Project, described her instruction based on the use of a formalist approach:

> I provided a template where students could "insert" information they gathered. They produced a claim and provided evidence to support the claim. I provided lesson plans that overemphasized structure; they followed the format and inserted information they found in their research... follow my instructions and create a well-written argument.
>
> (2017, n.p.; Beach & Beauchemin, 2019, p. 131)

Engaging in arguing-to-learn

Given her dissatisfaction with her students' writing based on this focus on structure, she focused more on engaging students in active debates and discussions about issues and topics (Newell et al., 2015). Her students were then engaged in arguing to learn so that they learn ways of formulating their developing positions related to vetting competing perspectives and information. For example, in addressing the question, "are humans equal?", students discussed different perspectives on the issues of human equality.

Analysis of The Ohio State University Argumentative Writing Project (2016) teachers' instruction based on a focus on arguing to learn in 31 classrooms over a four-year-period indicated that students learned to engage in critical inquiry based on interactions with peers as their potential audiences (Bloome et al., 2020; Newell et al., 2015).

Engaging in arguing-to-learn is a focus on creating a social context in which students interact with the teacher or peers to employ processes for discussing and employing writing as means of engaging and convincing audiences of the validity of their claims (Newell et al., 2014; 2015). The focus then is on the "construction of meaning that unfolds during talk and social interactions... but also the social practices of discussion" (Bloome et al., 2020, p. 27).

Arguing to learn involves going beyond simply determining whether the evidence supports a claim through focusing on how certain evidence or information leads to exploring several different claims. Students then test out the relationships between evidence and claims through exploring alternative perspectives on the validity of competing claims, leading to further critical inquiry between students. For example, in lieu of asking "What does this literary text mean?", a teacher may ask "Argue your understanding of this literary text," which invites students to formulate multiple understandings, unique to different students (Seymour et al., 2020, p. x).

Arguing to learn also involves a focus on "argument as conversation" in discussions through students acquiring ways of formulating arguments by responding to others' positions leading to counter-arguments (VanDerHeide & Juzwik, 2018).

Unpacking assumptions or warrants

As we noted in engaging students in critical response to reading texts in Chapter 5, students need to engage in unpacking the assumptions or warrants associated with the claim–reason relationship. One challenge in making explicit warrants is that they are "often taken-for-granted assumptions and rarely are people asked to justify the positions they take" (Seymour et al., 2020, p. 55). Students may then not be accustomed to surfacing their warrants unless their teachers ask them to do so. Arguing-to-learn for writing also involves students' self-reflection about their assumptions shaping their arguments, leading to revisions of their interpretations (Seymour et al., 2020).

As students engage in these interactions over time, they learn to anticipate their peers' counter-arguments to their claims, so that they can refute those counter-arguments with counter-claims/evidence. For example, students may discover competing perspectives regarding counter-arguments that eliminating fossil fuels will lose jobs and undermine the economy. At the same time, they may also find evidence that jobs associated with the implementation of clean energy options represent the fastest-growing segment of the economy. As they learn to articulate and share these competing perspectives through surfacing warrants and assumptions, they acquire the ability to engage in dialogic arguing to learn.

In supporting their claims, students, particularly middle-school students, will also often rely on narrative experiences as evidence for their claims. For example, in an analysis of a discussion of the pros and cons of snitching on their peers, the teacher asked students if they had ever witnessed a crime and/or engaged in snitching about that crime (Kim et al., 2014). In the discussion that ensued, students shared experiences supporting the position that snitching can be beneficial in identifying the culprit of a crime, while other students shared experiences of snitching as violating their alliance with peer group members resulting in their being ostracized from their group. One benefit of sharing these narratives is that they represent competing, dialogic points of view or perspectives on a problem or issue.

When students shared their experiences, the teacher was careful not to privilege or value one story's perspective over another to foster a range of different perspectives. As a result, the students then experienced tensions between the different perspectives. By validating these alternative perspectives, the teacher was also supporting the students by using narratives as a form of argument as valid evidence for supporting positions through their use of narratives. She was also valuing her students' lived-worlds, local experiences as significant to adopting their perspectives.

Entertaining competing perspectives

As in applying different critical perspectives in responding to literature as described in Chapter 4, students are also exposed to alternative perspectives on a topic or issue that invite them to formulate their position(s) or stance on these competing perspectives (Olsen et al., 2014). In doing so, students are enacting an identity as someone who is open to engaging in dialogic thinking about a topic or issue. For example, students writing their college admissions essays recognized the need to portray themselves as open-minded learners, something they assumed would achieve positive uptake from their college admissions audience readers (Aukerman & Beach, 2018).

For entertaining competing perspectives, students may engage in what is defined as "Listening Argument: an argument that listens to and explores multiple perspectives on an issue, including one's own multiple perspectives, in order to come to a decision or new understanding" (Vanderheide et al., 2021, p. 87). A "listening argument" differs from many arguments in online spaces that reflect only one singular, often biased perspective, as well as a simplistic, pro–con binary based on the need to generate what is assumed to be a one-sided superior stance.

By engaging in dialogue with others about a certain issue or problem, students explore alternative perspectives that require suspending one's biases to consider the value of perspectives that may challenge one's own. In one unit, students took notes based on reading their sources based on their perspective and from that of someone with an alternative, counter-perspective.

In considering these alternative perspectives, students addressed the questions, "'What types of people are these? What experiences brought them to be on that side? What motivates them?'" (p. 89). In some cases, while students began with adopting a certain stance on an issue, they began to empathize with these alternative perspectives. For example, one student initially argued that teachers should have the right to have guns in schools. However, after considering alternative perspectives, he recognized that students and teachers would experience discomfort with guns in schools, leading him to acknowledge why others would oppose teachers having guns.

Students also viewed the YouTube series, Middle Ground *t.ly/viPq*, with six participants, three of whom posit one perspective, and three, an alternative perspective, leading to students then discussing these alternative perspectives. (For more on teaching argumentative writing, see *Teaching argumentative writing* on the website.)

Activity: Generating Engaging Argumentative Writing Assignments

Generate an argumentative writing assignment building on your students' particular knowledge or interest in addressing a certain problem or issue as well as potential audiences, for example, their concern about the adverse effects of climate change on their region, to submit as letters to their town/city's paper as well as the option of writing scripts for creating videos. Specify some activities for engaging students in arguing-to-learn activities, such as engaging students in discussions in which they share potential objections to reducing the use of fossil fuels to generate counter-arguments. Include resources for students to access for providing evidence for their claims.

TEACHING EXPLANATORY/ANALYSIS WRITING

State ELA standards, particularly the CCSS, also include standards related to teaching explanatory or analysis writing. This writing involves explaining or analyzing a phenomenon in terms of causal relationships, for example, processes evident in the 9th–10th CCSS writing standard, "Develop a complex topic through well-chosen, relevant, and sufficient facts, concrete details, quotations, extended definitions, or other information and examples" (p. 41).

Explanatory writing addresses our critical inquiry framework in providing explanations for problems or issues based on alternative explanations. For example, students may explain why they engaged in creating their video games for use by younger students as a way of helping them learn certain physics concepts of gravity and force. As is the case with argumentative writing, this requires students' ability to analyze the validity of reasons or explanations for events in terms of their relevance or sufficiency of the evidence provided.

In formulating explanations for different phenomena or events, students need to entertain and evaluate different perspectives associated with identifying reasons for certain phenomena or events. For example, in providing explanations for the increased need to address issues associated with economic inequality in American society, students could engage in discussions that surface these competing explanations.

You can also provide students with prompts or heuristics to engage them in collaborative critical inquiry related to entertaining alternative perspectives. For example, Amber Simmons, who teaches at Brookwood High School, Snellville, Georgia, has students employ a QUEST heuristic for engaging in research projects: **Q**uestion and explore, **U**nderstand and analyze arguments, **E**valuate multiple perspectives, **S**ynthesize ideas, and **T**eam, **T**ransform and **T**ransmit to formulate and share their plans for conducting research projects (Beach & Beauchemin, 2019, p. 132).

Students in Amber's class then created posters describing their research projects to share their projects with peers visually. They included descriptions of their title, problem statement, research question(s), definitions, hypothesis, the significance of the study, methodology, and source list. Other students then attached Post-It notes to each other's posters to provide feedback, for example, that "Your research question is too broad. Further limiting/specifying your population would help narrow your research" (Beach & Beauchemin, 2019, p. 132).

Students could formulate alternative explanations for characters' actions for writing responses to literature based on their analysis of the beliefs and norms shaping those actions. For example, in Elizabeth Erdmann's 12th-grade class, students wrote responses to the novels *Lord of the Flies* (LOTF) (Golding, 2003) and *1984* (Orwell, 1961) related to analyzing issues of trust between characters. In LOTF, a group of boys trapped on an island attempt to devise a set of survival strategies that requires adherence to shared norms constituting trusting relations. In the novel, the boys splinter into two opposing groups—a group led by Ralph that includes Piggy and Simon who attempt to establish some norms related to the need to be rescued from the island, and a group, the "Hunters," led by Jack who challenge these social norms. In *1984*, the main character, Winston, works for The Ministry of Truth, to create propaganda and misinformation to maintain control of the people of Oceania by Big Brother, but then begins to critique his work leading to his challenging Big Brother.

Students then wrote reflections in response to prompts to explain characters' actions related to the level of trust between characters. They also drew on experiences in their own lives with different levels of trust in their relations, writing that required them to explain their contentions using evidence from the novels.

> **Activity: Generating Engaging Explanatory/Analysis Writing Assignments**
>
> Generate some explanatory/analysis writing assignments in which students formulate explanations for certain actions or phenomena, for example, formulating explanations as to why it is important to address a certain problem or why the main character acted in a certain manner in the world of a literary text. In formulating these examinations, as in argumentative writing, students need to unpack the assumptions or warrants underlying connections between their claims and the evidence for those claims. For example, in formulating reasons for the need to move start times up for their high school, students may cite evidence of the adverse impact of lack of sleep on adolescents' physical and mental health. In doing so, they may argue that adolescents' health is related to their overall academic success.

TEACHING INFORMATIONAL WRITING

Informational writing is designed primarily to provide audiences with specific, relevant information based on certain audience needs. For example, students may describe uses of iMovie editing techniques to enhance the quality of videos. While informational writing overlaps with argumentative and explanatory writing, its primary value is to provide audiences with certain information or knowledge to engage them in certain actions or tasks.

Therefore, students need to adopt their audience's perspective in determining what constitutes sufficient, relevant, valid information relative to performing these actions or tasks. You can do this by asking students to write directions for performing a task, for example, playing a simple online game. Then, with the writer watching, the audience performs the task, noting whether certain information was or was not helpful. They can also consider their audience's needs and interests by using questions they expect their audiences to be asking as subheadings, for example, "how can I purchase my tickets online?"

Students are more likely to be engaged in informational writing through problem-based learning (PBL). They are addressing problems or issues that interest them requiring their acquisition of information or data (Murphy & Smith, 2015). To gain a sense of effective investigation, students can study examples of investigative news reporting or documentaries such as PBS Frontline related to acquiring relevant, alternative perspectives on a problem or issue.

For example, students can *identify problems* related to the adverse effects of climate change in their regions related to increased temperatures/heat, sea rise, flooding, droughts, and wildfires/air pollution, etc. They can then *contextualize* a specific problem in terms of the larger institutional systems shaping the problem. For example, they may examine how the fossil fuel system for energy production depends on a transportation system based on cars/trucks, creating high CO_2 emissions impacting climate change. Students then *analyze* data or information related to the causes of the problem or issue, including the use of online database searches and/or interviews and informational searches. For their interviews, students can prepare questions in advance and audio record interviews for later transcribing.

Once students identify a problem or issue they want to investigate, they also need to consider whether or how to engage their audiences who may or may not be interested in knowing more about a certain problem or issue. Ideally, students can share their writing with peers, teachers, and other outside audiences (Hoffman, 2014).

They then can consider ways of best presenting their findings to audiences in a manner that will engage those audiences—sharing that enhances their sense of engagement with potential audiences (Marciano & Warren, 2019). They can create class newspapers or newsletters as well as contribute to the school newspaper. Students can learn to create effective news headlines by summarizing different scenes in *Romeo and Juliet* using direct quotes to create headlines (Styslinger et al., 2014). They can then access newspaper generator sites, Locsei *tinyurl.com/crwyubc* or Fodey (limited to 65 words) *tinyurl.com/v5dns* to create mock newspaper front pages as JPEGs to add to their class website.

> **Activity: Generating Engaging Informational Writing Assignments**
>
> You can generate some informational writing assignments involving communicating information about a topic or issue to certain audiences, particularly using online/digital tools. This requires that students know how to clearly and concisely focus and convey information relevant to informing their audiences about their topic or issue, including the use of multimodal/digital tools/figures to convey their information visually.

FOSTERING ONLINE WRITING INSTRUCTION

With the shift to totally online instruction during the pandemic, teachers often simply asked students to post their writing online without recognizing how online writing instruction also requires creating a supportive online space or community. They can do so by "adding a photo to emails, uploading a video introduction, and combining voice with written feedback for assignments [that] all help establish the instructor's presence and personality at the beginning of the class" (Collopy, 2020, p. 23). One book-length description of an online writing course written by a student and the instructor highlighted the importance of fostering shared, online discussions for creating a sense of community (Gasiewski & Warnock, 2018) (for methods of teaching online writing courses, see the Online Writing Instruction Community website *owicommunity.org*).

Students are often engaged in online writing outside of school on social media for social purposes, as contrasted with their writing in school to achieve grades, a disconnect between alternative purposes for writing (Dredger et al., 2010). This suggests the need to create purposeful online/digital writing that builds on the social purposes driving students' social media writing outside of school. (For resources and links to writing apps *usingipads.pbworks.com* and digital writing tools *digitalwriting.pbworks.com*).

You can also use Google Docs and Google Forms on Google Drive for Google Classroom *edu.google.com/products/classroom* to have students share, collaborate, and/or respond to each other's writing during a course through organizing assignments/topics in folders in Drive (Dail & Vásquez, 2018. Students can revise each other's text and/or add comments using these tools, which, as indicated in one study, enhanced students' revisions and sharing of feedback (Brodahl & Hansen, 2014). You can also use Google Forms, where students enter for addressing specific topics within categories on a table you create *bit.ly/writtenresponse*.

It's also important to have students share their writing not only with teachers but also their peers. One teacher used Padlet *padlet.com* as a discussion board for students to share their writing with peers (National Writing Project, 2021). The teacher also highlighted students' comments and inferred connections between comments. She noted,

> I've come to see Padlet as an effective, user-friendly, and aesthetically pleasing discussion board that helps us all come together in one space and bounce ideas off of one another without showing our faces on screen or speaking up in a sea of quiet voices.

In teaching *Macbeth*, a teacher, Althea, had students study the legend of a curse that actors in Macbeth productions actually used instead of fake daggers or dying because of illnesses in the play productions (Marlatt, 2019). Students used Google Docs to discuss this curse, including how the class itself may have been cursed when students heard the word Macbeth in a quiet classroom through the Voice Typing tool students were using.

Students then created presentations to the class that included a video and connections to curses in movies. They then shared their presentations using Google Hangouts with students in a another similar British literature class. Althea also connected with another teacher who teaches British literature in a high school in another city using Google Hangouts to share their presentations with the students in the other high school.

Students can also share their writing using Blogger *www.blogger.com*, Kidblog *kidblog.org*, Edublogs *edublogs.org*, or Wordpress.org *wordpress.org* or for blogging on iPads—BlogPress, Tumblr for iPad, or Blogsy apps or Blogger-droid, Tumblr, Weebly, LiveJournal, or Bloglovin on Android tablets (for links on blogging and blog platforms: *tinyurl.com/mdnjgmf*). Students benefit from reading/subscribing to blogs through the use of features such as layout, profiles, links, comments, tags, blogrolls, and contact information. In creating blog posts, students are writing about topics or issues that interest them. Kristin Wallace, an English teacher at Westonka High School; Mound, Minnesota, noted that: "students are writing for a real audience and about topics which inspire them. It doesn't matter if their passion is politics, snowboarding or Disney, they all have something to say when it is a subject they choose" (Beach et al., 2015, p. 145).

To foster responses to posts, students could serve as "blog partners" to ensure that one of their peers would respond to their posts. They can also share their informal writing on digital whiteboards to respond to each other for viewing by all class members.

You can also create a Twitter class account as different from your personal account or a Twitter hashtag for a specific class for students to follow students in their class and retweet their peers' tweets.

Students could also share their responses to online texts using social bookmarking/annotation tools such as Diigo Education sticky notes, Evernote, VoiceThread, Del.icos.us, Reddit, Pinterest, Pearltrees, Symbaloo, A.annotate, Crocodoc, or Bounce (for links to these tools *goo.gl/FZJBkf* and related resources *goo.gl/aeRNKD*).

> **Activity: Employing Online Writing**
>
> Based on your previous experience of using certain online writing tools and platforms, generate an engaging writing activity that exploits the affordances of these tools and platforms. For example, you may create a class blog in which students post entries and share reactions to each other's entries in ways that enhance the construction of a dialogic classroom community. Students can serve as "blog partners" working in pairs to comment on each other's posts to create dialogic interactions.

EDITING TEXTS

Students often have difficulty knowing how to vary their syntax in editing sentences so that their sentences enhance readability. As we note in Chapter 10, the use of direct grammar instruction through teaching rules or diagramming sentences will not enhance students' editing, given decades of research demonstrating that traditional grammar instruction has a minimal positive effect on improving writing quality (Graham, 2019; Graham et al., 2020; Hillocks, 2002).

The limitations of decontextualized grammar instruction

A recent review of research into decontextualized grammar instruction for students in grades three to seven found, in six different studies, that the writing quality actually deteriorated for students who were taught grammar versus students who were not taught grammar—possibly due to the disconnect between knowledge about rules versus an intuitive knowing-how sense of syntax acquiring through reading and language use (Graham 2019; Graham et al., 2020).

Adopting prescriptive grammar rules can also devalue students' use of African American Vernacular English (AAVE) as "'ungrammatical,' or 'broken English'" (Linguistics Society of America, 2002, p. 224), even though AAVE is based on regular, syntactic rules.

This suggests the need to distinguish between grammar as focusing on *syntax* and *usage* as focused on how people use language and punctuation in everyday interactions—for example, the use of more informal language in certain contexts. It is also the case that syntax may change over time due to usage, such as how writers in the past did not use contractions, while more current writers do use contractions.

Focusing on editing for readability

For helping students in editing their writing, we recommend integrating reading and writing instruction to help students focus on issues of *readability* related to the use of language to engage their audiences. This does not preclude a focus on a knowing-how, descriptive use of syntax related to enhancing readability. Students can learn to assess differences in their syntax through sentence combining activities (Anderson & Dean, 2014; Hudson, 2016).

In combining sentences, students are reflecting on reasons for combining or employing certain syntactical options in certain ways, given the rhetorical context. For example, students may decide to employ a passive tense, as in "the river was polluted by runoff from the chemical factory." They may do so to shift the blame away from the factory as the active agent causing the pollution in "runoff from the chemical factory polluted the river."

These options reflect an issue of readability with how subjects in an active voice generally enhance readability. However, writers may also want to shift the focus away from actors in the subject position for rhetorical reasons to deflect attention from those actors. Republican Senators in the 2021 Senate impeachment trial may prefer to state "President Trump was acquitted" versus "we acquitted President Trump" in addressing their Republican voters. This means that in editing their writing, students need to focus on their intended meanings related to achieving certain audience responses.

Troy Hicks (2014) records his writing and decision-making using the screencasting tool, Camtasia, to model his sentence combining processes for students by reflecting on reasons for selecting specific options. Students can then employ screencasting apps such as Explain Everything for iPad or Screenr for desktops to record their decision-making processes for sharing with the teacher or peers.

Students also benefit from reading aloud their writing in peer conferences so that they can listen for instances of using too many words or elongated sentences, leading to a recognition of the need to edit their text. To foster students' self-reflections as they are reading, you can have students engage in think-aloud responses when they are reading texts in which they make explicit their thoughts on specific language in a text (Beck, 2018).

Students can also use free online editing tools that provide feedback on the readability of their writing, for example, Wordtune *t.ly/nQUf*, Analyze My Writing *www.analyzemywriting.com*, Hemingway App *hemingwayapp.com*, and Slick Write *www.slickwrite.com/#!home* (Byrne, 2021). They can also use the subscription tool, Grammarly *app.grammarly.com* (for more on editing texts, see *Editing texts* on the website).

> **Activity: Responding to Readability in Texts**
>
> To help students attend to issues of readability in texts, you can provide students with texts with high versus low readability. Students can then identify specific aspects of syntax or usage that enhance or limit the readability of these texts and give reasons for differences in their perceptions of readability. They can also reflect on how their prior knowledge of a certain topic, subject, or discipline influences their comprehension of a text as a factor shaping readability.

PROVIDING FEEDBACK TO STUDENTS' WRITING

As we describe in more detail in Chapter 11 on assessment, providing feedback to students' writing involves describing your responses as a reader to their drafts, so that students then experience how an audience is experiencing their writing using reader-based feedback (Elbow, 1973). This includes noting instances in which you were engaged versus confused/puzzled about ideas' implied meaning or organization.

You are also enhancing your relationships with students through your individual interactions with a student based on describing your responses. For example, one teacher responded to her engagement with a student's writing by saying,

> "My stomach is dropping in this part of your story! The tension you build is palpable because you keep holding back from telling us what happened! It's as if being silent, by not telling us everything, you are making me feel nervous, scared, anxious and even angry for this character."
> (Bomer, 2010, p. 66)

Through the use of this "reader-based" feedback, you are modeling a vocabulary of composing processes so that students acquire meta-cognitive language to reflect on their writing (for activities to foster metacognitive reflection: Sweetland Center for Writing, *tinyurl.com/tbs3djn*). Students then internalize the "external dialogue" based on their interactions with you either in writing conferences or from your written comments for use as their own "internal dialogue" (Grossen & Salazar-Orvig, 2011). For example, in noting that "I appreciated how you cited evidence from a range of different sources," students may then reflect on their use of alternative sources in their subsequent writing.

Fostering students' self-reflections

For engaging in productive self-reflection, students need to focus on addressing a certain problem or issue that requires them to engage in problem-solving, ideally through an interaction with a peer or teacher (Sweetland Center for Writing, n.d.). If students have set certain goals for addressing these problems or issues in a course or for a particular assignment, they may then identify problems or issues in meeting those goals.

Students and peers can also engage in role-playing activities where they assume roles as writers and audiences to reflect on their processes, goals, audience perceptions, and shared knowledge of the topic or issue (Sweetland Center for Writing, n.d.). For example, in writing narratives, students could assume the roles of narrators of their stories and other characters and audiences to rehearse first-person narrating and dialogue between characters to receive responses from audiences.

After you provide feedback, they could then write a memo or verbally share with you responses answering the following questions: "What was most clear and helpful to you? What was your biggest take-away? What revision suggestions do you agree with? Why? How will you put those into practice?"

It's also important to focus your responses on only a few specific aspects instead of overwhelming students with numerous aspects. You can then select one or two issues in their draft that you believe students should work on so that you can have students focus on reflecting on those particular issues (Beck, 2018). For example, in giving feedback, Nancie Atwell (2014) poses only one question in her conferencing to model self-reflection about a particular issue in a student's draft.

For providing students with feedback at the editing phase of their writing as distinct from earlier drafting phases, you can model the application of metalinguistic knowledge about how grammar depends on their purposes and audience. An analysis of teachers' feedback to students' writing found that simply telling students to vary syntax in their sentences without providing reasons for doing so was perceived by students as not helping them in their editing

(Myhill et al., 2013). Teachers who provided effective feedback always contextualized implied revisions in terms of the purpose and audience shaping the students' writing. They did so through modeling their meta-commentary reflection on formulating purposes designed to achieve certain audience uptakes.

Using peer feedback for fostering reflections and revisions

Teachers may not have time to provide feedback on students' writing, so one alternative involves using peer feedback. Most research has found that students receiving peer feedback are more likely to make revisions, particularly when peers receive training (Huisman et al., 2018; Patchan et al., 2016). In addition, a study on whether peer feedback also improves writing quality over time examined revisions of 185 students in a Title 1 and a non-Title 1 high school (Wu & Schunn, 2021).

Students read a persuasive text to write an essay describing the rhetorical strategies employed in the texts; they then repeated the same task later. Students then received training on how to employ peerceptiv *peerceptiv.com*, an online peer-assessment tool to provide written comments to first drafts as well as ratings designed by a teacher.

Analysis of the results indicated that students improved the quality of their writing through their revisions, with a higher number and more high-level comments resulting in the implementation of high-level revisions. Students receiving more low-level comments focusing primarily on editing language made more low-level revisions. Students who received more comments also made more revisions. These results suggest that students benefit from simply engaging in revisions and receiving helpful feedback. Giving feedback to peers may transfer to enhancing their self-reflection of their writing (Wu & Schunn, 2021).

Training peers to give feedback

Because you may have only limited time during classes to conference with students, you can also train peers to provide feedback in their own conferences in pairs or small groups, particularly given the value of peer feedback for improving writing over time. For example, in a comparison of how college instructors versus peers respond to writing, peers were more likely to focus on global concerns than instructors and were less directive than instructors (Melzer, 2020).

Peers also gain as much from reading each other's drafts as they do from receiving comments from peers, suggesting the value of focusing on and training peers to give feedback as central to effective writing instruction. Without this training on effective, reader-based feedback to substantive aspects of a draft, students may focus more on voicing vague judgments as in "good job" or editing matters instead of engaging in a conversation about a draft to address a writer's primary concerns.

Analysis of high school students' perceptions of the value of peer feedback finds that they learned about the strengths and weaknesses of writing from reading their peers' writing and obtaining feedback based on a range of different perspectives (Loretto et al., 2018); 90% of some 500 students surveyed indicated that they believed their feedback was helpful for their peers.

In modeling feedback as part of this training, you are stressing the importance of relational framing of your interaction with a student by letting them set the agenda for the conference and providing them with positive comments about specific aspects of their draft. You are also focusing on just a few issues so that students can identify specific changes to address those issues at the end of the conference.

> **Activity: Providing Feedback Instruction for Students**
>
> To assist students in providing peer feedback on their writing, you can train students for peer conferencing by focusing on reader-based feedback as well as editing feedback based on readability. For example, you can have one student read aloud their text to a peer or have a peer provide read-aloud responses to their peer's text. You could model this feedback by sharing your responses to a student's text and making explicit reasons for editing feedback you provide students.

SUMMARY

In this chapter, we focused on general approaches for teaching writing in ways that go beyond the formalist orientation of the CCSS writing standards. We then delineated methods for teaching argumentative, informational, and explanatory writing based on activities emphasizing the social and rhetorical purposes for writing to engage audiences.

REFERENCES

Addison, J., & McGee, S. J. (2016). *Writing and school reform: Writing instruction in the age of Common Core and standardized testing.* The WAC Clearinghouse; University Press of Colorado.

American Psychological Assocation. (2020). *The publication manual of the American Psychological Association*, 7th ed. Author.

Anderson, J., & Dean, D. (2014). *Revision decisions: Talking through sentences and beyond.* Stenhouse.

Applebee, A., & Langer, J. (2011). A snapshot of writing instruction in middle schools and high schools. *English Journal, 100*(6), 14–27.

Atwell, N. (2014). *In the middle, third edition: A lifetime of learning about writing, reading, and adolescents.* Heinemann.

Aukerman, M., & Beach, R. (2018). Student conceptualizations of task, audience, and self in writing college admissions essays. *Journal of Adolescent & Adult Literacy, 62*(3), 320–327.

Bawarshi, A. (2003). *Genre and the invention of the writer.* Utah State University Press.

Beach, R., Anson, C., Kastman-Breuch, L., & Reynolds, T. (2015). *Understanding and creating digital texts: An activity-based approach.* Rowman & Littlefield.

Beach, R., & Beauchemin, F. (2019). *Teaching language as action in the ELA classroom.* Routledge.

Beck, S. W. (2018). *A think-aloud approach to writing assessment: Analyzing process & product with adolescent writers.* Teachers College Press.

Bloome, D., Newell, G., Hirvela, A., & Lin, T-J. (2020). *Dialogic literary argumentation in high school language arts classrooms: A social perspective for teaching, learning, and reading literature.* Routledge.

Bomer, K. (2010). *Hidden gems: Naming and teaching from the brilliance in every student's writing.* Heinemann.

Brodahl, C., & Hansen, N. K. (2014). Education students' use of collaborative writing tools in collectively reflective essay papers. *Journal of Information Technology Education: Research, 13*, 91–120.

Byrne, R. (2021, April 20). Tools to help students analyze their own writing [Web log post]. Retrieved from t.ly/3QZW

Collopy, T. (2020). Pivoting in a pandemic: Online writing strategies to help us all "do it better." *Council Chronicle, 30*(2), 22–25.

Dail, J. S., & Vásquez, A. (2018). Google Drive: Facilitating collaboration and authentic community beyond the classroom. *Voices From the Middle, 25*(4), 24–28.

Dredger, K., Woods, D., Beach, C., & Sagstetter, V. (2010). Engage me: Using new literacies to create third space classrooms that engage student writers. *Journal of Media Literacy Education, 2*(2), 85–100. Retrieved from tinyurl.com/y8dz853k

Elbow, P. (1973). *Writing without teachers*. Oxford University Press.
Eodice, M., Geller, A. E. & Lerne, N. (2017). *The meaningful writing project: Learning, teaching, and writing in higher education*. Utah State University Press.
Fanetti, S., Bushrow, K. M., & DeWeese, D. L. (2010). Closing the gap between high school writing instruction and college writing expectations. *English Journal, 99*(4), 77–83.
Flores, T. (2018). Breaking silence and amplifying voices: Youths writing and performing their worlds. *Journal of Adolescent & Adult Literacy, 61*, 653–661.
Gasiewski, D., & Warnock, S. (2018). *Writing together: Ten weeks teaching and studenting in an online writing course*. National Council of Teachers of English.
Golding, W. (2003). *Lord of the flies*. Penguin.
Graham, S. (2019). Changing how writing is taught. *Review of Research in Education, 43*, 277–303.
Graham, S., Kiuhara, S. A., & MacKay, M. (2020). The effects of writing on learning in science, social studies, and mathematics: A meta-analysis. *Review of Educational Research, 90*(2), 179–226.
Grossen, M., & Salazar-Orvig, A. (2011). Dialogism and dialogicality in the study of the self. *Culture & Psychology, 17*(4), 491–509.
Hicks, T. (2014, September 3). Lesson idea: Using technology to teach sentence combining [Web log post]. Retrieved from http://tinyurl.com/qd8nrhk
Hillocks, G. (2002). *The testing trap: How state writing assessments control learning*. Teachers College Press.
Hoffman, A. (2014). High school journalism, media literacy, and the Common Core State Standards. *The Journal of Media Literacy, 61*(1–2), 57–61.
Hudson, R. (2016). Grammar instruction. In C. A. MacArthur, S. Graham, & J. Fitzgerald (Eds.), *Handbook of writing research*, 2nd ed. (pp. 288–300). Guilford Press.
Huisman, R., Saab, N., van Driel, J., & van den Broek, P. (2018). Peer feedback on academic writing: Undergraduate students' peer feedback role, peer feedback perceptions and essay performance. *Assessment & Evaluation in Higher Education, 43*(6), 955–968.
Kent, T. (1993). *Paralogic rhetoric*. Associated University Press.
Kim, M-Y., Buescher, E., & Bloome, D. (2014, December 6). Crafting argument through the narration of local experience. Paper presented at the meeting of the Literacy Research Association, Marco Island, Florida.
Kittle, P., & Gallagher, K. (2021). *4 essential studies beliefs and practices to reclaim student agency*. Heinemann.
Lee, H. (1988). *To kill a mockingbird*. Warner Books.
Linguistics Society of America (2002). Resolution on the Oakland "Ebonics" issue. In L. Delpit & J. Kilgour Dowdy (Eds.), *The skin we speak: Thoughts on language and culture in the classroom* (pp. 223–224). The New Press.
Loretto, A., DeMartino, S., & Godley, A. (2018, March 19). What do high school students think about peer review? [Web log post]. Retrieved from https://goo.gl/Lt5b4f
Marciano, J. E., & Warren, C. A. (2019). Writing toward change across youth participatory action research projects. *Journal of Adolescent & Adult Literacy, 62*(6), 485–494.
Marlatt, R. (2019). "I didn't say, 'Macbeth,' it was my Google Doc!"; A secondary English case study of redefining learning in the 21st Century. *E-Learning and Digital Media, 16*(1), 46–62.
Melzer, D. (2020). Placing peer response at the center of the response construct. *Journal of Response to Writing, 6*(2), 7–41. https://scholarsarchive.byu.edu/journalrw/vol6/iss2/2
Modern Language Association. (2009). *MLA handbook for writers of research papers, 7th edition*. Author.
Murphy, S., & Smith, M. A. (2015). *Uncommonly good ideas: Teaching writing in the Common Core*. Teachers College Press.
Myhill, D., Jones, S., & Watson, A. (2013). Grammar matters: How teachers' grammatical subject knowledge impacts on the teaching of writing. *Teaching and Teacher Education, 16*, 72–91.
National Writing Project (2021, April 12). Teaching writing to support social & emotional learning [Web log post]. Retrieved from http://t.ly/2VdU
Newell, G. E., Bloome, D., & Hirvela, A. (2015). *Teaching and learning argumentative writing in high school English language arts classrooms*. Routledge.
Newell, G. E., VanDerHeide, J., & Wynhoff Olsen, A. (2014). High school English language arts teachers' argumentative epistemologies for teaching writing. *Research in the Teaching of English, 49*(2), 95–119.
Olsen, A. H., Ryu, S., & Bloome, D. (2014). (Re)constructing rationality and social relations in the teaching and learning of argumentative writing in two high school English language arts classrooms. In P. J. Dunston, S. K. Fullerton, C. C. Bates, P. M. Stecker, M. W. Cole, A. H. Hall, K. N. Headley, & R. P. Tennebaum (Eds.), *63rd Yearbook of the Literacy Research Association* (pp. 360–377). Literacy Research Association.
Orwell, G. (1961). *1984*. Penguin.
Patchan, M. M., Schunn, C. D., & Correnti, R. J. (2016). The nature of feedback: How peer feedback features affect students' implementation rate and quality of revisions. *Journal of Educational Psychology, 108*(8), 1098–1120.
Rejan, A. (2017). The "true meaning" of argument: Conflicting definitions of argument in the Common Core State Standards. *English Journal, 106*(5), 18–26.

Rex, L. A., Thomas, E. E. & Engel, S. (2010). Applying Toulmin: Teaching logical reasoning and argumentative writing. *English Journal, 99*(6), 56–61.

Schulten, K. (2020). *Student voice: 100 argument essays by teens on issues that matter to them.* Norton Professional Books.

Seymour, M., Thanos, T., Newell, G., & Bloome, D. (2020). *Teaching literature using dialogic literary argumentation.* Routledge.

Sheehy, M. (2003). The social life of an essay: Standardizing forces in writing. *Written Communication, 20*(3), 333–385.

Styslinger, M. E., Walker, N. L., &. Lenker, T. K. (2014). Beyond the sticky note and Venn diagram. *Voices from the Middle, 22*(2), 13–20.

Sweetland Center for Writing, University of Michigan (n.d.) Metacognition: Cultivating reflection to help: students become self-directed learners [Web log post]. Retrieved from http://t.ly/VwXU

The Ohio State University Argumentative Writing Project. (2016). Principled practices for teaching dialogic literary argumentation in high school English language arts classrooms. Author.

VanDerHeide, J., & Juzwik, M. M. (2018). Argument as conversation: Students responding through writing to significant conversations across time and place. *Journal of Adolescent & Adult Literacy, 62,* 67–77.

Vanderheide, J., Beaton, E. L., Olsen, A. W. (2021). Making others' perspectives present: Arguments that listen. *English Journal, 110*(5), 87–93.

Wilcox, K. C., & Jeffery, J. V. (2014). Adolescents' writing in the content areas: National study results. *Research in the Teaching of English, 49*(2), 168–176.

Wilcox, K. C., Dacus, L. C., & Yu, F. (2021). Adolescent writing development in the united states pre and post the implementation of the Common Core. In J. V. Jeffery & J. M. Parr (Eds.), *International perspectives on writing curricula and development: A cross-case comparison* (pp. 78–100). Routledge.

Wu, Y., & Schunn, C. D. (2021). The effects of providing and receiving peer feedback on writing performance and learning of secondary school students. *American Educational Research Journal, 58*(3), 492–526.

7

Writing and Enacting Narratives, Drama, and Poetry

Most state ELA standards, as does the CCSS, include standards related to composing narratives. For example, the CCSS standards for grades 9 and 10 include the standards:

- Engage and orient the reader by setting out a problem, situation, or observations establishing one or multiple point(s) of view, and introducing a narrator and/or characters; create a smooth progression of experiences or events.
- Use narrative techniques, such as dialogue, pacing, description, reflection, and multiple plot lines, to develop experiences, events, and/or characters.

(Common Core Standards, 2010, p. 46)

WRITING NARRATIVES

To engage students in writing short stories or autobiographical narrative writing, you have them portray or dramatize specific events through *showing* rather than *telling* based descriptions of setting, actions, dialogue, and narrator reflection.

In dramatizing events through their narratives, students are evoking their audiences' or readers' concern or sympathy about these problems or issues portrayed in these events. For example, in her book, *Nickel and Dimed: On (Not) Getting by in America*, described in Chapter 4, Barbara Ehrenreich (2010) uses narratives to portray her own experience of working in a discount retail store. She describes how she has real difficulty simply paying her rent and purchasing food on her low wages. The power of her narrative emerges from a difference between the reality she describes and the assumed belief of her reader that people who play by the rules and work hard at a full-time job ought to be able to earn enough money to support themselves. Today, many workers in America, particularly women in service jobs, earn only minimum wages resulting in difficulty paying for basic needs. Ehrenreich evokes a change in readers' thinking or attitudes by *showing* her difficulties in living on low wages instead of *telling* the reader what to think.

Creating settings based on norms

As with oral narratives, a key concept in creating settings for narratives is that of "tellability"— what makes a narrative worth telling. In creating a narrative, you are conveying the fact that

DOI: 10.4324/9781003177364-9

something unusual or extraordinary occurs in your story based on deviations or violations of certain norms (Labov, 1972). For example, you may share with peers the fact that you drove to your university, an event that lacks "tellability." Or, you may describe how, in driving to your university, another car came within inches of side-swiping your car, an event that now has more "tellability" given that your audience would perceive it as worth sharing with them—what Bakhtin (1981) defined as "eventness."

This concept of "tellability" points to the importance of creating settings in ways that highlight certain norms constituting characters' actions within the world of the narrative. These norms become evident when characters engage in actions that deviate from or violate those norms, leading to conflicts central to dramatizing the narratives.

To help students understand the concept of "tellability," you can then have students share oral narratives representing deviations from norms. Students could reflect on how they portrayed the setting for these narratives that implied certain norms that are violated. For example, a student shares a story about working at Starbucks and experiencing tensions with a customer. In doing so, she implies how Starbucks' corporate norms shape her actions to placate her customers. In reflecting on these norms, students become aware of the importance of creating a setting so that their readers infer norms constituting persons' actions.

Creating dialogue to portray characters' relations

Consistent with the notion of "show, don't tell," the use of dialogue serves to portray relations between characters. When Allen taught historically under-served high school sophomores, one of his first assignments was to have his students simply write down an imaginary conversation between two characters. Before they began to write, Allen's students brainstormed two or three characters, fictional but loosely based on people that they knew.

The more students were able to imagine these characters and what they might talk about, the better. To get the rhythm of the spoken word, students could experiment with recording and transcribing conversations. Allen also used the document camera to show students how to punctuate and paragraph conversations. Students who had been reluctant writers were encouraged when they were told that they simply had to write as people talk.

Writing short stories was the next step. By now, Allen's students already had experience creating dialogue and using it to develop character and action. For writing fictional narratives, students can draw on their experience reading short stories. They may then note examples of the narrator's point of view, creation of setting, use of dialogue, and the recognition that there is typically little explicit character description or development in a short story (as compared to a novel).

Drawing on and mimicking genres

Students can also acquire ideas for stories from a wide range of different literary or media genres for inspiration: science fiction, adventure, romance, horror, adventure/travel, comedy, satire/parody, detective/mystery, etc. For instance, reading examples of science fiction stories can lead students to envision a future world leading to a science fiction story in which characters are coping with challenges of life in the future: climate change, overpopulation, technological breakdowns, and so on. Noah Swanson, a 10th-grade student in Elizabeth Erdmann's class, drew on the time-travel narrative genre to write a story, "Jerry the Janitor," who is working in a university lab, only to interact with a machine in the lab that transports him back to Athens, Greece, 453 BC. In Athens, he is confronted with a mob who want to sacrifice him to the gods, but he interacts with a professor who created the machine who tells him that he needs to jump off a cliff to reactivate the machine batteries so that he is then transported back to the university.

To dramatize the deviation of norms associated with his work as a janitor, Noah describes how, as Jerry, "mopping the floors, he saw a bright light coming from around the corner of his hallway." He then opens the door to the machine. "It didn't take him long to lay down comfortably and wish to sleep forever. That was before the machine began to talk. 'Setting route to Athens, 453 BC,' the machine blasted into his ears" (unpublished student writing).

Rewriting or remixing narratives

Consistent with the standard, "create and present a text or artwork in response to literary work," students can rewrite or remix narratives by revising, adding events, inserting dialogue, altering settings, or changing endings of existing stories (Pope, 2006). They can also draw on, mimic, remix, or parody certain authors or genres in performing or writing stories, for example, creating suspense stories based on their reading of Edgar Allen Poe or Shirley Jackson stories.

One of Allen's students worked with a collection of Garcia Lorca poems, hyperlinking them to each other around key images and metaphors and adding images that the poems referred to. Another student took Poe's short story, "The Tell-Tale Heart," and, by linking several words in the work, created a series of the narrator's inner thoughts and provided a psychological justification for the murder (Rozema & Webb, 2008). (For a TED talk video on remix *tinyurl.com/mxgseveraly7ljII*.) (For more on writing fictional narratives, see *writing fictional narratives* on the website.)

WRITING AUTOBIOGRAPHICAL NARRATIVES/MEMOIRS

Writing autobiographical narratives or memoirs allows students to recall and examine certain past events that shaped their identities in a particular developmental phase or turning point in their lives; for example, moving from accepting others' beliefs to voicing their own beliefs.

Rather than creating a highlighted laundry list of events during their past lifetime, resulting in superficial portrayals, students benefit from focusing on and fleshing out one or two specific past events in some detail through actions and dialogue to explore how they have grown or changed. Students need to think about their past identity and perspectives to portray the earlier perspectives and identities when writing about the past. To select these events in their lives, students can create a timeline and then focus on a key moment when they were coping with certain problems or issues.

Students could read examples of autobiographical narratives or memoirs to gain an understanding of how writers focus on specific events. For example, students could read examples of autobiographies/memoirs such as *I Know Why the Caged Bird Sings* (Angelou, 2009) or *Between the World and Me* (Coates, 2015). They could also read *We Are Here to Stay: Voices of Undocumented Young Adults* (Kuklin, 2019) with writing by nine undocumented adolescents coping with the threat of being reported to legal authorities (for a unit with writing about adolescents coping with adversities *bit.ly/366wlwp* (Ford, 2019).

Acquiring information about past events

To acquire specific information about these past events, students can interview people who knew them in the past and talk about their prior perceptions (for examples of interviews with 1,750 African Americans, *www.storycorps.net/initiatives/griot*). They can also find photos of themselves, mementos, or documents from a certain time period to evoke memories of their actions or beliefs. In addition, teachers often have students create maps of the home or neighborhood where they grew up and mark sites of significant events that could be addressed in their writing.

In recalling details about past events, students may be concerned about the need to recall events exactly as they happened. To address this concern, you can help them recognize that their memories of the past often change as they acquire new understandings or ways of thinking.

Contextualizing past events based on cultural and historical worlds

Through their writing, students are portraying how their identities are shaped by their families, peers, school, and communities. They are also reflecting on the development of certain attitudes or ethics, given how they "are not creating a merely random identity, rather, they are actively narrating themselves relative to a moral ideal of what it is to be a good person" (Rymes, 2001, p. 498).

One 6–12 history/social studies writing standard focuses on students' ability "to incorporate narrative elements effectively into arguments and informative/explanatory texts. In history, students must be able to write narrative accounts about individuals or events of historical import" (Common Core Standards, 2010, p. 65). To have her students reflect on the influence of larger cultural context on their six-word memoir as part of a unit on "What Is the United States of America's Story," Tanya Hodge has her students think about the questions, "How does society see you? How does our US American Society view you? In what ways are you truly free or truly imprisoned in the United States? What is your role in our society?" (Beach et al., 2021, p. 185).

Students in Corinth Matera's 12th-grade class at South High School, Minneapolis, wrote racial autobiographies portraying their experiences with racial identities (for the assignment: *goo.gl/AwBuQL*) in response to the following questions:

- What events and influences have most shaped your understanding of your own racial identity OR your understanding of race in the US?
- What is your understanding of your own racial identity in the US? How has it changed over time?
- How do other parts of your identity—gender, class, national origin, religion, language—intersect with and shape that racial identity?
- How have you come to understand racial politics in the US?

(Beach & Beauchemin, 2019, p. 136)

Students could also respond to the following questions developed by Elizabeth Erdmann to have her students reflect on how their narrative/autobiographical writing represents their portrayals of their emotions constituting their relations with others:

1. For the particular event, you chose to write about, describe the nature of your relationship with the other person(s) in your narrative. What is your relationship with the other person like?
2. How would you describe (and how certain are you of) your own emotions or sense of trust in this relationship?
3. How would you describe and how certain are you of the other person(s) emotions or sense of trust in this relationship?
4. Do you think that your descriptions captured these emotions or a sense of trust? If so, what kinds of dialogue or language did you use to portray these emotions and/or a sense of trust that shaped the relationships in your narrative?
5. What did you learn, if anything, from your relationship with others in this event in terms of changes in how you relate to others in your daily life?

(Beach & Beauchemin, 2019, p. 51)

> **Activity: Having Students Write Narratives**
>
> You can have your students write a range of different types of narratives associated with different genres noted above—mystery, crime, adventure, romance, etc., as well as autobiographical/memoir narratives. Students could focus on their use of setting, dialogue, and descriptions of characters and events for portraying story development associated with enhancing "tellability" for engaging their readers. They can then share their narratives with peers to assess their peers' uptake related to their dramatized events for enacting "tellability."

CREATING DIGITAL STORIES

One of the Speaking and Listening CCSS standards involves making "strategic use of digital media and visual displays of data to express information and enhance understanding of presentations" (Common Core Standards, 2010). To address this standard, students can create digital fiction by combining words with images, sounds, music, and video to create an interactive experience for a reader.

They can study examples of digital fiction such as *Starting Harry Potter wizardingworld.com/collections/starting-harry-potter* or *For Inanimate Alice: The Last Gas Station* (Pillinger, 2014/2016) that follows Alice through a series of adventures *inanimatealice.com* (for teaching resources t.ly/7eA4). (for examples of digital stories, *tinyurl.com/lhyglfh* and *tinyurl.com/45xfohc*; for resources, see *goo.gl/gTjKkv*; *goo.gl/T1YRQc*; the Center for Digital Storytelling, *www.storycenter.org*; Alan Levine's 50+ Ways To Tell a Story, *50ways.wikispaces.com* (Lambert, 2012; Ohler, 2013).

Students can draw on their literary responses to write digital stories based on characters or create alternative versions of events or story endings. For responding to events and characters in the novel, *The Hunger Games* (Collins, 2008), participants engaged in an online role-play game in which they wrote backstories based on characters' identities. Players then revised their stories to have these characters interact with each other. Players then voted to have certain characters removed from the game.

Tools for creating digital stories

For creating digital stories, students can use Metta *www.metta.io* or Meograph *www.meograph.com*; apps such as Inklewriter *tinyurl.com/ksxqojn* or Storyrobe *storyrobe.wordpress.com*. Students can also employ iBooks Author *www.apple.com/ibooks-author* or Book Creator *digitalvaults.org* (for a video by Richard Byrne (2014) on the use of Book Creator, see *tinyurl.com/u5ngm68*).

One particularly useful tool for creating digital stories for the iPad is the free iOS Adobe Voice app, *tinyurl.com/lmmmlh5*. To use this app, students

- select a template for their story based on the options of Explain Something, Follow a Hero's Journey, Promote an Idea, Tell What Happened, or the open-ended Make Up My Own template,
- upload images from the site as well as their images, photos,
- record their commentary as well as music about those images to create a video,
- publish their video using email, Facebook, Apple Message, Twitter, or Adobe's cloud.

For filming and editing their stories, they can use video tools such as Flipgrid, Instagram, iMovie, Videolicious, Vidify, Imotion HD, Magisto Video Editor, Viddy, Andromedia Video Editor, Director, or Quiki.

EXAMPLES OF DIGITAL STORIES

Students in Fawn Canady's (Canady et al., 2018) classes created nonfiction digital stories about their daily lives that they then submitted to the Digital Storymakers Award hosted by Atavist (*atavist.com/examples*; for her teaching activities *goo.gl/jh3ct2*). For example, a Latino student created his story about coping with stereotypes connecting him to his low-income neighborhood versus his success in school.

Preservice teachers (PTs) at the University of Delaware created digital stories for responding to a young adult novel (Lewis & Flynn, 2014). They first employed the bubbl.us mind mapping tool to portray their analysis of the book. They then created a storyboard for their video and analyzed examples of digital poetry on the Electronic Literature Collection *eliterature.org*). They then used iMovie and VoiceThread for creating their video productions. Similarly, PTs at California State University, Long Beach created a digital story about a novel *tinyurl.com/kwx8an9* (for resources *tinyurl.com/mso2ju9*) (Pandya, 2014).

PTs created digital stories about their literacy development over time for modeling for their growth for future students. To do so, they addressed the questions "'What kinds of literacy practices and cultural traditions did you grow up with?' and 'How does your background shape the kind of writer and thinker you are?'" (Marlatt, 2019, p. 134). One PT portrayed his identity development associated with literacies acquired in his Spanish culture. He noted the importance of sharing his experience, particularly for Latinx students. Doing so would "inspire" future students to "'be proud of who they are' and to 'never be afraid to learn new things' [through] "seeing someone who believed in them and talked and looked like them at the same time'" (p. 143).

CREATING COMICS AND GRAPHIC NOVELS

Students can also create comics or graphic novels using Comic Life, *plasq.com*; Storybird, *storybird.com*; MakeBeliefsComix, *makebeliefscomix.com*; Pixton, *edu.pixton.com/educators*; Canva, *canva.com/create/comic-strips*; ReadWriteThink.org Comic Creator, *tinyurl.com/yauu9zj*; Seedling Comic Studio, *tinyurl.com/yddxccex*; MakeBeliefsComix, *makebeliefscomix.com* (for a tutorial, see *tinyurl.com/uu8tuon*); StoryBoardThat, *www.storyboardthat.com* (for a tutorial, see *tinyurl.com/sdmuhp7*); and Google Slides (for a tutorial, see *tinyurl.com/rxerxcu*).

For creating comics/graphic novels, students can study the use of multimodal formatting in comics and graphic novels through the use of panels, frames, balloons, gutters, and positioning of readers through close-up versus long shots or different angles (Bitz, 2010) in graphic novels such as the Maus series (Spiegelman, 1986; 1991), *Persepolis: The Story of a Childhood* (Satpari, 2004), *American Born Chinese* (Yang, 2008), and *The Adventures of Johnny Bunko: The Last Career Guide You'll Ever Need* (Pink & Pas, 2008), as well as the Scholastic Comix series for middle-school students (for resources, see *Comixology.com*, *wikihow.com/Make-a-Comic*, and *graphicnovelresources.blogspot.com*).

Students can also use comics for responding to texts. For example, for responding to *The Outsiders* (Hinton, 2006), 8th-grade students employed Comic Life to portray conflicts between the Socs and the Greasers (Wissman & Costello, 2014). Students in Elizabeth Erdmann's classes created their autobiographical memoirs using Comic Life based on reading autobiographical texts. They visually portrayed certain events in their lives using photos, speech bubbles, and written captions about those events (for the unit: *goo.gl/qpGRJe*) (Beach et al., 2021).

Activity: Creating Multimodal/Digital Narratives

You can develop some activities for students creating multimodal/digital narratives that may include digital video stories based on animated characters or actual live persons. Students could also create comics/graphic novels based on their autobiographical experiences or characters from novels, movies, or television shows. For example, they could create comics/graphic novels about their school, sports, or extra-curricular worlds portraying events that impacted their development over time.

WRITING AND ENACTING DRAMA

Based on their experiences in responding to drama and dramatic inquiry as described in Chapter 4, students can also create drama scripts for skits or plays to be performed within their classes or school (for resources on writing drama scripts, see *goo.gl/7dMMBP*). In writing drama scripts, students portray tensions between their articulated values and their actions, leading to the critique of the systemic, structural forces shaping their decisions (Iverson & Filipan, 2011).

To assist students in devising scripts, you can draw on their experiences with dramatic inquiry activities. You can create imagined "what-if" situations or dilemmas in which students adopt roles and attempt to address problems or challenges created by the teacher, described in Chapter 4 (Edmiston, 2014).

In his use of informal "dramatic inquiry" activities, Brian Edmiston (2014), engages students in addressing challenges, for example, setting up an organization to assist homeless people on the street to find food or shelter. As the activity unfolds, he then poses further complications requiring students to revise and adopt alternative strategies. For example, as members of this organization interact with a homeless person, what do they do when they find that a homeless person who is mentally ill has difficulty understanding the student offering assistance. Edmiston notes that: "Over time, inquiry opens up meaning to new possibilities as inquirers learn from and with one another in ongoing, authentic, substantive, polyphonic, dialogic conversations focused on implicit or explicit inquiry questions" (p. 40).

For example, 8th-grade students engaged in teams to solve a murder that occurred in the school library by taking photos and notes about evidence in the library, as well as examining text messages, fake financial documents, and suspects' fingerprints (Youman, 2018). Based on the evidence they collected, they then formulated a hypothesis as to who committed the murder to share with their English teacher who was assuming the role of police commissioner (Beach & Beauchemin, 2019, p. 146).

You can also insert new information or further complications requiring students to engage in further problem-solving. For example, in an activity in which students are setting up an organization to assist homeless people to find shelter and food, you may insert the complication of how to assist homeless people who are mentally ill who do not comprehend how they are being helped (Edmiston, 2014).

Based on these enactments, students can begin by writing down conversations and explore the move from oral to written language. Fostering students practice with dialogue addressing issues in the community can evolve into student-created theatrical pieces. For example, two 16-year-olds in an East Los Angeles high school interviewed former student activists who walked out of their classes in 1968 to protest the poor conditions of their schools (Tobar, 2011). Drawing on these interviews, they created the script, *2011 Meets 1968*. In the play, the students portrayed these students as arguing with their parents, confronting teachers who assumed that they shouldn't be educating Mexican American students, and being humiliated for speaking Spanish, leading to a two-hour production with professional actors.

In an activity based on *Something about America* (Testa, 2005), in which anti-immigrant protests target a Kosovan girl and her family, students are asked to assume the roles of newspaper reporters writing about protests with anti-immigration slogans: "'This is my America.'" "'But people come to America for freedom.'"/"'Get out of my country.'" "'Maybe your ancestors were immigrants.'"/ "'I am American.'" (Enciso, 2014, p. 186; Beach et al., 2021, p. 193). Students then recorded videos portraying discrimination against immigrants to share with students in another class and created posters about immigration to display in their school hallways.

In a drama production class in a suburban Midwestern high school taught by Sam Tanner (2014), students built their scripts around problems they perceived in their school. One script written by Laura (pseudonym), *High School Musical*, that reframes the school world as a prison in which a warden readily punishes deviant inmates, portrays the application of a "strict father" cultural model (Lakoff, 2016; Tanner, 2014). Both the warden and the prisoners adopt an "incarcerated discourse" of individualized self-degradation and blame for their difficulties as opposed to critiquing public institutions causing these difficulties (Winn, 2010). In her play, the prisoners ultimately challenge the warden's harsh control through resistance.

Laura also drew on the television program, *Jersey Shore*, that portrays tensions between rival gangs—the female "Mean girls" and male gang "Jocks." These gangs are continually fighting for power in the prison and focusing on physical aspects of gender identity, reframing gender roles in school that accentuates gender stereotypes. Laura also employed intertextual links to lyrics to add to *High School Musical*, when Ms. Warden attempts to have the prisoners celebrate a false sense of unity at the end of the play by singing, "We're All In This Together," an ironic comment on the conflicts between the warden/guards and prisoners. Laura noted that "writing the script gave me a more critical eye for the world around me; things that were serious now seem humorous to me."

In *Theater of the Oppressed* (1993) and *Games for Actors and Non-Actors* (2002), Brazilian theater director Augusto Boal has developed dramatic strategies that transform audiences into active participants in the theatrical experience and are perfect for a critical inquiry classroom. One Boal technique, as adapted by teachers, involves having student performers freeze actions, and having the audience (or rest of the class), brainstorm different actions or endings that offer various solutions to real-world social problems, which the students then perform (Boal, 1998).

Engaging in role-playing games (RPGs)

Students can also engage in role-playing games (RPG) in which they assume roles associated with coping with a challenge. Based on their roles, players interact with each other in a circle or around a table to verbally narrate their actions to reflect on the success or failure of those actions to cope with the challenge. For example, associated with a youth participatory action research (YPAR) project related to addressing issues of social equity and justice when playing the RPG *Dungeons & Dragons* (D&D) game, high school students interacted with each other about how the D&D rules themselves reify certain racist or sexist norms based on reflecting transcripts of their interactions (Jones et al., 2021).

In another RPG, for responding to *The House on Mango Street* (Cisneros, 1991), students addressed the issue of why the characters didn't assume more agency to deal with their problems (Jones et al., 2021). To reflect on the issue of assuming agency, students assumed roles in which they are engaged in medieval quests associated with Arthurian legends related to defeating a "Green Bandit" and protecting a princess. The students then reflected on how their actions did or did not involve assuming agency for achieving success. They then applied their reflections to respond to the characters' actions in *The House on Mango Street*.

Using tableaux or pantomime focus on embodied actions

In writing scripts, students also portray emotions of sadness, anger, fear, surprise, disgust, joy, envy, love, sadness, etc., as enacted through characters' embodied actions/gestures or facial expressions. Students understand the centrality of emotions as actions through participating in tableaux or pantomime activities that revolve solely around the use of embodied actions. For example, students could view drama films by turning off the sound to identify how certain embodied actions convey certain meanings, for example, maintaining physical distance related to a sense of detachment or withdrawal.

Students could also participate in tableau and pantomime sculpting activities. Students pair up with one student being the sculptor who positions the other student's body to convey certain meanings; for example, holding up arms as an expression of joy or placing hands on one's eyes as an expression of grief or sadness (Macro, 2019).

Eighth-grade students formed an inner circle as the "clay" figures while students in the outer circle acted as the sculptors who serve as models by adopting certain physical gestures as their teacher reads aloud students writing in response to *Diary of a Young Girl* (Frank, 2012; Chisholm & Whitmore, 2018). Students then freeze the poses of the students in the inner circle as sculptures as other students describe the meaning of these sculptures as representing certain meanings in response to *Diary*. In doing so, the students infer "how others use their bodies to respond to the meanings of the diary entries; students perceive their bodies as powerful texts in themselves" (Chisholm & Whitmore, 2018, p. 47).

Through this activity, students are thinking about how their peers' certain embodied actions imply certain meanings/emotions related to understanding the characters' actions. For example, a student in the outer circle assuming the role of Anne Frank may enact a stance of someone who is bent over as someone who is trying to hide from being discovered by Nazi soldiers that the "clay" student in the inner circle may then mirror. For example, in response to students' written response to *Diary*, "when we are changing from one place to another, those are the times when we really need to hold tight to who we really are. You can't move if you are lost," David, as "sculpture," grabs his chin to look away into the future and has Arianna as the "clay" figure mirror this action, along with placing her hand over her heart, followed by then freezing her as a sculpture. The sculptures and other students then move around the sculptures, describing their perceptions of the meaning of their embodied actions (Chisholm & Whitmore, 2018, p. 46). Through these sculpting activities, students are learning to appreciate the importance of enacting embodied, nonverbal actions for portraying characters' attitudes and emotions as central to engaging in drama activities.

Using improvisation to experience open-ended interactions

Given the centrality of emotions and embodied as actions shaping drama, it is also useful to engage students in improvisation drama activities as a means of enacting these emotions or embodied actions. In these improv activities, students engage in unfolding, indeterminate, and inventive interactions that build on each other's novel utterances based on the practice of "Yes, and . . . ." Improv unfolds in unpredictable ways, requiring participants to be continually attuned to each other's utterances, emotions, and embodied actions. In doing so, they "accept and add to offers made during the improv. This is the idea that everything that happens in an improvised scene must be accepted, affirmed, and added onto" (Tanner et al., 2020, p. 239). Through engaging in improv, teachers and students are attending and building on each other to create a classroom space that is "more about ways of being together, an ethos" (p. 251).

Julie Blaha, a teacher in the Anoka-Hennepin Minnesota School District, employs a "spacewalk" activity where students walked around in the classroom practicing connecting with students nonverbally (Beach et al., 2015). So, "'The next day at school, walking down the hallway, I noticed students smiling at me,'" she says. "'I was communicating that I noticed them'" (p. 102). She also recognizes that when students insult each other, they are actually attempting to fit in with their peers: "'It's giving people the ability to be funny with you versus against you,'" she explains. "'Not everyone has to laugh but no one can cry. Think about that in the classroom. If we could make people feel comfortable and feel welcomed?'" (p. 102).

Teachers in a methods course on improvisation devoted two hours in each class session engaging in improv interactions, followed by inferring implications for their teaching (Carter-Stone et al., 2021). They often focused on how improv practices are related to engaging open-ended dialogic teaching through attunement to emotions and embodied actions.

This course suggests the value of PTs in methods courses engaging in improv activities associated with potentially positive or challenging classroom events that could occur in practicum or student teaching. For example, PTs could engage in improv related to ways of building on students' high level of engagement versus a lack of interest in an activity requiring spontaneous reactions.

Students could also participate in "cyberdrama" activities based on uses of texting, email, online discussion, websites, or digital videos for communicating before, during, or after a drama activity (Davis, 2011). For example, groups of students in one activity receive an email indicating that they were selected to be immortal, requiring that they collaboratively create a response using a blog post and video to create a character who must decide whether they accept the invitation to be immortal. The groups then were asked to create a news or current affairs story involving their character or other related characters. They then engaged in a large-group role-play that was videotaped where the teacher and another adult interview students to request assistance in locating the immortal characters, who themselves are posting video clips about their experiences of being immortal.

> **Activity: Engaging Students in Drama Activities**
>
> Based on their responses to literature or movies/videos, you can create role-play or improv activities related to engaging students in critical inquiry about certain issues or topics. For example, in studying issues of racial tensions portrayed in a novel that students are reading, you can create a situation associated with students of color in a school receiving higher numbers of suspensions than White students. Students would assume roles of administrators, teachers, students, parents, community members, and law enforcement personnel who voice competing perspectives on this issue, leading to determining whether or not these suspensions were justified and whether administrators need to change their policies on suspensions.

WRITING AND PERFORMING POETRY

Students can write poems based on a range of different poetic forms or genres: haiku, lyrics, sonnets, ballads, graffiti, or spoken-word poetry. Students are most likely to engage in writing poetry when they can then perform poetry, particularly given their interest in hip-hop and rap (Alim, 2006).

Students may be more willing to write or perform poems about their everyday, familiar experiences. In recommending the poetry collection, *Love from the Vortex and Other Poems* (Sealy-Ruiz, 2020a), David Lennington (2021) noted that many of the poems in the book portray relationships. He described how the poet portrays her experience with six different relationships, something that would appeal to adolescents, given how they will also experience relationships that begin and end. He also notes how the poet uses language in her poems that are "easy in that they allow ready access to thinking about their complication" (p. 104), quoting lines from the poet's poem, "Motorcycle Rain" (Sealy-Ruiz, 2020b, p. 123):

> Your love is like the rain;
> it cleanses me.
> Your water clarifies the work of
> The sun—and
> the sun always returns.

Given that poetry often adheres to certain set forms or rules, students may benefit from exploring tensions related to both adhering to and violating those set forms or rules in performing and writing poems (Garvoille, 2021). Students can respond to different poetry types/genres such as a found poem that "allows poets to make order from a random or meaningless world." Haiku "portrays a moment in time with an unexpected lift." Sonnet that "explores a problem or contradiction the poet wants to reason through." Spoken word that "allows for an exploration of sound devices, punning, expressive emotion" (p. 33).

One popular poetry form is the "where I'm from" autobiographical poem in which students recall specific aspects of their upbringing (Christensen, 2009). Students write poems about who they were "raised by," about activities they were involved in at certain ages, about the people they view as their community, and about how they can heal the pain in their lives. The poems are shared in "read-arounds" where students sit in a circle, and, as students finish reading, the others write positive comments about their fellow student's work on strips of paper and share their comments with the author.

One benefit of having students write poetry is that students need to think about their use of syntax and usage in selecting words to convey their meanings. For example, students can create "cut-up poetry" by drawing on language from different sources related to thinking about the uses of different types of language (Simmons, 2014). For teaching about the use of syntax in poetry, students can identify the use of verbs to portray activity and movement; for example, use of verbs in the poem "Poem for Magic," Troupe's (1996) *tinyurl.com/orr6x46* that includes verbs portraying watching basketball, leading to students writing their own poems portraying movement (Christensen, 2009; Beach et al., 2021).

Performing poetry

Through performing poetry, students physically perform particular interpretations of poems through the use of pitch, alliteration, assonance, rhythm, metaphor, pauses, emphasis, sounds, and alternating voices. This requires that they reflect on the meaning of a poem to envision and rehearse how they will convey that meaning through their performance.

Students can perform poems by reading them aloud to convey certain meanings of words in poems. To do so, they can underline certain words to say them louder or insert vertical lines to add pauses (O'Connor, 2004). For effective examples of performing poems, they can also listen to The Slowdown podcast *schooledthepodcast.com* produced by the former US Poet Laureate, Tracy K. Smith (O'Connor, 2021).

Because students may be apprehensive about publicly reading aloud their work to their peers, it is important to address students' potential fears. In describing one poetry-performance community, Korina Jocson (2007) noted that mentors in helping students practice their performances shared their own fears about public performances by performing:

> different scenarios such as reading too fast or too slowly, reading while chewing gum, reading behind a piece of paper or book, reading while fidgeting or playing with one's hair, among others. [The mentors] reminded students what the most important aspect in the whole public reading experience was—to own their words, deliver them with an air of confidence, and have fun with them.
> (p. 145)

Students may also use their poetry to voice their opinions about ways to improve their school. Valerie Kinloch (2005) cites the example of a student, Jackie, who described how writing a poem involved use of writing to portray her thoughts and feelings, given how

> "writing is a means of expression/Expression is a way to get and remain/in conversation with oneself/It is,/in fact,/a way to be sane in a world of terror, greed, and war/But is it really democratic/to speak of writing, expression, terror, greed, and war/at the same time? Do I/have a right/ to speak?"
>
> After reading her writing, I asked Jackie to share it with the class, and she did. The results were amazing: one student, using his Spanish language before translating his ideas into English, said he feels the same way—not poor and not disadvantaged, but afraid. Someone else talked about his brother being unfairly tracked in slow paced classrooms; another student raised the issue of power and access; a final student asked the student near the back of the room what his name was—she had forgotten it, marked him as invisible, but now wanted to know, to remember.
> (p. 109)

Positioning students as agents of change requires listening to students' expression of their honest opinions and then demonstrating a commitment to addressing problems identified by students. Freire (1968) argued that this requires a shift in power relationships between teachers and students, so that students believe that they actually have the power to recommend changes.

Creating and performing spoken word/rap poetry

Given the popularity of spoken word/rap poetry, students may also write or employ spoken word/rap poetry as a form of social action or protest to engage audiences to address certain issues in their community.

An important source for spoken word performance is hip-hop culture constituting certain identities, performance, dress, languages, attitudes, and stances, particularly for African-American students (Alim, 2006; Chang, 2007). Rather than marginalize the expression of hip-hop culture in the classroom, it is important that teachers be open to capitalizing on the multiple literacies involved in hip-hop practices. By drawing on these practices, students create lyrics and performance practices for creating spoken word poetry (Jocson, 2007). They can employ spoken-word poetry or engage in poetry slams to express their concerns about social issues in their lives.

Students can study examples of rap and spoken-word poetry on sites such as Youth Speaks, Urban Word, Poetry Slam, Inc., e-Poets Network, DefPoetry series on HBO, or Poetic License. They can also access numerous poetry journals that include spoken-word performances and examples on YouTube. They can also study examples of connections between canonical poems and contemporary spoken word/hip-hop texts, for example, Walt Whitman's "Oh me, Oh Life" and Public Enemy's "Don't Believe the Hype" (Morrell & Duncan-Andrade, 2005).

In describing her experience as a student teacher in Rebecca Oberg's class when they engaged in a poetry-slam event, Natalie Pederson noted how when the students performed their poems:

> You feel that emotion and for students to see that done well makes them feel a lot more confident in their ability to do it . . . So it got them thinking deeply about how their gestures would make these words more powerful or could make them less powerful. I had students literally coming up to me saying like this hand or this hand, which worked better for that, and I'm like, oh my gosh, that's like, just the fact that you're being careful . . . So, for some students, it was a really great opportunity to learn the power of this kinesthetic movement and how words and movement come together to make something even more powerful.
>
> (Beach & Beauchemin, 2019, p. 155)

Creating digital poetry

Students can also create digital poems based on reading examples of digital poems on sites such as PowerPoetry, *www.powerpoetry.org*; the Electronic Literature Association collections, *collection.eliterature.org/1* and *collection.eliterature.org/2*; PBS Poetry Everywhere, *tinyurl.com/cpa299*; the Electronic Poetry Center, *epc.buffalo.edu/e-poetry/e-authors.html*; or Moving Poems poetry videos, *movingpoems.com*.

Students created multimodal poems by combining images, audio, and connections to other texts to create video productions of their poems (Curwood & Cowell, 2011). To do so, they reflected on the following questions:

- What visual images does each line of the poem bring to mind?
- What role might different colors or artistic styles play in enhancing the message?
- What motion or transitions support the mood of the piece?
- What musical genres may lend greater emotional impact to the piece?

(p. 118)

They can also share their poetry on social media platforms, as did adolescents using Instagram (Kovalik & Curwood, 2019).

Students can record their own performances using Garageband or Audacity, or employ tools such iMovie or Voicethread *www.voicethread.com* to create digital poetry that combines audio with images or video. When students are writing, particularly at the editing phase, they may be internally listening to enactment of "how it sounds." (For more on writing poetry, see *Writing poetry* on the website.)

SUMMARY

This chapter described methods for fostering students' writing narratives, including autobiographical narratives and digital stories, drama, and poetry. We emphasized the importance of creating engaging rhetorical contexts to foster critical inquiry and providing students with a sense of purpose and concern for their audience.

REFERENCES

Alim, H. S. (2006). *Roc the mic right: The language of hip hop culture*. Routledge.
Angelou, M. (1969). *I know why the caged bird sings*. Bantam Books.
Angelou, M. (2009). *I know why the caged bird sings*. Ballentine.
Bakhtin, M. M. (1981). *The dialogic imagination: Four essays* (Ed. M. Holquist, trans. C. Emerson). University of Texas Press.
Beach, R., Appleman, D., Fecho, B., & Simon, R. (2021). *Teaching literature to adolescents*, 4th ed. Routledge.
Beach, R., & Beauchemin, F. (2019). *Teaching language as action in the ELA classroom*. Routledge.
Beach, R., Johnston, A., & Thein, A. H. (2015). *Identity-focused ELA teaching: A curriculum framework for diverse learners and contexts*. Routledge.
Bitz, M. (2010). *When commas meet Kryptonite: Lessons from the comic book project*. Teachers College Press.
Boal, A. (1998). *Legislative theatre: Using performance to make politics*. Routledge.
Byrne, R. (2014, May 9). 7 web-based tools for creating short video stories [Web log post]. http://tinyurl.com/khfbj22
Canady, F., Martin, K., & Scott, C. E. (2018). "Song of Myself": A digital unit of study remix. In J. S. Dail, S. Witte, & S. T. Bickmore (Eds.), *Toward a more visual literacy: Shifting the paradigm with digital tools and young adult literature* (pp. 101–118). Rowman & Littlefield.
Carter-Stone, L., Meston, H., & Galloway, E.P. (2021). Yes-and-ing teacher and student talk: exploring the affordances of dramatic improvisation to support dialogic teaching. Paper presented at the annual meeting of the American Educational Research Association.
Chang, J. (Ed.). (2007). *Total chaos: The art and aesthetics of hip-hop*. Basic Civitas Books.
Chisholm, J. S., & Whitmore, K. F. (2018). *Reading challenging texts: Layering literacies through the arts*. National Council of Teachers of English.
Christensen, L. (2009). *Teaching for joy and justice*. Rethinking Schools.
Cisneros, S. (1991). *The house on Mango Street*. Vintage.
Coates, T-A. (2015). *Between the world and me*. One World.
Collins, S. (2008). *The hunger games*. Scholastic Press.
Common Core Standards. (2010). Common Core State Standards for English language arts & literacy in history/social studies, science, and technical subjects. Council of Chief State School Officers and the National Governors Association.
Curwood, J. S., & Cowell, L. L. H. (2011). iPoetry: Creating space for new literacies in the English curriculum. *Journal of Adolescent & Adult Literacy, 55*(2), 110–120.
Davis, S. (2011). Digital drama: Toolkits, dilemmas, and preferences. *Youth Theatre Journal, 25*(2), 103–119.
Edmiston, B. (2014). *Transforming teaching and learning with active and dramatic approaches: Engaging students across the curriculum*. Routledge.
Ehrenreich, B. (2010). *Nickel and dimed: On (not) getting by in America*. Metropolitan Books.
Enciso, P. (2014). Prolepsis and educational change: Interrupting inequities through drama. In S. Davis, H. G. Clemson, B. Ferholt, S-M. Jansson, & A. Marjanovic-Shane (Eds.), *Dramatic interactions in education: Vygotskian and sociocultural approaches to drama, education, and research* (pp. 171–188). Bloomsbury Academic.
Ford, C. (2019, November 29). *Build your stack: Memoir and reading choice*. National Council of Teachers of English. Retrieved from http://bit.ly/366wlwp
Frank, A. (2012). *Diary of a young girl*. Viking.
Freire, P. (1968). *Pedagogy of the oppressed*. Seabury Press.
Garvoille, A. (2021). Break the rules, already! Opening up closed form poetry. *English Journal, 110*(5), 27–35.
Haynes-Moore, S. (2015). Trading spaces: An educator's ethnographic exploration of adolescents' digital role-play. *Journal of Language and Literacy Education, 11*(1). Retrieved from http://jolle.coe.uga.edu
Hinton, S. E. (2006). *The outsiders*. Speak.
Iverson, S. V., & Filipan, R. S. (2011). Scripting success: Using dialogue writing to help students find their voice. In J. K. Dowdy and S. Kaplan (Eds.), *Teaching drama in the classroom* (pp. 123–129). Sense.
Jocson, K. (2007). *Urban youth as poets: Empowering literacies in/outside of schools*. Peter Lang.
Jones, K., Storm, S., Castillo, J., & Karbachinskiy, S. (2021). Chasing new worlds: Stories of roleplaying in classroom spaces. *Journal of Language and Literacy Education, 17*(1), 1–17.
Kinloch, V. (2005). Poetry, literacy, and creativity: Fostering effective learning strategies in an urban classroom. *English Education, 37*(2), 96–114.
Kovalik, K., & Curwood, JS (2019). #poetryisnotdead: Understanding Instagram poetry within a transliteracies framework. *Literacy, 53*(4), 185–195.
Kuklin, L. (2019). *We are here to stay: Voices of undocumented young adults*. Candlewick Press.
Labov, W. (1972). *The language of the inner city*. University of Pennsylvania Press.
Lakoff, G. (2016). *Moral politics: How liberals and conservatives think*, 3rd ed. University of Chicago Press.

Lambert, J. (2012). *Digital storytelling: Capturing lives, creating community*, 4th ed. Routledge.
Lennington, D. (2021). Saying the unsayable and making poetry legible. *English Journal, 110*(5), 103–105.
Lewis, W., & Flynn, J. E. (2014, November 15). Using digital tools to tell and understand stories. Presentation at the annual meeting of the National Council of Teachers of English, Washington, DC.
Macro, K. J. (2019). Integrating drama: An embodied pedagogy. In K. J. Macro & M. Zoss (Eds.), *A symphony of possibilities: A handbook for arts integration in secondary English language arts* (pp. 65-78). National Council of Teachers of English.
Marlatt, R. (2019). This is my story: Preservice English teachers create welcome videos to navigate the places and spaces of their literacy lives. *Contemporary Issues in Technology & Teacher Education, 19*(2), 129–155. Retrieved from https://tinyurl.com/y8h2u7ze
Morrell, E., & Duncan-Andrade, J. (2005). Popular culture and critical media pedagogy in secondary literacy classrooms. *International Journal of Learning, 12*(9), 273–280.
O'Connor, J. S. (2004). *Wordplaygrounds: Reading, writing, and performing poetry in the English classroom*. National Council of Teachers of English.
O'Connor, J. (2021). Waking up with The Slowdown: Daily poetry in the classroom. *English Journal, 110*(5), 20–26.
Ohler, J. B. (2013). *Digital storytelling in the classroom: New media pathways literacy, learning, and creativity*, 2nd ed. Corwin.
Pandya, J. Z. (2014). Towards critical participatory literacies through digital video composition in an elementary literacy capstone course. In J. Brass & A. Webb (Eds.), *Reclaiming English language arts methods courses: Critical issues and challenges for teacher educators in top-down times* (pp. 40–53). Routledge.
Pink, D. H., & Pas, R. T. (2008). *The adventures of Johnny Bunko: The last career guide you'll ever need*. Riverhead Trade.
Pillinger, K. 2014/2016). *For inanimate Alice: The last gas station*. Bradfield.
Pope, R. (2006). *Textual intervention: Critical and creative strategies for literacy studies*. Routledge.
Rozema, R., & Webb, A. (2008). *Literature and the Web: Reading and responding with new technologies*. Heinemann.
Rymes, B. (2001). *Conversational borderlands: Language and identity in an alternative suburban high school*. Teachers College Press.
Sealy-Ruiz, Y. (2020a). *Love from the Vortex and other poems*. Kaleidoscope Vibrations.
Sealy-Ruiz, Y. (2020b). "Motorcycle Rain." In Y. Sealy-Ruiz, *Love from the Vorte and other poems* (p. 123). Kaleidoscope Vibrations.
Satpari, M. (2004). *Persepolis: The story of a childhood*. Pantheon.
Simmons, A. (2014, April 8). Why teaching poetry is so important. *The Atlantic*. Retrieved from http://tinyurl.com/ohap655
Spiegelman, A. (1986). *Maus I. A survivor's tale*. Pantheon.
Spiegelman, A. (1991). *Maus II. A survivor's tale*. Pantheon.
Tanner, S. J. (2014). A youth participatory action research (YPAR), theatrical inquiry into whiteness. Unpublished Doctoral Dissertation, University of Minnesota.
Tanner, S. J., Leander, K. M., & Carter-Stone, L. (2020). Ways with worlds: Bringing improvisational theater into play with reading. *Reading Research Quarterly, 56*(2), 237–252.
Testa, M. (2005). *Something about America*. Candlewick.
Tobar, H. (2011, March 8). Learning the power of art to uplift, inspire. *The Los Angeles Times*. Retrieved from http://tinyurl.com/la9qd3s
Troupe, Q. (1996). Poem for magic. In *Avalanche* (pp. 40–42). Coffee House Press.
Winn, M. T. (2010). "Betwixt and between": Literacy, liminality, and the celling of Black girls. *Race Ethnicity and Education, 13*(4), 425–447.
Wissman, K. K., & Costello, S. (2014). Creating digital comics in response to literature: Linking the arts, aesthetic transactions, and meaning-making. *Language Arts, 92*(2), 103–117.
Yang, G. L. (2008). *American born Chinese*. Square Fish.
Youman, K. (2018, August 21). Killer lesson: Olentangy students use evidence to determine whodunit. [Web log post]. Retrieved from https://goo.gl/bqaymC

8

Implementing Digital/Media Literacy Standards

One of the major developments in teaching ELA is the increased focus on using digital/media tools for responding to and creating texts given the increased time that adolescents devote to the consumption of online media/communication and video gaming. 12th graders in 2016 spent an average of six hours a day, twice as much time online as in 2006 (Twenge et al., 2019). Another survey indicated that adolescents devote an average of about seven-and-a-half hours daily on their screens, not including screen time for school work (Rideout & Robb, 2019).

Adolescents from lower-income homes devote an average of two hours more screen time than adolescents from higher-income homes, while 63% of all adolescents employ social media "every day." In addition, twice as many adolescents view videos as they did in 2015, averaging an hour a day, while there is also a decline in TV viewing. At the same time, only 10% indicated that they enjoy generating their own digital content (Rideout & Robb, 2019).

This increased use of digital media parallels a decline in print reading, with 60% of 12th graders engaged in the daily reading of a book or magazine in the late 1970s compared to 16% in 2016 (Twenge et al., 2019). Only 32% of adolescents indicate that they had read books for pleasure in the past month, with older adolescents devoting less time than younger adolescents (Rideout & Robb, 2019). In the year prior to the pandemic, 89% of students indicated that they used digital tools a few days a week and 42% want to use them more often, with 85% of teachers and 96% of principals supporting the increased use of digital tools (Calderon & Carlson, 2019).

LIMITATIONS OF STANDARDS RELATED TO DIGITAL/MEDIA INSTRUCTION

Given adolescents' extensive use of digital media both outside and in school, there is only minimal focus on the use of digital/media tools in the Common Core Standards (2010) ("use technology, including the Internet, to produce and publish writing and to interact and collaborate with others" p. 41; and "make strategic use of digital media and visual displays of data to express information and enhance understanding of presentations" p. 48).

DOI: 10.4324/9781003177364-10

The CCSS do refer to these digital and media literacies in grades 6–12 (Common Core Standards, 2010):

- reading standard, "Integrate and evaluate content presented in diverse formats and media, including visually and quantitatively, as well as in words." (p. 35)
- writing standard, "Use technology, including the Internet, to produce and publish writing and to interact and collaborate with others." (p. 41)
- speaking/listening standard, "Make strategic use of digital media and visual displays of data to express information and enhance understanding of presentations." (p. 48)

However, there is then little focus on comprehending multimodal texts through images, sound, and color (Brauer, 2018). Teaching about popular/social media texts based on graphic images or emotions is often marginalized based on the assumption that "'if a message uses simple language or activates strong emotions or attacks enemies, it is not worth bringing into the classroom'" (Collopy, 2021, p. 11).

As a result, preservice students engaged in imaginative uses of digital story writing and gaming tools were still concerned in their student teaching about how these activities may not be consistent with a focus on achieving traditional literacy standards related to preparing students for mandated standardized tests (Mirra, 2019). One preservice teacher noted that students may express the concern that "'I don't know how to write the essay because you didn't show me how to write an essay; you showed me how to make a video'" (p. 282).

As noted in Chapter 1, the NCTE standards go beyond the CCSS digital media standards to emphasize the importance of students actively engaging in responding to and creating digital texts as evident in their standard: "Candidates apply and demonstrate knowledge of learning processes that involve individually, collaboratively, and critically accessing, consuming, curating, and creating texts (e.g., print, digital, media) (National Council of Teachers of English, 2021, p. 1).

LIMITATIONS OF INSTRUCTIONAL USES OF DIGITAL MEDIA/TOOLS

One of the underlying assumptions related to the use of digital/media tools in the classroom is whether it will transform and democratize instruction, particularly from the perspectives of technology corporations prompting their technology tools. However, one limitation of this assumption is that it fails to acknowledge that the disparity between the access and use of technology tools in upper-income families and schools with students from those families may increase the disparities between upper-and-lower-income students (Reich, 2020).

Underlying this assumption is a neoliberal belief that acquiring use of technology skills is essential for achieving economic success in a knowledge economy. The belief is that students need "21st-century skills" related to "creativity, communication, collaboration, and critical thinking (Partnership for 21st Century Learning, 2016)" as promoted by business, education, and governments, as well as articulated in the Common Core State Standards (National Governors Association, 2010; Mirra, 2019, p. 264).

This focus on a "21st-century skills" model posits how technology tools enhance instruction based on an individualistic, neoliberal focus on schooling to prepare students for the free market as opposed to a focus on digital media for engaging in addressing societal problems through civic engagement (Garcia & Mirra, 2019). "In sum, the Common Core ignores the economic, regulatory, and technological contexts in which all texts are created, limiting student questions about text production, access, industry, and equity" (Brauer, 2018, p. 635).

ADOPTING A "CONNECTED LEARNING" FRAMEWORK

An alternative "connected learning" framework (Garcia, 2014) "advocates the use of new media to broaden student access to experiences that are interest-driven, peer-supported, and academically-oriented" (Ito et al., 2013). This framework "refers to the transformation that occurs when academic learning is linked to the rich, overlapping ecologies of students' lives and fosters personal and social transformation" (Mirra, 2019, p. 264).

A "connected learning" framework has been essential for thinking about the increased focus on hybrid online learning during the pandemic, when teachers and students increased their use of online learning tools such as Zoom, Microsoft Meets, Skype Meet Now, Cisco Jabber, Google Meet, TeamViewer, Vimeo Live, Adobe Connect, etc. The use of these tools can "more easily link home, school, community, and peer contexts of learning; support peer and intergenerational connections based on shared interests; and create more connections with non-dominant youth, drawing from capacities of diverse communities" (Mirra, 2019, p. 264). In addition, these tools involve using alternative instruction that differs from face-to-face instruction (Karchmer-Klein, 2020; Warnock & Gasiewski, 2018.

Teachers can also organize their instruction and submission of student work using Google Classroom, Canvas LMS, Bridge, Moodle, Absorb, SuccessNet Plus, Thinkific, LearnWorlds, Schoology, Blackboard, Desire2Learn, etc. Teachers report most frequently employing Google Classroom, Canvas, and Moodle as learning management systems (LMSs) (Vega & Robb, 2020) (for a ranking of the most popular digital instructional tools for 2021, see *www.top tools4learning.com/ed150*).

At the same time, a survey of students ages 14–18 in Massachusetts during the pandemic found that 50% still prefer to learn face-to-face; 34% prefer hybrid remote/in-person learning; and only 16% prefer remote learning (Crabtree, 2021). Students in lower-income families were more likely to be learning remotely despite the lack of high-speed internet connections in their homes

Moreover, 12% of teachers indicated that their students lacked home online access, particularly for students in Title I and/or diverse schools (Vega & Robb, 2020). This suggests the need to recognize the need for equity in online instruction based on more inclusive practices so that students from non-dominant families are not disadvantaged by a lack of connections or knowledge of digital tools (Kelly & Zakrajsek, 2020).

For providing online or hybrid instruction using digital practices, it's important to distinguish between practices constituting effective online instruction from practices for face-to-face instruction. You can enhance online instruction by establishing your online physical presence through creating a video about yourself; responding promptly to students' emails/messages; being a participant in online discussions; using breakout rooms for small-group discussions; posting weekly topics; creating partners for students to share their work, including videos of guest lectures; and making sure that you are available online based on virtual office hours (Darby, 2019; Flaherty, 2020),

STUDENTS' USE OF SOCIAL MEDIA/YOUTUBE

Another major shift in adolescents' use of digital media involves a shift in their preferred social media platforms, with Snapchat, YouTube, and Instagram being the most popular online platforms rather than Facebook (Anderson & Jiang, 2018). One-third of social media users (36%) say they have used social media sites in the past month to voice their support for a cause. They also look up information about rallies or protests happening in their area (35%) or encourage others to take action on issues they regard as important (32%), with Latinx and Black users being more likely to do so (Auxier, 2020). While adolescents gain much from being online, this daily use of screen time can lead to a habitual dependency on social media. They, therefore, need to reflect how and why they are using social media through resources available from the LiveMoreScreenLessTM organization *www.livemorescreenless.org*.

Effects of social uses of social media

Research on adolescents' use of social media finds that those adolescents who spend less time interacting face-to-face due to dependency on social media report being less happy (Twenge, 2017). In addition, undisclosed research by Facebook found that adolescent females' use of its Instagram platform causes adverse mental health issues based on their perceptions of themselves (Wells et al., 2021).

You may assume that consistent with the connection model, participation on social media may connect people. However, people may also become housed within their media bubbles, resulting in a lack of exposure to alterative perspectives. For example, a study found that when Twitter users who identified as Democrats or Republicans were asked to follow prominent members of the opposite party, rather than becoming more considerate of their alternative perspectives, these users actually became more entrenched in their positions, with liberals becoming more liberal and conservatives becoming more conservative (Goldberg, 2021). As a result, users' alignment within their media bubbles only increased, a reflection of the lack of interaction between people due to their political perspectives.

At the same time, other research finds that despite concerns about the negative effects of social media, 31% of adolescents believe that social media has positive effects; 24%, negative effects; and 45%, neither positive nor negative effects (Anderson & Jiang, 2018). Online sharing with peers also serves as an outlet or "relief valve" from the pressures of schoolwork (boyd, 2016). An analysis of the relationships between adolescents' amount of social media, device use, and TV viewing and their experience of depression, behavioral issues, and suicidal tendencies found no difference in these relationships from 2010 to 2019 (Vuorre et al., 2021).

Pedagogical uses of online media

You can have students interact online for pedagogical purposes using Twitter, Instagram, Snapchat, TikTok, or Facebook (using a private class account). For example, two middle school ELA teachers, Michelle Falter *@michellefalter* and Michell Forbes *@toocoolformiddleschool* employ Instagram for sharing teaching ideas (Falter & Forbes, 2020). In addition, students can access the YA Authors Twitter list, *tinyurl.com/y9v49euv* for interacting with YA authors (Ferlazzo, 2019). For interacting on Twitter, students benefited from the teachers and their use of hashtags to determine topics and themes in their subjects and themes in ways that focused their discussion (Loomis, 2018).

Fostering middle-school students' supportive online interaction in small groups in the classroom involves use of supportive synchronous or synchronous comments to blog posts leading to sharing of comments in response to videos using Padlet *padlet.com* or Video-Ant *ant.umn.edu*. (Ciccone, 2019). Students identified these practices as supportive of productive interactions—they need to

- Be respectful of others' opinions
- Disagree with ideas and not make it personal
- Represent a give and take of ideas
- Take the other person's ideas seriously
- Build on the original post's ideas
- Be on topic
- Not be anonymous
- Distribute comments equally amongst posts
- Bring together multiple perspectives
- Seem to anticipate/consider the feelings and potential responses of others (Ciccone, 2019, p. 175).

Activity: Students' Perceptions of Using Social Media

You can have students discuss the degree to which they perceive their interactions on social media as enacting authentic relations with others, particularly with little or no face-to-face interactions. They can cite instances in which posts served as building support versus problematic posts that contain misinformation. For example, Aubrey created a digital comic portraying positive and negative aspects of her use of social media. In her comic, the narrator holds up emoji masks indexing positive versus negative experiences using social media. She concludes her digital comic by portraying herself as an avatar from the video game Skyrim, with the statement, "'I feel like when I'm in a game, it's like I want to be that person in the game, so I should be who I am'" (Canady et al., 2020, p. 12).

USING DIGITAL TOOLS FOR RESPONDING TO TEXTS

As noted in Chapters 4 and 5 on responding to texts, you can have students employ a range of digital tools to respond to texts in ways beyond simply writing essays or talking about texts.

Sharing online responses to texts

To have students interact with students in another school for responding to the same text, you can have students share responses on Zoom, *zoom.us*; Microsoft Teams, *tinyurl.com/y9xmp7yx*; or Web room, *webroom.net*; or, for synchronous interactions, on Padlet, *padlet.com*; or Flipgrid, *flipgrid.com* (Ferlazzo, 2019).

Students can also share their thoughts or questions during a discussion with an entire class using backchannel tools such as Backchannel Chat *backchannelchat.com* or the Collaborate feature of Nearpod *nearpod.com* as well as a screencasting tool such as Explain Everything *explaineverything.com/* (Burns, 2017).

Students can also share their responses to texts in online book club discussions (Colwell et al., 2018). In responding to *Delirium* (Oliver, 2016) in an online discussion, a student responded that "'It was so touching that I actually cried when Alex was shot [in *Delirium*]. It was like killing of [*sic*] Peeta (from the *Hunger Games*) or Edward (from *Twilight*)'" (Colwell et al., 2018, p. 235). Students also posed questions, for example, "'I like *Delirium*, because it creates a world in the future so different from ours. . . . This is an interesting world . . ., but it's not a world I'd want to live in. Would you want to live in this world?'" (Colwell et al., 2018, p. 236).

Use of digital annotations

As noted in Chapter 5 and 6, students can also collaboratively share their responses to digital texts using digital annotation tools *tinyurl.com/6oqgm2m*. For example, they can employ Diigo Sticky Notes, Evernote, VoiceThread, iAnnotate, A.nnotate, or Viewbiz; A.nnotate, AnnotDoc Lite, or WebNotes iOS apps; or Adobe Reader, iAnnotate pdf, or PDF Annotation Android apps.

They can then collaboratively respond to each other's annotations to discuss a specific part of a text. To respond to the e-book version of *All American Boys* (Reynolds & Kiely, 2015), students added written responses, images, and video annotations using Glose.com, *glose.com* to share their responses with peers, who then responded with their own annotations (Kajder, 2018).

One useful tool for having students share and respond to each other's annotations is Diigo Sticky Notes. You can set up an education Diigo account as *www.diigo.com/eduction* that also allows you to share bookmarks to websites with your students. To have students respond to a text, students highlight sections of a text and then add "sticky note" annotations to then respond to each other's annotations to create a discussion about the text.

Use of digital illustrations

You can also have students add digital illustrations or artwork for responding to texts. For responding to Anne Frank's *The Diary of a Young Girl* (Frank, 2012), students added photos to respond to characters' actions in the novel (Chisholm & Whitmore, 2018). For responding to *The Pearl* (Steinbeck, 2000), middle school students created comic images by using cinematic techniques to focus on certain characters' actions (Beach, 2019). One student varied images based on long shots versus close-ups to note that "'this would make a really good movie . . . it wasn't super hard to visualize what some of these scenes look like'" (p. 12).

High school students engaged in a project that combined poetry with comic images to portray their identities as "nerds" (Kersulov & Henze, 2021). Students read examples of comics/graphic novels such as *Maus Volume 1* (Spiegelman, 1992), *Persepolis* (Satrapi, 2000), and *American Born Chinese* (Yang, 2006). Students then wrote poems about their identities and created an inventory of their "nerd identities" to create images that portray those identities in a comic. (For methods for creating comics, see Byrne (2020) *tinyurl.com/y3ofgadn* and *tinyurl.com/wax9zmj*).

Use of hyperlinks

You can also have students add hyperlinks to texts that connect specific words or phrases to websites or PowerPoint slides. For example, for responding to the poem "I, Too," students created hyperlinked connections to "speeches, literature, plays, artwork, famous people, songs, television shows, and video games. Associations with contemporary culture and political issues mediated through multiple modes also fostered personal connections to literature" (Smith, 2019, p. 212). For example, one Black student connected the poem to his writing about his personal experiences as a Black male.

Use of memes and hashtags

Teachers in a YA literature class shared their multimodal responses to YA novels on Google Drive (Smith & Seglem, 2018). Given their critique of the portrayals of adults in YA novels, one group of teachers created the "Y U no" meme (Smith & Seglem, 2018, p. 87) to share with others in the class. Another teacher accessed Tumblr and blogs to discover that many adolescents shared their multimodal responses to YA literature. Preservice teachers in one study taught multimodal/digital poetry within digital/media contexts using Slack to search for and add words or phrases, including the use of hashtags (Jones, 2020).

CREATING MULTIMODAL TEXTS

Students can also create multimodal texts as infographics, posters, or comics based on combining text with images or sound using Adobe Photoshop, Canva, Mediabang Paint, or Piktochart (Jensen, & Shaughnessy, 2021). Students employed Glogster (*eduGlogster* for teachers) to create digital posters to share with audiences on the Glogster website, *www.edu.glogster.com* (Dail & Vásquez, 2018). Students also create multimodal texts using the Instagram Stor tool *about.instagram.com/features/stories* in which they combine images or video clips with texts as a form of snapshots that include just a few words (Valdivia, 2021). For example, a student may create a text about Black Lives Matter protests with images from those protests along with descriptions of participants' messages related to reasons for engaging in protests.

To create remixes of texts, students could examine examples of remixes of Shakespeare's plays. These include the OMG Shakespeare remixes of *Romeo and Juliet*, *Macbeth*, *Hamlet*, and *A Midsummer Night's Dream* (Carbone & Shakespeare, 2015; Falter & Beach, 2018). They can also respond to the novel, *Inanimate Alice inanimatealice.com* (Bradfield Company, 2005–14), in which the main character, Alice, employs technology on her journey to cope with challenges.

Students can then use a tool such as Mozilla Popcorn Maker, *popcorn.webmaker.org* to import texts to create a remixed text. Drawing on images and texts from his own life, Ian O'Byrne (2014) employed Popcorn Maker to create a "Six Word Memoir" (for the assignment *t.ly/1k7D*).

ENGAGING IN INTERACTIVE FICTION VIDEO GAMES

Students also engage in interactive fiction (IF) video games that involve them in making decisions about characters' actions, practices that can then be connected to literary texts students are reading (Batchelor et al., 2021). In teaching ninth-graders, a teacher, Megan, connected her computer to a projector so that students in her class could collaboratively engage in playing video games. For example, students shared their decisions in responding to the IF game, Life Is Strange *t.ly/vBod*, in which a high school senior, Max, had to make her own decisions about relations with her peers. She then had students infer connections between Max and characters in the mystery novel, *And Then There Were None* (Christie, 2011). One student noted that "Making connections between the video game and the book allowed me to understand the deeper concepts of both texts" (p. 97). Other IF games include:

Papers, Please! *t.ly/GTFA*
Walden: A Game *www.waldengame.com*
80 Days *www.inklestudios.com/80days*
Homer's Odyssey t.ly/DYMn
Orwell: Keeping an Eye on You *t.ly/dC68*
Shelley's Frankenstein *www.inklestudios.com/frankenstein/*
Attentat 1942 (about World War II) *attentat1942.com*
Brukel (about a grandmother's memories) *brukelgame.com*
Nancy Drew: Midnight in Salem *t.ly/yUP*
What Remains of Edith Finch? *t.ly/SaVq* (Batchelor et al., 2021).

RESPONDING TO AND PRODUCING VIDEOS

Videos have emerged as a primary digital/media tool for engaging students in the classroom. In a 2019 survey, 60% of teachers employ video streaming services such as YouTube, SchoolTube, or Netflix for use in their instruction (Vega & Robb, 2020). In using videos, it is important to foster students' active engagement in responding to online videos such as YouTube EDU *www.youtube.com/education*, TED Talks, Khan Academy, TeacherTube, BrainPOP Featured Movie, Discovery Channel, Vimeo, Frequency, Snagfilms, Hulu+, PBS Videos, Amazon Instant Video, WatchKnow Educational Videos, Video Science, Video2Brain, Coursera, Udacity, and edX.

For providing online instruction using videos, you can generate videos as short mini-lectures or demonstrations of the use of response techniques or digital production practices to provide students with instruction on these techniques or production practices in your courses. You can employ Flipgrid, *flipgrid.com* (for a guide on the use of Flipgrid, see *tinyurl.com/y28t4q5r*) to create your videos or have students create their videos. Students can also use Google ThreadIt *t.ly/SyqF* for creating videos for sharing based on Google sharing options.

Ian O'Byrne (2015) uses EDpuzzle, *edpuzzle.com*, in his methods courses to create videos of instructional methods in which he adds his oral comments and questions to the videos. He also adds his videos to Vialogues *www.vialogues.com*, as a space for online discussions about videos on their site. For editing videos, you or your students can employ iMovie, WeVideo, VideoEditor, Animoto, Popcorn, Windows Movie Maker, StoryRobe, or other video-editing tools or apps.

Responding to videos

It is also important to foster students' active versus passive responses in viewing videos. To do so, you can have students employ video annotation tools to create annotations to specific content in a video. Students can use VoiceThread *voicethread.com*, VideoAnt *ant.umn.edu*, Educano *www.educanon.com*, Metta *www.metta.io*, or EDpuzzle *edpuzzle.com* to create annotations. For example, in using VideoAnt, students import a video URL into VideoAnt. They then view the video on a screen on the left side and stop their video to insert annotations in a sidebar on the right (for an introduction for using VideoAnt created by Richard, *tinyurl.com/y9srmcn*).

Students can also employ digital think-alouds on their own or with peers for responding to videos of literary texts (Karchmer-Klein, 2020). First, they copy the videos using screen capture tools such as Digital Tool Purpose, Quicktime, Explain Everything, Show Me, Vittle Lite, Screencastif, or Screencast-o-Matic Screen Capture to engage in think-alouds.

Video responses to texts

For sharing their responses to texts, students can create digital book trailers by drawing on Nancy Keane's site, *www.nancykeane.com*; the Digital Booktalk site, *tinyurl.com/ab2ssl*; or Crystal Booth's tutorial on creating book trailers, *www.squidoo.com/booktrailers*. Students in one project "preferred to interpret literature through a multimodal project compared to a written literary analysis essay" (B. Smith, 2019, p. 215).

Students can also create video clips linked to specific events or settings in a text to contextualize the meaning of those events or settings. For responding to the short story "Harrison Bergeron" (Vonnegut, 1961) that portrays a dystopian world of the future, students created video clips that were connected to the historical period of the 1960s related to the Cuban missile crisis (B. Smith, 2019). For responding to the book, *Into the Wild* (Krakauer, 1997), a 12th-grade student created a ten-minute video for sharing with his literature circle as a means of sharing his engagement with the book through portraying connections between the text and his own life (Marlatt, 2019).

Producing videos

For creating videos, students should plan their use of shots and angles through scripts using ScriptWrite, *tinyurl.com/6pnvtxw* and storyboards using Storyboards, *tinyurl.com/852zj9l*.

They can draw on their experience with comics or graphic novels to note the value of employing a range of different shots (close-ups, mid-shots, establishing) to position their viewers in relation to actors/persons or objects. For example, to portray a person as powerful, they may employ an angle shooting up on that person. Or, to portray a person as alone or lost, they may employ a long shot. One incentive for writing scripts for their videos is that students are able to actually experience how their reading aloud of a script where they "'say the stuff instead of write stuff'" leads to further revisions (Pandya, 2021, p. 12). After completing their filming, they can then edit using the previously mentioned editing tools on page 150 to crop shots or add transitions as well as music or soundtracks.

Creating digital stories

Students can also create digital stories using Flipgrid, Instagram, iMovie, Videolicious, Vidify, Imotion HD, Magisto Video Editor, Viddy, Andromedia Video Editor, Director, or Quiki (for resources on creating digital stories *goo.gl/gTjKkv* and *goo.gl/T1YRQc*). Fawn Canady

(2018) had her students create digital stories as nonfiction narratives for publication/submission to the Digital Storymakers Award hosted by Atavist (*atavist.com/examples*; for her description of her use of digital tools in her teaching *goo.gl/jh3ct2*). One Latino student portrays how he deals with the difficulties of coping with stereotypes of himself associated with his low-income neighborhood versus himself as being successful in his school world (Canady et al., 2018).

Students participating in the Compose Our Worlds project (*goo.gl/TBVz4n*) created drawings/posters, artwork, and videos for display in a virtual museum as a means of sharing the results of their projects (Boardman et al., 2021). In creating digital stories based on events in their lives, they interviewed people associated with the event as well as images portraying the event to address the question, "How do authors use time, place, and perspective to tell a compelling story of what happened?"

Middle school students as members of the Imagine the Future project at the University of Miami *imaginefuture.org* worked collaboratively in teams to create digital stories with a focus on issues of environmental sustainability (Smith, B., 2019). Team members included the scriptwriter, director, scientist, and video producer.

Activity: Producing Videos

You can have your students create videos about topics, issues, or themes they are studying in your classes, in some cases, as alternatives to final essays or presentations. Students can then share their videos to audiences beyond the classroom. For example, to respond to portrayals of the climate crisis in cli-fi literature, students could create videos documenting climate change effects in their community, such as droughts on farming or flooding of rivers. (For examples of adolescents' videos about climate change *vimeo.com/youngvoicesfortheplanet/videos* and *www.youtube.com/c/YpteOrgUk/videos*)

AUDIO LISTENING AND RECORDING

Students also listen to and create podcasts, audiobooks, and/or music and record audio files or podcasts such as CNN Student News to gain knowledge of current events related to issues or problems they are studying or podcasts about young adult novels *blog.feedspot.com/young_adult_book_podcasts* or *player.FM/podcasts/Ya-Literature*. Students can also listen to productions by adolescents from the Youth Radio project *https://yr.media* on current issues or topics. They can also create audio responses to literacy texts, using Vocooroo, GarageBand, or videos, as did students in Molly Vanish's students at Washburn High School, Minneapolis for responding to texts (for Molly's modeling responses to texts, see *tinyurl.com/ocse8yf*). They can also create music to add to texts, as did students for responding to *The Odyssey*, *youtu.be/znoN_3Vb1hk* (Blom, 2017).

Producing audio files

Students can create their own audio files and podcasts using Garageband for Mac *tinyurl.com/lemswvx*, iOS Garageband *tinyurl.com/mmkcto3*, Audacity for Windows *tinyurl.com/3jcmr*, or Mac *tinyurl.com/5b8w7*. They can also use Seesaw *web.seesaw.me*, Screencastify *screencastify.*

com, or Flipgrid *info.flipgrid.com* (audio record only), as well as creating a podcast using Anchor *anchor.fm* (Bergman, 2021). Students at South High School in Minneapolis teamed up with members of the local Minnesota Public Radio to create podcast stories about activities involving responses to the killing and upkeep of the memorials at the site of the killing of George Floyd in Minneapolis *t.ly/nDOt*).

Students could record interviews with grandparents and parents as part of a family history project or interview peers or adults about their interests in certain hobbies, topics, issues, or events. The StoryCorps app *https://storycorps.me* is particularly useful for conducting these interviews. In addition, their sample interviews *https://storycorps.me/interviews* can be used to demonstrate the interviewing process for students.

In one project, college students produced 13 short radio productions that were broadcast on a university campus and on an overseas radio station about their perceptions of multiculturalism. Students also wrote essays describing their productions in terms of how they addressed issues related to multiculturalism in their productions (Todorova, 2015). These productions functioned as "soundscapes" that "involved the use of vocal and electronically generated sounds to express a feeling, make an impression, or tell a story" (p. 49). In addition, students in one classroom engaged in a weekly, Open Mic space *https://go.osu.edu/openmic* that they organized for sharing their perceptions of issues such as White supremacy or heteronormative norms (Clark & Williams, 2020). Students also shared videos, music, and narratives related to their experience with these issues.

Creating podcasts

For creating podcasts, students can address issues facing them in their school or community (Guggenheim et al., 2021). To model this process for her classroom, a teacher shared a video about how a school district banned radio stations on the school bus that were playing rap songs, leading to parents objecting to the ban as racist *t.ly/QM9z*. Students then shared their own experiences of being judged in public as well as how the local all-White city council in a city of 25% Latinx passed ordinances regarding control of music/car engines. One student who created a podcast on being a teen parent noted how

> I [Alexia] have found it difficult to enjoy writing assignments in school. Many writing assignments did not have a meaning or purpose. It often seemed I could not even express myself in the writing that I was writing. Yet, with our narrative podcasting project, I loved how everyone got to appreciate my work the way I was making it. I was so proud and so excited because I got to choose to talk about our experiences as teen parents.
>
> (p. 42)

Students also created songs and soundtracks about their experiences living in the pandemic to create a podcast about their experiences creating their song and soundtracks (Evans et al., 2021).

RESPONDING TO AND ASSESSING STUDENTS' DIGITAL PRODUCTIONS

For responding to and assessing students' multimodal digital productions, you can draw on criteria from the National Writing Project (2011) Multimodal Assessment project. These criteria include: "artifact (finished product), context, substance (content, quality, and significance of ideas presented), process management and skills, and habits of mind" (Beach et al., 2018, p. 303).

To engage in self-reflections about their multimodal texts, students can employ ShowMe or Explain Everything screencasting apps to record think-aloud reflections about their work (Abrams, 2014). You can also create videos to model self-reflection processes related to reflecting on goals, genres, materials, and intended audience uptake (Rankins-Robertson et al., 2015). You can also employ previously mentioned video annotation tools such as YouTube Annotations or VideoAnt *ant.umn.edu* to add specific comments to particular images in students' videos as well as also use audio feedback tools such as Jing, Camtasia, CamStudio, SoundCloud, Audacity, or Kaizena (for use with Google Drive files) to provide feedback (Beach et al., 2018).

ENGAGING IN CRITICAL MEDIA LITERACY

Given the marked proliferation of information in the media, media outlets compete for audience' attention associated with what Renee Hobbs describes as the "commodification of their attention . . . to reach audiences, you must appeal to their deepest hopes, fears, and dreams" to influence the audience's actions and opinions (Collopy, 2020, p. 10). (See Beach, 2007, *teachingmedialiteracy.pbworks.com*.)

Students need to acquire critical media literacy practices to respond critically to misinformation or disinformation in the media. A small number of media conglomerates frame their media content in ways that are consistent with the preferences of their company sponsors. These sponsors prefer having the program content as consistent with promoting their products; for example, the use of beer commercials for sports events in which fans may purchase beer.

While there is a focus in the CCSS on critical thinking related to teaching argumentative writing, teachers may focus less on critical media analysis of the use of persuasion in media texts as a different set of literacy practices than a focus on argument (Hobbs, 2021). Students need to be able to assess the validity of online information, given increases in online misinformation in political campaigns (Baumgartner & Towner, 2017). 35% of teachers have "frequently" or "very frequently" engaged students in critical analysis of online information (Vega & Robb, 2020). You can foster students' critical responses to online information through addressing these questions derived from #digcitcommit:

1. How can I stay informed by evaluating the accuracy, perspective, and validity of online sources?
2. How can I locate and/or develop spaces online where I can engage respectfully with people who have different beliefs and experiences than me?
3. How can I use technology to engage, participate, and be a force for good in my community?
4. How can I learn to balance my screen time with other activities and social interaction?

(Buchholz et al., 2020, p. 13)

For her methods courses, Nicole Mirra created the Digital Democratic Dialogue (3D) Project *bit.ly/DDD-more* involving online civic engagement to address issues in their lives, for example, gun control (for an interview with Mirra about the project *bit.ly/DDD-project*) (Collopy, 2021).

To address issues of media representations, students can also draw on the questions developed by the National Association of Media Literacy Education (NAMLE) *namle.net*: Key Questions: *t.ly/TpRS*

Authorship: Who made this message?
Purpose: Why was this made? Who is the target audience (and how do you know?)
Economics: Who paid for this?
Impact: Who might benefit from this message? Who might be harmed by it? Why might this message matter to me?
Response: What kinds of actions might I take in response to this message?
Content: What is this about (and what makes you think that)? What ideas, values, information, and/or points of view are overt? Implied? What is left out of this message that might be important to know?

Activity: Sharing Examples of Online Misinformation

Students could collect and share examples of online misinformation on a class website or blog. Hobbs (2021) has her students engage in the "To Share or Not Share" activity for analysis of media texts. Students select which messages they would share with peers versus messages they would upload to an online propaganda gallery (Collopy, 2020). Given that making this selection requires that students consider the purpose and context constituting the meaning of a message, she has her students create their propaganda message about an issue or cause.

CRITIQUING STEREOTYPICAL MEDIA REPRESENTATIONS

Students could also critique stereotypical media representations based on race, class, gender, sexuality, age, or social status that often occur in genres. Students can engage in racebending practices *racebending.com* as well as stereotypical representations of gender through genderbending or queerbending as well as through the use of hashtags such as #BlackLivesMatter or #LoveWins (Stornaiuolo & Thomas, 2017).

Engaging in civic activism to critique these practices involves "restorying" stereotypical narratives to create counter-narratives evident, for example, in the Broadway production of *Hamilton* that portrays an alternative version of racist practices by White males in early American history (Stornaiuolo & Thomas, 2017). For example, students created their own animation counter-narrative to critique the gendered, all-White portrayals in the movie *Frozen* (Buck & Lee, 2013).

Largely White college students who received instruction on critical media analysis of media representations of Blacks and Latinos adopted more positive attitudes towards Blacks and Latinos than students who did not receive this instruction (Erba et al., 2019). High school students adopted a feminist critical analysis of the *Toy Story* and *Pocahontas* films and created collages based on magazine covers and ads that enhanced their awareness of stereotypical gender representations (Friesem, 2017). (For videos on gender representations, see *Killing Us Softly 3*, tinyurl.com/d37y5h, and Representations of Gender in Advertising, tinyurl.com/n632a8z.)

To engage in critical analysis of these media representations, students can combine photos or images to create collages to then discern certain consistent patterns in these photos or images reflecting, for example, how female athletes are often portrayed just as much in terms of their appearance as they are in terms of their athletic prowess, or how females are portrayed in advertising or media primarily in terms of their appearance or as physically thin (Smith et al., 2015).

To critique these images, students could pose the questions:

- Where do these representations come from?
- Who produces these representations?
- Why are they producing these representations?
- How is complexity limited by these representations?
- What is missing or what is silenced in these representations?

(Beach et al., 2021, p. 114).

Students could also analyze how media portrayals of racial violence/protests often employ stereotypical representations. These representations may include "Humanizing White Criminals—Dehumanizing Black Victims," "Compromising Photos of Black Victims," "Lone Wolf Characterization of White Criminals," "Black Children Represented as Adults," "Self-Defense vs. Guilty Until Proven Innocent" and "Double Standard Depictions of Justice Movements" (Johnson, 2015; Baker-Bell et al., 2017, pp. 133–135).

Students can also critique these patterns through the use of Twitter hashtags such as #BlackLivesMatter, #AmINext, #ShutItDown, and #ICantBreathe (Ibid., p. 137). To share their perceptions of these stereotypes, students can pass pieces of paper with a description of their identity without their names around to peers who write an image, idea, or widely held view used to categorize people with this identity marker. The rotations continue until each student has added a remark to each of their peers' papers. Once students receive their original sheet of paperback, they will be asked to take a few moments to review the remarks written on their paper and be prepared to discuss as a whole class (Ibid., p. 142).

CRITIQUING ADVERTISING AND CORPORATE BRANDING

Students can also engage in critical analysis of advertising in terms of how ads target audiences to equate their use of certain products to achieve personal satisfaction or social status, such as wearing certain brand-name clothes as markers of class identity. To critique this audience appeal, students can ask:

- Who is the intended or target audience?
- What signs, markers, images, language, social practices imply that audience?
- How is the audience linked to the use of the product?
- What are the underlying value assumptions connecting the use of a product/activity and satisfaction/social status? (Beach et al., 2016, p. 167).

For critiquing sports teams' branding, students can also examine how sports commentary often focuses primarily on portraying the team as a brand in ways that limit a focus on individual players' unique identities or attitudes versus defining their identities as contributing to the team (Beach & Caraballo, 2021). For example, Colin Kaepernick engaged in kneeling during games as an expression of concern over racial justice. He was then not only not hired by other teams, but sports commentators downplayed the meaning of his actions as inconsistent with the overall corporate branding of the National Football League. In contrast, professional players created The Players' Tribune blog *www.theplayerstribune.com/en-us* to voice their unique perspective about the sport; for example, professional basketball player Blake Griffen voicing his critique of the owner of the Los Angeles Clippers for his racist perspectives.

Critiquing news reporting

Critiquing misinformation and disinformation in the news requires going beyond traditional notions of persuasion evident in the CCSS. Those standards define persuasion as primarily involving a focus on logical argumentation based on analysis of claims and supporting evidence. The CCSS did not include persuasion related to tapping into emotions or fears associated with the use of misinformation and disinformation (Anderson, 2021). Instead, analysis of misinformation and disinformation requires the ability to adopt multiple, alternative perspectives based on different value assumptions, as expressed in the NCTE Resolution on English Education for Critical Literacy in Politics *t.ly/4cfe* that posits the need for critical inquiry of use of falsehoods and lies in politics.

One of the reasons for the increase in misinformation and disinformation relates to a shift in television news in the past few decades to cable news networks that frame news more on certain ideological perspectives. A Fox News versus MSNBC/CNN report on the same news topic may frame these topics totally differently.

Another reason for the superficial, often biased coverage of news has to do with the ownership of television stations by large media conglomerates such as Sinclair, Nexstar, Gray, Tegna, and Tribune who owned 443 stations in 2016 (Mats, 2017). Stations owned by these companies may report news based on perspectives consistent with their corporate agendas; for example, providing a more conservative analysis of political events (see Figure 8.1).

A shift from print to online news

There has also been a decline in the distribution or sales of print newspapers. This decline results in newspapers shutting down or reducing staff due to declines in advertising and circulation, leading to less substantive coverage of local news and a loss of 25% or 33,000 in print newspaper jobs (Geiger, 2019).

One reason for this decline is that a Pew Research Center survey found that 53% of US adults obtain their news from social media sites such as Facebook, YouTube, Twitter, and Instagram, who do not have to pay, as of 2021, for those news stories (Shearer & Mitchell, 2021). Of those who rarely get their news on social media, 59% expect it to be largely inaccurate, with only 39% expecting it to be largely accurate (Shearer & Mitchell, 2021). As a result, people who rely on these social media outlets for news are more likely to be exposed to misinformation, resulting in not having correct information about current events or politics (Mitchell et al., 2020).

Of 5,844 college students, 89% accessed news from social media; 76% from online newspapers; and 55% from news feeds (Head et al., 2018). Given the high amount of news, students often relied on news digests such as BuzzFeed or Skimm, but often only focused on the

FIGURE 8.1 You Write What You're Told (used with permission from Micah Ian Wright)

news they perceived as related to their lives, such as weather/traffic or national politics. Most were aware of the need to distrust misinformation and 36% indicated that "fake news" led them to distrust all of the news; whilst 58% shared or retweeted news, particularly related to commitments to certain causes.

Critical inquiry responses to online news

This research suggests the need for students to engage in critical analysis of online news. In one study, one group of students created videos representing inaccurate news reporting, while a second group only viewed these videos, and a third just received instruction on new media (Geers et al., 2020). The group who created the videos demonstrated the highest level of critical understanding of politics presented in the news, suggesting the value of actively engaging students in producing news to acquire a critical stance. To do so, students can access the KQED Do Now site, *www.kqed.org/learning/category/do-now* or the Youth Voices, *www.youthvoices.live* site to access online discussion of current news topics—for example, discussions of teen suicide—leading to students creating a public service announcement video (Turner & Reed, 2018).

Teachers can access the Civic Online Reasoning site *cor.stanford.edu* developed by Sam Wineburg at Stanford University, which includes critical analysis of online information. These activities are based on analysis of practices employed by expert fact-checkers who examine websites related to determining the author's expertise and credentials as well as political alignments.

To assist teachers and students in analyzing the news, Project Information Literacy *projectinfolit.org* examined how the news covered the first 100 days of the Covid pandemic (Boudreau, 2020). This included a focus on "information agency" and "visual literacy" related to the analysis of data and graphs to track changes in coverage over time.

Students can discuss issues using the previously-mentioned Digital Democratic Dialogue (3D) Project developed by Nicole Mirra *bit.ly/DDD-more*. In an interview with Mirra about the project (Collopy, 2021; *t.ly/fMhgi*), she noted the importance of going beyond the analysis of factual evidence in the news. Students could pose "questions such as: 'Why does this speak to me in my world? Why does that not speak to you? What do we have in common and where are we diverging?'" Students interacted with each other based on questions shaping three units:

1. Who am I? How do I see myself? What are stereotypes others have about me and my community?
2. What are the issues I care about? How do these issues affect me and my community? How does the news media talk about these issues? Is it helping or hurting the dialogue?
3. What are your dreams about what the future of civic community could and should look like? What kind of future do you see?

To teach her college students about fact-checking online information by drawing on Caufield's (2021) book on fact-checking, Annie Mendenhall

> was shocked to hear students tell her that this was the first time anyone had taught them techniques like tracking down the original source for a piece of information, researching the author or publisher, and reading what others say about their validity.
> (McMurtrie, 2021)

Activity: Conducting Media Ethnographies

Students engage with media through active social participation as members of digital fan clubs, shared viewing of television/movies, participating on social media sites, playing video games, etc. Students can conduct media ethnographies to study the meaning of their own and/or others' social practices involved in participating in these spaces (for examples, *tinyurl.com/t9ppmyf;*, 2018; Garcia, 2016 *goo.gl/Z56CZx*). (To engage in media ethnographies, students can use a questionnaire that was employed for a study in Europe of adolescents' media use with a particular focus on video games *t.ly/Lsb6* (Scolari et al., 2020)).

Students can observe as well as interview participants regarding their responses to and participation in response to TV shows, movies, music, chat rooms, blogs, online fan club activities (soap opera/Star Trek/fan.fiction.net), magazines/e-zines, as well as participation in media events (sports broadcasts, rock concerts) or playing video games.

In doing so, they can examine how members of these sites define their identities through participation in these sites. Middle-school students may study how, for example, the Barbiegirl *www.barbiegirls.com* online virtual site invites tween females to enjoy the experience of "fashion, fun, friendship" by creating their own avatars and talking or shopping with other tweens (For resources on critical media literacy, see Critical Media Literacy organizations on the website.)

SUMMARY

In this chapter, we described the use of various digital/media production tools for engaging students in responding to and creating multimodal, digital texts in ways that assist them in communicating with a range of different audiences. In addition, given adolescents' extensive use of media, we suggested methods for engaging them in critical analysis of their use of media and how they can use digital media to promote change.

REFERENCES

Abrams, S. S. (2014). *Integrating virtual and traditional learning in 6–12 classrooms: A layered literacies approach to multimodal meaning making*. Routledge.

Anderson, J. (2021, March 4). *Why teaching about propaganda and all the ways it is disseminated is an important step toward understanding and strengthening our democracy*. Harvard EdCAST. Retrieved from http://t.ly/8mhE

Anderson, M., & Jiang, J. (2018, May 31). *Teens, social media & technology, 2018*. Pew Research Center. Retrieved from www.pewresearch.org/internet/2018/05/31/teens-social-media-technology-2018/

Auxier, B. (2020, July 13). *Activism on social media varies by race and ethnicity, age, political party*. Pew Research Center. Retrieved from http://t.ly/ATjw

Baker-Bell, A., Stanbrough, R. J., & Everett, S. (2017). The stories they tell: Mainstream media, pedagogies of healing, and critical media literacy. *English Education, 49*(2), 130–152.

Batchelor, K., Bissinger, N., Corcoran, C., & Dorsey, M. (2021). Choose wisely! Interactive fiction video games in the English classroom. *English Journal, 110*(5), 94–102.

Baumgartner, J. C., & Towner, T. L. (Eds). (2017). *The Internet and the 2016 presidential campaign*. Lexington Press.

Beach, R. (2007). *Teachingmedialiteracy.com: A guide to links and activities*. Teachers College Press.

Beach, R. (2019). Engaging students in shared inquiry. *Voices from the Middle, 26*(3), 9–13.

Beach, R., & Caraballo, L. (2021). Languaging actions in sports media and students' writing about sports. In K. Garland, K. S. Dredger, C. L. Beach, & C. Leogrande (Eds.), *Stories of sports: Critical literacy in media production, consumption, and dissemination* (pp. 145–170). Lexington Books.

Beach, R., Castek, J., & Scott, J. (2018). Acquiring processes for responding to and creating multimodal digital productions. In K. Hinchman & D. Appleman (Eds.), *Adolescent literacies: A handbook of practice-based research* (pp. 292–309). Guilford Press.

Beach, R., Thein, A. H., & Webb, A. (2016). *The English language arts Common Core state standards: A critical inquiry approach for 6–12 classrooms*, 2nd ed. Routledge

Bergman, M. (2021, June 2). 5 podcasting tools you can use for next school year [Web log post]. Retrieved from http://t.ly/8uJy

Blom, N. (2017). Creative criticism: Dialogue and aesthetics in the English language arts classroom. *Journal of Adolescent & Adult Literacy, 61*(1), 45–54.

Boardman, A. G., Garcia, A., Dalton, B., & Polman, J. L. (2021). *Compose our world: Project-based learning in secondary English language arts*. Teachers College Press.

Boudreau, E. (2020, October 28). The shape of news: How educators can use news coverage as a tool to foster critical thinking skills [Web log post]. Retrieved from http://t.ly/rIwM

boyd, d. (2016, July 11). Blame society, not the screen time. *The New York Times*. Retrieved from https://goo.fl/ohgbVt

Bradfield Company. (2005–2014). *Inanimate Alice*. Retrieved from www.inanimatealice.com

Brauer, L. (2018). Access to what? English, texts, and social justice pedagogy. *Journal of Adolescent & Adult Literacy, 61*(6), 632–642.

Buchholz, B. A., DeHart, J., & Moorman, G. (2020). Digital citizenship during a global pandemic: Moving beyond digital literacy. *Journal of Adolescent & Adult Literacy, 64*(1), 11–17.

Buck, J., & Lee, B. (2013). *Frozen* [Film]. Walt Disney Productions.

Burns, M. (2017, May 2). Tech-based formative assessment [Web log post]. Retrieved from http://t.ly/g0FS

Byrne, R. (2020, January 17). Three ways to create online comics. Retrieved from https://tinyurl.com/y3ofgadn

Calderon, V. J., & Carlson, M. (2019, September 12). Educators agree on the value of ed-tech [Web log post]. Retrieved from http://T.Ly/H76y

Canady, F., Martin, K., & Scott, C. E. (2018). "Song of Myself": A digital unit of study remix. In J. S. Dail, S. Witte, & S. T. Bickmore (Eds.), *Toward a more visual literacy: Shifting the paradigm with digital tools and young adult literature* (pp. 101–118). Rowman & Littlefield.

Canady F., Scott, C. E., & Hicks, T. (2020). "Walking a thin line": Exploring the tensions between composition curriculum and students' lives as digital writers. *Journal of Language and Literacy Education, 16*(2), 1–20.

Carbone, C., & Shakespeare, W. (2015). *Srsly Hamlet. OMG Shakespeare*. Random House.

Caufield, M. (2021). *Web literacy for student fact-checkers*. Pressbooks. Retrieved from https://webliteracy.pressbooks.com

Chisholm, J. S., & Whitmore, K. F. (2018). *Reading challenging texts: Layering literacies through the arts*. Routledge; National Council of Teachers of English.

Christie, A. (2011). *And then there were none*. William Morrow.

Ciccone, M. (2019). Teaching adolescents to communicate (better) online: Best practices from a middle school classroom. *Journal of Media Literacy Education, 11*(2), 167–178.

Clark, C. T., & Williams, J. M. (2020). Making a "safe" and subversive space for students' lives through Open Mic. In J. Dyches, B. Sams, & A. S. Boyd (Eds.), *Acts of resistance: Subversive teaching in the English language arts classroom* (pp. 95–108). Myers Education Press.

Collopy, T. (2020). Zines in the classroom: Finding an audience of one—or 100. *Council Chronicle, 29*(3), 26–29.

Collopy, T. (2021). Media literacy: Urgent work for our ELA classrooms and our democracy. *Council Chronicle, 30*(3), 9–13.

Colwell, J., Woodward, L., & Hutchinson, A. (2018). Out-of-school reading and literature discussion: An exploration of adolescents' participation in digital book clubs. *Online Learning, 22*(2), 221–247.

Common Core Standards. (2010). *Common Core State Standards for English language arts & literacy in history/social studies, science, and technical subjects*. Council of Chief State School Officers and the National Governors Association.

Crabtree, S. (2021, February 2). Few Massachusetts students prefer remote learning [Web log post]. Retrieved from http://t.ly/sva3

Dail, J. S., & Vásquez, A. (2018). Seeing the world differently: Remixing young adult literature through critical lenses. In J. S. Dail, S. Witte, & S. T. Bickmore (Eds.), *Toward a more visual literacy: Shifting the paradigm with digital tools and young adult literature* (pp. 91–100). Rowman & Littlefield.

Darby, F. (2019, April 17). How to be a better online teacher. *The Chronicle of Higher Education*. Retrieved from http://tinyurl.com/ycok926n

Erba, J., Chen, Y., & Kang, M. H. (2019). Using media literacy to counter stereotypical images of Blacks and Latinos at a predominantly White university. *Howard Journal of Communications, 30*(1), 1–22.

Evans, R. A., Goering, C. Z., & French, S. D. (2021). Soundtracks, songwriting, and soundscapes: Producing the podcast of our lives. *English Journal, 110*(4), 69–76.

Falter, M. M., & Beach, C. L. (2018). Oh my!: Remixing Shakespeare in the ELA classroom. In J. J. Dail, S. Witte, & S. T. Bickmore (Eds.), *Young adult literature and the digital world* (pp. 3–16). Rowman & Littlefield.

Falter, M. F., & Forbes, M. D. (2020). Amplifying teacher voices through Instagram: Subversive teaching meets the 21st century. In J. Dyches, B. Sams, & A. S. Boyd (Eds.), *Acts of resistance: Subversive teaching in the English language arts classroom* (pp. 79–94). Myers Education Press.

Ferlazzo, L. (2019, April 14). Ways to use tech effectively in English classes. *Education Week: Teacher*. https://tinyurl.com/y8nt7rke

Flaherty, C. (2020, March 16). As human as possible. *Inside Higher Education*. Retrieved from http://tinyurl.com/y8rumpgw

Frank, A. (2012). *Diary of a young girl*. Viking.

Friesem, E. (2017). Developing media and gender literacy in the high school classroom. *Journal of Literacy & Technology, 18*(2), 154–191.

Garcia, A. (Ed.). (2014). *Teaching in the connected learning classroom*. Irvine, CA: Digital Media and Learning Research Hub.

Garcia, A. (2016). *Good reception: Teens, teachers, and mobile media in a Los Angeles high school*. MIT Press. https://goo.gl/Z56CZx

Garcia, A., & Mirra, N. (2019). "Signifying nothing": Identifying conceptions of youth civic identity in the English language arts Common Core State Standards and the National Assessment of Educational Progress' Reading Framework. *Berkeley Review of Education, 8*(2), 195–223. Retrieved from https://escholarship.org/uc/item/9048x2kh

Geers, S., Boukes, M., & Moeller, J. (2020). Bridging the gap? The impact of a media literacy educational intervention on news media literacy, political knowledge, political efficacy among lower-educated youth. *Journal of Media Literacy Education, 12*(2), 41–53.

Geiger, A. W. (2019, September 11). *Key findings about the online news landscape in America*. Washington, DC: Pew Research Center. Retrieved from https://tinyurl.com/yyqb9ars

Goldberg, M. (2021, November 2). Social media brings us together. That's the problem. *Minneapolis Star Tribune*. Retrieved from http://t.ly/0rql

Guggenheim, A., Glover, D., & Gisel Alvarado Mejia, A. (2021). Voices and sounds heard: Composing through narrative podcasting. *English Journal, 110*(4), 37–44.

Head, A. J., Wihbey, J., Metaxas, P. T., MacMillan, M., & Cohen, D. (2018). How students engage with news: Five takeaways for educators, journalists, and librarians, Project Information Literacy Research Institute. Retrieved from https://projectinfolit.org/publications/news-study

Hobbs, R. (2021). *Media literacy in action: Questioning the media*. Rowman & Littlefield.

Ito, M., Gutiérrez, K., Livingstone, S., Penuel, B., Rhodes, J., Salen, K., . . . Watkins, S. C. (2013). Connected learning: An agenda for research and design. Retrieved from Digital Media and Learning Research Hub website: http://dmlhub.net/sites/default/files/ConnectedLearning_report.pdf

Jensen, A., & Shaughnessy, M. (2021). "Experimenting fearlessly" in twenty-first-century writing and teaching. *English Journal, 110*(4), 83–91.

Johnson, M. (2015, July 22). 8 ways the media upholds White privilege and demonizes people of color. *Everyday Feminism*. Retrieved from http://everydayfeminism.com/2015/07/the-media-white-privilege/

Jones, K. (2020). Preservice teacher cognitive conflict around poetic discourse in digital spaces and implications for equitable teaching. *Contemporary Issues in Technology and Teacher Education, 20*(4). Retrieved from http://t.ly/enc1

Kajder, S. B. (2018). "It's about more than words": Reading *All American Boys* in a social digital reading environment. In J. S. Dail, S. Witte, & S. T. Bickmore (Eds.), *Toward a morevisual literacy: Shifting the paradigm with digital tools and young adult literature* (pp. 9–18). Rowman & Littlefield.

Karchmer-Klein, R. (2020). *Improving online teacher prep evidence-based practices for learning in the digital environment*. Teachers College Press.

Kelly, K., & Zakrajsek, T. D. (2020). *Advancing online teaching creating equity-based digital learning environments*. Stylus.

Kersulov, M. L., & Henze, A. (2021). Where image and text meet identity: Gifted students' poetry comics and the crafting of "nerd identities." *Journal of Media Literacy Education, 13*(1), 92–105. https://doi.org/10.23860/JMLE-2021-13-1-8

Krakauer, J. (1997). *Into the wild*. Anchor Books.

Loomis, S. (2018). #Twitter: A pedagogical tool in the high school classroom. *Journal of Language and Literacy Education, 14*(1), 1–10.

Marlatt, R. (2019). "Ditch the Study Guide": Creating short films to analyze literature circle texts. *Journal of Adolescent & Adult Literacy, 63*(1), 311–321.

Mats, K. E. (2017, May 11). Buying spree brings more local TV stations to fewer big companies. Pew Research Center [Web log post]. Retrieved from http://t.ly/UCV6

McMurtrie, B. (2021, January 12). Teaching in the Age of Disinformation: Propaganda and conspiracy theories are everywhere. What's a professor to do? [Web log post]. Retrieved from www.chronicle.com/article/teaching-in-the-age-of-disinformation?

Mitchell, A., Jurkowitz, M., Oliphant, J. B., & Shearer, E. (2020, July 30). *Americans who mainly get their news on social media are less engaged, less knowledgeable*. Pew Research Center. Retrieved from http://t.ly/zj70

Mirra, N. (2019). From connected learning to connected teaching: Reimagining digital literacy pedagogy in English teacher education. *English Education, 51*(3), 261–291.

National Council of Teachers of English. (2021). NCTE standards for the initial preparation of teachers of English language arts 7–12 (initial license). Author.

National Writing Project. (2011). Planning to test the framework in practice. Retrieved from http://digitalis.nwp.org/resource/2751.

O'Byrne, I. (2014, September 26). Remix online content with Mozilla Popcorn. *Literacy Now*. Retrieved from https://tinyurl.com/y3rofukh.

O'Byrne, I. (2015, September 6). *Using Vialogues to scaffold student use of video and dialogue in the classroom.* Retrieved from http://tinyurl.com/rqqr4bl.

Oliver, L. (2016). *Delirium.* HarperCollins.

Pandya, J. Z. (2021): The uses of writing for digital video. *Theory Into Practice*, 60(2), 194–201.

Pertierra, A. C. (2018). *Media anthropology for the digital age.* Polity.

Rankins-Robertson, S., Bourelle, T., Bourelle, A., Fisher, D. (2015). Multimodal instruction: Pedagogy and practice for enhancing multimodal composition online. *KAIROS*, 19(1). Retrieved from http://tinyurl.com/lwauxuj

Reich, J. (2020). *Failure to disrupt: Why technology alone can't transform education.* Harvard University Press.

Reynolds, J., & Kiely, B. (2015). *All American boys.* Atheneum/Caitlyn Dlouhy Books.

Rideout, V., & Robb, M. B. (2019). *The Common Sense Census: Media use by tweens and teens, 2019.* San Francisco, CA: Common Sense Media. Retrieved from www.commonsensemedia.org/research/the-common-sense-census-media-use-by-tweens-and-teens-2019

Satrapi, M. (2000). *Persepolis.* Pantheon Books.

Scolari, C. A., Ardèvol, E., Pérez-Latorre, O., Masanet, M.-J., & Rodríguez, N. L. (2020). What are teens doing with media? An ethnographic approach for identifying transmedia skills and informal learning strategies. *Digital Education Review*, 37, 269–287.

Shearer, E., & Mitchell, A. (2021, January 12). News use across social media platforms in 2020. Washington, DC: Pew Research Center. Retrieved from http://t.ly/sm4S

Smith, A., & Seglem, R. (2018). Emerging media, evolving engagement: Expanding teachers' Repertoires of young adult literary study and response. In J. S. Dail, S. Witte, & S. T. Bickmore (Eds.), *Toward a more visual literacy: Shifting the paradigm with digital tools and young adult literature* (pp. 79–90). Rowman & Littlefield.

Smith, B. E. (2019). Mediational modalities: Adolescents collaboratively interpreting literature through digital multimodal composing. *Research in the Teaching of English*, 53(3), 197–222.

Smith, L. R. (2015). What's the best exposure? examining media representations of female athletes and the impact on collegiate athletes' self-objectification. *Communication & Sports*, 4(3), 282–302.

Spiegelman, A. (1992). *Maus I: My father bleeds history.* Pantheon Books.

Steinbeck, J. (2000). *The pearl.* Penguin.

Stornaiuolo, A., & Thomas, E. E. (2016). Restorying the self: Bending toward textual justice. *Harvard Educational Review*, 86(3), 313–338.

Todorova, M. (2015). Dusty but mighty: Using radio in the critical media literacy classroom. *Journal of Media Literacy Education*, 6(3), 46–56.

Turner, K. H., & Reed, D. (2018). Responding to young adult literature through civic engagement. In J. S. Dail, S. Witte, & S. T. Bickmore (Eds.), *Toward a more visual literacy: Shifting the paradigm with digital tools and young adult literature* (pp. 41–52). Rowman & Littlefield.

Twenge, J. M. (2017, November 19). Teenage depression and suicide are way up—and so is smartphone use. *The Washington Post*. Retrieved from http://t.ly/Er7H s

Twenge, J. M., Martin, G. N., & Spitzberg, B. H. (2019). Trends in US adolescents' media use, 1976–2016: The rise of digital media, the decline of TV, and the (near) demise of print. *Psychology of Popular Media Culture*, 8(4), 329–345.

Valdivia, A. (2021). Digital production on Instagram: Vernacular literacies and challenges to schools. *Theory Into Practice*, 60(2), 172–182.

Vega, V., & Robb, M. B. (2020). *The Common Sense census: Inside the 21st-century classroom.* Common Sense Media. Retrieved from www.commonsensemedia.org/research/the-common-sense-census-inside-the-21st-century-classroom-2019

Vonnegut, K. (1961). *Harrison Burgerson.* Retrieved from www.tnellen.com/cybereng/harrison.html

Vuorre, M., Orben, A., & Przybylski, A. K. (2021). There is no evidence that associations between adolescents' digital technology engagement and mental health problems have increased [Web log post]. Retrieved from https://doi.org/10.1177/2167702621994549

Warnock, S., & Gasiewski, D. (2018). *Writing together: Ten weeks teaching and studenting in an online writing course.* National Council of Teachers of English.

Wells, G., Horwitz, J., & Seetharaman, D. (2021, Sept. 14). Facebook knows Instagram is toxic for teen girls, company documents show. *The Wall Street Journal*. Retrieved from http://t.ly/gOsM

Yang, G. L. (2006). *American born Chinese.* First Second.

9

Implementing Speaking and Listening Standards

Most state speaking/listening standards go beyond traditional speech instruction that typically focuses on students giving public speeches to a larger perspective on fostering rich, open-ended classroom conversations through which students adopt dialogic stances through:

- meshing the personal with the academic so that students draw on their experiences to inform their academic work.
- applying multiple voices acquired from a range of different sources and texts to discussion and writing.
- thinking and reflecting based on connections within and across experiences and texts in specific places and time.
- reflecting on these experiences to support meaning-making (Fecho, 2011, pp. 7–9) (Beach et al., 2021, p. 129).

Teacher-dominated discussions often limit the expression of alternative perspectives. In contrast, dialogic discussions involve listening to students' diverse voices and being open to and encouraging unscripted, unanticipated contributions. They also involve encouraging explicit thinking aloud and student questions, avoiding teacher-centered control of discussions, and the use of writing and drama activities to support discussions (Juzwik et al., 2013).

POSITIONING OTHERS THROUGH SPEAKING/LISTENING

Speakers position audiences based on how they assume these audiences will respond to them. For example, suppose a speaker assumes that their audience will respond negatively. In that case, they will employ language differently than if they assume that their audience will respond positively.

Speakers also position others relative to their social status or authority (Harré & Van Langenhove, 1999). "As people position one another in social interactions, I argue that people are always answering an implicit positioning question addressed to them: 'Who am I and who are you in relation to others in this event?'" (Edmiston, 2014, p. 87).

In facilitating classroom discussions, you can position students in monologic ways through posing closed "correct answer" questions that limit open-ended interactions fostering students' expression of their ideas (Dean & Coombs, 2014). Interacting with students in a supportive manner serves to establish your relationships with them for their entire school career and model ways for them to interact in supportive ways with their peers.

SINGLE PUBLIC PRESENTATIONS

One focus of speaking/listening standards is the single public presentation associated with the familiar public speech. In making these speeches, students need to know how to clearly present their ideas to an audience and sequence their ideas so audiences can follow their reasoning. To assist students in preparing for presentations, you can encourage students to engage in critical analysis of oral presentations to address the CCSS "evaluate a speaker's point of view, reasoning, and use of evidence and rhetoric" (Common Core State Standards, 2010, p. 48).

By viewing examples of TED talk presentations *www.ted.com/talks*, students acquire strategies associated with body language, voice, pauses, and gestures; highlighting and summarizing key points; and effective use of slides. Students can also analyze speakers' positions in terms of clear formulation of claims and effective use of evidence by listening to talk-show radio or podcasts such as Serial *serialpodcast.org*, a podcast based on formulating arguments based on different sets of evidence (Keigan, 2014).

In having students prepare for public presentations, they should select topics about which they have a strong interest to feel some purpose for giving their speeches. For example, to prepare for speaking before a group, students could first record themselves using a webcam or screencasting tool to create a video of their presentation. They can then review that video to note instances in which they were effective and make needed revisions in their presentation. To do so, they could apply the following tips (Palmer, 2011):

> Poise: Appear calm and confident.
> Voice: Make every word heard.
> Life: Put passion into your voice.
> Eye contact: Visually engage each listener.
> Gestures: Make motions match your words.
> Speed: Adjust your pace for a powerful performance.
>
> (p. 3)

Students also need to know how to employ presentation tools such as PowerPoint, Keynote, Prezi, Google Slides, or Haiku Deck. This includes avoiding using too much language on their slides that students simply read to their audiences as opposed to using images or video clips to convey their ideas.

To generate more interaction between you and/or students and audience members using their mobile devices, you and/or your students can employ interactive presentation tools such as LiveSlide *atlaslearning.net*, or the iOS Doceri *tinyurl.com/kmmnkyw*, iOS *tinyurl.com/mnsh8mk* and Android *tinyurl.com/mjjuuqq* Celly, or iOS Socrative *tinyurl.com/n4vgbym* apps. For the use of LiveSlide, you can project your slides on both the classroom screen and students' devices to have students insert their responses that are then shared with the class.

You can also integrate open-ended questions or survey/poll prompts into your face-to-face or online presentation slides. Using tools such as Collaborize Classroom, Socrative,

EdPuzzle, SurveyMonkey, PollEverywhere, or Nearpod invites students to respond to your presentations (Krahenbuhl & Smith, 2015). For example, in using Nearpod, you upload your presentation file to Nearpod, embed questions throughout the presentation slides, select the "live session" option, and invite students to join the session using a code. Your questions appear on students' devices and then students provide answers that can be aggregated and shared with the class (Krahenbuhl & Smith, 2015). You can then project the results on a screen and have students discuss some reasons for these results.

CRITERIA FOR EVALUATING PUBLIC SPEECHES

It is useful to provide students with clearly defined criteria or rubrics for their self-assessment and peer and/or teacher assessment. These criteria may include:

- *Use of voice and non-verbal cues.* Students employ variations in voice and pitch, as well as pauses, to convey their ideas. They also use non-verbal cues such as eye contact or gestures to build a relationship with their audience.
- *Adoption of a persona and stance.* Students adopt the persona of a believable, knowledgeable spokesperson with a clearly defined stance on a topic or issue.
- *Gaining audience identification.* Students seek audience identification through referencing their audience's knowledge, beliefs, or interests in a topic or issue.
- *Logical organization of ideas.* Students organize and present their ideas logically, forecasting their overall structure and providing a summary conclusion.
- *Use of illustrative examples.* Students provide illustrative examples of their ideas based on consideration of their audiences' prior knowledge, interests, and beliefs.
- *Use of visual/digital presentation tools.* In using presentation tools (PowerPoint, Keynote, Prezi, etc.), students use language and/or images in a manner that supports versus substitutes for their presentation. (For more on public speeches, see *Public speeches* on the website.)

ALTERNATIVES TO CLASSROOM PUBLIC SPEECHES

The traditional classroom public speech can be intimidating for some students, given that it is not all that dialogic and can consume considerable class time. Plus, it is more meaningful to students when they informally speak to real audiences about the knowledge/expertise they are developing in your class. Therefore, here are some alternatives to large-group classroom presentations.

Podcast or vodcast presentations

You can ask students to create podcasts or video presentations as described in Chapter 8 for sharing with the class, other students in the school, or community members. For example, they could record a vodcast (video-podcast) through their computer's Webcam using iMovie or Windows Movie Maker. To do this, students simply need to click on the "Record" button to record themselves. Then, when they are done recording, they can click "Share" to compress and save the file to the desktop. You might also ask students to use vodcasts to share autobiographical narratives, their positions on certain issues, or book/media recommendations.

Or, rather than engaging in face-to-face presentations, students could import their slides into the iOS 9Slides *9slides.com* app to record an audio or video presentation to post on a class blog or website.

Spoken word presentations

Students could perform poems, rap lyrics, or narratives by recording them as spoken word presentations (for examples: *tinyurl.com/3n6p875*). Recording spoken-word presentations involves employing their voice, pitch, pauses, non-verbal cues, and gestures to convey unique meanings, as well as the use of musical instruments. Students can also present in different classes, at student assemblies, teachers' meetings, professional conferences, community organizations, town halls, and various public settings. These can all be excellent opportunities to engage students to consider appropriate speaking genres for addressing specific audiences.

To assist LD, blind, or deaf and ELL students in making presentations, they can employ speech-to-text or text-to-speech software tools that help them move between reading and orally performing text. For example, if they have difficulty publicly sharing their ideas, they can first dictate their thoughts using speech-to-text tools such as Dragon Dictate to create a written text to read aloud. Or, they can write out their thoughts to then use text-to-speech tools to present an oral version of their written thoughts. (For more on alternatives to public speeches, see *Alternatives to public speeches* on the website.)

> **Activity: Having Students Engage in Alternative Presentation Modes**
>
> You can have your students consider engaging in alternatives to the traditional classroom speech. That might include creating a recorded podcast/vodcast for online sharing, a video using Flipgrid for sharing presentations to the class, or a rap/spoken word performance that may even include musical performances. Students can also consider group performances in which members assume and perform certain roles—for example, acting as a Greek chorus or jury members responding to characters' actions in literary texts.

ONE-TO-ONE SOCIAL INTERACTION: ACTIVE LISTENING AND SUPPORT

One important aspect of addressing the speaking/listening standards involves one-to-one oral interactions between yourself and students. Listening to the other is critical to the success of these interactions. You may interact with students coping with a challenge or provide them with feedback about their work. In these one-to-one interactions, careful listening to reasons for their difficulties can provide them with useful suggestions on coping with those difficulties.

Restating or playing back students' words can help them understand what they are communicating. In some cases, students may have difficulty formulating their thoughts and feelings. For example, they are having difficulty knowing how to formulate their original ideas for their presentation. You can restate what they are saying—"You seem to be saying that you're having difficulty formulating your original ideas for your presentation." Thus, you're assisting students to clarify their thoughts and feelings. You're also giving them a sense of your ability to empathize with their difficulties.

Such interactions are particularly important for supporting students who are struggling in your class or who are reticent to talk in class, requiring consideration of particular ways to support those students. This includes recognizing cultural differences in students' use of conversational interactions. (For more on one-to-one social interactions, see *One-to-one social interactions* on the website.)

FACILITATING DIALOGIC INTERACTIONS FOR CLASS DISCUSSIONS

For struggling middle school readers who do not enjoy reading, participating in discussions served to enhance their enjoyment and understanding of reading as well as when they could make connections between their own lives and the text (Pittman & Honchelle, 2014). To enhance their engagement, you can facilitate class discussions in ways that foster dialogic interactions between students (Juzwik et al., 2013). Unfortunately, teacher-led discussions often involve *one-to-one* student-to-teacher interactions instead of interactions *between* students that surface a range of different dialogic voices and perspectives on a topic (Bakhtin, 1981). One reason for the lack of dialogic interaction is that teachers use discussions to have students achieve what the teacher assumes to be the "right answer" (Aukerman, 2013).

Preservice teachers reflecting on their experiences facilitating teacher-led large-group, small-group, and Socratic seminar discussions led to their identifying productive practices versus other practices for which they needed to provide more support for their students (Athanases et al., 2020). In doing so, they recognized different advantages for using these three different discussion types. For example, they noted how large group discussions allow for teacher facilitation and assessment, how small group discussions fostered high student participation, and how Socratic seminar discussion generated interpretative insights.

Observing the limitations of her cooperating teacher's large group discussion, one preservice teacher decided to have students talk in pairs for rehearsals of ideas prior to their large group discussion. She also recognized the limitation of teachers' overuse of scaffolding of discussion as limiting students' development of their ideas. The preservice teacher also noted the need to "'work with Ss [on] teaching them to respond, agree, and disagree respectfully,'" to "'encourage Ss to make the connections on their own, without my help,'" and "'to give thorough explanations of their claims inferences by drawing evidence from the text, . . . to explain themselves without teacher prompting'" (p. 11).

Changing seating arrangements

Assuming that the chairs in your classroom can be moved, you can shift the seating arrangements so that rather than students all facing you in the front of the room, they could sit in a circle facing each other. Students may then be more likely to respond to each other rather than assume that they need to respond just to you. You can then also have students go around the circle to share their initial responses to a text (Beach et al., 2021).

Posing open-ended questions

Teacher-led discussions often involve the use of the Initiate–Respond–Evaluate (IRE) teaching where the teacher poses a question, a student answers, and the teacher evaluates their answer, as in "Jill, what was the setting for *The Crucible*?" Jill: "Salem, Massachusetts"; teacher: "very good, Jill." In using of the IRE pattern, the teacher maintains total control of the discussion.

This use of the I–R–E pattern and closed questions (questions with just one correct answer) predominate in classroom discussions, with only a few instances of students responding to each other. One study of hundreds of classrooms found that three or more students only interact with each other an average of 1.7 minutes per every 60 minutes of class time (Applebee et al., 2003). The lack of student interaction with each other has to do with the use of closed questions. Of the questions posed in the study, only 19% of their questions were authentic, open questions—questions with no predetermined answers.

In posing questions, it is therefore important to ask open-ended questions eliciting students' opinions or ideas that have no predetermined "right" answer. It is also useful to employ longer pauses after posing open-ended questions to give students time to formulate their responses (Goodwin, 2014). In one study, the use of higher-level questions was correlated with longer wait times (Larson & Lovelace, 2013).

It is also important to support students' tentative, exploratory thinking instead of assuming that they need to voice definitive "right answers." For example, suppose students perceive the discussion as a space to share their tentative, exploratory thinking. In that case, students may then be more willing to share publicly their thinking and how they are thinking about their thinking (Kim & Bloome, 2021).

It is also useful to begin with engagement questions such as "What emotions did the story evoke?" or autobiographical response questions on students' related experiences instead of higher-level interpretation questions.

You can also have students collaboratively generate their own list of questions to share on their devices or whiteboard. You can also model the generation of certain questions using question-asking heuristics such as The Critical Response Protocol based on the following questions: "What are you noticing?" "What did you see that makes you say that?" "What does it remind you of?" "How do you feel?" "What questions does the 'text' raise for you? What did you learn?" (Beach et al., 2010, p. 27).

When discussions do seem to stall, you can ask students follow-up questions such as "What do you mean by . . ." "Can you tell me more about . . ." "What makes you think that?" "Can you give me an example from the text?" "What is a real-world example?" or "Are there any cases of that?" (Zwiers & Crawford, 2011, p. 32).

Fostering exploratory, tentative thinking and disagreements

As noted in Chapter 6, students may perceive discussions for sharing their tentative thinking through their use of "passing theories" (Kent, 1993) as in voicing "I'm not sure about this" hypotheses or hunches. By framing their thoughts as tentative hypotheses or hunches, other students perceiving that a speaker is testing out their ideas may then want to chime in with their equally tentative thoughts or listening to others "external dialogue," to then internalize that dialogue as "inner dialogue" or new ways of thinking that they may then make explicit in a discussion (Grossen & Salazar Orvig, 2011).

You can model exploratory, tentative thinking by making explicit your own inner dialogue about how you are thinking about a question, problem, or issue (Kim & Bloome, 2021). For example, in her 8th-grade classroom, Amber Damm shares her thoughts for how she is thinking about her thinking to foster growth in her students' inner dialogue (Beach, 2019):

> It's never just like, "Oh, you didn't put this here." It's like, "Here's what you could have put here," or, "Here's how something could have worked here," or maybe, "I think you should look at this," and that could actually help you . . . It's helpful 'cause then every time you do it you go back smarter than you were last time, so you'll come back with new ideas and new ways to look at things than you did the last time.
>
> (p. 10)

It is also useful to encourage productive disagreements in which students are willing to challenge each other. Analysis of "collaborative conflict talk" fostered by a teacher's use of indirect challenges and provocative paraphrases based on conflict talk associated with her students' familiarity with "the dozens" resulted in 10th-grade students engaging in productive collaborative disagreement during whole-class discussion (Sherry, 2014).

Attending to different language dialect participation styles

Students may differ in their use of language participation styles based on differences in race or class. For example, Black students employing African American Vernacular English (AAVE) may be more likely to employ figurative/exaggerated language, wordplay, signifying, repetition, gestures, call-and-response, aphorisms, and overlapping talk (Lee, 2007; Smitherman, 2000). Therefore, it is important to support students' use of different language dialect styles to be more comfortable participating in a discussion (Beach et al., 2021).

PRACTICES FOR FOSTERING DIALOGIC DISCUSSIONS

You can also employ the following practices for fostering dialogic discussions.

Initial free-writes

Students could engage in some informal free-writes to help them spontaneously generate some thoughts about a topic or text. You might then ask them to share what they wrote and have other students react to their peers' ideas. You can also provide students with a prompt for their free-writes related to the topic or issue being discussed. Writing can also be used during a discussion ("Let's everyone write about the response student X just made") or at the end of a discussion ("What are the most important things you learned from our discussion today?").

Sharing narratives

Students could share narratives about their everyday experiences. For example, in responding to a novel or story, students may recall experiences related to the events in a novel or story. It's important that students elaborate on their narratives rather than simply summarizing a related event. Elaborating on a related narrative event can help students develop their perspectives or beliefs associated with that event.

Charts, graphs, or maps

One approach to fostering interaction between students is to employ paper or online charts, graphs, or maps and the Groupboard app and SyncPad apps to share using a collaborative whiteboard. For example, you or your students can identify the key questions, topics, problems, or issues under discussion and add related information, subtopics, examples, or illustrations to a chart, graph, or map. In discussing issues of government intervention or control of people's private lives related to studying *1984* (Orwell, 1961) described in Chapter 6, Elizabeth Erdmann put up sheets of paper around her classroom listing different potential types of intervention. Students listed, for example, outlawing all guns, mandatory DNA files, or requiring licenses to have children. Students then walked around the room and added their comments on whether or not they agreed with these interventions, which served to foster further discussion.

"Backchannel" comments

For students who may be reluctant to contribute to a discussion, you can have them post "backchannel" comments using tools such as Chatzy *www.chatzy.com*; *Talkwall, talkwall.uio.no*; Google *Forms*; or a whiteboard using Mural, *mural.co/education*; Explain Everything Whiteboard, *tinyurl.com/yccx7tjh*; or Whiteboard.fi, *whiteboard.fi*. During a discussion, students' comments are projected on a screen or whiteboard. Students can also employ Padlet, *padlet.com*, a popular online bulletin board for sharing comments.

These tools serve to encourage those students who are reticent to share thoughts to participate in a discussion. As one student noted, "'When we have class discussions, I don't really feel the need to speak up or anything . . . When you type something down, it's a lot easier to say what I feel'" (Gabriel, 2011, p. 1).

Taking class notes

One strategy for shifting away from a teacher-directed discussion is for you to take notes of your students' discussion. Chris Friend (2014) creates a "'class notes'" document on Google Drive for students to share notes for his classes. Then, during class, his primary role is that of note-taker where he projects his notes on a screen and has other students taking notes that are also on the screen. In doing so:

> I leave them to survive the conversation on the merits of their own contributions, not my guidance. I write what I hear everyone saying. I occasionally write a question in the notes. Sometimes students see them and respond; sometimes I refer back to them in a conversational lull; sometimes they simply go unanswered. By taking notes, I show I'm listening. By asking the occasional question, I show I'm attentive. By looking at my screen and not at them, I show that I really do want them to be in charge of the conversation.

> **Activity: Analyzing Classroom Discussions**
>
> Observe some large-group classroom discussions, taking notes of specific instances of student talk and teacher use of facilitation techniques. You can note the frequency and types (open-versus-closed) of teacher questions and how many students talk, along with how often they interact with each other. You can also compare differences between these discussions in the level of student participation related to differences in the teacher's use of facilitation techniques and activities to determine reasons why use of certain techniques served to foster student engagement and interaction. You can then reflect on how you might employ these techniques to foster facilitating your own classroom discussions.

ONLINE GROUP DISCUSSIONS

As described in Chapter 8, during the pandemic, students largely engaged in instruction through online group interactions using sites such as Zoom, *zoom.us*; Skype, *www.skype.com*; WebEx, *www.webex.com*; Microsoft Teams, *tinyurl.com/zzoon4o*; or Google Meet, *meet.google.com*, as well as Google Hangouts, for iOS, *tinyurl.com/tbuaaos*, or Android, *tinyurl.com/j5mfdd4*.

Students can also engage in online sites such as Share Board, Fring: Video Calls + Chat, BT Chat HD, ooVoo Video Chat, Vtok: Google Talk Video, FaceTime, ClickMe Online Meetings, GoToMeeting, and Adobe Connect for iOS. The Skype for Educators *www.skypeforeducators.com/educators.htm* service, ePals *www.epals.com*, Youth Voices *youthvoices.net*, and TakingitGlobal *www.tigweb.org* lets you set up connections for students to communicate with other students in different parts of the country or world.

While synchronous discussions are more spontaneous, having to write out their responses in an asynchronous chat also means that students are more likely to reflect on others' written responses prior to reacting to those responses. Collaborize Classroom *www.collaborizeclassroom.com* and the Collaborize Classroom Pro iOS app *tinyurl.com/mk4t36w* provide students with different discussion roles for engaging in asynchronous online discussions. Students assume the "silent moderator" role, who poses questions, or the "involved participant" who facilitates discussion. They can also use tools on the platform to conduct surveys or polls to determine their attitudes on certain topics or issues that can spark further discussion.

You can also employ Twitter for online interactions by you and your students and between students by creating your own Twitter class account or creating a Twitter hashtag for your specific class(es) instead of using your personal Twitter account.

For online discussion starters, Pear Deck *peardeck.com*, Let's Geddit *www.letsgeddit.com*, Answergarden *answergarden.ch*, or Socrative *m.socrative.com* can be employed to pose questions. Or, you can use the game-based Kahoot *getkahoot.com* to create questions for game-like activities.

One advantage of using online discussions is that students who are intimidated by the nonverbal aspects of sharing thoughts in face-to-face discussions are often more comfortable sharing their thoughts in online discussions. Students can also engage in online discussion after school hours so that they are not limited to discussion during classroom hours, so that, for example, they can therefore engage in book club discussions at any time.

In using online discussions, you need to establish some "netiquette" guidelines constituting respectful, safe interactions to avoid students' use of cyberbullying/flaming, ridicule or hurtful comments, or sharing private/personal information. Similar guidelines were enacted by the New York City Department of Education (2013) *tinyurl.com/n343e5o*.

For sharing literary responses or book recommendations as well as thoughts on topics or issues, students can also use the Flipgrid *tinyurl.com/m52e9ck* iOS app to create a 90-second video clip response to a topic, problem, or issue for posting on class blogs or websites. There are also online posters tools such as Padlet *padlet.com* for students to post notes on a collaborative online bulletin or use Google Forms to project students' contributions to a shared screen. (For more on using online group discussions, see *Using online group discussions* on the website.)

USING SMALL-GROUP OR BOOK CLUB/LITERATURE CIRCLES DISCUSSIONS

One alternative to large-group discussions involves the use of small group or book club/literature circles discussions, with ideal group sizes of 3–5 students (Appleman, 2006; Bowers-Campbell, 2011). In small group discussions, students can set their discussion agendas or pose their questions to each other, often resulting in more development of topics than in large group discussions (Hulan, 2010).

To assist students in working effectively in small groups, you can model ways of posing questions and assuming the roles of facilitator, note-taker, summarizer, devil's advocate/challenger, etc. (Daniels & Steineke, 2004). You can also have students share summaries of their discussions back to the large group, reporting that fosters some accountability to complete their tasks in their groups.

In having students engage in book club/literature circles discussions, students should have some say about the books they select to read so that they experience a sense of ownership and engagement (Bernadowski & Morgano, 2011; Beach & Yussen, 2011). Students also need to build on others' responses to move beyond their individual responses to generate new composite interpretations that transcend their individual responses.

For creating groups, you can consider the option of assigning students to groups so that groups consist of a range of different talents or ability levels as well as a mixture of gender and race to avoid having all the students of a certain type in their segregated groups.

As noted above, students can assume different roles in their groups (Harvey & Daniels, 2009) as:

- *facilitator*, who poses questions, asks for reactions to members' statements, summarizes members' positions, encourages all members to participate, and restates others' perspectives.
- *leader*, who initiates and concludes discussions.
- *scribe*, who takes notes to report on the group's focus to the large group.
- *devil's advocate*, who challenges the group with alternative perspectives or position.
- *connector*, who makes connections to other texts or experiences.
- *summarizer*, who provides summaries of the discussion.

For example, one teacher had students assume similar roles as a "discussion leader" as facilitator, as "bridge-builder" for making connections between their experiences and the text, and as "discussion detective" who shares specific parts of the text that imply the larger meaning of the overall text (Beach & Beauchemin, 2019, p. 117). At the same time, it's important that students not adhere too rigidly to these roles so that they assume different roles within a discussion.

One small-group discussion activity, "save the last word" involves a student selecting a certain passage or sentence from a text perceived to be significant for other students' responses (City, 2014). Then, this student gets the "last word" in describing reasons they selected this passage or sentence for inferring connections between their responses and other students' responses.

Teachers often choose literature circles for teaching texts that may not be approved for use in their school—typically multicultural and political texts. However, students often struggle to take up the critical invitations such books encourage, suggesting the need for some teacher support (Thein et al., 2015). Moreover, critical discussion of political and multicultural texts requires careful and consistent teacher scaffolding that student-directed small groups typically cannot accommodate. (For more on the use of small-group discussions or literature circles, see *Small-group discussions or literature circles* on the website.)

USING THINK-ALOUDS IN STUDENT PAIRS

One alternative to small-group discussions involves pairing students to engage in think-alouds as described in Chapters 5 and 6 to share their thoughts with each other as they read a short text (Beck, 2018; Wilhelm, 2001). For example, one student A makes their thinking explicit to the other student B, who supports A to continue to share their thoughts. After student A has completed their think-alouds, student B begins their think-alouds with A providing support.

As described on pages 90/91, so that students go beyond simply summarizing their responses to describe how they are thinking as they are reading, you may want to model your own think-aloud processes with a student in responding to a short text.

You can also have students record their think-alouds to provide you with information about their comprehension processes, particularly for students who may have difficulty making explicit their thinking or simply recounting story or novel events without elaboration (Abrams, 2014).

FOSTERING STUDENTS' SELF-REFLECTIONS ON THEIR DISCUSSION PRACTICES

To foster students' improvement in their use of discussion practices, at the completion of discussions, you can have them discuss or free-write about their perceptions of effective or productive versus less effective or productive discussion practices (Beach et al., 2021). Students are then reflecting on differences in their engagement in their classroom discussions.

In one class, 12th-grade students shared the following self-reflections:

Katie: I latch onto something, and then I premeditate it a little . . .
Bailey: Oh, I think about it a lot. I observe for quite some time before I interject my own comment. I think it through, and I have a very thorough thought process. It doesn't always come out like I want it to, but I still observe for a long time before I make my comment.

Donovan: I have like a 5% success rate. I cherish those 5% moments.

Kayleigh: I feel like if I'm going to throw something out, I want it to be something that's going to contribute to the conversation. I don't want to just throw something out, be random and stuff. I like also seeing what other people pull out from the reading, because what I pull out is totally different from what you guys pull out.

(Beach & Beauchemin, 2019, p. 187)

These students noted the importance of listening to each other to extend or build off each other's responses.

Activity: Using "Fishbowl" Observations of Small Group Discussions

You can also employ "fishbowl" reflection activities in which students sit in an outer ring around a small-group discussion of 4–6 students seated in inner rings. Students in the outer ring then record examples of inner-ring students' discussion practices to provide them with their descriptive feedback about their discussion practices. In her middle school classroom, based on their "fishbowl" observations, Anne Richardson (2010, p. 85) had students identify practices and norms for "accountable talk" to then identify six basic "rules of conduct" associated with "accountable talk":

1. One person speaks at a time.
2. Use a one-foot voice (a voice that can be heard only from a foot away or less).
3. Stay on topic.
4. Listen actively to each other.
5. Keep eyes on the speaker.
6. Make connections to the previous speaker's ideas before moving on to another idea.

ASSESSING STUDENTS' DISCUSSION PARTICIPATION

There are both advantages and disadvantages to assessing students' discussion participation by recording the amount or nature of individual students' contributions. While students' writing is typically assessed, their discussion contributions are less likely to be assessed; assessing their contributions conveys the importance of discussion to students. However, assessing contributions may simply lead to students attempting to perform for a positive evaluation through "'display talk'" (Juzwik et al., 2013, p. 65). Moreover, attempting to keep track of each student's talk in large classes while also facilitating a discussion can be difficult, if not impossible. One value of using small-group discussions is that you can move around the classroom to observe students' interactions to then provide momentary feedback, particularly in terms of perceiving their use of effective interaction practices.

To assess students' discussions, you can share with them what you value in their discussions to stress the importance of active listening, formulating responses in some depth in ways that reflect an insightful understanding of the problem or issue, an openness to entering alternative perspectives that may differ from their own perspectives, a willingness to restate and respond to positive ways to peers' contributions, and the ability to synthesize the direction or key points of a discussion. For her classes, Alexis Wiggins (2014) developed the following criteria that she shared with her students so that they run the discussion and then self-assess the discussion based on these criteria:

- Everyone has participated in a meaningful and substantive way and more or less equally.
- There is a sense of balance and order; the focus is on one speaker at a time and one idea at a time.
- The discussion is lively, and the pace is right (not hyper or boring).
- Students back up what they say with examples and quotations regularly throughout the discussion from dialectical journals and/or the text which are read from out loud often to support arguments.

(p. 80)

Her students sit in a circle, and she notes instances of the students' contributions to the discussion. She then uses this data to note patterns in the students' talk, for example, noting that a student shared only story summaries, leading her to recommend to the student that she draw on her journal responses to provide deeper responses.

REFLECTING ON YOUR DISCUSSION FACILITATION

You are most likely to improve your facilitation strategies by creating audio or video recordings of you leading discussions in your methods courses' microteaching discussions and/or your practicum or student teaching. (For recording your classroom discussions for research purposes, you should obtain written permissions from your students, and, given that they are under 18, a parent or guardian's signature on a permission form). You can also create transcripts of your recordings using text-to-speech tools such as oTranscribe *otranscribe.com*, the ftw transcriber *www.theftwtranscriber.com*, or iOS TEMI app *tinyurl.com/yx6cvfkp* or Android TEMI app *tinyurl.com/vjvjqyf* ($0.10 a minute).

In reviewing these recordings and/or transcripts, you can note instances of posing open versus closed questions related to the degree to which students developed their ideas. You can also identify instances in which different students collaboratively developed their thoughts on the same topics instead of jumping around superficially from topic to topic. To determine students' development of topics, for each topic, you can count the number of turns (change in speakers), reflecting the fact that different students are interacting with each other to develop a topic (Beach & Yussen, 2011).

You can also have your peers respond to these recordings to obtain their feedback and perceptions of your facilitation strategies either in face-to-face interactions or through online annotations using *VideoAnt, ant.umn.edu* or VoiceThread *voicethread.com*. For example, teachers in one study were giving feedback to each other's five-minute video clips of their teaching using VoiceThread (Heintz et al., 2010). Teachers were asked to pose questions about their own clips; their peers then reviewed the clips, responded to these questions, and made other comments, and posed other questions. For example, peers made the following responses to a discussion led by Matt on *Lord of the Flies*, in which he began the discussion with the question, "What is social Darwinism":

Alexis: I noticed that your question, "What is social Darwinism," and you're getting kids to think about what that means; I think your question was too difficult. And, I didn't see you ask many probing questions, so it seemed the conversation sort of lulled, until one student brought up some textual support, and then you saw several students participate.

June: I think you demonstrate the importance of enthusiasm, like the way a student asked you a question, and you responded, "I don't know!" Just the way you said it seemed to engage many of the students who didn't talk. And even though it's a bit theatrical, I think that's needed every now and then.

Matt: In the beginning, all the students were asking me questions, so part of doing that was to turn it back to them. I got the impression that not many of them have had much experience in that sort of discussion.

Maggie: I saw that too, how they seemed to look at you, but then I also thought, well maybe they were just trying to get their points, since you were grading them based on their participation. And that's how participation points can sometimes get in the way.

(Arver, 2011, p. 23)

From sharing their feedback, Matt and his peers recognized the need to provide structure and provide a safe space for students to participate. They also realized that teachers' beliefs about teachers' roles in discussions strongly influenced how they facilitated discussions. And, they learned that while they had different, conflicting perspectives about effective discussions, such conflicts were important to share in formulating their beliefs about facilitating discussions. In reflecting on her facilitation of discussions, one teacher noted how students "don't always do a great job of listening and responding to each other's comments. And I thought that was evident from the transcript. There wasn't a lot of following up on what other people said" (Schieble et al., 2020, p. 115). This suggests the need to model ways of listening to others leading to attending to and restating their ideas.

You may also want to reflect on changes in your facilitation of discussions over time to determine the effects of altering your questioning or use of pre-discussion activities. For example, in one action-research project, teachers analyzed changes in 45 whole-class discussion videos over time (Wells, 2011). Over time, they found they were asking more open-ended questions and fewer closed questions and evaluations of students' responses—using the I–R–E pattern. As a result, their students voiced more alternative opinions and more frequently initiated discussions.

While the teachers retained control of the discussions, there was also a shift in the teachers' stance from being the primary expert on a topic or issue to adopting a more inquiry-based, dialogic stance in which both teacher and student collaboratively constructed knowledge. This suggests that it is important to alter your facilitation techniques and not assume that you are the primary source of all knowledge, but rather, acknowledge that your students are contributing their knowledge. (For more on reflecting on discussion facilitation, see *Reflecting on discussion facilitation* on the website.)

REFERENCES

Abrams, S. S. (2014). *Integrating virtual and traditional learning in 6–12 classrooms: A layered literacies approach to multimodal meaning making*. Routledge.

Applebee, A. N., Langer, J. A., Nystrand, M., & Gamoran, A. (2003). Discussion-based approaches to developing understanding: Classroom instruction and student performance in middle and high school English. *American Educational Research Journal, 40*, 685–730.

Appleman, D. (2006). *Reading for themselves: How to transform adolescents into lifelong readers through out-of-class book clubs*. Heinemann.

Arver, C. (2011). A virtual world for *Lord of the Flies*: Engaging students and meeting Common Core Standards. In A. Webb (Ed.), *Teaching literature in virtual worlds: Immersive learning in English studies* (pp. 14–25). Routledge.

Athanases, S. Z., Sanchez, S. L., & Martin, L. E. (2020). Saturate, situate, synthesize: Fostering preservice teachers' conceptual and practical knowledge for learning to lead class discussion. *Teaching and Teacher Education, 88*, 1–16.

Aukerman, M. (2013). Rereading comprehension pedagogies: Toward a dialogic teaching ethic that honors student sensemaking. *Dialogic Pedagogy: An International Online Journal, 1.* Retrieved from http://dpj.pitt.edu/ojs/index.php/dpj1/article/view/9

Bakhtin, M. A. (1981). *The dialogic imagination: Four essays* (M. Holquist, Ed., C. Emerson, Trans.). University of Texas Press.

Beach, R. (2019). Engaging students in shared inquiry. *Voices from the Middle, 26*(3), 9–13.

Beach. R., Appleman, D., Fecho, B., & Simon, R. (2021). *Teaching literature to adolescents*, 4th ed. Routledge.

Beach, R., & Beauchemin, F. (2019). *Teaching language as action in the ELA classroom.* Routledge.

Beach, R., Campano, G., Edmiston, B., & Borgmann, M. (2010). *Literacy tools in the classroom: Teaching through critical inquiry in Grades 6–12.* Teachers College Press.

Beach, R., & Yussen, S. (2011). Practices of productive adult book clubs. *Journal of Adolescent & Adult Literacy, 55*, 121–131.

Beck, S. W. (2018). *A think-aloud approach to writing assessment: Analyzing process & product with adolescent writers.* Teachers College Press.

Bernadowski, C., & Morgano, K. (2011). *Teaching historical fiction with ready-made literature circles for secondary readers.* Libraries Unlimited.

Bowers-Campbell, J. (2011). Take it out of class: Exploring virtual literature circles. *Journal of Adolescent & Adult Literacy, 54*(8), 557–567.

City, E. A. (2014). Talking to learn. *Educational Leadership, 72*(3), 10–16.

Common Core Standards. (2010). Common Core State Standards for English language arts & literacy in history/social studies, science, and technical subjects. Washington, DC: Council of Chief State School Officers and the National Governors Association.

Daniels, H., & Steineke, N. (2004). *Mini-lessons for literature circles.* Heinemann.

Dean, A., & Coombs, D. (2014). From pledging allegiance to your flag to sharing beignets: Call- and-response as critical pedagogy. In S. Jones (Ed.), *Writing and teaching to change the world: Connecting with our most vulnerable students* (pp. 100–122). Teachers College Press.

Edmiston, B. (2014). Dialogue and social positioning in dramatic inquiry: Creating with Prospero. In S. Davis, H. G. Clemson, B. Ferholt, S-M. Jansson, & A. Marjanovic-Shane (Eds.), *Dramatic interactions in education: Vygotskian and sociocultural approaches to drama, education and research* (pp. 79–96). Bloomsbury.

Fecho, B. (2011). *Writing in the dialogical classroom: Students and teachers responding to the texts of their lives.* National Council of Teachers of English.

Friend, C. (2014, September 11). Learning to let go: Listening to students in discussion [Web log post]. Retrieved from http://tinyurl.com/pmmwk8p

Gabriel, T. (2011, May 12). Speaking up in class, silently: Using social media. *New York Times Learning Lesson, The New York Times.* Retrieved from www.nytimes.com/2011/05/13/education/13social.html

Goodwin, B. (2014). Research says get all students to speak up. *Educational Leadership, 72*(3), 82–83.

Grossen, M., & Salazar Orvig, A. (2011). Dialogism and dialogicality in the study of the self. *Culture & Psychology, 17*(4), 491–509.

Harré, R., & Van Langenhove, L. (Eds). (1999). *Positioning theory: Moral contexts of intentional action.* Blackwell.

Harvey, S., & Daniels, H. (2009). *Comprehension and collaboration: Inquiry circles in action.* Heinemann.

Heintz, A., Borsheim, C., Caughlan, S., Juzwik, M. M., & Sherry, M. B. (2010). Video-based response & revision: Dialogic instruction using video and web 2.0 technologies. *Contemporary Issues in Technology and Teacher Education, 10*(2). Retrieved from https://citejournal.org/volume-10/issue-2-10/english-language-arts/video-based-response-revision-dialogic-instruction-using-video-and-web-2-0-technologies

Hulan, N. (2010). What the students will say while the teacher is away: An investigation into student-led and teacher-led discussion within guided reading groups. *Literacy Teaching and Learning, 14*(1–2), 41–64.

Juzwik, M., Borsheim-Black, C., Caughlan, S., & Heintz, A. (2013). *Inspiring dialogue: Talking to learn in the English classroom.* Teachers College Press.

Keigan, J. (2014, December 30). Three (Common Core) justifications for binge listening to serial [Web log post]. Retrieved from http://tinyurl.com/nbyqmm

Kent, T. (1993). *Paralogic rhetoric.* Associated University Press.

Kim, Y-M., & Bloome, D. (2021). When thinking becomes a topic of classroom conversations: languaging thinking practices in a high school English classroom. *Research in the Teaching of English, 56*(2), 177–199.

Krahenbuhl, K. S., & Smith, K. (2015). Nearpod: A technology tool to engage students in inquiry *ASCD Express, 10*(9). Retrieved from http://tinyurl.com/k4xzus2

Larson, L. R., & Lovelace, M. D. (2013). Evaluating the efficacy of questioning strategies in lecture-based classroom environments: Are we asking the right questions? *Journal on Excellence in College Teaching, 24*(1), 105–122.

Lee, C. D. (2007). *Culture, literacy, and learning: Taking bloom in the midst of the whirlwind.* Teachers College Press.

New York City Department of Education (2013, Fall). *Social media use guidelines.* Author. Retrieved from http://tinyurl.com/n343e5o

Orwell, G. (1961). *1984.* Penguin.

Palmer, E. (2011). *Well spoken: Teaching speaking to all students.* Stenhouse.

Pittman, P., & Honchell, B. (2014). Literature discussion: encouraging reading interest and comprehension in struggling middle school readers. *Journal of Language and Literacy Education, 10*(2). Retrieved from http://jolle.coe.uga.edu/current-issue

Richardson, A. E. (2010). Exploring text through student discussions: Accountable talk in the middle school classroom. *English Journal, 100*(1), 83–88.

Schieble, M., Vetter, A., & Martin, K. M. (2020). *Classroom talk for social change: Critical conversations in English language arts.* Teachers College Press.

Sherry, M. B. (2014). Challenges and provocative paraphrases: Using cultural conflict-talk practices to promote students' dialogic participation in whole-class discussion. *Research in the Teaching of English, 49*(2), 141–167.

Smitherman, G. (2000). *Talkin that talk: Language, culture, and education in African America.* Routledge.

Thein, A. H., Guise, M., & Sloan, D. L. (2015). Examining emotional rules in the English Classroom: A critical discourse analysis of one student's literary responses in two academic contexts. *Research in the Teaching of English, 49*(3), 200–223.

Wells, G. (2011). Integrating CHAT and action research. *Mind, Culture, and Activity, 18*(2), 161–180.

Wiggins, A. (2014). Spinning the web. *Educational Leadership, 72*(3), 78–81.

Wilhelm, J. D. (2001). *Improving comprehension with think aloud strategies.* Scholastic Press.

Zwiers, J., & Crawford, M. (2011). *Academic conversations: Classroom talk that fosters critical thinking and content understandings.* Stenhouse.

10

Implementing the Language Standards

English teachers are often associated with the need to use "proper" grammar, spelling, and mechanics. It is the primary job of the English teacher to teach students to speak and write in Standard English, isn't it? The answer to this question isn't a simple one, especially when our goals are to engage students in critical inquiry, justice, and action as well as address language, grammar, and usage standards.

In this chapter, we discuss current theory and research on language variation, vernacular dialects, and English language learning with the goal of making sense of this complex issue. At the same time, we consider what standards often ask of English teachers about the teaching of language, grammar, and usage, and we highlight ways that you can both meet and exceed these standards as you acknowledge and build upon students' language and literacy practices.

INTERROGATING ASSUMPTIONS ABOUT LANGUAGE INSTRUCTION

Teaching about language, grammar, and usage in a way that supports students in critical inquiry, justice, and action will require you to think carefully about some common-sense assumptions about language. This section discusses several key language concepts that are often confused or conflated in language instruction. Thinking carefully about these concepts can help you begin to interrogate common-sense assumptions about language.

Grammar versus usage

One important distinction related to language instruction involves the difference between grammar and usage—concepts people often conflate and confuse. Grammar is based on a set of internal norms or patterns, while usage is better understood as rules related to taste. And, as Zuidema (2005) explains, "most people believe that observing the rules of taste is the same as knowing the rules of a language" (p. 668). A rule of taste or usage might be using the word "ain't" or ending a sentence in a preposition. Neither of these forms of usage impedes understanding and they are therefore not grammatically incorrect from a linguistic standpoint. Instead, this sort of usage is frowned upon in certain contexts based strictly on taste. Such confusion causes people to see the English language as far more "rule" laden than it is in reality. By understanding language usage as rules of taste, you can lead your students in critical inquiry about language that considers questions about whose rules of taste matter and in what context and how those rules might be disrupted.

"Knowing-that" versus "knowing how"

Another assumption people often make about language is that being able to explain and identify grammar rules, or "knowing that" about language, is necessary for being able to use language, or "knowing how" about language. This assumption is based on the perceived need for direct instruction on traditional school grammar, naming parts of speech, grammar exercises, and worksheets, and extensive correction of student errors of grammar and usage. The belief is that this instruction on "knowing that" knowledge of language would enhance a "knowing how" ability to write effectively.

However, decades of research on the effects of instruction in traditional school grammar on writing quality find that such instruction has little or no effect on writing quality. George Hillocks's (1984) analysis of over 500 studies of the teaching of composition puts it this way:

> The study of traditional school grammar (i.e., the definition of parts of speech, the parsing of sentences, etc.) has no effect on raising the quality of student writing. Every other focus of instruction examined in this review is stronger. Taught in certain ways, grammar and mechanics instruction has a deleterious effect on student writing. In some cases a heavy emphasis on mechanics and usage (e.g. marking every error) results in significant losses in overall quality. School boards, administrators, and teachers who impose the systematic study of traditional school grammar on their students over lengthy periods of time in the name of teaching writing do them a gross disservice that should not be tolerated by anyone concerned with the effective teaching of good writing. Teachers concerned with teaching standard usage and typographical conventions should teach them in the context of real writing problems.
>
> (p. 160)

One reason for the lack of transfer is that many traditional grammar rules are invalid, as is the case with the definition of a noun as naming a person, place, or thing, when in fact, gerunds such as "swimming" can function as nouns, as can other names of actions.

At first glance, the Common Core Standards and many state standards documents only describe a traditional approach to language, grammar, and usage. For instance, the CCCS anchor standards for language state that students should "demonstrate command of the conventions of standard English grammar and usage when writing or speaking." Indeed, this emphasis on knowledge and command of Standard English is found throughout the language standards across grade levels. By contrast, the National Council of Teachers of English Standards for the Initial Preparation of Teachers of English Language Arts 7–12 (Initial Licensure) highlight the importance of preparing teachers to value students' language diversity: "Candidates apply and demonstrate knowledge and theoretical perspectives of language and languaging, including language acquisition, conventions, dialect, grammar systems, and the impact of languages on society as they relate to various rhetorical situations (e.g., journalism, social media, popular culture) and audiences" (National Council of Teachers of English, 2021).

Prescriptive versus descriptive perspectives on language use

Another assumption involves the difference between a *prescriptive* perspective that dictates the need to conform to certain assumed, uniformed norms or rules for using language versus a *descriptive* perspective that posits the need to consider variation in uses of language across different social and cultural contexts (Wolfram, 2019). A key consideration related to this distinction involves who is formulating certain perspectives, and how. For example, people may prescribe the need for students to learn and use Standard or Academic English in schools, assuming that such language is neutral, somehow more grammatically correct than other forms of language, and therefore most appropriate for school.

However, scholars have long argued that Standard or Academic English is in fact synonymous with White, middle-class forms of language (Alim & Smitherman, 2012; Baker-Bell, 2017). The uniform rules and norms that a prescriptive approach to language supports, therefore, implicitly, and often explicitly, suggest that the use of African American English (AAE), for instance, is not "proper English" or acceptable in schools (Metz, 2019). Such a suggestion is deeply harmful and dismisses AAE's rich, complex, and valuable linguistic and cultural resources.

A more descriptive perspective moves away from these prescriptive stances based on social hierarchies to value language variation associated with race, class, and/or gender differences. To have his students reflect on assumptions about language use, Mike Metz (2019) shows audio clips from movies of different characters' speeches to then identify attributes related to race/ethnicity, class, gender, and age based on their language. Based on these perceptions, his students then reflect on whether or not they are applying stereotyped assumptions to their attribution—for example, perceiving characters with Southern accents as inferior. Students then examine how they may have acquired these prescriptive suppositions shaping their perceptions.

A descriptive perspective recognizes the need to value language variation across different social and cultural contexts. For example, one of the Speaking and Listening CCSS standards references the idea of varying one's language according to different contexts, that students "adapt speech to a variety of contexts and communicative tasks, demonstrating a command of formal English when indicated or appropriate" (Common Core State Standards, 2010, p. 45). In other words, while state ELA standards certainly place a high value on Standard English, they also importantly suggest that students must be able to understand and use language variation within the English language across different social and academic contexts.

Recognizing and valuing language variation

In order to teach your students how language functions in different contexts, you will first need to consider how language varies and changes. In order to consider this phenomenon, let us take the example of English as it is spoken in the United States. Most Americans recognize that English speakers in the United States speak differently in various regions. Americans also know that English-speaking young adults in the United States use different words, turns of phrase, and even sentence construction in 2021 than they did in 1980. How do these differences happen, and what do they suggest about Standard English?

People often imagine that there is one correct, formal, or standard form of any language that anyone can acquire through education. Variations on the standard form of a language—for instance, African American English or Chicano English—are then considered to be informal, colloquial, or even improper or incorrect. Research has found that Americans who see themselves as speaking Standard English—typically White, middle-class people—tend to hold negative views of people who speak vernacular Englishes (Blake & Cutler, 2003; Perry & Delpit, 1998). Likewise, research suggests that teachers often have lower expectations for students who speak in vernacular forms of English (Cazden, 2001; Ferguson, 1998). However, linguists and literacy scholars have widely debunked these common beliefs about how language works and the value of vernacular dialects. For instance, Godley et al. (2006) explain that:

> Scientific research on language demonstrates that standard dialects are not linguistically better by any objective measures; they are socially preferred simply because they are the language varieties used by those who are most powerful and affluent in society. In addition, although schools often refer to Standard English as if it were a single dialect, there are numerous regional standard dialects in the United States and around the world, as well as significant structural differences between written and spoken Standard Englishes.
>
> (p. 30)

It has often been assumed that Standard English is the language of the majority. We know that Standard English is a White, middle-class form of English (Alim & Smitherman, 2012), but the reality is that by 2030, the majority of students in American schools will be students of color. This massive demographic shift towards a more diverse American population means that the idea of Standard English as the norm needs to be challenged.

In his seminal book, James Gee (1996) persuasively argued that even people who see themselves as Standard English speakers rarely, if ever, speak standard English. Instead, all English speakers (and speakers of any language) speak a range of informal variations of English that vary in their faithfulness to Standard English across different social contexts. For example, you almost certainly speak a different variation of English in your classroom as a teacher than you do at home with your friends or family. And, even in your most formal teaching moments, an audio-recording of your speech would quickly convince you that you do not speak perfect Standard English in this context.

Ultimately Standard English—like the standard form of any living language—is an abstract ideal or model for writing, but not something the people actually speak (Lippi-Green, 1997). Moreover, the rules and norms related to usage vary across contexts with regard to Standard English. In other words, even Standard English is not "standard" (Wolfram et al., 1999).

Gee also notes that people vary their use of formal versus informal language depending on how they frame the social contexts in which they are participating. For example, in giving a formal talk about the representation of women in Hollywood films, a teacher notes that "formal content analysis of Hollywood films indicates that female characters are generally portrayed in limited, often subservient ways"; while in talking with her peers, the teacher may state that, "there's not a lot of strong women in Hollywood films."

These differences in the use of formal versus informal language use reflect the ways in which the meanings and use of language vary according to differences in social and cultural contexts constituted by different discourses. In her formal language use, the teacher is drawing on a discourse of media/feminist analysis associated with her identity in an academic context. In talking with her friends, she is simply assuming her identity as a friend sharing her thoughts. (For more on critical discourse analysis, see *Critical discourse analysis* on the website.)

> **Activity: Reflecting on Variation in Language Use**
>
> Consider the variation in your language use even within your role as an English teacher. Working with a partner, audio-record yourself role-playing three different scenarios. In each scenario, you should attempt to describe your goals for the year in one of your classes or your teaching philosophy. In the first scenario, imagine that you are talking with a student. In the second scenario, imagine that you are talking with your principal. In the third scenario, imagine that you are talking with a parent. Transcribe each of your role-play discussions and analyze the transcripts for patterns in your language. What kinds of differences and similarities do you find in your word choice, grammar/usage, affect, and tone? What information do you include or omit in each scenario? Is your language consistent with Standard English in each scenario? What other social practices is your language use linked to in each scenario? What kinds of social access might you gain through your use of language variation in each scenario?

LANGUAGE AS A SYSTEM VERSUS LANGUAGING AS ACTIONS

Many of the state ELA standards frame language as a codified system of grammar rules. An alternative perspective defines language as "languaging" based on how people employ *language as action* to enact relations with others to achieve certain social purposes, given that "languages are activities, not systems" based on a bundle of social practices in certain contexts (Pennycook, 2010). For example, the meaning of "friend" or "unfriend," associated with social networking derives from their unique use of social practices in that online context.

Examining languaging for enacting relations shifts from individuals' use of language to how the meaning of language lies in the "in-between" within relations similar to how members of a jazz band improvise off of each other's playing (Beach & Bloome, 2019; Bertau, 2014). These meanings evolve through shared interaction, given how "truth is not born nor is it to be found inside the head of an individual person; it is born between people collectively searching for truth, in the process of their dialogic interaction" (Bakhtin, 1984, p. 110). One 12th-grade student noted how she uses languaging to enact trusting relations with her peers:

> I think because we joke and play around that is the way we talk in a positive manner. I think that because we are teens, we relate with our peers because we use the same vocabulary. I think my group has a good trust with each other because we talk about all of the things we have going on even if they are personal.
>
> (Beach & Beauchemin, 2019, p. 6)

In any interaction, the meaning of one person's utterance depends on previous and subsequent utterances. In languaging relations, people enact "in-between" meanings through "answerability" associated with the use of these past and anticipated utterances as well as actual uptake from others (Bakhtin, 1984).

The nature of these "in-between" meanings also depends on adhering to certain ethical norms based on enacting an "I–thou" sense of caring and trust versus an interpersonal "I–it" relation with the other (Buber, 1970). Enacting these "I–thou" relations with students involves using languaging to create caring, trusting relations with your students by enacting safe classroom spaces. As one ELA teacher noted,

> The more a person displays characteristics that are deemed to be safe and familiar, the more likely it is that we will agree to become vulnerable to their actions. Determining another's trustworthiness, therefore, requires observation, experience, and good old-fashioned time. Given how vulnerable students are to our moods, evaluations, and decisions, students need to determine whether we are worthy of risking interpersonal engagement before they agree to learn from us.
>
> (Toshalis, 2016, p. 19)

It is also the case that the "in-between" meanings of languaging depend on how languaging is enacted in a specific event or situation associated with the question, "what is going on here?" related to the kinds of relations being enacted in that event or situation (Goffman, 1986). Contextualizing the meaning of languaging in an event involves thinking about the purposes, norms, discourses, and identities shaping that event. For instance, the meaning of a question in a marriage proposal differs from the meaning of asking a question of a witness in a courtroom.

Use of languaging also includes expressions of emotions as well as the use of embodied actions. Given the focus on the in-between meanings, the meaning of languaging emotions and embodiment lies not with individual actions but rather in how emotions such as anger, envy, joy, fear, etc., or facial expressions, gestures, eye contact, etc., have certain meaning *within* an interaction.

Reflecting on languaging through "languaging thinking"

Students grow in their languaging through continually reflecting on their languaging actions using "languaging thinking" as "meta-commentary" (Rymes, 2014). They do so by making explicit how they are thinking about languaging relations with others or in their writing (The Ohio State University Argumentative Writing Project, 2016). You may model "languaging thinking" by sharing your thoughts on *how* you were thinking about planning an activity for the class or how you would be responding to a text for teaching that text.

Shelly Mann has her students respond to the following questions to reflect on the languaging actions for enacting relations with others:

1. What is MY relation to others (friends, family, the "inner circles" of my life)?
2. How do I use texts to construct relationships with others (friends, family, the "inner circles" of my life)?
3. How do our actions impact our friends and family?
4. How does society construct identity (gender, race, ethnicity, and class)?

5. What are the different ways you enact different identities according different relational ways of being through languaging?

(Beach & Beauchemin, 2019, p. 12)

12th-grade students engaged in "mini-ethnography" writing about their interaction with others in peer groups, sports teams, clubs, families, etc. (Beach & Caraballo, 2021). They were then given prompts asking them to reflect on their use of languaging actions in their interactions. Students most frequently reflected on how their languaging served to support relations with others, followed by languaging creating a sense of belonging, and use of "insider language" to enact specific identities and roles in their interactions (for a video summary ila.onlinelibrary.wiley.com/doi/10.1002/jaal.1190). For example, Kyle Wendorf described the insider language use of members of his hockey team:

> We have developed our own language of grunts, names, and noises. Every player on the team is fluent in this secret complicated language. We use the language to call to our teammates on the ice. It is necessary for the team to speak the tongue of puck so that the other team doesn't know who we were calling to or what we are planning to do. For instance a, "YA YA YA YA" means quick hurry pass the puck. Even though this seems like a simple call, no two hockey players sound alike while calling for the puck.

(For more on theories of social language use, see *Theories of social language use* on the website).

SHOULD WE TEACH STANDARD ENGLISH IN TODAY'S SCHOOLS?

In the last few pages, we've made the case that all language includes variation, that no one form of English is linguistically superior to another, that language and languaging are in fact social practices that achieve different purposes in relationships and interaction, and that Standard or Academic English is not neutral and is closely associated with White, middle-class norms. Is it still important for students to learn Standard English in schools with all of this in mind?

We argue that, yes, students do need to learn about Standard English in school—but as a concept and as part of a complex and critical understanding of language use and variation (Alim, 2005; Baker-Bell, 2020; Godley & Reaser, 2018; Kirkland & Jackson, 2008). And, indeed, students should always be taught first and foremost about the value of their home language. Learning about Standard English includes understanding what it looks like and its gatekeeping role in allowing some people access to power while denying it to others. Lisa Delpit (2006) has written about Standard English as part of "codes of power" that we should ensure our students are able to access. She states:

> To act as if power does not exist is to ensure the power status quo remains the same. To imply to children . . . that it doesn't matter how you talk or how you write is to ensure their ultimate failure. I prefer to be honest with my students. I tell them that their language and cultural style is unique and wonderful but that there is a political power game that is also being played, and if they want to be in on that game there are certain games they too must play.

(pp. 39–40)

To be clear, Delpit is not suggesting a prescriptive view of language—one that would ask students to give up their home languages or variations in favor of Standard English. Instead, Delpit argues that students be taught to learn to effectively use Standard English—as one of several equally valuable variations or languages in their linguistic repertoire—to gain access to power structures and ultimately change the status quo.

Kirkland (2010) provides a useful extension of Delpit's ideas. Kirkland argues that the English language might more accurately be thought of as Englishes because of the intense plurality of its variations. He also argues that although it is useful to teach all students Standard English, teachers should also focus on how other Englishes (and variations of languages other than English) provide access to particular kinds of social power or status.

Moreover, rather than centering the study of Standard English, current scholars who study critical language teaching in the English classroom argue that English teachers should focus first on developing, supporting, and valuing the linguistic repertoires and resources that multilingual students bring to the classroom (e.g., Baker-Bell, 2017; Haddix, 2015; Johnson et al., 2017; Martinez, 2017). Further, Baker-Bell (2020) makes the compelling case that Black students and other students who have been linguistically marginalized in schools need and deserve instruction that helps them understand and disrupt the linguistic oppression they've experienced in schools.

> **Activity: Identifying Language Differences in a School World**
>
> Based on our discussion of language differences, in your practicum experience in a school, listen to students talking in the hallways, lunchroom, sports/extra-curricular activities, and classrooms to identify differences in their language use. Note differences in how they may talk with peers versus teachers/adults and differences based on their race/ethnicity and/or class. You could also interview students related to these differences in terms of how they determine whether and how to employ different language uses based on reading norms in social contexts—for example, norms in a classroom discussion versus talk in the lunchroom or hallway.

LEARNING DISCIPLINARY LANGUAGES

As students learn about language variation, it is also important that they learn about how language varies across academic disciplines. While disciplinary language tends toward Standard English, the focus in learning about disciplinary language is different from that of learning Standard English. Rather than teaching a set of rules for grammar, teaching about disciplinary language is about how different disciplines use particular vocabulary, abstract concepts, figurative language, and syntactical features that are specific to knowledge and learning in a particular domain. For example, in a math class, students learn to employ words associated with mathematical analysis such as plot, graph, calculate, estimate, convert, substitute, etc. (Zwiers, 2014, p. 105).

Unless students are familiar with the concepts and typical uses of language associated with a particular discipline or domain, they will struggle when they need to comprehend texts with unfamiliar academic language. For example, the following passage from Leakey and

Lewin's (1992) book, *Origins Reconsidered: In Search of What Makes Us Human,* refers to the concept of territoriality as used in the field of paleoanthropology:

> Territoriality is a flexible behavioral trait in many animals, often influenced by ecological circumstance. And human behavior, of course, is flexible in the extreme. Humans do not march in lockstep to the demands of aggressive genes. Our behavior as a species is complex, always shaped by cultural context, and always amenable to choice, to free will. We argued that a willingness to accept the notion that *Homo sapiens* is driven to violent conflict by biological imperative is itself a cultural manifestation.
>
> (p. xvii)

Understanding this passage requires understanding concepts of ecology, genes, cultural context, free will, Homo sapiens, biological imperative, cultural manifestation, and larger prior knowledge of a cultural anthropological perspective on explaining human behavior that differs from a biological explanation.

Students may vary in terms of their uses of disciplinary language within their school contexts, communities, or home context. For instance, if a student lives in a family of physicians, they may be more familiar with medical and scientific language than their peers. Or, if a student has a family member who is a farmer, they may have more knowledge of the agricultural language and discourse practices than their peers. Jeff Zwiers (2014, pp. 7–8) identifies four types of capital shaping differences in students' understandings and uses of language:

- *Social* capital has to do with students' interactions with other adults or peers in which certain types of languages may be used.
- *Cultural* capital reflects socioeconomic class differences having to do with parental education, literacy practice in the home, exposure to particular forms of art or music, or travel opportunities.
- *Knowledge* capital is derived from previous reading, viewing or interactions with others, resulting in knowledge of disciplinary or academic practices.
- *Linguistic* capital comprises the ability to employ abstract or complex language or discourses as well as to know how and when to employ certain kinds of languages in certain contexts.

Uses of these different types of capital serve to define students' identities as constituted by the ability to employ certain discourses as ways of knowing and thinking (Gee, 1996)—for example, the discourse of physics related to explaining aspects of gravitation and force.

Students learn the use of different languages through acquiring these different types of capital. Students who aren't as familiar with Standard English (and the White, middle-class practices that accompany Standard English) often have linguistic and cultural resources that are overlooked in schools and are perceived to disadvantage them when faced with tasks involving the use of Standard English. In addition, students from higher-income family backgrounds are more likely to have access to these different types of capital employed in school subject matter areas than students from lower-income family backgrounds (Flynn, 2011). These White, middle-class students know that they benefit from the linguistic prejudices of schools so they have the incentive to employ Standard English.

This suggests the need to help all students understand linguistic diversity and the role of power and privilege in teaching Standard English by engaging them in active use of various languages in discussions or in their writing instead of relying only on direct language instruction. In discussions, you can employ prompts that invite or model uses of particular languages. Over time, students acquire facility through active uses of a variety of languages in discussions.

ENGAGING STUDENTS IN CRITICAL INQUIRY RELATED TO LANGUAGE USE

There are a number of ways that you can engage your students' critical inquiry into language use. Below, we illustrate some of these approaches through our three critical inquiry practices.

Adopting a critical stance toward language variation

A first step in helping students understand language variation is to encourage them to adopt a critical stance toward the role of varieties of English and other languages within the larger scope of history, politics, and grammar (Zuidema, 2005). This suggests the need to help students understand that Standard English is not a static system that is somehow indicative of intellectual or moral superiority. Rather, it is a continually shifting, abstract model that should be understood as a tool that provides certain kinds of social access (Flynn, 2011).

Goodman (2011) suggests that a close examination of language in Shakespeare's plays can illustrate for students the dynamic, fluid nature of the English language. She points out how Shakespeare's use of functional shifts in words—for instance, using a word commonly used as a noun as a verb—led to functional shifts in those words in everyday use. Similarly, Zuidema (2005) suggests that teachers might show students the same poem written in Old English, Middle English, and Modern English as a means of demonstrating the useful and necessary evolution of the English language. She explains that:

> Some words or phrases become linguistic fads; others fall into disuse or "misuse." Rules of taste change, and the pronunciations, uses, conjugations, and spellings of words are altered over time to adjust to new contexts, speakers, purposes, and audiences. We call this adaptability "survival of the fittest" when we discuss other kinds of evolution; it is evidence of the resilience of language and not a matter for concern.
>
> (p. 872)

Once students begin to take a critical stance toward the idea that English is static, you can engage them in activities that "de-center" and question Standard English and center other Englishes like AAE (White, 2011). For example, White (2011) asked his students to translate a section of Tupac Shakur's "Just Me Against the World," which is written in a variation of African American Vernacular English, into Standard English. He explained:

> Though each passage—the original and its translation—says the same thing (each has the same literal message), the original, non-Standard English passage inevitably holds far more

emotional and rhetorical power regardless of audience . . . via different translations of the same texts, my students experienced firsthand how meaning can be lost when we insist on a rigid form of English for making meaning.

(p. 47)

You can also help your students to de-center and question Standard English by guiding them through activities that shed light on linguistic prejudice and racism. Wilson (2001) suggests that students can learn how particular regional, racial, cultural, and generational variations of English and variations on languages such as Spanish become stigmatized by examining how people who use particular variations are portrayed in popular culture in the media. She suggests that students "tape-record sitcoms in which certain dialects are used to delineate particular character types and how those linguistic features suggest character, level of education, degree of intelligence, etc." (34). She recommends that students "record evidence of language prejudice in cartoons, newspaper or magazine articles, or editorials" (34).

Finally, you can help your students adopt a critical stance toward language variation by asking them to examine their uses of language within the larger context of language variation. For instance, Hagemann (2001) suggests engaging students in a role-playing activity in which they describe a car accident to their parents, a friend, and an insurance agent. In her own work with this activity, she found that, "depending on the audience, [students] chose different words, added/deleted particular details, used a different tone, etc." (78). Hagemann argued that this sort of role-playing activity illustrates for students that we all use different variations of language all the time to suit different purposes and to perform various aspects of our identities.

Similarly, Flynn (2011) detailed a unit in which a teacher asked students to brainstorm a list of dialects that they hear and speak in their everyday lives—for instance, "dinner table," "church," and "military" as well as those that are most overtly racial, cultural, or regional. Students in this classroom also studied Gary Soto's (1997) play *Novio Boy* with the goal of examining how and for what purposes characters in the novel chose to speak particular variations of English and Spanish. Overall, students in this study learned that no one language, dialect, or variation is correct, but instead that all dialects and variations of any language can be appropriate and useful depending on audience and purpose.

In her Language in Cultural Context class, Molly Vanish helped her 11th-grade students develop a critical stance toward language. Her students examined language related to politics, race, gender, and social class in hip-hop music, poetry, and documentary film. Below, Molly explains this work:

Today we were talking about language and regionalism and we watched a clip from the movie, *Snatch*, with Brad Pitt and we looked at the ways that the in-group had power even though they didn't have power in an official sense so how language is used in that way. Having film is really important in showing students what is real so that their awareness shifts a little bit.

Some students have that awareness so having chances to share that awareness through presentations and conversations helps. So, [I might ask] "Did anyone have a time when they were in the out-group because of how people were using dialect or slang and hearing different examples?" [A student might respond], "Oh, I volunteer at the hospital and the doctors use all these words and I have no idea about what they are saying. And I can't always answer everybody's questions." And [another student might say], "I worked at some Mexican restaurant and I didn't speak Spanish fluently so I wasn't able to create friendships with the people there." (Beach et al., 2016, p. 202)

Considering alternative perspectives through the study of language variation

Once you have helped your students adopt a critical stance toward languages and language variations, you can begin to lead them through activities that help them understand how their identities are constructed through their uses of language as social practice. In doing so, you are challenging them to consider alternative perspectives regarding uses of language as they impact their ability to access particular kinds of power. This kind of instruction is particularly important for students who are English language learners (ELLs).

In order to help students understand how their identities are constructed through language use, you first need to acknowledge and value students' home languages. Hollie (2001) offers several useful suggestions for valuing students' home languages that are supported by the Linguistic Affirmation Program (LAP). This LAP program is "a comprehensive nonstandard language awareness program designed to serve the language needs of African American, Mexican American, Hawaiian American, and Native American students who are not proficient in Standard American English (SAE)" (54). In this program, students are encouraged to use home languages whenever possible in the classroom "as an acknowledgement of their culture and history" (57). Hollie also recommends that teachers value and bolster students' cultures and histories by using culturally relevant literature. For instance, Hollie's teachers used literature in which authors use African American English, such as works by Julius Lester and Virginia Hamilton.

Studying such literature moves beyond acknowledging students' linguistic backgrounds toward providing students with a means of exploring connections between language practices and identity construction. Hollie explained that

> these works give the students the opportunity to see the language in the text versus simply hearing it all the time. Then they are able to make comparisons and contrasts with the language they read and the language they speak, as well as with Standard American English.
>
> (2001, p. 58)

Finally Hollie recommends that teachers engage students in activities with a significant amount of physical movement such as role-play and reader's theater, which allow for expressions of identity and diversity in language use.

Medina and Campano's (2006) study of linguistically diverse students engaging in drama and role-play activities corroborates Hollie's recommendation. In their study, students used role-play scenarios to critically examine the treatment of linguistically diverse students by teachers and administrators in one school. They also detail a unit in which students read a bilingual text, *My Diary from Here to There* (Pérez, 2002); kept character journals in either English, Spanish, or both; and then engaged in dramatic dialogues based on their journals. After examining these drama activities, Medina and Campano surmised that "drama affords a generative nexus between the students' own identities and more expansive understandings of school-based literacy practices" (333). Further, they concluded that text and selves work together in a productive dialectic that creates a dynamic, in-between space where students explore characters' fictional lives but also their own actual lives and identities in schools. In the process, the students mine their cultural experiences to arrive at more complete and incisive understandings of how they are positioned by others, including educators, administrators, and policymakers (pp. 339–340). (For more on studying language variation, see *Studying language variation* on the website.)

ADOPTING ALTERNATIVE PERSPECTIVES ON LANGUAGE USE

As students begin to understand how their identities are constructed and positioned in relation to the languages and dialects they use, you will want to engage students in activities that encourage them to collaborate with and relate to others to explore multiple perspectives on social practices related to language use. A productive place to begin involves dialogic, student-centered discussions of language variation. For instance, Godley and Minnici (2008) found that by engaging in dialogic discussions of language variation, the primarily African American students in their study were able to identify nuances and variations in the use of African American Vernacular English across various neighborhoods in their city.

Because students were encouraged to express conflicting ideas, even ideas that challenged their teacher, their collaborative work in these discussions led them to understand language variation and identity beyond their teacher's initial goals. Godley and Minnici explained that

> With this discussion, students moved from the curriculum's framing of language variation on a national scale to language variation on a much more local scale . . . The students' depiction of their linguistic identities, therefore, emphasized distinct identities within an African American community rather than a linguistic identity constructed primarily in opposition to White identities.
>
> (2008, p. 336)

What is important to notice here is that through students' collaborative, dialogic discussion in this classroom, they began to see how language is used as a social practice that identifies one as being a member of a particular community with particular beliefs and values.

Language diversity and variation are not only topics for English in North America, but are issues around the world. Linda Christensen (2009) has created a curriculum on language and power that examines the "colonial roots of linguistic genocide and analyzed how schools continue to perpetuate the myths of inferiority or invisibility of some languages" (p. 209). She explains that "over half of the world's languages have become extinct in the last 500 years."

To help her high school students experiment with and understand different perspectives relative to language and power, Christensen holds a "linguistic tea party." She has created a set of carefully described roles based on the stories of real people in the present and in history that includes: Hector Pieterson, a student from South Africa forced to learn Africaans; Damien O-Donovan, an Irishman whose friend was beaten to death by the British Army for speaking Irish; Gloria Anzuldua, a Mexican American writer hit as a child by a teacher for speaking Spanish; Lois-Ann Yamanaka, a native Hawaiian; Ngugi wa Thiong'o, a Kenyan novelist who stopped writing in English and instead writes in his native Kikuyu; Molly Craig, an Aboriginal from Australia; Bud Lane, a Native American from Oregon and one of the last speakers of Coastal Athabaskan; and others (Christensen, 2009, pp. 218–225).

At the "tea party" Christensen provides her students with a list of questions, such as "Find someone who was forced to speak another language. Who is this person? How did this affect the person?" or "Find someone who started or joined an organization to preserve his or her language. Who is this person? Why did the individual decide to take this action?" After the tea party, students first write about questions like, "What do the people who are forced to change their language have in common? How do they feel about their language?" They then engage in additional research, reading essays and stories, and watching a film about Native American boarding schools, *In the White Man's Image* (Lesiak, 1992). They study the Soweto Uprising, write poetry and short pieces, create symbolic drawings, and study the language restoration movement.

Another activity that may help students understand alternative perspectives on language involves doing language ethnographies. In this activity, students observe and describe how particular types of language use constituted their own or others' identities, roles, and relationships based on certain norms, beliefs, and social practices in a given social context, group, or community.

As part of her mini-ethnography assignment previously noted, Elizabeth Erdmann had students identify their participants' characteristic language use. For example, Gabriel Lindquist described the use of language references by avid movie goers or cinephiles:

> A Cinephile's terminology is somewhat limited to the films they have seen. They use references from film old and new. It can be used in both casual and proper discussion. It adds a sense of seclusion and individuality that can be matched by few other things. It is also vital that both parties understand the film reference, if not it may cause one of the party members to become disgruntled. But when they do perceive it, it can be a thing of beauty. An example of cinephile lingo may come in many forms, such as: Say that you find a friend yours that was injured in some fashion, the incident itself is irrelevant.
>
> "Sorry to bother you, but would you be willing to take me to the hospital. I seemed to have gotten myself scraped up a bit".
> "Are you alright" I would ask.
> "Oh I'm fine, 'tis but a flesh wound. As long as you are not taking me to the castle Anthrax I can't complain".
> The quotes "'tis but a flesh wound" and "castle anthrax" are both popular references to Monty Python's *The Holy Grail*. This shows how engrained a reference may be. To the point where it comes off as natural. Which many cinephile's can quote from for hours on end. (Beach et al., 2016, p. 205)

By conducting these ethnographies, students learned how language establishes shared knowledge and defines identities within groups or events. (For more on conducting ethnographies of language use, see *Conducting ethnographies of language use* on the website.)

> **Activity: Reflecting on your language ideologies**
>
> You can reflect on your language ideologies by responding to the following quotes:
>
> 1. And my thing is, you come to this country, it's an English-speaking country, you need to learn English. Not for us to go and learn Spanish, nah! I got to learn your language, see, because I am in your country now.
> 2. I think it is great [that the students use Spanish]. Like my kids use it all the time amongst each other, whether it is inside the classroom or outside of the classroom, and I want to embrace that. I don't want them to lose that. As long as they are trying to learn English, I am happy.
> 3. With the ESL population, I don't see mainstream teachers really knowing them that well. I think they take the language barrier as a way out to just say, "Well, I don't speak their language so I'm not going to, I don't ha-, I can't get involved."
>
> (Beauchemin, 2021; quotes from Gallo et al. 2014).

TRANSFORMING THINKING ABOUT LANGUAGE USE

We have discussed the value of guiding your students through instruction that helps them adopt a critical stance toward language use and consider alternative perspectives on how people use language. Your students will then be ready to synthesize what they have learned toward transforming their thinking about language use and experimenting with the acquisition of new language varieties and dialects. This includes treating your students' various home languages and dialects as "resources" rather than "problems" (Ruíz, 1998).

Doing so acknowledges that many of your students' identities are constructed through their linguistic experiences as people who are multilingual. According to Cummins et al. (2006),

> One of the most consistent findings in the literature on bilingualism is that literacy skills in a student's first language (L1) and second language (L2) are strongly related. In other words, L1 and L2 literacy are interdependent or manifestations of a common underlying proficiency.
>
> (p. 299)

Based on this research, the authors suggest that investing time in helping your students understand their use of their first languages (or dialects) has the potential to improve their proficiency in other Englishes including the disciplinary languages of schooling.

A student's knowledge of their home language or dialect is useful in making connections and building proficiency in other Englishes through comparison, or what some scholars refer to as "contrastive analysis" (Godley & Minnici, 2008; Wheeler & Swords, 2006). For instance, scholars have found that students may struggle to understand particular features of new language variations. For example, a subtle distinction between words in different disciplines can be difficult to distinguish. Students can then be taught to better understand those features by having a teacher explicitly point them out so that they, first, notice and pay attention to these features.

Students could then compare those features to their current uses of language and consider how linguistic choices affect their ability to community effectively (Hagemann, 2001; Siegel, 1999). For instance, AAE linguistic variations often use double negation in a phrase like, "I don't know nothing about that." Standard English variations would more likely use a phrase like, "I don't know *anything* about that." Drawing attention to the specific differences in a feature like negation can help your students determine with which audiences particular linguistic choices will be most effective.

You can also ask your students to view documentaries about language use such as *American Tongues* (Alvarez & Kolker, 1986), *The Story of English* (Cran, 1997), or *Do You Speak American?* (Cran, 2005) in order to study patterns and rules in varieties of English that they may use in their home lives versus variations of Standard English that will provide them with different kinds of social access (Zudeima, 2005). For instance, *Do You Speak American* takes viewers on a journey around the United States, providing a glimpse into the history and social purposes behind language use in various regions and among various peoples. After viewing the film, students could be asked to study different regional, generational, or racial/ethnic variations that were discussed, constructing a list of rules for each variation that includes a comparison with rules of Standard English. (For more on studying dialect differences, see *Dialect differences* on the website.)

It is critical that, as you begin to ask students to explore the conventions of linguistic variation including Standard English, you are clear that you are not asking them to give up their home languages or related identities. As Hagemann (2001) reminds us, our goal as teachers should be "expanding" rather than "erasing" a student's linguistic repertoire (78).

With this goal in mind, it is useful to teach students to consider how people vary their use of language across social contexts. In earlier editions of this book, we suggested teaching students about the concept of "code-switching"—or using different languages, discourses, and variations in different contexts.

However, recent scholarship challenges code-switching, arguing that it continues to center Standard English while marginalizing non-dominant Englishes by sidelining discussions of race in ways that do more harm than good for linguistically marginalized students (Baker-Bell, 2013; 2017; Canagarajah, 2006; Kirkland & Jackson, 2008; Young, 2009). Rather than teaching students about code-switching, we recommend focusing on critical language pedagogy by focusing on helping students see language as related to power, identity, history, culture, and politics (Alim, 2007; Baker-Bell, 2013; Godley & Minnici, 2008; Godley & Reaser, 2018).

Examining literary texts in which characters explicitly discuss their own language variation can help students understand how language is associated with power and identity (Zuidema, 2005). Zuidema (2005) recommends *A Lesson Before Dying* (Gaines, 1993) or chapter 12 of *To Kill a Mockingbird* (Lee, 1960) as possible texts for this work. Other research has also found *To Kill a Mockingbird* to be a useful text for examining how characters use language (Godley & Minnici, 2008; Thein et al., 2010). Students studied how Calpurnia, the African American housekeeper who worked in the White, upper-middle-class Finch household, not only used different language, demeanor, and dispositions but also held different norms for the Finch children's behavior in the Finch's home than she did in her own church community (Thein et al., 2010).

You could engage your students in this type of literary activity by asking small groups of students to study various characters in a novel. Students could examine first how a character's language use, affect, discourse, and identity are depicted across contexts in a novel. They could then look for how the character is depicted as gaining access to certain kinds of power by way of adapting various identities through language use.

As students understand characters' use of linguistic variation and the usefulness of particular languages and varieties for particular audiences and purposes, they will need practice with constructing and producing texts that incorporate language variation. A useful entry point into this type of work might be to ask students to write and perform skits that incorporate various dialects (Flynn, 2011). In Flynn's study, students tried to construct lists of rules for each of the dialects they used. Another useful addition to this project would be to ask students to explain why each dialect was appropriate (or inappropriate) for each character in the skit to gain particular kinds of access or meet particular goals.

Activity: Employing Language Consistent with Community Norms

You might also ask your students to construct texts that will help them solve authentic problems in their own community. For example, suppose budget cuts threatened to dissolve your school's music programs. In that case, you could ask students to construct texts that would persuasively communicate with three different audiences to argue for help in keeping the programs. You might ask students to consider both the mode and the language/variation that would be most appropriate and persuasive for each audience.

For instance, in trying to gain ground with the school board, students might write a formal letter in Standard English that makes arguments based on reason. In seeking the support of their peers, they might send a text or a Tweet written with texting symbols and abbreviations and with language variation that is common among adolescents in their community. Spanish-speaking students could create a translation of the message including Spanish phrases commonly used by students in the school. (For more on studying dialect differences, see *Studying dialect differences* on the website.)

THE IMPORTANCE OF ELL INSTRUCTION.

Students who are English language learners represent just over 10% of the public school population, and often more in schools hiring new teachers. Given problems with traditional methods and materials for ELL instruction, the Council of the Great City Schools (2014) representing 67 large-city school districts, generated a framework statement regarding the need to mesh ELL instruction with the CCSS along with a set of criteria for assessing instructional materials and resources (Maxwell, 2014). This includes the use of daily "focused language study" on English-language acquisition related to the CCSS in either separate or ELA classes and a focus on "discipline-specific and academic language expansion" (DALE) by acquiring the use of formal, academic language in all subject matter classes.

This also includes the use of culturally responsive teaching that builds on students' cultural backgrounds perceived to be assets as well as use of texts that provide authentic, non-stereotypical portrayals of students' cultural worlds—for example, the use of high quality, authentic instructional materials and texts in Spanish.

Culturally responsive teaching includes investigating your students' families' literacy practices to determine their uses of language. In some cases, students themselves may serve as translators for their parents—a process involving extensive translanguaging practices (Orellana, & García-Sánchez, 2019.

Adopting a translanguaging perspective involves going beyond *external* perspectives on language focus naming different categories of types of language such as "English," "French," "Arabic," or "Mandarin," to adopt an *internal* perspective that perceives language itself as a set of features of repertoire employed to express oneself (Beauchemin, 2021).

These external perspectives are often based on language ideologies shaping categories such as "limited-English-proficient" (LEP) to label students. These labels fail to consider how bi/multilingual students have certain valuable literacy practices, instead of using the category, English language learner (ELL), to highlight students' accomplishments in learning English (Beauchemin, 2021). A translanguaging perspective—like a critical language pedagogy perspective—involves more than code-switching from one language to another (Beauchemin, 2021). Code-switching assumes that bilinguals' two languages are two separate monolingual codes that could be used without reference to each other. Instead, translanguaging posits that bilinguals have one linguistic repertoire from which they select features strategically to communicate effectively (Goodman & Tastanbek, 2021).

This requires challenging stereotypes you may have about students from non-dominant communities as lacking academic abilities given their use of language (García-Sánchez & Orellana, 2019). It also involves inquiring about students' families' "funds of knowledge" related to literacy and cultural practices that you build on in creating classroom activities (Moll & González, 2004). This includes finding out

> what kids do when they are not in school: who they talk with; where they go; what games they play; what they read, write, listen and view . . . youth do engage in rich and complex practices every day. They play, read, write, talk and work with their peers and families, using language (often multiple linguistic varieties) to do a wide range of things including to entertain, argue, compare, contrast, and take action in the world. They observe and participate in a wide range of relationships, activities, and tasks. They learn from that engagement.
> (García-Sánchez & Orellana, 2019, pp. 19–20)

A translanguaging framework also recommends purposeful use of technology based on students' needs as opposed to technology for its own sake (Parker, 2007). One useful resource for addressing ELL instruction related to the CCSS is the Colorin Colorado blog Common Core and ELLs *blog.colorincolorado.org*.

ELL students need highly individualized assistance in learning English, particularly to engage in meaningful practice in using English in contexts in which they are using language to achieve a certain goal, for example, requesting or sharing information on how to do something. There are a number of different apps such as iOS HGP 2.0, Hello English, Basic Pronunciation: Clear Speech from the Start, or Beginner English or Android English Training or Speak English that provide students with activities for practicing language use in conversational contexts (Beach & O'Brien, 2014; see also resources *tinyurl.com/lldfxb7*). And, students can employ translation apps such as iOS or Android Google Translate, iOS Translator with Voice, or iOS Communilator Free translation apps for dictating in their primary language to hear or read translations to self-assess their translation abilities (Beach & O'Brien, 2014, p. 162). (For more on teaching English Language Learners, see *Teaching English Language Learners* on the website.)

> **Activity: Responding to Bilingual Texts**
>
> You can also have students read bilingual texts in the classroom, particularly in working with younger secondary students, given that more bilingual texts are available for those students (Beauchemin, 2021). Students with the same home language, but at different levels of proficiency, could pair up and read aloud to each other in both languages.
>
> Students could also respond to bilingual texts using sticky notes written in their home language. They can also employ Google Translate to listen to translations or translations of the written work in another language. (For slides on Translanguaging in Comprehension Instruction (Part I) *http://t.ly/59DI* and Part II *http://t.ly/EwcD* created by Faythe Beauchemin for her reading methods course at the University of Arkansas that include lists of books for use with younger students.)

SUMMARY

State ELA and the Common Core standards for language and usage broadly convey two key points. First, they ask that you help your students gain an understanding of the concept Standard Academic English in both written and oral forms. Second, they ask that you ensure that your students value their own languages and variations and understand the contextual nature of language and usage. It is also important that they are prepared to communicate appropriately and effectively across social contexts. In this chapter, we have argued that both of these standards can be met and exceeded by guiding your students through critical inquiry practices that help them understand language variation and the role of Standard English within that variation.

Beyond meeting these standards, this approach will aid you in acknowledging the linguistic resources that all of your students bring to your classroom and it will provide you with tools for helping all of your students understand the socially constructed, fluid nature of language and its ability to constrain or empower people.

REFERENCES

Alim, H. S. (2005). Critical language awareness in the United States: Revisiting issues and revising pedagogies in a resegregated society. *Educational Researcher, 34*(7), 24–31.

Alim, H. S. (2007). Critical hip-hop language pedagogies: Combat, consciousness, and the cultural politics of communication. *Journal of Language, Identity, and Education, 6*(2), 161–176.

Alim, H. S., & Smitherman, G. (2012). *Articulate while Black: Barack Obama, language, and race in the US.* Oxford University Press.

Alvarez, L, & Kolker, A. (Directors). (1988). *American tongues* [Motion picture]. United States. Center for New American Media.

Baker-Bell, A. (2013). "I never really knew the history behind African American language": Critical language pedagogy in an advanced placement English language arts class. *Equity & Excellence in Education, 46*(3), 355–370.

Baker-Bell, A. (2017). I can switch my language, but I can't switch my skin: What teachers must understand about linguistic racism. In E. Moore, A. Michael Jr., & M. W. Penick-Parks (Eds.), *The guide for white women who teach black boys* (pp. 97–107). Corwin Press.

Baker-Bell, A. (2020). *Linguistic justice: Black language, literacy, identity, and pedagogy.* Routledge.

Bakhtin, M. M. (1984). Problems of Dostoevsky's Poetics (C. Emerson, Ed. & Trans.). University of Minnesota Press.

Beach, R., & Beauchemin, F. (2019). *Teaching language as action in the ELA classroom.* Routledge.

Beach, R., & Bloome, D. (Eds.). (2019). *Languaging relations for transforming the literacy and language arts classroom.* Routledge.

Beach, R., & Caraballo, L. (2021). How language matters: Using ethnographic writing to portray and reflect on languaging actions. *Journal of Adolescent & Adult Literacy, 65*(2), 139–148.

Beach, R., & O'Brien, D. (2014). *Using apps for learning across the curriculum: A literacy-based framework and guide.* Routledge.

Beach, R., Thein, A. H., & Webb, A. (2016). *The English language arts Common Core state standards: A critical inquiry approach for 6–12 classrooms*, 2nd ed. Routledge.

Beauchemin, F. (2021). Literacy as social: Relational-keys in literacy events. *English Teaching: Practice and Critique, 20*(3), 328–340.

Bertau, M. C. (2014). Exploring language as the "in-between". *Theory & Psychology, 24*(4), 524–541.

Blake, R., & Cutler, C. (2003). AAE and variation in teachers' attitudes: A question of school philosophy? *Linguistics and Education, 14*(2), 163–194.

Buber, M. (1970). *I and thou* (W. Kaufmann, Trans.). Charles Scribner's Sons.

Canagarajah, S. (2006). *The place of world Englishes in composition: Pluralization continued.* Norton.

Cazden, C. B. (2001). *Classroom discourse: The language of teaching and learning*, 2nd ed. Heinemann.

Christensen, L. (2009). *Teaching for joy and justice.* Rethinking Schools.

Common Core Standards. (2010). *Common Core State Standards for English language arts & literacy in history/social studies, science, and technical subjects.* Washington, DC: Council of Chief State School Officers and the National Governors Association.

Council of the Great City Schools. (2014). A framework for raising expectations and instructional rigor for ELLs: A project of the Council of the Great City Schools. Author.

Cran, W. (Director) (1997). *The story of English.* [Motion Picture]. United States. Home Vision Entertainment.

Cran, W. (Director). (2005). *Do you speak American?* [Television Series] New York: WNET.

Cummins, J., Chow, P. & Schecter, S. (2006). Community as curriculum. *Language Arts, 83*(4), 297–307.

Delpit, L. (2006). *Other people's children: Cultural conflict in the classroom.* New Press.

Ferguson, R. F. (1998). Teachers' perceptions and expectations and the Black–White test score gap. In C. Jencks & M. Phillips (Eds.), *The Black–White test score gap* (pp. 273–317). Brookings Institute Press.

Flynn, J. E. (2011). The language of power: Beyond the grammar workbook. *English Journal, 100*(4), 27–30.

Gaines, E. J. (1993). *A lesson before dying.* Knopf.

Gallo, S., Link, H., Allard, E., Wortham, S., & Mortimer, K. (2014). Conflicting ideologies of Mexican immigrant English across levels of schooling. *International Multilingual Research Journal, 8*(2), 124–140.

García-Sánchez, I. M.,& Orellana, M. F. (Eds.) (2019).*Language and cultural practices in communities and schools: Bridging learning for students from non-dominant groups.* Routledge.

Gee, J. P. (1996). *Social linguistics and literacies: Ideology in discourses*, 2nd ed. Taylor & Francis.

Godley, A., Sweetland, J., Wheeler, R., Minnici, A., & Carpenter, B. (2006). Preparing teachers for dialectically diverse classrooms. *Educational Researcher, 35*(8), 30–37.

Godley, A., & Minnici, A. (2008). Critical language pedagogy in an urban high school English class. *Urban Education, 43*(3), 319–346.

Godley, A. J., & Reaser, J. (2018). *Critical language pedagogy: Interrogating language, dialects, and power in teacher education.* Peter Lang/International Academic Publishers.

Goffman, E. (1986). *Frame analysis: An essay on the organization of experience.* Northeastern University Press.

Goodman, B. (2011). Linguistic audacity: Shakespeare's language and student writing. *English Journal, 100*(4), 39–43.

Goodman, B., & Tastanbek, S. (2021). Making the shift from a codeswitching to a translanguaging lens in English language teacher education. *TESOL Quarterly, 55*(1), 29–53.

Haddix, M. (2015). *Cultivating racial and linguistic diversity in literacy teacher education: Teachers like me.* Routledge/National Council of Teachers of English.

Hagemann, J. (2001). A bridge from home to school: Helping working class students acquire school literacy. *English Journal, 90*(4), 74–81.

Hillocks, G. (1984). What works in teaching composition: A meta-analysis of experimental treatment studies. *American Journal of Education, 93*(1), 133–170.

Hollie, S. (2001). Acknowledging the language of African American students: Instructional strategies. *English Journal, 90*(4), 54–59.

Johnson, L. L., Jackson, J., Stovall, D., & Baszile, D. T. (2017). "Loving Blackness to Death": (Re)Imagining ELA classrooms in a time of racial chaos. *English Journal, 106*(4), 60–66.

Kirkland, D. (2010). English(es) in urban contexts: Politics, pluralism, and possibilities. *English Education, 42*(3), 293–306.

Kirkland, D. E., and Jackson, A. (2008). Beyond the silence: Instructional approaches and students' attitudes. In J. Scott, D. Y. Straker, & L. Katz (Eds.), *Affirming students' right to their own language: Bridging educational policies and language/language arts teaching practices* (pp. 160–180). National Council of Teachers of English.

Leakey, R. E., & Lewin, R. (1992). *Origins reconsidered: In search of what makes us human.* Doubleday.

Lee, H. (1960). *To kill a mockingbird*. Lippincott.
Lesiak, C. (Director). (1992). "*In the White man's image.*" [Television series episode]. WBGH American Experience.
Lippi-Green, R. (1997). *English with an accent: Language, ideology, and discrimination in the United States*. Routledge.
Martinez, D. (2017). Imagining a language of solidarity for Black and Latinx youth in English language arts classrooms. *English Education, 49*(2), 179–196.
Maxwell, L. A. (2014, September 9). Urban districts develop Common-Core guide for teaching ELLs [Web log post]. Retrieved from http://tinyurl.com/q96t3nq
Medina, C., & Campano, G. (2006). Performing identities through drama and teatro practices in multilingual classrooms. *Language Arts, 83*(4), 332–341.
Metz, M. (2019). Principles to navigate the challenges of teaching English language variation: A guide for nonlinguists. In M. D. Devereaux & C. C. Palmer (Eds.), *Teaching language variation in the classroom: Strategies and models from teachers and linguists* (pp. 69–75). Routledge.
Moll, L. C., & González, N. (2004). Engaging life: A funds of knowledge approach to multicultural education. In J. Banks & C. McGee Banks (Eds.), *Handbook of research on multicultural education*, 2nd ed. (pp. 699–715). Jossey-Bass.
National Council of Teachers of English (2021). NCTE standards for the initial preparation of teachers of English language arts 7–12 (Initial Licensure). Author. Retrieved from https://ncte.org/wpcontent/uploads/2021/11/2021_NCTE_Standards.pdf.
Orellana, M. F., & García-Sánchez, I. (2019). *Language and cultural processes in communities and schools: Bridging learning for students from non-dominant groups*. Routledge.
Parker, L. L. (Ed.) (2007). *Technology-mediated learning environments for young English learners*. Routledge.
Pennycook, A. (2010). *Language as local practice*. Routledge.
Pérez, A. I. (2002). *My diary from here to there*. Children's Books
Perry, T., & Delpit, L. (Eds.) (1998). *The real Ebonics debate: Power, language and the education of African-American children*. Beacon Press.
Ruíz, R. (1998). Orientations in language planning. In S. McKay & S. L. Wong (Eds.), *Language diversity: Problem or resource?* (pp. 3–25). Newbury House.
Rymes, B. (2014). *Communicating beyond language: Everyday encounters with diversity*. Routledge.
Siegel, J. (1999). Stigmatized and standardized varieties in the classroom: Interference or separation? *TESOL Quarterly, 33*, 701–728.
Soto, G. (1997). *Novio boy: A play*. Graphia.
The Ohio State University Argumentative Writing Project. (2016). Principled practices for teaching dialogic literary argumentation in high school English language arts classrooms. Author.
Thein, A. H., Guise, M. & Sloan, D. L. (2011). Problematizing literature circles as forums for discussion of multicultural and political texts. *Journal of Adolescent & Adult Literacy, 55*(1), 15–24.
Thein, A. H., Oldakowski, T., & Sloan, D. L. (2010). Using blogs to teach strategies for inquiry into the construction of lived and text worlds. *Journal of Media Literacy Education, 2*(1), 23–36.
Toshalis, E. (2016). Correcting Our Connecting. *Educational Leadership, 74*(1), 16–20.
Wheeler, R., & Swords, R. (2006). *Code-switching: Teaching Standard English in urban classrooms*. National Council of Teachers of English.
White, J. (2011). De-centering English: Highlighting the dynamic nature of the English language to promote the teaching of code-switching. *English Journal, 100*(4), 44–49.
Wilson, M. (2001). The changing discourse of language study. *English Journal, 90*(4), 31–36.
Wolfram, W. (2019). Language awareness in education: A linguist's response to teachers. In M. D. Devereaux & C. C. Palmer (Eds.), *Teaching language variation in the classroom: Strategies and models from teachers and linguists* (pp. 61–66). Routledge.
Wolfram, W., Adger, C. T., & Christian, D. (1999). *Dialects in schools and communities*. Erlbaum.
Young, V. A. (2009). "Nah we straight": An argument against code switching. *Journal of Advanced Composition, 29*(1–2), 49–76.
Zuidema, L. (2005). Myth education: Rationale and strategies for teaching against linguistic prejudice. *Journal of Adolescent & Adult Literacy, 48*(8), 666–675.
Zwiers, J. (2014). *Building academic language: Meeting Common Core Standards across disciplines, grades 5–12*. John Wiley & Sons.

Section III

Evaluation, Assessment, and Reflection

11

Assessing Students' Learning

Assessment is a crucial part of teaching. Regular assessment provides data about student progress in achieving learning goals. It also provides teachers with crucial information about their instruction and about changes that you need to make in focus, approach, pacing, and differentiation. Effective teachers rely on testing and formal assessment; they observe and evaluate student progress and constantly modify instruction to support inclusion and success.

One key aspect of evaluating students' growth involves *formative assessment* that provides students with continuous feedback about their work. Formative assessment differs from summative assessment in that it focuses on students learning as students are engaged in an activity or project over time. Formative assessment emphasizes:

- recognizing individual differences in students' achievement versus the assumption that all students should be achieving at the same rate and time.
- providing immediate versus delayed feedback.
- fostering progress or growth over time versus test scores or labels.
- helping students formulate goals for students' self-assessment versus reliance on external, outside summative assessment tools (Ryan, 2014).

Central to any consideration of the use of formative assessment is the larger focus on how assessment contributes to fostering learning. The 2021 NCTE ELA standards include the standard "candidates identify and/or design formative and summative assessments that reflect ELA research, align with intended learning outcomes, and engage learners in monitoring their progress toward established goals" (National Council of Teachers of English, 2021, p. 3).

Formative assessment involves providing feedback for "assessing for" learning—to help students enhance their learning of literacy practices over time (Black et al., 2003). In contrast, summative assessment involves "assessing" students to provide them with a snapshot indication of their abilities at a particular moment or point in time, such as a standardized reading test designed to measure students' reading ability.

This chapter describes various ways to assess students through ongoing, descriptive, supportive, formative assessment of students as they are engaged in various activities (Swaffield, 2008). This means that you, as a teacher, are not just assessing students based on their

DOI: 10.4324/9781003177364-14

performance of isolated skills or on a standardized test or as isolated individuals. You are also assessing students' work over time in meaningful contexts, such as how effectively students collaborate with others to achieve certain goals.

We also examine issues with summative assessment related to the limitations of standardized assessments associated with determining whether students have achieved certain standards.

USE OF FORMATIVE ASSESSMENT WITHIN LEARNING CONTEXTS

Defining the purpose of formative assessment requires understanding the kinds of learning occurring in a classroom context. In that context, students bring certain status-quo literacy practices that they have already acquired. They are then participating in activities designed to foster acquiring new practices. The difference or gap between the practices students already know and what new practices they may acquire has been defined in terms of Vygotsky's (1978) concept of the zone of proximal development (ZPD) (Dann, 2018; 2019). (For a video series on formative assessment by Professor Heidi Andrade as part of the Arts Assessment for Learning Project *artsassessmentforlearning.org/about-assessment*, with examples of formative assessments for use with theater instruction *t.ly/SKC6*; Andrade & Heritage, 2018.)

Responding to students within their zone of proximal development

Teachers learn about their students' current knowledge and practices to create and scaffold activities that promote their development of new knowledge and practices within their zone of proximal development (ZPD) (Vygotsky, 1986). Knowing that a student has a particular interest in creating comic books, in teaching a literary text, a teacher may build on that interest to have the student respond to a text using comic-book images. The teachers may also have the student share her responses with her peers to foster her competence to bolster her sense of agency.

The purpose of assessment is to foster learning by providing helpful feedback within a student's ZPD. This involves determining students' status-quo level of their knowledge or use of literacy practices to foster their growth in ways that lead them to acquire new knowledge or employ new literacy practices over time within their ZPD. You are then framing your descriptive feedback within this ZPD learning gap so that you're nudging the student to go beyond their status-quo level. At the same time, you are still considering their potential, current ceiling in order that students will understand the meaning of your feedback so that you're not overwhelming them with feedback beyond their potential level that they may not be able to address.

For example, in responding to middle-school students' narratives, you may describe your engagement with the students' descriptions of characters in their narrative. At the same time, you also want them to go beyond descriptions to, consistent with "show–don't tell," portray their characters' actions or dialogue to flesh out those descriptions. Given your sense of the student's writing ability—that they may understand how to portray character traits through dialogue, you may then describe how you gain a fuller understanding of one of their characters through knowing how they talk to others. Based on the student's description of a character's traits, you may then have the student verbalize some dialogue that portrays that character's traits.

Institutional conceptions of ZPDs as "achievement gaps"

The concept of gap is also used in references to "achievement gaps" between high-versus low-achieving students based on standardized test scores (Dann, 2018). Administrators' concern about "achievement gaps" leads them to posit the need for test-preparation instruction in ways that foster standardization of curriculum. Administrators then ask teachers to teach relatively low-level literacy practices related to grammar, usage, and "correct-answer" reading comprehension skills at the expense of more open-ended, constructivist instruction.

Stephanie Shelton and Tamara Brooks described how these administrative demands to increase test scores impacted their teaching (Shelton & Brooks, 2019). They participated in frequent faculty meetings in which administrators admonished teachers with statements such as "'Our scores have got to be better; they're below the regression line'" (p. 6). They both describe how, given the focus on preparing students for tests that consist of short reading passages from literary texts, they would then have students read primarily shorter texts. So when they would teach novels, they were told by administrators that they need to "'focus on shorter passages and multiple choice. We need to get our reading scores up'" (p. 7). As a result, they were less likely to have students read novels that may enhance their literature engagement. This focus on test-preparation also reinforced the need to teach primarily short texts based on adherence to the 11th- and 12th-grade Common Core State Standards (2010) that refer to reading only dramas, stories, and poems as opposed to novels.

The result of this focus on the "achievement gap" is that teachers experience the need to adhere to these top-down administrative demands, resulting in an increased demoralization of teachers who no longer perceive themselves as having the autonomy to plan their curriculum (Santoro, 2018).

Activity: Reflecting on the Purpose of Assessment

Reflect back over your experience with being assessed on your work in schools over time. What assessment experiences enhanced your learning and growth over time, and what experiences were counter-productive? Were the assessments relevant or not relevant to what you were supposed to be learning in a unit or course? Based on those experiences, how do you plan to assess your students in ways that will foster their learning?

FOSTERING STUDENTS' VALUING OF FORMATIVE ASSESSMENT

In thinking about students receiving assessments, it's also important to consider how students understand, value, and use assessments to foster new ways of learning and thinking based on how they learn (Dann, 2018). If students do not value your assessments, they may not draw on your feedback to make changes in their learning.

Being open to change shaping their perceptions of assessment requires that students go beyond a "fixed mindset" to adopting a "growth mindset" related to knowing that, based on receiving supportive feedback, they can change (Dweck, 2012). (For information about the application of the "growth mindset" concept (Ackerman, 2019) t.ly/lAUf and *mindset works.com*.)

Students are more likely to understand and value assessment to adopt a "growth mindset" when they experience collaborative, supportive relations with teachers and peers, resulting in their perceiving feedback as useful (Dann, 2019). This suggests the need for teachers and peers to enact supportive relations with students based on being co-learners engaged in shared, supportive interactions to enhance students' sense of agency to improve their literacy practices.

If they lack that sense of agency as someone who can develop their literacy practice, they may not perceive the value or need to use feedback to enhance their learning (Dann, 2018). It is also the case that continually correcting students for their English use may only result in their developing a more negative self-perception of their student identity. They may then lack confidence in sharing their talk in the classroom (Smagorinsky, 2013).

ENGAGING IN FEEDBACK TO BUILD RELATIONSHIPS AS SUPPORTIVE CO-LEARNERS

In giving feedback, teachers enact certain identities associated with building relations with students to foster students' development of their own identities over time (Dann, 2018). Students are less likely to value feedback based on external, standardized criteria that shift the focus away from their relations with their teacher. Students may then perceive the teacher's feedback as a form of ventriloquism of these standardized criteria in ways that limit enacting a close relation with their teacher (Dann, 2019).

As a result, giving "feedback as a process which is as much about shaping identity(ies) in action as about specific curriculum messages is important" for development over time (Dann, 2019, p. 369). For example, in responding to a high school student's narrative portraying her challenges in middle school with reading difficulties, a teacher may share similar experiences with reading difficulties. In responding to his student's writing, Ian Thompson (2013) described his use of feedback in working with a student in crafting narrative writing through both adopting the role of "equal partner in the negotiation of meaning" as well as "critical partner who could prompt and question" (p. 260). As the student was writing his narrative, Thompson voiced responses and posed questions that helped the student revise his narrative in ways that engaged Thompson.

As students interact with teachers or peers, they are exposed to "external dialogue" from others that they then internalize as "inner dialogue" constituted by different alternative voices and perspectives to engage in looping their new way of thinking as "external dialogue" (Zittoun, 2017, p. 132). For example, one student, Ashley, was struggling with challenges in her life, but she did not want to share those difficulties with peers (Beach & Aukerman, 2019). However, members of her peer group insisted on talking with her, noting that "'Ashley, tell us what's wrong and we'll make it better'" (p. 62). She describes how internalizing her peers' supportive "external dialogue" led to developing her confidence in interacting with others. By internalizing her peers' "external dialogue" to develop her "inner dialogue," she developed an increased sense of social agency in her use of "external dialogue." She noted that "this group of people became aware of my social anxiety and how bad it was and they helped me order food at fast-food places and talk in front of strangers. Now, I can be more myself in class and out in public" (p. 62).

When teachers or peers provide feedback with students as "external dialogue," students then internalize that feedback as "inner dialogue" for reflecting on their writing. By framing descriptive feedback as tentative, exploratory thoughts instead of definitive, authoritative perceptions, students may be more likely to draw on that feedback to engage in "inner dialogue" to reflect on their writing.

"FEED-UP"

To foster students' self-assessment, you are having students reflect on their purposes, expectations, and criteria by engaging them in "feed-up," "feedback," and "feed-forward" formative assessment for thinking ahead about their use of literacy practices (Fisher & Frey, 2014; Hattie & Timperley, 2007).

In engaging students in "feed-up" formative assessment, you have students continually clarify their goals and expectations to self-assess whether they are accomplishing their purposes and expectations through their use of certain literacy practices. To identify their purposes and expectations, students may ask themselves, "where am I/are we going?" or "what am I/are we trying to accomplish?" (Fisher & Frey, 2014). For example, students creating a video documentary may determine that they want to capture how students perceive the influence of cliques in their school on bullying based on interviews of members aligned to different cliques.

For having students formulate goals related to motivation, it is useful to distinguish between performance goals associated with external markers of achievement versus mastery goals related to reflection on one's practices and growth (Emery, 2021). When students focus on *performance goals*, they are concerned about achieving success based on external measures of success in ways that may limit their focus on difficulties or challenges. In contrast, in formulating *mastery goals*, students are focusing more on addressing challenges in ways that lead to growth based on adopting a growth mindset (Dweck, 2012).

Mastery goals involve a focus on deep learning and gaining understanding related to improvement over time (Soylu et al., 2017). Performance goals involve a focus on being perceived as competent as opposed to incompetent—in some cases related to performance on standardized tests, even though articulating those goals may not enhance performance (Soylu et al., 2017). To focus on mastery goals, you have students identify goals they want to address based on what they want to learn in a course based on their previous experiences and needs (Emery, 2021).

You may also have students formulate their goals for work on a specific writing or response task to reflect on whether they have achieved their goals. For setting goals of their writing, students could pose the following questions:

- What is your goal with this piece? What do you hope readers take away?
- What are your biggest strengths in this draft? What feels right to you, and why?
- What might be the merits of this opening (x), rather than another (y)?
- How do your language choices help you achieve your aims? Where and how might you experiment further?
- What sections concern you in terms of organization, and why?
- Are there any other ways of making an impact in the closing (z)?
- What lingering concerns do you have about the direction of your writing?

(Song, 2017, p. 236)

You can also interact with students to discuss goals for developing their reading interests and experiences in your course. You may ask them to identify books they have most versus least enjoyed reading and reasons for differences in their reading experiences. Based on the identification of books they enjoyed, you can recommend other books in the same genre, with similar themes, or the same author.

You can also have them create narrative descriptions or "learning stories" (Swaffield, 2008) describing their experiences of responding to specific texts. For example, students can describe texts they perceived to be challenging and what practices they employed to cope with these challenges. They may also describe instances in discussions when they believed they were making a positive contribution and instances in which they felt that they were not involved in the discussion.

They may use "learning stories" to describe positive experiences. For example, a 9th-grade student at Jefferson High School, Bloomington, Minnesota, Abby Trevor, reflected on writing a fantasy short story:

> I almost always write medieval fantasy stories. This story seemed like a good chance to vary from that a little bit, so I wrote a modern fantasy instead. It might not seem like that much of a change, but the style is different nonetheless, especially as this story was set on our Earth while most of my other stories are not. My goal was to gain more experience with a different kind of writing and improve my style in general.
>
> It soon became clear, however, that I couldn't fit [my original ideas] in with the limits on the story's length . . . I actually think that that was somewhat lucky. Hopefully, this way, the reader can use their imagination to come up with some of the [characters'] previous adventures, but there's enough in the story so that they're not totally bewildered. My options are also open if I ever want to write a prequel or a sequel. Overall, I ended up getting rid of my broader ideas and focusing more on a few key scenes. This naturally changed my perspective as well. I realized that I had to focus my attention and writing on the scenes that were absolutely necessary to the story.
>
> (Beach et al. 2010, p. 153)

"FEEDBACK"

In providing feedback, you and/or your students are asking "how am I doing" or "where am I now?" related to the use of certain literacy practices (Fisher & Frey, 2014). For example, as students are working on their documentary, they may be continually asking themselves whether they are capturing the kinds of material that will convey their ideas about cliques in their school.

In giving dialogic feedback in conferences, teachers can encourage students to verbalize their thinking processes so that conferences are collaborative spaces for enacting productive thinking (Beck et al., 2020). For example, in a conference with a student related to issues in the organization of Darius's draft, the teacher, Ms. Miller, had him read aloud his draft to then identify the different sections of his draft:

> Ms. Miller: Do you think that this is for your discussion part, where you're writing that [checks understanding]?
> Darius: Um, this is for the introduction.

Ms. Miller: OK, so how do you feel like you might be able to expand on this a little bit [locates part of the text needing improvement]? Do you think that you included the 5Ws in this part: who, what, where, when, why [provides metalinguistic clues]?
Darius: No.
Ms. Miller: OK, so what ways do you think that you would be able to expand on that [elicits ideas]?
Darius: Well, state the specific event that was going on.

With this subtle direction, Darius was able to determine what was missing and how to fix it.
(Beck et al., 2020, p. 654).

As we noted in Chapter 6 on giving feedback to students' writing, it's important to provide descriptive "reader-based" rather than judgmental feedback. In providing descriptive feedback, you are responding as a reader to how you are engaged, entranced, moved, involved, disturbed, struck by, intrigued, puzzled, overwhelmed, lost, or expecting support or evidence and not finding it (Elbow, 1998). Peter Elbow calls this approach providing students with "movies of the reader's mind," and he talks about "pointing," "summarizing," "telling," and "showing." Rather than judging their work, students then use your feedback to make their judgments about whether they have achieved their purposes, so they are learning to self-assess.

In giving feedback, you continually describe how students perceive and construct their purpose, audience, text, and language based on your assignment. In some cases, students may need further clarification about your assignment to provide them with some leeway in creatively interpreting your assignment consistent with their purposes, interests, or needs.

You can examine examples of how teachers created assignments resulting in students writing and teachers' responses to that writing by accessing an online database of student writing and interviews with teachers about how their approaches shape their responses to that writing (Sherry, 2014). To do so, sign in to *23.21.225.52* as "citeuser" with password "Sw@p2013" and click "Submit."

If students express difficulties in their responses in a conference, you can have students engage in certain activities. For example, in working with a student who had difficulty understanding the characters' relationships in the novel, *The Dead and the Gone* (Pfeffer, 2010), Tina Cassidy (2013) had the student create a chart of the characters' relationships using Evernote *evernote.com*, and then return to reading aloud the novel, which the student recorded on Evernote. Tina then asked the student to take notes about the next character he encountered, notes that provided her with evidence of his understanding of the character.

How can you provide this descriptive feedback, particularly with a large number of students and limited classroom time to meet with individual students? You can schedule brief individual one-to-one conferences with students that focus on only salient aspects of their work, aspects that students can then focus on in revising their work. Another approach is to wander around that room, asking students to raise their hands when they are ready for some feedback and/or need assistance so that you're only briefly interacting with students.

As we noted in Chapter 6, a third approach is to train peers to provide descriptive feedback, recognizing that without training, students typically resort to providing only general, positive comments that may not be useful (Beach & Friedrich, 2006). To teach your students about providing feedback to others, you can model giving reader-based feedback or fostering self-assessing and revisions, followed by students practicing feedback and self-assessing in one-to-one conferences or small groups.

For giving peer feedback, students can also employ think-alouds normally associated with use for reading instruction as described in Chapters 5, 6, and 9 for verbally fostering specific responses to texts (Beck, 2018). To engage in think-alouds, students need specific training that includes modeling think-alouds. (For instructions on the use of think-alouds, see Wilhelm, 2013, *tinyurl.com/y79grf6g*.)

Students could share think-alouds as they are composing with you or a peer in ways that reveal how they are making explicit decisions about composing in ways that reveal certain challenges in composing texts (Beck, 2018). For example, students may share their concerns about not knowing their audience's knowledge or attitudes about a topic to determine what background information they need to include or whether to address their audience's concerns about the stances they are taking on the issue.

Activity: Training Peers to Provide Feedback

Given the need to have students receive feedback during their drafting/revision process, you can provide them with training on how to provide descriptive, reader-based feedback in pairs or small groups. You can model giving feedback by demonstrating your own feedback to a student and/or create videos modeling your feedback processes. This includes beginning with having students sharing their own concerns or questions about their writing so that the interaction revolves around their voice, as opposed to you controlling the interaction. It is also important to focus on just a few substantive aspects of their writing, including delaying editing feedback, to avoid overwhelming students with too many issues. In describing your perceptions of their writing, you can also model how you invite students to respond to those reactions to share ways of revisions for your comments. You can also end the conferences with their summarizing changes they plan to make in their writing.

USE OF DIGITAL TOOLS FOR PROVIDING FEEDBACK

In addition to the use of face-to-face conferences, there are several digital tools that can be used to provide descriptive feedback:

- Comments in Word or Google Docs along with Google Forms *docs.google.com/forms* can be employed to provide open-ended written feedback to students' writing. Forms can also be used in conjunction with Flubaroo *www.flubaroo.com* to assign, compute, share, and display assessments of students' writing on Forms. You can also use Kaizena *kaizena.com* to provide verbal feedback to Google Docs files or PeerMark for Turnitin. (You first need to authorize the use of Kaisena with Google Docs; you then select the Google Docs file to which you want to add audio comments to specific places in a student's writing.)
- Classkick *www.getclasskick.com* can also be used to provide immediate feedback to students as they are working on their iPads. You and/or peers can view students' writing on their iPads to then write comments about that writing or students can request teacher feedback.

- Annotations on students' digital writing using Diigo sticky notes, *diigo.com/education*; desktop iAnnotate PDF, *tinyurl.com/2whcqsj*; iOS iAnnotate, *tinyurl.com/mmdw2mr*; Android iAnnotate, *tinyurl.com/kgwd4ad*; iOS Adobe Reader, *tinyurl.com/lhoyya2*; or Android Adobe Reader, *tinyurl.com/7g373kq*
- Digital audio files recorded on Garageband (Macs) or Audacity (Macs and Windows) that students can listen to as they are reviewing their work.
- Screencasting tools such as Jing *www.techsmith.com/jing* or CamStudio *camstudio.org* to record comments of the students' writing on the screen.
- iOS *tinyurl.com/kvqpxhl* and Android *tinyurl.com/lqcjbor* Coach's Eye app to record a student's performance for providing feedback to students' drama or speech performances. You can then slow down their physical movements by providing recorded feedback about the students' techniques or form.
- For using online peer-feedback, you can use PeerGrade *peergrade.io*, PeerStudio *peerstudio.org*, PeerAssessment *peerassessment.com*, or TeamMates *teammatesv4.appsort.com*. You can also create an online writing lab in your school and train students to give online feedback to their peers.

Teachers can also use social media to assess students' writing. Two teachers created a final course assessment. Students determined how they would be assessed by selecting their topics to address on Twitter and formulating criteria related to determining the validity of their Tweets (Forzani et al., 2020).

They also had students engaged in critical analysis of problematic online content often found on Twitter. When students then used hashtags to garner responses from people outside their classroom, they could assess those responses' validity. The teachers knew that they were having students take risks in participating in an online space. However, they perceived that "the risk was worth taking because it made it possible for them to reconnect the literacies of their classroom with real-world literacies, enabling their students to experience all the attendant benefits that accompany that shift" (p. 354). (For more on the use of digital tools for giving feedback, see *Digital tools for giving feedback* on the website.)

DEFINING CRITERIA FOR SELF-ASSESSING

To assist students in self-assessing their use of literacy practices, you can provide them with criteria relevant to their participation in your activities. For example, a hypothetical, 12th-grade student, Bill, is writing a letter to the school board arguing that they need to allow the high school to experiment with offering "hybrid classes" that combine time in class with time spent working in an online space. Bill likes to work on his own in the school media center on his computer. In his letter, he posits that participating in these "hybrid classes" would allow him to complete more of his work during school hours in the media center without physically attending his classes every day.

Bill knows that he needs to consider the rhetorical context and genre conventions involved in writing a letter to the school board. In addition, he knows that he has to provide relevant background information about "hybrid classes" to school board members who may have little knowledge of how "hybrid classes" operate.

He also anticipates school board members' potential skepticism about whether students would devote time outside of class to completing their schoolwork in a relatively unsupervised context. Given his status as a student, he knows that he needs to document support from teachers and/or administrators. Therefore, formulating criteria for writing such as Bill's letter involves considering the social context constituting his writing based on criteria related to consideration of one's audience's beliefs and knowledge, use of appropriate language given those audiences, formulation of one's claims, and providing supporting evidence.

At the same time, unless students have also had some experience in these events or contexts, they may not understand how to apply these criteria. While Bill's teacher may have provided him with criteria such as "considers audience's prior knowledge and beliefs in formulating an argument," unless Bill has had some experience in the domain of writing for actual adult audiences, he may not understand the meaning of these criteria. In Bill's case, he transferred his experiences serving on the student council in which he had to pose arguments to teachers and administrators to crafting his letter to the school board. Therefore, it would be helpful, rather than simply informing students of the criteria for an assignment, to formulate criteria with your students so that they have some input and understanding of the nature of those criteria. (For more on defining criteria, see *Defining criteria* on the website.)

Defining criteria for assessing critical inquiry practices

To engage students in self-assessing use of the critical inquiry practices featured in this book, the following are some criteria for having students reflect on their use of such critical inquiry practices.

For identifying *problems or issues*, students need to assess the significance, relevance, sufficiency, validity, and coherence of their formulation of those problems or issues (Grice, 1975).

In considering *significance*, students need to effectively demonstrate the significance of the problem or issue as requiring serious consideration. To do so, they may describe how people's lives have been impacted by the problem or issue—for example, how the problem of stagnant wages since the 1970s has resulted in economic inequality associated with many Americans struggling economically.

In considering *relevance*, students need to be able to provide information, reasons, and ideas relevant to the nature of the problem or issue being addressed in a certain context and their rhetorical goals for convincing their audience about the seriousness of the problem or issue. For example, in addressing the problem of economic inequality, a student may cite evidence of the number of Americans living in poverty—one in five children—and the number of middle-class Americans with little or no savings.

In assessing *sufficiency*, students consider whether they have enough information or evidence to support their positions or contentions. Students often do not have enough information simply because they did not adequately search material or engage in enough research on their topics, issues, or text. On the other hand, students may have too much information on other cases, requiring that they sort through that information to find the most useful information.

In providing information, students also need to determine the *validity* of that information based on vetting sources and author credentials. Students may draw information from sources that are not credible or that skew the information based on their ideological orientation.

To assess their ability to determine validity, you or your students could determine the degree to which students are actually testing the validity of their resources.

They also need to assess the *coherence* of their texts, recognizing that notions of coherence or effective organization vary markedly according to genre conventions and philosophies of text meaning. For example, while it is assumed that the traditional school essay is typically organized based on a defined, logical, thesis/support progression, the organization of a postmodern digital story with multiple alternative pathways entails quite different notions of coherence.

To assess the coherence of their oral or written narratives, students consider the degree to which their use of certain cues, titles, beginnings, endings, complications in characters' plans, or conflicts serve to imply certain themes effectively.

Formulating solutions to problems or issues

For self-assessing their ability to formulate solutions to problems or issues, students need to determine whether their proposed solutions will be perceived as viable by their audiences. For example, they may address the lack of access to grocery stores located in low-income urban neighborhoods that provide healthy food options to those neighborhoods. They then need to prove that, if people did have access to these stores, they would select healthy food options and could afford to purchase those options.

"FEED-FORWARD"

In providing "feed-forward" formative assessment, you and/or your students are reflecting on the future direction of their work over time by posing the questions, "Where am I going next?" (Fisher & Frey, 2014). Students then reflect on how they can change or improve on their uses of literacy practices in the future, providing some direction for their future development. For example, students may determine that, in adopting roles in drama activities, they need to experiment more with adopting alternative language and perspective consistent with their roles. Or, in revising their writing, they may determine that they need to adopt a different stance.

During a unit or course, students can note whether and how they are achieving their goals. In her Humanities courses, Tanya Hodge asked her students to respond to these questions:

- What are three goals you have for yourself for quarter 2 Humanities 2 English Language Arts class?
- What worked well this quarter in English? Consider sources, instruction, lessons, activities, etc.
- What did not work well this quarter in English?
- What do you need from us as your teachers to help you progress and be prepared for postsecondary/college-level reading, writing, and thinking?

(Beach & Beauchemin, 2019, p. 191)

One of her student's, Catherine Matejeck, reflected on how she was "getting more and better work in and learning how to annotate was very helpful ... I strengthened my skills in real life note-taking and thoughtful writing, as well my annotations" (p. 192).

Then, during the course, students can reflect on the degree to which they are making progress in addressing those goals. For example, in the beginning of a course, a student may note that they want to develop their ability to attend to their peers' emotions and perspectives in small-group classroom discussion through careful listening. They may then note how they experienced growth in attending to others' emotions and perspectives, as evidenced by their ability to restate their peers' perspectives as in "you seem to be looking at X in Y way."

They can also address the following questions related to the extent and how they are achieving their goals:

- How am I progressing toward my learning goal?
- Are the strategies I am using working?
- Is my work at the level of quality I am hoping to achieve?
- What can I do to improve my work?
- Do I need to seek help from a peer or the teacher?

(Harris & Brown, 2018, p. 19)

USES OF E-PORTFOLIOS FOR REFLECTING ON GROWTH OVER TIME

Students can employ e-portfolios that include their work during a course to reflect on their growth over time for addressing their "feed-forward" goals. Based on their goals, students can then select certain texts to include in their portfolio as examples of how they are achieving those goals. For example, given that they set a goal to develop their ability to support their thesis statements using specific evidence, students could include examples of an initial essay that lacked supporting evidence and then a later essay that included ample supporting evidence. They could then compare these essays, noting how they learned to access and develop their supporting evidence during the course.

In addition to using commercial portfolio platforms, students can create their portfolios using the Google Sites (in Google Drive) website (for video tutorials by Sam Kary *t.ly/hzv3* and Brett Case *t.ly/3qIw*). Students can also e-portfolios through use of Google Docs, blogs, wikis, or e-portfolio desktop platforms such as Dropr, *dropr.com*; Desire To Learn, *brightspace.com/products/eportfolio*; Portfoliogen, *portfoliogen.com*; Pathbrite, *pathbrite.com*; or Three Ring (iOS, *tinyurl.com/k789t5u/*, and Android *tinyurl.com/knsm4ml*); iOS Portfolio for iPad, *tinyurl.com/mhdl9tt*; iOS Philio, *tinyurl.com/kf7s42x*; or Android Easy Portfolio, *tinyurl.com/maql5l3*, apps.

Students may include all of their writing or image/video productions completed in a course or school year. They then create a separate showcase portfolio that includes what they perceive to be their strongest work for submission for final course evaluations with reasons for their selections. They then reflect on their development of specific literacy practices, dispositions, reading interests, and how their work enacts their identities as learners. You can then assess these showcase portfolios based on the quality of their work and their reflections on their development over time. (For more on the use of e-portfolios, see *Using e-portfolios* on the website.)

EMPLOYING RUBRICS FOR RATING STUDENTS' WORK

Based on the use of criteria, you may also develop rubrics that provide students with rating scales or checklists in which you rate students' work or students' rate their work. There are three basic types of rubrics—holistic, analytic, and primary trait. Holistic rubrics rate the text or work based on an overall score. For example, in scoring a student's essay, you may rate that essay on a scale of "1" to "6" in terms of your overall subjective assessment of an essay's quality—drawing on specific criteria for what constitutes a "1", "2," etc.

Analytic rubrics break out specific criteria for assessing student performance on their text production or performance on a task. For example, the frequently used "6-trait" rubric provides specific criteria for rating students' writing on a scale of "1" to "6" for "ideas," "organization," "voice," "word choice," "sentence fluency," and "conventions"—for example, the 6 + 1 Trait rubric employed by EducationNorthwest *t.ly/YdmL*. Primary-trait rubrics identify those traits and specific criteria for those traits unique to a particular assignment or writing.

Limitations in using rubrics

There is considerable debate about the value and use of rubrics for rating students' work (Wilson, 2006). Rubrics are often used in assessments to achieve high reliability, defined as high levels of agreement between judges or scorers. However, to achieve high agreement, rubrics are often framed in terms of formalist or quantitative criteria. For example, in writing an essay, a student employs a thesis statement and provides supporting reasons or uses a certain number of reasons to support their thesis. They do so because judges or scorers are often more likely to agree on more formalist or quantitative criteria than with more subjective criteria such as the use of voice or clarity of their stance (Mabry, 1999).

As a result, rubrics often comprise of these formalist or quantitative criteria, resulting in an emphasis on these criteria in assignments or instruction related to the assignment. This can result in an evaluation of writing that focuses on employing the desired organizational structure, such as using the five-paragraph theme structure. Students then focus more on simply conforming to the organizational structure rather than developing or expressing their ideas (Mabry, 1999). At the same time, poorly designed, vague, or restrictive rubrics may undermine thoughtful self-assessment or your assessment (Broad et al., 2009). For example, prepackaged, generic criteria available on the Web (*Rubicon.com*) may not be relevant to your specific assignment expectations.

While providing students with rubrics can certainly be helpful for them in clarifying the criteria by which their work will be evaluated, it can also serve to limit their focus to conforming to these criteria. As a result, you or your students may find that the rubrics may not capture the unique qualities of students' particular work.

In her critique of rubrics, Maja Wilson (2006) cites the example of assessing what she perceived to be one of her students' narratives describing her experiences with her family, thunderstorms, and visiting Texas. She notes that: "She then attempted to apply the Michigan Educational Assessment Program (MEAP) six-point rubrics to assess her writing, rubrics based on whether the writing was engaging, clear, and focused" (p. 109). She might have assigned a failing two score, to quote the criteria, that the "limited control over writing conventions may make the writing difficult" in that "the writing was a bit of a mess: inconsistent paragraphing, full of unintended fragments, unclear transitions, and rife with spelling, punctuation, and sentence structure errors" (p. 109).

However, she was personally moved by the writing, noting that "*this* paper was what made being a writing teacher the best job in the world" (p. 110). Maja noted that her student:

> stumbled onto some rather large insights as she wrote. While her description of thunderstorms was interesting in itself, she surprised herself and me as she began to connect the sound of the rain to her search for an answer and reliance on herself in the midst of uncertainty and rejection. Her writing brought both of us somewhere new.
>
> (p. 111)

Maja was also concerned that making revisions to her writing according to the rubrics' emphasis on the coherent organization "would have changed the loose, poetic structure of what she had begun to do" (p. 112).

Difficulty understanding the meaning of criteria

Another limitation of rubrics is that students may not understand the criteria underlying certain rubrics, suggesting the need to discuss or model these criteria with students (Beach et al., 2021). You can also help students understand these criteria or rubrics by having students propose or negotiate specific criteria or rubrics. Students may also be more likely to benefit from the use of rubrics when they are involved in co-constructing their rubrics, given that they are then more likely to understand the language used in the rubrics (Brown, 2018).

Use of rubrics with multimodal digital practices

The use of rubrics may also not adequately capture the processes associated with multimodal digital writing or media production. Drawing on The National Writing Project's Multimodal Assessment Project *digitalis.nwp.org/resource/1577* (Whithaus et al., n.d.) that identified five domains for assessing multimodal production: context, artifact, substance, process management/technical skills, and habits of mind, Troy Hicks (2013) describes his assessment of Justine Maag's (2010) digital book trailer *tinyurl.com/mkal67g* for the book, *Ninth Ward* (Rhodes, 2010):

- Context ... provide[s] initial information to the viewer about the disaster before the response to the book begins.
- Artifact ... employs effective transitions, captions, panning and zooming, and a musical background.
- Substance. By bringing in the voice of Hurricane Katrina and choosing images from the disaster itself, Maag adds significance through an alternative, significant interpretation of the text.
- Process/skills ... makes an effort to be academically and ethically responsible by citing her sources.
- Habits of mind ... using images that situate the Hurricane Katrina disaster in the broader context of American history.

(p. 13)

In summary, rubrics can certainly be useful in providing feedback to students based on rating their effectiveness in addressing certain criteria. However, because the criteria employed in rubrics are often formalist or quantitative, rubrics may be less useful in terms of assessing students in their engagement in critical inquiry and literacy practices. While rubrics may appear to help teachers justify the grades they assign, they may significantly detract from your most important task as a teacher: listening well to your students and understanding their work. (For more on employing rubrics, see *Employing rubrics* on the website.)

> **Activity: Devising Criteria and/or Rubrics for Student Self-Assessing**
>
> Based on a writing assignment you have developed for use in your practicum or student teaching, formulate some criteria and/or rubrics for students to self-assess their writing. Consider your students' age/grade level in terms of their understanding of the meaning of language in your criteria/rubrics. Also, consider focusing on criteria/rubrics based on the relevant features for their writing at the drafting phase instead of focusing on too many editing features. If you're creating rubrics, limit the number of optional rating choices based on clearly defined categories that avoid an emphasis on negative self-assessments.

SUMMATIVE ASSESSMENTS

In contrast to ongoing, formative assessments, summative assessments provide information about students' long-term learning and abilities. They also serve to assess students' performances as groups to judge the effectiveness of the instruction students are receiving.

There are a number of different types of summative assessments—your own tests or exams or portfolio assessments that may or may not lead to assigning grades, as well as the use of district, state, or national standardized assessments to determine students' performance within a school, district, state, or nation related to the need for "accountability." Some of these assessments are "performance-based" in that they require students to demonstrate their use of certain literacy practices as a means of demonstrating their abilities or knowledge. Others are standardized tests based largely on multiple-choice test items.

The limitations of grades

One purpose for summative assessment involves assigning grades to students. The recent "ungrading" movement raises questions about the value and use of grades related to potential negative impact on student motivation and learning as when students receive failing or "D"/"C" grades (Blum, 2020). Students grades can impact their potential for college admissions. Given California universities policies indicating that they need to complete certain courses with a C or higher, in 2018–19, 59% of students could meet those requirements, while for the class of 2022, only 46% of students could meet those requirements—with also a gap of 17% difference between Black/Latinx and White/Asian American students (Khan, 2021).

One issue in the use of grades is that teachers may assign grades related to students work habits, missing deadlines, or classroom behavior, which can be related to perceptions of race, class, or gender differences, as opposed to a focus on students' learning, resulting in the Los Angeles and San Diego Unified districts informing their teachers of the need to base grades on learning (Khan, 2021). Teachers may also provide students who receive low grades on tests or writing assignments to retake tests or rewrite an assignment as well as provide students with extra time to complete work.

Use of multiple-choice tests

While there are certain limitations to using multiple-choice tests, one option is to have students create their own multiple-choice questions employing the PeerWise online platform *PeerWise.cs.auckland.ac.nz*. Creating their own questions requires that students demonstrate an understanding of the topic or ideas being addressed in their questions to create a bank of questions organized by topics within a course (for an introductory video *t.ly/6gne*).

Their peers then answering the questions have access to explanations for certain answers being correct versus incorrect. Peers can also rate the difficulty level and quality of the questions and anonymously post comments about the questions. Research on PeerWise found that it contributed to students' demonstration of their learning (Kelley et al., 2019).

Given the pressure from administrators to increase test scores, particularly for "low-scoring schools," teachers then focus their reading and writing instruction based on goals and practices associated with those tests. In describing their outcomes for teaching writing, five teachers framed their instruction based on the skills associated with their state's writing test—for example, a focus on providing relevant evidence for claims (Howe, 2020).

In an interview reflection on the use of standardized assessments in her Bloomington, Minnesota suburban district, Elizabeth Erdmann noted that:

> They want us to teach the same texts, have the same tests, and have the same final exams, and the same papers. The school is getting it from the district and the district is getting it from the school board, so there's all of this control that didn't exist before.

She also expressed concern about how she, as a teacher, is perceived when her students may not demonstrate improvements in their test scores:

> It's really hard to show change in student achievement when you get a certain group of kids and they are not your kids forever. So if you look at the students you're teaching, and I'm teaching a lot of students with 504s and IEPs, so another teacher with AP students will always have higher scores than I would. So then you have to come up with a common goal—so like the rate of increase or we're going to have more students graduate. (Beach et al., 2016, p. 226).

Determining the validity and reliability of assessments

Determining the *validity* of these assessments involves asking whether particular assessment measures actually measure what they purport to measure; for example, a student's "reading comprehension" level or "writing ability." One issue with the validity of multiple-choice items reading tests is that students may or may not have prior knowledge of the topics in test items. As a result, students with certain previous knowledge of those topics can apply their prior knowledge to select the "correct answer" without even reading the passage (Beach et al.,

2021). Determining the *reliability* of summative assessments involves determining whether students will achieve the same results in taking the same assessment over time. If not, then there are issues with the assessment's validity.

Even based on a single test, these assessment results may then be used to label a student as, for example, a "struggling reader." However, that student may be highly proficient in reading certain types of texts, such as the sports page, that are not included in these tests (Alvermann, 2006).

It is also the case that students' background social status influences their test performance as well as their writing, as evident in an analysis of 60,000 students' household income, SAT scores, and the content of their admissions essay for application to the University of California in 2016 (Alvero et al., 2021). Students from higher-income families had higher SAT scores than students from lower-income families.

Students from higher-income families also wrote about different topics that may have been more relevant and/or appealing based on college admissions criteria. For example, they may have described their ability to successfully engage in completing a task or project, while students from lower-income families wrote more about some limitations in their lives. (One reason that many colleges and universities no longer require the SAT/ACT for admissions is the recognition that these tests scores may give students from higher socio-economic backgrounds certain advantages, including the ability to pay for test preparation training.)

One limitation of summative assessments related to validity is that they generally do not include items related to students' use of digital/multimodal practices, even though they are central to students' everyday communications (Unsworth et al., 2019). (For resources on assessing these practices: National Writing Project's Multimodal Assessment Project, *tinyurl.com/y7kkbphsI* (Jimerson, 2011.)

One example of the use of multimodal tools for course assessment involves using digital badges to represent success in a unit or course. To help their peers understand the concept of "rhetorical knowledge," students created a website, digital essay, ignite talk, and digital badges as visual representations of specific practices associated with the effective application of "rhetorical knowledge" (West-Puckett, 2016). For a digital badge that represented "rhetorical knowledge," students used the image of a compass related to the notion of having a clear sense of direction for determining one's audience, context, and strategy for achieving uptake. Students themselves then determine whether or not their peers earn certain badges. The teacher then assigns grades based on students achieving a certain number of badges.

It may also be the case that, given mandated testing, schools have to devote some days for testing that can detract from classroom instruction time. It may also be the case that, given the de-contextualized nature of assessment tasks, students may not be engaged in tasks for which they perceive no purpose other than doing well on a test.

The Common Core State Standards assessments

The Smarter Balanced Assessment Consortium has developed one set of standardized assessments based on the CCSS (SMAC) consortium *www.smarterbalanced.org* consisting of 14 states as of 2021. These states administer summative assessments in the final 12 weeks of the school year for grades 11 and 3–8. They also assess students based on optional interim performative and computer-adaptive assessments throughout the school year using items and tasks developed and scored by teachers *smarterbalanced.org/our-system/assessments*.

One advantage of the SMAC assessments is that they include computer-based performance tasks that involve students in active demonstrations of their abilities in addition to multiple-choice items. (For information on their scoring of narrative, informational/explanatory, and opinion/argumentative writing using the Smarter Annotated Response Tool (SmART) *smart.smarterbalanced.org*).

It is important to note that these assessments are based on addressing the CCSS instead of individual teachers' own unique curriculums. Students may then experience issues with these assessments if teachers are not focusing on or adequately addressing the CCSS. These assessments may also have validity and reliability issues associated with computer scoring of students' writing. (For more on summative assessments, see *Summative assessments* on the website.)

USE OF E-PORTFOLIOS FOR SUMMATIVE ASSESSMENT

One effective alternative to these standardized assessments involves the use of e-portfolios, as previously described on page 216. For example, students may select essays in their e-portfolio from the beginning and end of the school year to reflect on changes in their writing, for example, their increased use of revisions. While students may assume that they hadn't made many changes, Corinth Matera cites an example of a student sharing her reflection in a conference by stating:

> I don't know if I've really grown a lot and she'll pull out their portfolio and you wrote this last fall and look at this, this essay, this creative nonfiction you just produced. It's amazing, you know. And so just being able to remind them of what they've done and show that growth has been really powerful.
>
> (Beach & Beauchemin, 2019, p. 194)

Students may create *process-based* or *storage* e-portfolios (Cambridge et al., 2009) that include all of their work over a semester or year. They then reflect on changes in that work over time, such as changing their argumentative writing to formulate alternative perspectives supporting their claims. They may also create *product-based* or *showcase* e-portfolios that contain only certain selected content designed to demonstrate how they have achieved course objectives or assessment criteria (Cambridge et al., 2009).

A primary purpose for the use of e-portfolios involves fostering students' reflections on their learning over time. For example, you can provide students with prompts or criteria for fostering their reflection on reasons for selecting certain items, changes in their amount or quality of writing or reading, shifts in their attitudes towards their learning, increased use of critical inquiry practices, etc. (Mueller, 2008).

Activity: Creating Summative Student Assessments

Based on a unit you plan to teach in your student teaching, develop a summative assessment that will provide you with an understanding of whether or not your students have learned what you wanted them to learn. This assessment could be an exam and/or it could be a final paper or e-portfolio. For example, based on teaching the critical

> perspectives described in Chapter 5, you may want to determine whether students could effectively apply one of those perspectives to a text or texts they were reading in your course. For example, you may want to determine whether students can apply a gender perspective to critiquing portrayals of characters in a novel or novels they were reading.

SUMMARY

In this chapter, we noted the need to employ formative assessment methods to provide students with ongoing feedback about their work to enhance their learning, while at the same time recognizing the limitations of the use of rubrics employed in formative assessment. We also reviewed the current status of summative assessments associated with issues of standardized testing as well as the use of the PARCC consortium assessments associated with the CCSS. While these assessments include more performance assessment tasks, there are major limitations to any such assessments, limitations that can be reduced by using e-portfolios to determine students' growth in learning over time.

REFERENCES

Ackerman, C. E. (2019, August 11). Growth mindset vs. fixed + key takeaways from Dweck's book [Web log post]. Retrieved from http://t.ly/lAUf

Alvermann, D. E. (2006). Struggling adolescent readers: A cultural construction. In A. McKeough, L. M. Phillips, V. Timmons, & J. L. Lupart (Eds.), *Understanding literacy development: A global view* (pp. 95–111). Erlbaum.

Alvero, A. J., Giebel, S., Gebre-Medhin, B., Antonio, A. L., Stevens, M. L., & Domingue, B. W. (2021). Essay content is strongly related to household income and sat scores: Evidence from 60,000 undergraduate applications. (CEPA Working Paper No. 21-03). Retrieved from Stanford Center for Education Policy Analysis: http://cepa.stanford.edu/wp21-03

Andrade, H., & Heritage, M. (2018). *Using formative assessment to enhance learning, achievement, and academic self-regulation*. Routledge.

Beach, R., Appleman, D., Fecho, B., & Simon, R. (2021). *Teaching literature to adolescents*, 4th ed. Routledge.

Beach, R., & Aukerman, M. (2019). Portraying and enacting trust through writing in a high school classroom. In R. Beach & D. Bloome (Eds.), *Languaging relations for transforming the literacy and language arts classroom* (pp. 49–68). Routledge.

Beach, R., & Beauchemin, F. (2019). *Teaching language as action in the ELA classroom*. Routledge.

Beach, R., Campano, G., Edmiston, B., & Borgmann, M. (2010). *Literacy tools in the classroom: Teaching through critical inquiry, grades 5–12*. Teachers College Press.

Beach, R., & Friedrich, T. (2006). Response to writing. In C. A. MacArthur, S. Graham, & J. Fitzgerald (Eds.), *Handbook of writing research* (pp. 222–234). Guilford Press.

Beach, R., Thein, A. H., & Webb, A. (2016). *The English language arts Common Core state standards: A critical inquiry approach for 6–12 classrooms*, 2nd ed. Routledge.

Beck, S. W. (2018). *A think-aloud approach to writing assessment: Analyzing process & product with adolescent writers*. Teachers College Press.

Beck, S. W., Jones, K., Storm, S., & Smith, H. (2020). Scaffolding students' writing processes through dialogic assessment. *Journal of Adolescent & Adult Literacy, 63*(6), 651–660.

Black, P., Harrison, C., Lee, C., Marshall B., & William, D. (2003). *Assessment for learning: Putting it into practice*. Open University Press.

Blum, S. D. (Ed.). (2020). *Ungrading: Why rating students undermines learning (and what to do instead)*. West Virginia University Press.

Broad, B., Adler-Kassner, L., Alford, B., & Detweiler, J. (2009). *Organic writing assessment: Dynamic criteria mapping in action*. Utah State University Press.

Brown, G. T. L. (2018). *Assessment of student achievement*. Routledge.

Cambridge, D., Cambridge, B. L., & Yancey, K. B. (2009). *Electronic portfolios 2.0: Emergent research on implementation and impact.* Stylus.

Cassidy, T. (2013, July 5). Reading conferences and Evernote [Web log post]. Retrieved from http://tinyurl.com/ok3d77c

Common Core State Standards (2010). *Common Core State Standards for English Language Arts.* Retrieved January 10, 2015 from www.corestandards.org

Dann, R. (2018). *Developing feedback for pupil learning: Teaching, learning and assessment in schools.* Routledge.

Dann, R. (2019). Feedback as a relational concept in the classroom. *The Curriculum Journal, 30*(4), 352–374.

Dweck, C. (2012). *Mindset: How you can fulfill your potential.* Robinson.

Elbow, P. (1998). *Writing with power.* Oxford University Press.

Emery, D. (2021, January 11). Using writing to promote learning goals: A focused start to a new semester [Web log post]. Retrieved from http://t.ly/anRL

Fisher, D., & Frey, N. (2014). *Checking for understanding: Formative assessment techniques for your classroom.* ASCD.

Forzani, E., Corrigan, J. A., & Slomp, D. (2020). Reimagining literacy assessment through a new literacies lens. *Journal of Adolescent & Adult Literacy, 64*(3), 351–355.

Grice, H. P. (1975). Logic and conversation. In A. Jaworski & N. Coupland (Eds.), *The discourse reader* (pp. 76–87). New York: Routledge.

Harris, L. R., & Brown, G. T. L. (2018). *Using self-assessment to improve student learning.* Routledge.

Hattie, J. & Timperley, H. (2007). The power of feedback. *Review of Educational Research, 77*(1), 81–112.

Hicks, T. (2013, February). May the journey continue: A response to Kevin Cordi's work on teaching the digital book trailer. *Adolescent Literacy in Perpective*, pp. 10–14. Ohio Resource Center.

Howe, E. (2020). Alignment and convergence for what? and how? Tensions of writing instruction within a test-based accountability system. In M. Gresalfi & I. S. Horn (Eds.), *The interdisciplinarity of the learning sciences*, 14th International Conference of the Learning Sciences (ICLS), 4 (pp. 2225–2228). International Society of the Learning Sciences.

Jimerson, L. (2011, September 22). *The NWP Multimodal Assessment Project.* The Current. https://tinyurl.com/y7kkbphs

Kelley, M. R., Chapman-Orr, E. K., Calkins, S., & Lemke, R. (2019). Generation and retrieval practice effects in the classroom using PeerWise, *Teaching of Psychology, 46*(2), 121–126.

Khan, I. (2021, November 8). Faced with soaring Ds and Fs, schools are ditching the old way of grading [Web log post]. *The Los Angeles Times.* Retrieved from www.latimes.com/california/story/2021-11-08/as-ds-and-fs-soar-schools-ditch-inequitable-grade-systems

Mabry, L. (1999). Writing to the rubric: Lingering effects of traditional standardized testing on direct writing assessment. *Phi Delta Kappan, 80*(9), 673–679.

Maag, J. (2010). Ninth Ward trainer. [video]. Retrieved from www.youtube.com/watch?v=Ah6Ys51qHOg

Mueller, J. (2008). *Authentic assessment toolbox.* Retrieved from http://jfmueller.faculty.noctrl.edu/toolbox/index.htm

National Council of Teachers of English. (2021). *NCTE standards for the initial preparation of teachers of English language arts 7–12 (initial licensure).* Author.

Pfeffer, S. B. (2010). *The dead and the gone.* HMH Books.

Rhodes, J. P. (2010). *Ninth ward.* Little Brown.

Ryan, C. (2014)). Teaching in the present: Empowering teachers and students through formative assessment. *The Council Chronicle, 23*(3), 6–9.

Santoro, D. A. (2018). Is it burnout? Or demoralization? *Educational Leadership, 75*, 10–15.

Shelton, S. A., & Brooks, T. (2019). "We need to get these scores up": A narrative examination of the challenges of teaching literature in the age of standardized testing. *Journal of Language and Literacy Education, 15*(2), 1–17.

Sherry, M. B. (2014). The Student Writing Archive Project (SWAP): Designing a searchable database of student writing and teacher commentary for English teacher preparation courses. *Contemporary Issues in Technology and Teacher Education, 14*(3). Retrieved from http://t.ly/E0Dx

Smagorinsky, P. (2013). What does Vygotsky provide for the 21st-century language arts teacher? *Language Arts, 90*(3), 192–204.

Song, A-Y. (2017). "Meta-talk" as a composition tool: Promoting reflective dialogue during the drafting process. *Multiple perspectives, 19*(4), 234–238.

Soylu, M. Y., Zeleny, M. D., Zhao, R., Bruning, R. H., Dempsey, M. S., & Kauffman, D. F., (2017). Secondary students' writing achievement goals: Assessing the mediating effects of mastery and performance goals on writing self-efficacy, affect, and writing achievement. *Frontiers in Psychology, 8*(1406), 1–14.

Swaffield, S. (Ed.). (2008). *Unlocking assessment: Understanding for reflection and application.* Routledge.

Thompson, I. (2013). The mediation of learning in the zone of proximal development through a co-constructed writing activity. *Research in the Teaching of English, 47*(3), 247–276.

Unsworth, L., Cope, J., & Nicholls, L. (2019). Multimodal literacy and large-scale literacy tests: Curriculum relevance and responsibility. *Australian Journal of Language and Literacy, 42*(2), 128–139.

Vygotsky, L. S. (1978). *Mind in society: The development of higher psychological processes.* Harvard University Press.

Vygotsky, L. S. (1986). *Thought and language*. MIT Press.
West-Puckett, S. (2016). Making classroom writing assessment more visible, equitable, and portable through digital badging. *College English*, 79(2), 127–151.
Whithaus, C., Eidman-Aadahl, E., & other members of the MAP Committee. (n.d.). The NWP Multimodal Assessment Project. Berkeley, CA: National Writing Project. Retrieved from http://digitalis.nwp.org/resource/1577.
Wilhelm, J. D. (2013). *Improving comprehension with think aloud strategies: Modeling what good readers do*. Scholastic Press.
Wilson, M. (2006). *Rethinking rubrics in writing assessment*. Heinemann.
Zittoun, T. (2017). Symbolic resources and sense-making in learning and instruction. *European Journal of Psychology and Education*, 32, 1–20.

12

Fostering Teacher Reflection and Professional Development

In this final chapter, we discuss ways to foster reflection on your teaching. We also provide you with resources to enhance your professional development as a teacher. You are most likely to develop and improve as a teacher through your reflections on what you do well and what you need to do to enhance students' learning based on the development of your knowledge, beliefs, abilities, and dispositions related to ELA instruction. This chapter therefore addresses the National Council of Teachers of English standard for preservice teachers:

> Candidates reflect on their ELA practice, use knowledge and theoretical perspectives to collaborate with educational community members, and demonstrate readiness for leadership, professional learning, and advocacy.
>
> (National Council of Teachers of English, 2021, p. 4)

APPLYING A CRITICAL INQUIRY FOCUS TO YOURSELF AND YOUR STUDENTS

Given the overall focus of this book on critical inquiry on practices operating in schools, it's also appropriate to apply critical inquiry on your own practices to reflect on your strengths as well as areas for improvement. Your faculty instructors, cooperating teacher, and/or supervisors will perceive you favorably, given your willingness to critically reflect on your teaching practices to develop a sense of self-efficacy defined as your confidence in your ability to use your teaching to enhance students' learning (Guskey, 2021). Teachers with high levels of self-efficacy are more willing to be open to alternative instructional approaches, willingness to seek out support and coaching, and have more patience to assist students experiencing difficulties in learning, resulting in higher levels of students' learning, enhanced job satisfaction, increased parental involvement, and lower levels of apathy and burnout (Mielke, 2021).

Developing self-efficacy as a preservice or new teacher through engaging in innovative teaching also entails taking risks which may be perceived as problematic by cooperating teachers or administrators reifying status-quo norms and practices (Anderson & Schuh, 2021). Cooperating teachers and administrators therefore need to provide supportive feedback

DOI: 10.4324/9781003177364-15

and suggestions that invite you to achieve some autonomy by taking risks associated with innovative teaching. Cooperating teachers and administrators also need to help you balance the inevitable stresses of teaching to avoid burnout, as well as set boundaries between one's teaching and one's personal life (Anderson & Schuh, 2021).

Consistent with our framework, developing self-efficacy entails identifying problems or issues in your planning and execution of your instructional activities, and then changing those activities to address those problems or issues. For example, you may sense that many of your students aren't participating in class discussions. You can then consider ways to alter your facilitation strategies to encourage those students to participate. For example, you may have students jot down thoughts prior to the discussion and then ask those students to share what they wrote. Or, you may have students engage in small group discussions to have members of those groups share what they discussed in the large group.

Based on implementing the activities in this book, in reflecting on your ability to foster students' own critical inquiry, related, for example, to address issues associated with the impact of climate change (Beach, 2015; Beach et al., 2017), you can determine the degree to which you:

- *foster students' identification of problems or issues* significant to their lives, leading them to engage in critical inquiry. You can then determine their level of motivation based on their enthusiasm to address a problem or issues that matter to them—for example, the issue of the impact of climate change on their future lives.
- *model formulation of specific reasons for problems or issues* so that students can convince audiences of the seriousness of those problems or issues. You can then determine students' ability to formulate these reasons for the significance of a problem or issue. For example, you may note their ability to cite reasons for the seriousness of climate change impacts relative to extreme weather patterns, warming of oceans, rising sea levels, and drought.
- encourage students to effectively *apply a range of different perspectives* to understand the nature of certain problems or issues as evident in students applying different perspectives. For example, they could examine the failure to address causes for increased carbon dioxide emissions related to the political, economic, agriculture, and media systems.
- assist students in identifying *ways to address their problems or issues* through taking action to address those problems or issues to communicate with relevant stakeholders. For example, students may communicate with owners of local fossil fuel or alternative energy companies regarding their plans to reduce fossil fuel emissions.
- socialize students into acquiring disciplinary literacy practices constituting English languages by going beyond a focus on methods for engaging students in discussion or writing to acquiring these disciplinary literacies practices (Kavanagh & Rainey, 2017). This includes a larger focus on disciplinary aspects of engaging in social actions related to citizenship practices which may be a challenge (Spanke, 2021). One student teacher asked, "'What good is learning about social justice if we don't know who we are as individual people? (p. 132). Another noted that "'It's hard to find a way to teach citizenship in a structured [English] curriculum . . . I can't incorporate other historic aspects into my English classes. It's not realistic to be able to do all of that'" (p. 132).

ENGAGING IN METACOGNITIVE TEACHING: REFLECTING ON YOUR KNOWLEDGE, BELIEFS, AND DISPOSITIONS

Central to your development is your ability to engage in metacognitive teaching through reflecting on your knowledge, beliefs, and dispositions shaping your instruction (Scales et al., 2020).

In reflecting on your knowledge about teaching English, you are reflecting on what you know about literature, composition, speaking/listening, media/digital literacies, and language, as well as your knowledge about different methods for teaching these subjects relative to addressing the CCSS. For example, you may infer that while you have extensive knowledge about contemporary literature associated with the CCSS reading standards, you may lack knowledge of current young-adult literature, particularly if you are working with middle-school students.

You are also acquiring knowledge of your students' abilities, interests, literacy practices, and attitudes to tailor your instruction based on that knowledge. This includes understanding the developmental differences between, for example, a 6th grader and a 12th grader. It also involves acquiring information about their interests related to activities and media/reading outside of school and their ability to employ certain literacy practices. Given that you are addressing issues of race, class, gender, and sexuality in your classes, you also need to understand their attitudes towards these issues so that you can anticipate them.

You also benefit from reflecting on your beliefs and attitudes about how and why to teach English. In your student teaching and first years of teaching, you need to be able to justify your use of certain methods to your students, cooperating teacher(s), and/or college supervisors, for example, your beliefs about the value of adopting a critical inquiry approach. Being able to justify your beliefs about the value of using certain methods is particularly important in classrooms or schools employing traditional methods that may differ from your own methods, resulting in their reluctance to support your use of critical inquiry activities (Smagorinsky et al., 2004). You may have acquired relatively innovative teaching methods in your teacher preparation program. However, unless you have also developed a strong set of beliefs to justify those methods, you may simply conform to their school's more traditional methods, given pressure to do so (Smagorinsky et al., 2004).

Addressing potential tensions between theories/practices you acquire in your teacher education program versus the theories/practices valued in your student teaching/initial years of teaching requires understanding any differences between the cultural norms and attitudes operating in your student teaching/teaching contexts versus those norms and attitudes acquired in your teacher education program (Scales et al., 2020). For example, as she began her student teaching, Rosa devoted time to observing and talking with her mentor teacher to learn about her student teaching context, consistent with advice from her university supervisor that she "'build contextual knowledge and relationships first'" (Scales et al., 2020, p. 56). She learned that her mentor teacher shared her reservations about adopting the use of scripted instruction.

It is also useful to study the norms and practices valued in the larger school culture in which you are working, which may or may not be shaping your own classroom contexts (Scales et al., 2020). This includes norms and practices employed by administrators related to disciplinary policies and supervision/support of teachers. It also involves learning about the extra-curricular/sports activities your students are engaged in, such as participation in drama productions, debate/speech, clubs, or sports that you can draw on to have students discuss or write about experiences in those contexts (Beach, 2022).

You will also need to demonstrate your ability to reflect on your teaching as part of your program's certification recommendations and/or edTPA certification assessments operating in some states through reflections about your instruction evident in your teaching unit(s), videos, and/or evidence of student learning. Or, you may create e-portfolios often required for state certification and/or employment purposes. In those e-portfolios, you are demonstrating to reviewers your teaching philosophy, ability to address certain standards, evidence of instructional planning, and ability to foster student learning. For example, you may include activities of how you created accommodations for ELL and special-need learners. (For more on your state certification requirements, see *State certification requirements* on the website.)

While you have been thinking about implementing standards in reading this book and taking your ELA methods courses, you may also have opportunities to participate in professional development provided by districts or schools. Engaging in this professional development provides you with opportunities to interact with teachers you are working with who are themselves actively engaged in professional development on ways to implement standards.

METHODS FOR ENGAGING IN SELF-REFLECTION

There are several different methods you can employ to engage in self-reflection.

Using narratives for self-reflections

Allen has the students in his classes preparing to become teachers write autobiographical narratives about their own important experiences both in and outside of school learning to read and write. In addition to "telling stories" future teachers reflect on what they learn about good (and not so good) language arts teaching. His students focus not only on themselves but try to remember/research what was happening to other students in their classes or in other classes/tracks or how their social community or their social location have impacted their learning experiences (rural/urban/suburban, poor/wealthy/middle class, monoethnic/multicultural, etc.). (Teachers may also post their narratives about their teaching experience on the Storri blog site *edblogs.columbia.edu/storri*.)

Allen's students often explore how ability grouping/tracking affected their literacy learning. These literacy narratives may include samples of writing or teacher assignments, interviews with teachers, parents, or classmates, recreated dialogue, poetic expression/analysis, memories, illustrations, reportage, etc. One purpose of the exercise is to "know thyself" and become self-conscious about your own experience, and recognize how it may differ from many students you will teach. As future teachers share their literacy narratives, patterns emerge that point toward best practices in literacy instruction.

You can also write reflections in a personal narrative mode about specific instances in your teaching with yourself as the sole audience, or you can share your reflections on your own or a course blog for comments by your peers. You can then use these narratives to portray how your identity as a novice teacher is shaped by particular interactions with students, teachers, parents, and administrators. One preservice teacher, Sandy, interacted with her mentor teacher, who asked Sandy,

> "Who are you as a teacher?" I looked back at her, surprised. "What do you mean?" She responded. "I've watched you all day and I've seen an extension of myself in this classroom. Who are you? I want to challenge you to figure that out and show me yourself tomorrow."
> (Schultz & Ravitch, 2013, p. 42)

Based on her narratives about her teaching, Sandy reflected on how "'I was just like her, even though I'm not her. I don't want to be in her shadow; I wanted to explore and figure out who I am as a teacher'" (p. 42).

You can also benefit from interacting with students as well as their families to have them share narratives about their lives to garner insights into the strengths and challenges related to building on those strengths and challenges in the classroom (Newcomer & Cowin, 2021). For example, one preservice teacher learned that her student's father never completed school and spent time in prison. She then reflected on how "it is easy to judge based on stereotypes, but as I learned more about this family, I realized how I can help my future students with resources, compassion, and even parental advice" (n.p.).

In portraying your experiences, you may also portray instances of tensions associated with a sense of uncertainty or doubt described as "wobble" (Fecho et al., 2021). As one first-year teaching noted:

> But there is so much more to teaching today than just caring for the kids. I wish it was different; that I could plan, teach, grade, and use all my energy on the kids. But external demands like "teaching to the test" (we just got done with 6 days of testing and this coming week will be testing all 11th graders on the ACT) and analyzing data (the two topics of one of our latest PLC meetings) make it hard to do just that.
> (p. 25)

Analysis of written narratives by student teachers in a university-based teacher education program examined how, as student teachers, they shaped their narratives based on participation in different social relationships and the pedagogical methods in their program versus school (Schultz & Ravitch, 2013). One of the primary themes that emerged from these narratives is their need as student teachers to distinguish themselves from their mentor teachers. They often felt as if they were "teaching in the shadows" of their mentor teachers. For example, one student teacher's narrative portrayed her fears of adopting a teacher style distinct from her mentor teacher's style that worked well with the students she was teaching while also wanting to experiment with and establish her own style.

Student feedback about your instruction

You can acquire pupil perceptions of what they have gained from participating in your activities by having them write exit memos or notes asking them to briefly describe what they learned in your class at the end of a class. From reviewing their writing, you can then determine the extent to which you've achieved your learning objectives and what changes you need to make when you believe that you may not have achieved those objectives.

Recording and reviewing instruction

As previously noted regarding reflecting on your discussion facilitation, you can create audio or video recordings of your classroom activities or micro-teaching in methods courses. A study of the use of teacher-created videos in lieu of administrators' observations found that teachers benefited from the use of reflection on their videos (Yaffe, 2015). As previously noted, for reflecting on videos of your own and/or your peers' teaching, you and your peers can add annotations using Timelinely *www.timeline.ly*, Reclipped *www.reclipped.com*, TinyTake *tinytake.com*, or VideoAnt *ant.umn.edu*.

In reflecting on these recordings, it is useful for you to focus on your own practices and students' level of participation and engagement relative to specific aspects of your activities as evidence of their learning (van Es et al., 2014). You can have your peers share their perceptions of the recordings with you for them to apply alternative perspectives on classroom events, such as focusing on different students' actions during an activity. To avoid negative, judgmental feedback, your peers could employ the descriptive feedback methods described in Chapter 11; for example, describing how certain students reacted to an activity so that you then share your self-assessment as to possible reasons for those reactions.

De-briefing conversations about your teaching

During your practicum or student teaching, you could meet with your cooperating teacher, university supervisor, and/or other colleagues to verbally share your reflections on what went well in your activities and what needs work. In doing so, you can review recordings of the activities or verbally describe the nature of the activities to specify the particular aspects of those successful and those that were less successful. You can then identify some specific practices to focus on in your future teaching to determine improvements in use of those practices.

ENGAGING IN SYSTEMATIC SELF-REFLECTION

Much of your self-reflection occurs as momentary thoughts during or after your instruction. At the same time, there are several tools you can use to reflect on your instruction across activities and time.

Action research

Action research involves posing certain questions about your instruction or students to collect data systematically to address those questions. Thus, rather than engaging in random reflections, action research formalizes reflection through focusing your attention on certain issues of teaching and learning in some systematic manner.

To engage in action research, you can identify certain difficulties, challenges, or issues in your own or another teacher's classroom. You may examine why your students aren't engaged with a certain activity to step back and reflect on possible reasons for their lack of engagement. Central to action research is the ability to pose specific research questions that serve to frame your research. Rather than focus on *yourself*, you ask questions such as (a) What do you notice? (b) What's your evidence? (c) What's your interpretation of what took place? and (d) What questions do you have about what occurred? (Sherin & van Es, 2005, p. 480). For example, you may pose questions about individual differences in your students' engagement in activities given differences in their interests, knowledge, beliefs, and goals. To determine reasons for this variation, you can select some students who differ in their engagement and then interview them or have them write about their perceptions of their experience in your activities in terms of their interests, knowledge, beliefs, and goals related to participation in those activities. You can then use those perceptions to infer reasons for variations in their participation. For example, some students did not have a clear sense of purpose for engaging in an activity.

You may also be interested in determining whether students are effectively acquiring new practices over time due to your instruction, for example, their ability to apply alternative perspectives. To do so, you can track changes in students' use of certain practices by comparing their writing or recorded talk over time. For example, two teachers addressed the question, "What happens when kids are trained to ask the questions?" (Wilhelm, 2009). They tracked changes in the types of questions students would write at the beginning of class to determine changes in these question types. By the end of the year, students were employing both inferential and critical questions, questions connecting to their lived experience, and that focus on issues portrayed in texts, to infer how these questions shaped their interactions.

Once you've identified factors shaping your use of certain activities, the next time you employ this activity, you can make changes in how you conduct this activity based on those factors. Or, you may be intrigued with how certain new methods or approaches might contribute to certain kinds of learning. In doing so, you may examine what and whether students learned what you or the teacher hoped students would learn and how students perceived their learning experience in terms of engagement and interest. (For more on engaging in teacher action research, see *Teacher action research* on the website.)

Studying your school's community world

Your action research may also include studying your school's community world related to how certain local cultural norms and practices operating in your school and/or community may shape your teaching. For example, teaching in a small rural town may entail quite different approaches than if you are teaching in an urban setting. To do so, you can observe events in the school or community—teacher meetings, other teachers' classes, sports events, pep rallies, social events, school board meetings, etc., including interviewing participants about their perceptions of these events.

To determine the community's race and class demographics, you can conduct what Susan Groenke (2010) defines as an "equity audit" to collect data about student demographics in the school district. You may determine the make-up of the school demographics in terms of race and class for both students and teachers. You may acquire information about how the differences in these groups reflect differences within and across the community served by a school. For example, in Groenke's methods course, preservice teachers noted that there were no advanced placement classes in the more rural, low-income schools in a district. They also found that all ELL students in a district were sent to one of the poorer, understaffed schools in the district. And, they noted that there were no teachers of color in a school in a largely White, middle-class community and that the Honors students believed that they were superior to the other students.

Based on the data you collect, you can then infer the prevailing norms, beliefs, attitudes, and goals underlying the school's and/or community's culture and the differences in students' or teachers' perceptions of these norms, beliefs, attitudes, and goals. You can then reflect on:

- how do teachers or students differ in their perceptions of these norms, beliefs, attitudes, and goals?
- what are expressions of deviations from these norms, beliefs, attitudes, and goals, and what do these expressions represent?
- what are the different groups or cliques operating in the school and/or community and how and why do they differ in terms of their own norms, beliefs, attitudes, and goals?
- what are the different spaces in the school and/or community, who defines these spaces, and how?
- how are your own beliefs, attitudes, and identities consistent with your school's and/or community's norms, beliefs, attitudes, and goals? (Beach et al., 2016, pp. 239–240).

This may also involve participating in local community organizations serving diverse student populations to understand the community's diversity (Barnes & Boyd, 2021). This includes identifying issues experienced by adolescents in these organizations; for example, learning that LGBTQ adolescents expressed concern about not being able to address LGBTQ experiences in their school.

Creating e-portfolios

As noted in Chapter 11, you can also engage in systematic self-reflection by creating e-portfolios documenting your work during your program and student teaching, typically a program requirement related to addressing certain NCATE standards and/or for completion of the edTPA certification assessment in states employing edTPA. E-portfolios serve as a repository of your work: your lesson plans, units, teacher websites, course papers, evidence of your students' work, your teaching philosophy, ability to address certain of the CCSS, and biographical information about yourself.

As noted in the previous chapter, you can create E-portfolios using a website (Google Sites, Weebly), blog, wiki, or e-portfolio desktop platforms such as Dropr *dropr.com*, Desire To Learn *brightspace.com/products/eportfolio*, Portfoliogen *www.portfoliogen.com*, Pathbrite *pathbrite.com* desktop platforms, or use of apps: Three Ring iOS *tinyurl.com/k789t5u/* Android *tinyurl.com/knsm4ml*, iOS Portfolio for iPad *tinyurl.com/mhdl9tt*, iOS Philio *tinyurl.com/kf7s42x*, or Android Easy Portfolio *tinyurl.com/maql5l3*. In creating your e-portfolio, it's important to create clearly-defined categories on the front page for organizing your materials.

You may create your own more *process* or *program* version designed to foster your self-reflection throughout your program versus a *showcase* e-portfolio designed for use in seeking employment. For your process or program e-portfolio, you may focus on how and why you drew on certain teaching activities derived from your methods courses in your practicum or student teaching. You may also reflect on changes in your knowledge and beliefs based on your teaching philosophy, your ability to address different CCSS through sample lesson plans or units, and your reflections on your classroom instruction during student teaching accompanied by sample student work.

Your showcase e-portfolio would then contain those particular items from your program portfolio designed to impress future employers. For example, by including links to your use of your own teacher websites, course management systems, or class blog or wiki, you can demonstrate to future employers your ability to organize your instruction and provide information for both students and parents about course assignments, related online texts, resources, examples of student work, and contact information.

As you begin your e-portfolio, your self-reflection may seem awkward and artificial, but you may become more adept at reflecting on your work overtime. One study found that as preservice teachers began their portfolios, their writing was often descriptive, with little critical self-reflection (Çimer, 2011). However, due to instructor feedback and guidance overtime, their reflections became more self-critical. It is also the case that as you transition from a program to showcase e-portfolio, that you acquire an increased sense of agency and ownership regarding your teaching abilities (Boulton, 2014). (For examples of teacher portfolios, see *Teacher portfolios* on the website.)

BUILDING ONLINE PERSONAL LEARNING NETWORKS (PLNS)

It is also useful to create your own online personal learning networks (PLNs) (Richardson & Mancabelli, 2011) using social media/networking, blogs, podcasts, online conferences, and listservs such as the following:

- Twitter: using #edchats, #ntchat, #engchat, #rechat, #techeducator, #smedu, #edtech, #titletalk, #engchat, and #yalitchat
- Online PLNs/PLCs: TeacherVision *teachervision.com*, English Companion Ning *englishcompanion.ning.com*, Classroom 2.0 *classroom2.0.com*, The Educator's PLN *edupln.ning.com*, ReadWriteThink *readwritethink.org/professional development*, edWebNet *home.edweb.net*, Edutopia For New Teachers *goo.gl/ntxeXr*.
- For sharing videos about teaching: YouTube Teachers *youtube.com/user/teachers*, Teaching Channel *teachingchannel.org*, TeacherTube *teachertube.com*, SchoolTube *schooltube.com*, Edutopia Videos *edutopia.org/videos*.

For more online professional development sites, see *Online professional development sites* on the website.)

Your personal learning network may include membership in an organization such as NCTE (the National Council of Teachers of English *ncte.org*). As a member, you receive journals such as *Voices from the Middle* for middle school language arts teachers or *English Journal* for high school teachers. You can also become a member of the International Literary Association (ILA) *literacyworldwide.org* which entitles you to receive the *Journal of Adolescent and Adult Literacy* for educators of all adolescents and adults. In addition, these national organizations as well as state affiliates hold conferences and workshops that provide sharing of teaching ideas and resources, including the ReadWriteThink curriculum curation site *tinyurl.com/yb45dhu*.

SUMMARY AND CONCLUSION TO THIS BOOK

This chapter described various methods for engaging in both momentary and systematic self-reflection about your successes and challenges essential for your growth as an ELA teacher. We also noted the value of accessing readily available online professional development resources to create a personal learning network.

As we conclude this book, we hope that you have benefited from the ideas we've presented on teaching English and your participation with the virtual cases. We also hope that you recognize the need to address state standards and go beyond these standards by adopting a critical inquiry approach to engage your students in dialogic meaning-making. We also invite you to contribute your units or lesson plans to this book's wiki site *http://exceedinge lastatestandards* by contacting Richard at rbeach@umn.edu to request editing access to post your materials or by sending the materials to him for him to post.

REFERENCES

Anderson, W., & Schuh, K. (2021). Self-efficacy holds staying power for new teachers. *Educational Leadership, 79*(3), 65–69.

Barnes, M. E., & Boyd, A. (2021). Analysis before action: A framework for examining communities as texts. *Review of Education, Pedagogy, and Cultural Studies, 43*(4), 358–378.

Beach, R. (2015). Commentary: Imagining a future for the planet through literature, writing, images, and drama. *Journal of Adolescent and Adult Literacy, 59*(1), 7–13.

Beach, R., Thein, A. H., & Webb, A. (2016). *Teaching to exceed the English language arts Common Core state standards.* Routledge.

Beach, R. (2022). *Drawing on students' worlds in the ELA classroom: Toward critical engagement and deep learning.* Routledge.

Beach, R., Share, J., & Webb, A. (2017). *Teaching climate change to adolescents: Reading, writing, and making a difference.* Routledge.

Boulton, H. (2014). Portfolios beyond pre-service teacher education: A new dawn? *European Journal of Teacher Education, 37*(3), 161–176.

Çimer, S. O. (2011). The effect of portfolios on students' learning: Student teachers' views. *European Journal of Teacher Education, 37*(3), 161–176.

Fecho, B., Coombs, D., Stewart, T. T., & Hawley, T. S (2021). *Novice teachers embracing wobble in standardized schools: Using dialogue and inquiry for self-reflection and growth.* Routledge.

Groenke, S. L. (2010). Seeing, inquiring, witnessing: Using the equity audit in practitioner inquiry to rethink inequity in public schools. *English Education, 43*(1), 83–96.

Guskey, T. R. (2021). The past and future of teacher efficacy. *Educational Leadership, 79*(3), 20–25.

Kavanagh, S. S., & Rainey, E .C. (2017). Learning to support adolescent literacy: Teacher educator pedagogy and novice teacher take up in secondary English language arts teacher preparation. *American Educational Research Journal, 54*(5), 904–937.

Mielke, C. (2021). The critical element of self-efficacy. *Educational Leadership, 79*(3), 15–19.

National Council of Teachers of English. (2021). NCTE standards for the initial preparation of teachers of English language arts 7–12 (initial licensure). Author.

Newcomer, S. N., & Cowin, K. M. (2021). The power and possibility of stories: Learning to become culturally sustaining and socially just educators. *Review of Education, Pedagogy, and Cultural Studies,* doi: 10.1080/10714413.2020.1860407

Richardson, W., & Mancabelli, R. (2011). *Personal learning networks: Using the power of connections to transform education.* Solution Tree.

Scales, R. Q., Wolsey, T. D., & Parsons, S. A. (2020). *Becoming a metacognitive teacher: A guide for early and preservice teachers.* Teachers College Press.

Schultz, K., & Ravitch, S. M. (2013). Narratives of learning to teach: Taking on professional identities. *Journal of Teacher Education, 64*(1) 35–46.

Sherin, M. G., & van Es, E. A. (2005). Using video to support teachers' ability to noticeclassroom interactions. *Journal of Technology and Teacher Education, 13*(3), 475–491.

Smagorinsky, P., Gibson, N., Moore, C., Bickmore, S., & Cook, L. S. (2004). Praxis shock: Making the transition from a student-centered university program to the corporate climate of schools. *English Education, 36*(3), 214–245.

Spanke, J. (2021). Viral loads and downward spirals: English, citizenship, and a context of crises. *English Education, 53*(2), 123–144.

van Es, E. A., Tunney, J., Goldsmith, L. T., & Seago, N. (2014). A framework for the facilitation of teachers' analysis of video. *Journal of Teacher Education, 65*(4) 340–356.

Wilhelm, J. D. (2009). The power of teacher inquiry: Developing a critical literacy for teachers. *Voices from the Middle, 17*(2), 36–39.

Yaffe, D. (2015, May). A clearer view of the classroom. *District Administration.* Retrieved from http://tinyurl.com/o2qxh8y

Index

Note: The Index uses US spelling

1619 Project: A New Origin Story, The (Hannah-Jones et al.) 71
1984 (Orwell) 24, 116–117, 172
2011 Meets 1968 (play) 134

AAE *see* African American English (AAE)
AAVE *see* African American Vernacular English (AAVE)
Academic English 183, 199
Academy of American Poets 82
Accelerated Reader (AR) 74
accommodations 34
achievement gaps 207
action, taking 25, 31–32, 45, 102
action research 232–233
activity plans 21, 23, 24–33
advertising 31, 52, 155, 156–157
affect-based evaluations 78
African American English (AAE) 183, 190, 192; language variation 184, 196
African American Vernacular English (AAVE) 120, 171, 190–191, 193
alternative perspectives 13, 15, 16–18, 27–30, 31, 49, 77, 97–98; argumentative writing 112, 113, 114, 115, 222; language variation 192, 193–194, 195
American literature 7
American public schools 41, 42
American Verse Project 82
analysis writing 116–117
Anderson, L. A. 59
annotations 75, 95–96, 110
annotation tools 95–96, 148, 150–151, 154, 213, 232
Appleman, D. 51
AR *see* Accelerated Reader (AR)
arguing-to-learn 113–114
argumentative texts 100–101
argumentative writing 47, 112–115; alternative perspectives 112, 113, 114, 115, 222; arguing-to-learn 113–114

artwork 75, 129, 148
As I Lay Dying (Faulkner) 52
assessment 34, 205–206, 223; formative 205, 206, 207–216, 217–219, 223; online reading practices 94, 96–97; public speeches 167; self-assessment 213–214; summative 205, 219–223
asynchronous discussions 173
Atwell, N. 11, 73, 122
audio feedback tools 154
audio files production 152–153
audio listening 152
Aukerman, M. 12, 14
autobiographical narrative writing 127, 129–131, 133, 140
Autobiography of an Ex-Colored Man, The (Johnson) 97
Avila, J. 53

backchannel comments 172
Baghdad Burning: Girl Blog from Iraq (Riverbend) 98
Baker-Bell, A. 188
Bali, M. 13
banking model of education 8
Banks, M. A. 44
Banksy 32
Beach, R. 3, 44
Becker, T. 97–98
bilingual texts 199
biographical perspective 70
Blackburn, M. V. 72
Blaha, J. 136–137
Blau, S. 16
blogs 98, 119, 147, 157, 198
Boal, A. 135
book clubs 74, 174–175
Borsheim, C. 16
Borsheim-Black, C. 4
Boyd, Ashley S. 3, 58
British literature curriculum 6

Brooks, T. 207
Brown, J. S. 14

Cain, C. 77
Campano, G. 192–193
Canadian Teachers' Federation 18
Canady, F. 132, 151–152
Carpenter, B. 184
Cart, M. 72
Cassidy, T. 211
CCSS *see* Common Core State Standards (CCSS)
censorship 59–61
characters perspectives 76–77
charts 172
Chow, P. 195
Christensen, L. 193–194
civic activism 155
Civic Online Reasoning site 159
Civil Rights Movement 15
claim/reason–evidence relationships 101, 114
Clark, C. T. 72
class accounts, Twitter 119, 173
Classkick 212
class notes 172
class perspective 70
classroom discussions 12, 16–18, 108, 165–166, 169–171, 177–178
classroom public speeches 166–168
climate change 3, 15, 30, 44, 90, 101, 113, 228
closed questions 170, 177, 178
close reading 14–15, 68, 74–76, 88–89, 103
Coats, K. 79
code-switching 196, 198
coherence 215
Coleman, D. 88
collaboration 30–31
collaborative critical inquiry 116
collaborative interpretations 52
Colorin Colorado blog 198
Color Purple, The 72
comics 133, 149, 151
Common Core State Standards (CCSS) 4, 45–48, 50, 53, 54, 67, 131; argumentative writing 113; close reading 74, 88; digital media 143, 144, 157; informational texts 99; language standards 182, 183; learning progressions 48–50; multicultural literature 43; narrative writing 127; reading texts 52, 53; single public presentations 166; text complexity 8, 51; writing standards 10, 116
Commonlit 95
communication 57, 58, 59, 61
Compose Our Worlds project 152
conflict talk 171
connected learning framework 145
contemporary problems 22–23, 24–33
contextualizing texts 89–90
controversial topics 59–60, 61
Council of the Great City Schools 197
counter-storytelling 32

COVID pandemic 3
critical analysis 154–155, 156–157
Critical Canon Pedagogy model 7–8, 71
critical disabilities perspective 72
critical disabilities studies 72
critical inquiry 7, 13–14, 67, 69–70, 116, 227; argumentative writing 112–115; dramatic responses 77–78; informational texts 100–101; language usage 190–192; nonfiction texts 100–101; perspectives 70–72; problem solving 214, 215; self-assessment 214–215
critical language pedagogy 196
critical literacy 14–15
Critical Literature Pedagogy 70–71
critical media literacy 154–156
critical pedagogy 13
critical race perspective 71, 72
critical race theory 60, 71
Critical Response Protocol (CRP) 75, 170
critical Whiteness perspective 71
cultural knowledge 6, 7
cultural literacy 6, 8
cultural literacy model 7, 8
culturally responsive teaching 44–45, 197–198
cultural norms 233–234
cultural studies 15
cultural tradition 7
Cummins, J. 195
curricular freedom 56–57
curriculum 6–7, 8, 9–10, 21, 47–48; *see also* Common Core State Standards (CCSS); IRA/NCTE Standards for the English Language Arts; National Council of the Teachers of English (NCTE)
cyberdrama 137

Damm, A. 171
Darling-Hammond, L. 41–42
database use 93
Days of Rondo (Fairbanks) 102–103
decolonial perspective 71–72
deconstructivist/poststructuralist perspective 70
Delirium (Oliver) 148
Delpit, L. 187–188
descriptive feedback 183, 211, 212–213
destination literature 78–80
Dewey, J. 15
dialogic discussions 165–166, 169–172
dialogue 128
Diary of a Young Girl (Frank) 136, 148
digital and media literacies 143, 144
digital annotation tools 95–96, 148
digital audio files 213
digital book reports 76
digital book trailers 151
Digital Democratic Dialogue (3D) Project 154, 159
digital illustrations 148
digital maps 96
digital media 143, 144–145, 146, 157
digital note-taking tools *see* notetaking tools

digital poetry 140
digital stories 107, 131–132, 133, 144, 151–152
Digital Storymakers Award 152
digital think-alouds 151
digital tools 143, 144–145, 147–149, 212–213
Diigo Sticky Notes 148
disabilities studies perspective 83
disagreements 171
disciplinary languages 188–189
Discovering Wes Moore (Moore) 99
discrimination 43, 60, 71, 90, 100–101
discussion practices 16–18, 157–158, 175–177
diverse cultures 43
Do You Speak American? (Cran) 196
drama 80–82, 134–135, 140
drama activities: embodied actions 135–136; improvisation 77–78, 136–137
drama scripts 133–136
dramatic inquiry 77–78, 133, 134
dramatic responses 77–78
Dugan, M. 30
Dungeons & Dragons (D&D) game 135
Dunn, P. A. 72
Dyches, J. 7–8

editing texts 120–124
Edmiston, B. 134
EDpuzzle 150
Ehrenreich, B. 127
ELA standards (NCTE) *see* National Council of the Teachers of English (NCTE)
Elbow, P. 211
ELL *see* English language learners (ELL)
embodied actions 135–136
emotional responses 24–25
Engel, S. 112
English language arts 3–4, 5–6, 7
English language learners (ELL) 42, 103, 197–198
English literature 6–7
English teachers 3, 4–6
e-portfolios 216, 222, 230, 234–235
Epstein, S. 16
Erdmann, E. 24–25, 116, 130–131, 133, 172, 194, 220
essential questions 100
Everett-Cacopardo, H. 94
everyday experiences 109–110
experience sharing 58
explanatory writing 116–117
exploratory thinking 170–171
expository essays 108

Facebook 146
Faulkner, J. 76
Feed (Anderson) 52
feedback 121–124, 208–209; descriptive 183, 211, 212–213; formative assessment 210–215, 223; peer 123, 177–178, 211, 212, 213
feed-forward formative assessment 215–216
feed-up formative assessment 209–210

Fences (Wilson) 80–81
fictional narratives 128–129
Firekeeper's Daughter, The (Boulley) 76
fishbowl reflection activities 176
five-paragraph expository essays 108
Flipgrid 150
Flynn, J. E. 191, 197
formalism 9–10
formalist curriculum 9–10
formal language 184
formative assessment 205, 206, 207–216, 217–219, 223
Forzani, E. 94
free-reading programs 73
free-writes 171
Freire, P. 8, 13, 15, 139
Friedman, T. 97
Friend, C. 172

Gee, J. 29, 184
gender discrimination 90
gender perspective 70
genre knowledge 98–99, 111
genres 128–129
Gibson, A. 82
GLBTQ literature 72
global warming *see* climate change
Glogster 149
goals 209–210
Godley, A. 184, 193
Goodman, B. 190
Google Classroom 118–119
Google Docs 119, 212
Google Forms 119, 212
Google Hangouts 119
Google ThreadIt 150
Gorman, A. 82
grades 219–220
graffiti art 31, 32
grammar 120, 181, 182, 185
graphic novels 133, 149, 151
graphic organizers 96
graphs 172
Great Books 6, 8
Griffen, B. 157
Groenke, S. L. 233

Hagemann, J. 191, 196
Hamlet (Shakespeare) 80
Harrison Bergeron (Vonnegut) 151
Harste, J. C. 24
hashtags 149
Hess, D. E. 60
Hicks, L. 76
Hicks, T. 14–15, 121, 218
High School Musical (script) 134–135
Hillocks, G. 182
hip-hop culture 139
Hirsch, E. D. 7
Hobbs, R. 154

Hodge, T. 130, 215
Holland, D. 77
Hollie, S. 192
House on Mango Street, The (Cisneros) 135
Hunger Games, The (Collins) 71, 131
hybrid instruction 145
hyperlinks 92, 149

I Am Malala: How One Girl Stood Up for Education and Changed the World (Yousafzai) 99
I Am Malala: The Girl Who Stood Up for Education and Was Shot by the Taliban (Yousafzai) 99
identities 130, 192–193
IF *see* interactive fiction (IF)
ILA *see* International Literacy Association (ILA)
illustrations 148, 172
imagination 31
Imagine the Future project 152
improvisation 77–78, 136–137
inequality 37, 43
inferring connections 97–98, 101
informal language 184–185
informal writing 110
informational texts 67, 99–101, 102–103
informational writing 117–118
Initiate–Respond–Evaluate (IRE) teaching 170, 178
Instagram 146, 149
interactive fiction (IF) 149–150
interactive learning 30–31
interactive presentation tools 166
interactive tools 43, 75–76
International Literacy Association (ILA) 56, 235
International Reading Association (IRA) 56
interpretating texts 76–77, 78
interpretative complexity 51
intertextual connections 97–98, 101
Into the Wild (Krakauer) 151
iOS Adobe Voice app 132
IRA *see* International Reading Association (IRA)
IRA/NCTE Standards for the English Language Arts 55, 56
IRE teaching *see* Initiate–Respond–Evaluate (IRE) teaching

Jenkins, C. 72
Jersey Shore (television program) 135
Jim Crow laws 100–101
Jocson, K. 139
justice, inquiry, and action model 13, 18, 21, 22, 23, 24–30, 31–34, 37, 45, 69, 83

Kaepernick, C 156–157
Kennedy, C. 94
Kiili, C. 94
Kincheloe, J. L. 42
Kinloch, V. 139
Kirkland, D. 188
Kohn, A. 31

Lachicotte Jr., W. 77
language dialect styles 171
language ethnographies 194
language instruction 181, 199; grammar 120, 181, 182, 185; usage 181–182, 183
language standards 181, 182, 183, 185, 199
language usage 187–188, 199; critical inquiry 190–192; disciplinary languages 188–189; language variation 183–185, 189–190, 193–194, 195–197; social practice 192–193
language variation 187–188, 189–191, 195–197, 199; African American English 184, 196; alternative perspectives 192, 193–194, 195; language usage 183–185, 189–190, 193–194, 195–197
languaging 185–187
Leakey, R. E. 188–189
learning as social 16–18
learning goals 34
learning in context 16
learning progressions 48–50
learning stories 210
learning theory 16
Leland, L. 24
Lennington, D. 137–138
lesson plans 33–34, 35–37; activities 21, 23, 24–33
Leu, D. J. 94
Leveled Questions, Costa 74
Levine, S. 78
Lewin, R. 188–189
Lewison, M. 24
LGBT literature 72
Linguistic Affirmation Program (LAP) 192
literary interpretation 70–72, 78
literary texts 8–9, 67
literature 3, 5, 6–7
literature circles 174–175
literature standards 10
Lord of the Flies (LOTF) (Golding) 116–117, 177
Love from the Vortex and Other Poems (Sealy-Ruiz) 137–138

McAvoy, P. 60
Macbeth (Shakespeare) 71, 74, 119
McGee Banks, C. A. 44
McVerry, J. 94
Maher, S. 28–29, 110
Mann, S. 186–187
maps 172
Marciano J. E. 16
Martin, J. 60
Marxist perspective 70
Matera, C. 130
Maykel, C. 94
media representations 155–156
Medina, C. 192–193
memes 149
memoirs 99, 129–131; *see also* autobiographical narrative writing

INDEX

metacognitive teaching 229
metadiscursive practices 89–90
Metz, M. 183
Minnici, A. 184, 193
Mirra, N. 154, 159
misinformation 157–158
Moore, M. 53
Morrell, E. 14–15
Morris, J. 4, 8–9, 10, 12, 58, 80
Mozilla Popcorn Maker 149
multicultural children 43
multicultural education 44–45
multicultural literature 43
Multimodal Assessment project (2011) 153–154
multimodal digital productions 153–154
multimodal responses 75–76
multimodal texts 144, 149, 154
multimodal tools 221
multiple-choice tests 220–221
Myer, W. D. 51

NAEP *see* National Assessment of Educational Progress (NAEP)
NAMLE *see* National Association of Media Literacy Education (NAMLE)
narratives 171–172
narrative writing 109, 127–129, 140; autobiographical 127, 129–131, 133, 140; digital stories 133, 140; drama 80–82, 140; fictional narratives 128–129; poetry 82–83, 129, 137–140, 148
National Assessment of Educational Progress (NAEP) 46, 87
National Association of Media Literacy Education (NAMLE) 155
National Council of the Teachers of English (NCTE) 7, 41, 43, 50, 56, 144, 182, 205, 227, 235
National Writing Project (2011) 153–154
Native American literature 72
NCTE *see* National Council of the Teachers of English (NCTE)
Nearpod 167
Nemeth, E. A. 72
netiquette guidelines 174
#NeverAgain movement 15
New Critical literary analysis methods 88
New Criticism 68
newsletters 117–118
newspaper generator sites 117–118
newspapers 117–118, 157
news reporting 157–159
nonfiction digital stories 132
nonfiction texts 87, 88, 92–96, 97–101, 102–103, 157–159
NoodleTools 95
notetaking tools 95, 110, 148

Oberg, R. 76, 102, 140
O'Brien, T. 102
O'Byrne, W. I. 44, 94, 149, 150

Of Mice and Men (Steinbeck) 33, 83
Of Plymouth Plantation (Bradford) 72
Ohio State University Argumentative Writing Project 113
OMG Shakespeare remixes 149
one-to-one oral interactions 168–169
online book club discussions 148
online editing tools 121
online group interactions 173–175
online information 93–94, 154, 159
online instruction 118, 145
online interaction 146–149
online learning tools 145
online misinformation 154
online news 157–159
online nonfiction texts 92–96, 103, 157–159
online peer-feedback 213
online reading practices 92–97
online searches 110–111
online texts 7, 87, 92–96, 119; nonfiction texts 92–96, 103, 157–159
online tools 92–93, 95–96, 121
online writing 118–119, 147
open-ended questions 166, 170, 178
opportunity gap 41
Other Wes Moore: One Name, Two Fates, The (Moore) 99

Padlet 119
pantomime sculpting activities 136
parent/guardian communication 57, 58, 59, 61
Passionate Shepherd to His Love, The (Marlowe) 82–83
Paterson, J. 21–22
PBL *see* problem-based learning (PBL)
Pearl, The (Steinbeck) 148
Pearson, P. D. 51
pedagogy 12
Pederson, N. 140
peer conferences 121
peer feedback 123, 177–178, 211, 212, 213
personal learning networks (PLNs) 235
Petrone, R. 16
Pew Research Center 157
Piecing Me Together (Watson) 77
Pimental, S. 88
Players' Tribune blog, The 157
PLNs *see* personal learning networks (PLNs)
podcasts 152–153, 167
poetry 82–83, 129, 137–140, 148
Poet X, The (Acevedo) 78
postcolonial perspective 70
prescriptive perspective 183
presentation tools 166
preservice teachers (PTs) 132, 137, 144, 169, 227, 233–234
Pride and Prejudice (Austen) 69
problem-based learning (PBL) 117–118
problem posing model of inquiry 8, 13, 15
problem solving 77–78, 134, 214, 215
process model 11, 12
professional development 227, 229, 235

Project Information Literacy 159
psychoanalytic perspective 70
psychological perspective 70
PTs *see* preservice teachers (PTs)
public speeches 166–168

queer perspective 72
queer theory 72
questions 25–27; closed 170, 177, 178; essential 100; open-ended 166, 170, 178; text-dependent 88
Quicksand (Larsen) 97

racial autobiographies 130
racial groups 41, 42, 130
racial identities 130
racism 43, 60, 71, 100–101
Ravitch, D. 46, 48
readability 120–121
reader-based feedback 121–124
reader response theory 68–69
reading 11, 67–69, 73–76, 99–100, 103, 143; online 94, 96–97
reading abilities 52–53, 87–88
Reading Apprenticeship framework 100
reading comprehension practices 87–88
Reading for Understanding Initiative (RfU) 87
reading homework 34–37
reading texts 8, 34–37, 51, 52, 53, 54
reading workshops 73
Reciprocal Teaching methods 94–95
references 111
reflection 34
relevance 214
reliability 221
Resolution on English Education for Critical Literacy in Politics (NCTE) 157
Rex, L. A. 112
RfU *see* Reading for Understanding Initiative (RfU)
rhetorical modes 9
Rhoads, C. 94
role-playing activities 122, 135
role-playing games (RPGs) 135, 149–150
Romeo and Juliet (Shakespeare) 81
rubrics 217–219, 223

Sarigianides, S. 4
Scarlet Ibis, The (Hurst) 72
Schecter, S. 195
school community 233–234
school culture 229–230
school curriculum *see* curriculum
school policies 57
science fiction stories 128–129
screencasting tools 121, 213
sculpting activities 136
Scythe (Shusterman) 77
seating arrangements 169
segregation 100–101
self-assessment 213–215

self-efficacy 227–228
self-reflection 122–123, 175–176, 230–232, 234–235
Selma (DuVernay) 90
sense of purpose 109
service learning 33
Shakespeare, W. 6, 149, 190; *Hamlet* 80; *Macbeth* 71, 74, 119; *Romeo and Juliet* 81
Sharp, G. 32
Sheffer, M. 74–75
Shelton, S. 207
short stories 127, 128
significance 214
Simmons, A. 116
single public presentations 166–168
Sipe, R. 47
skills model 10–11, 12
Skinner, D. 77
SMAC assessments (Smarter Balanced Assessment Consortium) 221–222
Smagorinsky, P. 56
small group discussions 174–175, 176
Smith, M. W. 51
Smith, S. A. 44
social action 16, 18, 67
social media 76, 146–147, 157–158, 213
social movements 15
social practice 192–193
Something about America (Testa) 134
speaking/listening standards 165, 166, 168
special learning students 103
spoken word presentations 168
spoken word/rap poetry 139–140
Standard English 183, 184, 187, 188, 189, 190, 199
standardization 53
standards 34, 46, 48–50, 53; *see also* Common Core State Standards (CCSS); IRA/NCTE Standards for the English Language Arts; National Council of the Teachers of English (NCTE)
stereotypical representations 155–156
Stevens, L. P. 30
Stor tool, Instagram 149
strategy lessons 12
student achievement 46, 53
student demographics 233–234
student engagement 51, 52, 53–54, 67, 69
student motivation 50
style guidelines 111
sufficiency 214
Sulzer, M. A. 79
summative assessment 205, 219–223
supporting evidence 111
Swanson, N. 128–129
Sweetland, J. 184
symbolic meaning 78
synchronous discussions 173

tableau sculpting activities 136
teacher freedom 56–57, 61
teacher-led discussions 169, 170

INDEX

teachers 3, 21
teacher unions 61
teaching methods 4–6, 73–78, 79–83, 227–228, 229–233, 234–235
technology tools 144–145
TED talk presentations 166
tellability 127–128
tentative thinking 170–171
test-preparation 207
textbooks 6, 7–8, 23
text complexity 8, 51, 52
text comprehension 89–90
text-dependent questions 88
text selection 8–9, 51, 52, 53, 56–57, 59–61, 73–74
text structures 9
text-to-speech (TTS) tools 103
Thein, A. H. 3, 79
Things They Carried, The (O'Brien) 27, 102
think-alouds 90–91, 110, 151, 175, 212
Thomas, D. 14
Thomas, E. E. 112
Thompson, I. 208
Tienken, C. 53
Timbrell, N. 94
To Kill a Mockingbird (Lee) 25–26, 28, 29, 69, 71, 110, 196
translanguaging perspective 198
TTS tools *see* text-to-speech (TTS) tools
Twitter 119, 146–147, 173

usage 181–182, 183

validity 214–215, 220, 221
Vanish, M. 17–18, 152, 191–192
video annotation tools 150–151, 154, 232
video games 135, 149–150
video production 151, 154, 232
videos 150–151, 167

Vietnam War protests 15
Virginia Tech University (shootings) 88
vocabulary 91–92
voting rights 89–90

warrants 102, 114
Warren, C. A. 16
Webb, A. 3, 32–33, 44, 57–58, 82, 83, 128, 129, 230
websites 93–94; *see also* social media
Wendorf, K. 187
Wheeler, R. 184
White, J. 190–191
Wiggins, A. 177
Wikipedia 93
Wilhelm, J. D. 51, 56
Wilson, M. 191, 217–218
Word 212
World is Flat: A Brief History of the 21st Century, The (Friedman) 97–98
writing 31, 108–111
writing instruction 108–109
writing skills 11, 182
writing standards 10, 47, 107, 109, 116

young adult literature (YAL) 59, 78–80, 149
youth action 15–16, 18
youth engagement 59
youth lens perspective 71
youth participatory action research (YPAR) 16, 135

Zancanella, D. 53
Zawilinski, L. 94
Zentner, J. 59
zone of proximal development (ZPD) 206
Zuidema, L. 181, 190, 196
Zwiers, J. 189

CPSIA information can be obtained
at www.ICGtesting.com
Printed in the USA
BVHW061806240822
645433BV00010B/505